2ND EDITION

MEDIA CULTURE AND SOCIETY

PAUL HODKINSON

an introduction

SAGE

Los Angeles | London | New Delhi
Singapore | Washington DC | Melbourne

Los Angeles | London | New Delhi
Singapore | Washington DC | Melbourne

SAGE Publications Ltd
1 Oliver's Yard
55 City Road
London EC1Y 1SP

SAGE Publications Inc.
2455 Teller Road
Thousand Oaks, California 91320

SAGE Publications India Pvt Ltd
B 1/I 1 Mohan Cooperative Industrial Area
Mathura Road
New Delhi 110 044

SAGE Publications Asia-Pacific Pte Ltd
3 Church Street
#10-04 Samsung Hub
Singapore 049483

Editor: Michal Ainsley
Editorial assistant: Delayna Spencer
Production editor: Imogen Roome
Copyeditor: Kate Campbell
Proofreader: Jill Birch
Indexer: David Rudeforth
Marketing manager: Lucia Sweet
Cover design: Jen Crisp
Typeset by: C&M Digitals (P) Ltd, Chennai, India
Printed by CPI Group (UK) Ltd, Croydon, CR0 4YY

Library of Congress Control Number: 2016939482

British Library Cataloguing in Publication data

A catalogue record for this book is available from the British Library

ISBN 978-1-4739-0235-0
ISBN 978-1-4739-0236-7 (pbk)

At SAGE we take sustainability seriously. Most of our products are printed in the UK using FSC papers and boards. When we print overseas we ensure sustainable papers are used as measured by the PREPS grading system. We undertake an annual audit to monitor our sustainability.

CONTENTS

MEDIA CULTURE AND SOCIETY

SAGE was founded in 1965 by Sara Miller McCune to support the dissemination of usable knowledge by publishing innovative and high-quality research and teaching content. Today, we publish over 900 journals, including those of more than 400 learned societies, more than 800 new books per year, and a growing range of library products including archives, data, case studies, reports, and video. SAGE remains majority-owned by our founder, and after Sara's lifetime will become owned by a charitable trust that secures our continued independence.

Los Angeles | London | New Delhi | Singapore | Washington DC | Melbourne

LIST OF ILLUSTRATIONS

ABOUT THE AUTHOR

Paul Hodkinson is a sociologist whose work is focused upon youth cultures, online communications, contemporary fatherhood and the relationships between media and cultural identities. He is author of *Goth: Identity, Style and Subculture* and *Media, Culture and Society*. He is also co-editor of *Youth Cultures: Scenes, Subcultures and Tribes* (with Wolfgang Deike) and *Ageing and Youth Cultures* (with Andy Bennett). He has published a wide range of journal articles and book chapters across the range of his interests.

His most recent research projects have focused on ageing and youth cultures, experiences of targeted harassment among subcultural participants and fathers who are primary or equal carers for young children. He is based in the Department of Sociology at the University of Surrey where he teaches and supervises on media, music and youth cultures.

ACKNOWLEDGEMENTS

Thanks to the Department of Sociology at the University of Surrey for providing me with a wonderful place to work for the last 13 years. Thanks, specifically, to colleagues at Surrey and elsewhere connected to research and teaching on media, culture and society, including those who have offered advice or thoughts related to sections of this book. Acknowledgement is also due to Graham McBeath, from whom I learned so much at the University of Northampton and, most of all, to all those who first inspired my interest in the study of media, culture and society when I was a student in the Department of Cultural Studies at the University of Birmingham.

Thanks also to the team at Sage Publications for all the help and support provided throughout the process or producing the second edition of this book. And thanks to my students, without whom my enthusiasm and understanding would be so much less. Finally, thanks to my partner, Holly Cummins, for her love, support and ever-entertaining proof-reading, and to my little boys, Laurie and Asher, for making life so entertaining even in the midst of the most frantic of writing and editing.

CHAPTER 1
INTRODUCTION

FOCAL POINTS

- Introduction to the notions of media, culture and society
- The relationship between media representations and society
- Linear models of the communication process
- A suggested model of the elements of media in social context
- Summary of the chapters to follow

INTRODUCTION

Perhaps more than ever before, media and communication are at the centre of everyday lives. At work, at home, in public spaces or while travelling from one location to another, we are rarely far away from mediated sounds, images or words, whether in the form of television, websites, magazines, mobile apps, newspapers, music or social media. On our own and in the company of others, media entertain us, enable connections with friends and communities, provide interpretations of the world around us and offer resources for the forging of identities and imaginations. And their importance to everyday lives and routines suggests that media also must have the most significant implications for the nature and character of the broader culture and society that surround us. We live, it may be argued, in a media culture, a media society. This book provides an introduction to the relationships between media and the broader social and cultural world in which they operate.

MEDIA, CULTURE, SOCIETY

It is worth remembering that *media* is the plural of the term *medium*, which refers, essentially, to the means through which content is communicated between an origin and a destination. It could be argued that the human body acts as the first and most fundamental medium in this respect, transferring thoughts, ideas and emotions into speech or gestures audible or visible to others. Yet our concern here is with the use of artificial forms of media to enhance and extend our communicative capacity beyond the capabilities of our own bodies, transforming the range of expression open to us and mediating what we say over longer distances or to greater numbers of people, for example. At one extreme, such media may enable each of us to interact with friends or acquaintances without the need to be in the same room, city or even country, while on the other, they may enable a relatively small number of professional media producers to transmit large volumes of content to audiences of millions. Such producers, along with the technologies they utilise and content they distribute, are often collectively referred to as 'the media' and this certainly has become an acceptable use of the term. It remains important, however, to understand media as plural and diverse. Although contemporary large-scale 'mass media' figure heavily in our discussions, we'll focus on a broad range of different types and scales of communication involving a plethora of organisations, communities and individuals. This is of particular importance in the context of a digital media age in which the interrelationships between traditional forms of mass media and a range of more interactive forms of communication have become pivotal.

Two connected senses of the word *culture* are of importance to our discussions in this book, both of which are identified in the influential writings of Raymond Williams (1988; 1989) on the subject. First, culture is sometimes used in a specific sense to refer to the worlds of creative expression or, as Williams puts it, 'the works and practices of intellectual and especially artistic activity' (1988: 90). Traditionally this sense of the term was reserved for elite or 'high' forms of literature, music, art and theatre, but increasingly its use also encapsulates the larger realm of so-called *popular culture*, including pop music and popular fiction or drama, for example. As Williams puts it, 'culture is ordinary' (1989: 3). At certain points, we'll use the term culture in this more restricted sense, including as a means to refer to mediated forms and practices of expression.

Importantly, however, such creative forms and activities form just part of a crucial second sense of the word culture, as a way to refer to the whole way of life of a society or group, including values, meanings, identities, traditions, norms of behaviour and ways of understanding the world. As Williams argues, although they are different, the two senses of culture are closely related. After all, the practices of creative, artistic and intellectual expression in a given society encapsulate anything from the production and consumption of famous art, literature, music or television programmes to grassroots dancing, music-making, dress and acts of worship – all of which form an integral part of the overall ways of life of that society. The word culture, then, often refers simultaneously to creative practices and broader ways of life, whether in reference to the distinctive identities, rituals, practices and forms of expression associated with a particular group (as in 'punk culture'), or a certain activity (as in 'television culture'), or as a more general way to invoke the range of cultural features and practices across a broader range of people.

Society, meanwhile, is a closely related, but somewhat broader term, which refers to the whole social world in which we exist or 'the body of institutions and relationships within which a relatively large group of people live' (Williams 1988: 291). Society particularly invokes an emphasis on social relations, including the detail of everyday interactions and the operation of broader social groupings and categories of social differentiation, such as those based on class, ethnicity and gender. Patterns of wealth, power and inequality are a further core element of societies, as are social institutions, including the apparatus of government and law, education systems, religious organisations, commercial corporations and smaller-scale organisational units such as the family. Together with established hierarchies of wealth, power and control, such institutions form a complex set of *structures* through which social relations are lived out. Among those who study societies, a key question concerns the relationship between these established structures and human *agency*, which means people's ability to be self-determining. Are we shaped by the gender, social class or ethnic category into which we were born – or indeed by the family structure, education system or religious institutions which play a role in our lives? Or do we have the power to determine our own futures? The importance of media at so many levels of contemporary social life renders it a crucial consideration in such questions of structure and agency.

Crucially, it is difficult to envisage a study of such questions about the make-up of society, the arrangement of social relations or the balance of structure and agency, that omits the cultural ways of life and expression which lie at the heart of all societies – and equally difficult to imagine how one might examine questions about cultural rituals, understandings, identities or creative practices without reference to the society in which they take place. The emphasis of the terms culture and society is different in some respects, then, but there are extensive overlaps and ambiguities between them, something that particularly applies to the connection between society and the broader sense of culture as way of life. I would urge readers to feel comfortable with this fuzziness. For although the particular emphasis of one term or the other may be invoked at different stages of the discussions ahead, our ultimate concern is with the relationship of communications media with the range of phenomena covered by the two. We will explore the possibility, then, that media have, in one way or another, become integral to what we might term the broader social and cultural environment, something that includes the distribution of wealth, power and influence, the operation of social structures and institutions, class, gender and ethnic relations, patterns of identity and community, ideas and understandings, practices of intellectual, artistic and creative expression and broader ways of life.

STARTING POINTS: SHAPING, MIRRORING AND REPRESENTING

Needless to say, the development of a detailed understanding of the role of media in relation to these various features of the broader social and cultural environment in which we live is far from a simple task. So let's take things one step at a time and consider, by way of a starting point, two simple and contrasting approaches to the relationship between mass media content and society. For the purpose of the discussion, let's assume society here can be taken to include, amongst other things, culture in its broad sense as a reference to overall ways of life.

Some approaches regard media as constructors or *shapers*, arguing that the content they distribute has the power to influence people and affect the future of society (see Figure 1.1).

Figure 1.1   Media as shaper

There are all sorts of arguments that fit into this approach. Some suggest, for example, that media depictions of sex and violence are liable to influence viewers to the extent that people's real lives may become more dominated by promiscuity or danger, while others warn that stereotypical portrayals of ethnic or sexual minority groups might increase the marginalisation of such groups within society. Arguments that political or moral bias in the media may lead to a predominance of certain opinions among audiences also come into this category, as do assertions that the general quality of media content in a given society may affect how informed, engaged or creative its population is. Such perspectives all focus on the ways media may be affecting or influencing us.

Others focus, not on how media content shapes us, but on the way it reflects or *mirrors* society (see Figure 1.2). The predominant role of media, according to this view, is to reflect back to us events, behaviours, identities, social relations or values which are already important. Media, then, are deemed more significant for the way they follow rather than the way they lead.

Figure 1.2   Media as mirror

From this perspective, if media are dominated by sex and violence, this is because we already live in a society in which these are important – and if particular opinions or values are given prominence in media content, this reflects their existing currency. When accused of manipulating public opinion through bias, news media professionals often defend themselves by reciting the cliché 'don't shoot the messenger'. The implication is that news is neutrally reflecting the world and that, if we don't like it, we should seek to improve that world rather than blaming media.

As Alexander (2003) shows, the belief that media reflect society has prompted some analysts to try to learn about changing structures, cultural norms or politics within real society by studying media content. Such analysis can be instructive up to a point. For example, during the 1980s, the baddies in Hollywood action or war films (*Rocky*, *Top Gun*, *From Russia with Love*) often were from the former Soviet Union, reflecting real world Cold War tensions at the time between that country and the US. By the 1990s, the Cold War was largely over and a switch of US foreign policy towards the Middle East was apparently mirrored by a greater emphasis on Arab or African Hollywood enemies (*Patriot Games*, *Black Hawk Down*, *The Siege*).

In their extreme form, however, suggestions that media content either shapes or mirrors society are both simplistic. An improvement would be to understand the relationship as a circular one involving elements of both processes. The media-as-mirror approach is useful in reminding us that, rather than being invented out of thin air, media content often relates closely to real events and to prevailing social trends and cultural values. But media content does not reflect these perfectly or neutrally. Media producers are highly selective with respect to what they include, and they present those elements which they *do* include in very particular ways. They do not offer us a mirror but a selective, manufactured set of *representations* (or re-presentations) of the world. As Hall (1982: 64) explains: 'representation is a very different notion to reflection. It implies the active work of selecting and presenting, of structuring and shaping'.

The content of television drama series, for example, can often relate closely to scenarios and dilemmas already of significance within broader society. Such series do not simply mirror society, however, because only certain characters, issues and incidents are included and these are represented to audiences in particular, dramatically appealing ways. Likewise, there may indeed be a relationship between the race or nationality of Hollywood villains and real US foreign policy, but rather than comprising a neutral reflection of the world, this demonstrates a selective emphasis on particular US-oriented perspectives.

Because media representations are selective and manufactured, this makes them distinct from the world they sometimes are assumed to reflect. It is this which creates the possibility that media may also have the potential to influence us. Repeated emphasis upon certain opinions, themes, events or practices across media, and consistent exclusion of others, may have a bearing upon future attitudes, identities, behaviour and social patterns. Rather than deciding between the shaping and mirroring approaches, then, a more useful starting point is to conceive of an ongoing process whereby selective media representations constantly feed into and are themselves fed by the makeup and character of society (see Figure 1.3).

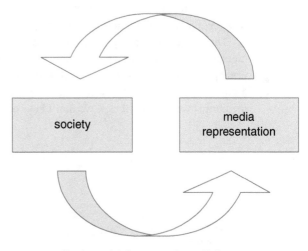

Figure 1.3 Circular model of representation and influence

THE COMMUNICATIONS PROCESS

The circular representations model outlined above provides a helpful starting point for an understanding of the socio-cultural significance of media, and it can be usefully applied to many of the specific topics covered throughout this book. Yet, as well as rather over-simplifying the complex range of phenomena included within our earlier discussion of culture and society, this model remains too general to facilitate a detailed analysis of the way media work. In order to take us a step further, we need to break the process of media communication into its core components and consider the significance of each one. This involves thinking not just about the content of media, but where such content comes from, how it is transmitted and what happens when people engage with it.

TRANSMITTERS, RECEIVERS AND NOISE

One of the first attempts to develop a systematic understanding of the relationship between different components in the communications process was developed by Shannon and Weaver (see Figure 1.4). The model was developed for the Bell telephone company, which wanted to improve the efficiency of communication using technology. It was not intended to represent broader processes of mass communication, but became highly influential in this respect. The model comprises a one-directional process whereby a message goes through a number of stages. It is created by an information source (e.g. somebody's voice), encoded into an electronic signal by a transmitter (e.g. their telephone), decoded back into its original form by a receiver (e.g. the other person's telephone) and received by a recipient at its destination.

The model also incorporates *noise*, which refers to interference which might distort the message en route so that what is received is different to what was sent. Shannon and Weaver's primary concern here were *technical problems* relating to faults or technological limitations – a poor connection can make it hard to understand what people are saying and, even if the medium is working perfectly, we don't hear people on the telephone in quite the same way as

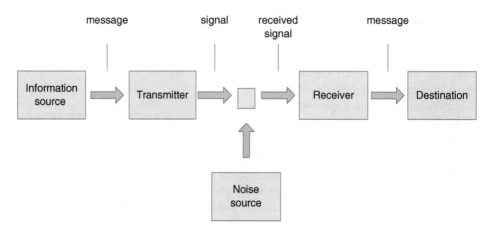

Figure 1.4   Shannon and Weaver's model of communication (1949)

we would if we were in the same room. However, they also considered the notion of *semantic problems*, which refers to the possibility that the recipient might misunderstand the message itself as a result of ambiguities in its content, and *effectiveness problems*, relating to the failure of the message to have the desired impact on the recipient. Shannon and Weaver's interest in semantic and effectiveness problems was largely focused on how such complications could be avoided through improving the technical efficiency with which messages are encoded and decoded (Fiske 1990). Nevertheless, their focus on such matters opened the doorway to important issues about the human interpretation or 'decoding' of different forms of media content by audiences and the ways media might influence people.

WHO SAYS WHAT IN WHICH CHANNEL TO WHOM WITH WHAT EFFECT?

Emphasis on communication as a human as well as a technical process was taken a stage further by Lasswell (1948), who produced a model oriented to the development of a broader under-standing of the role of mass media in society. The model is phrased as a question: 'Who says what in which channel to whom with what effect?' Memorable and deceptively concise, this question sets out an agenda for the understanding of media, through breaking up the communications process into its key components and formulating an interpretation of the relationships between them. If we separate out the components of the question and present them as a diagrammatic model, we can see clear similarities with the transmission model (see Figure 1.5).

Whereas Shannon and Weaver focused on the efficiency of the technical apparatus of communication, Lasswell's approach suggests each of the factors he identifies have equally important implications for the outcome of the communication process. I might conduct a detailed analysis of the content of a set of YouTube videos, then, but unless I also investigate the status and motivations of those who created and distributed them, the capacities and limitations of YouTube itself as a medium through which they are transmitted and the make-up and orientation of their audience, then my understanding will be partial and limited. One of the strengths of Lasswell's model is that it could potentially be applied to all manner of forms of communication, from music listening, to social media conversations, to magazine reading, or even university lectures.

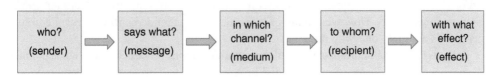

Figure 1.5 Diagrammatic representation of Lasswell's model (1948)

LINEAR AND ONE-DIMENSIONAL

Although valuable in breaking the communications process into components and considering the relationship between them, the models of Shannon and Weaver and Lasswell have been criticised for over-simplifying the communications process. According to Chandler (1994a),

Shannon and Weaver's model relies upon a 'postal metaphor' of communication. That is, it treats communication as something centred upon the effective (or ineffective) transport and delivery of a pre-existing message, complete with any meanings it contains, to a destination. Its overriding concern with the efficiency of the delivery system may make sense as a means for Bell to enhance its technical services, but provides a limited understanding of the broader operation of media in society.

As Chandler points out, the Shannon and Weaver model encourages us to view communication as an essentially one-way, linear process in which the sender of the message is active and the role of the receiver is limited to passively collecting and absorbing it. It implies what some have termed a *hypodermic syringe* approach to media, whereby messages are automatically injected into the mind of recipients, whether in the lounge, the cinema or the lecture theatre. What is not allowed for is the possibility that 'recipients' might do more than just receive, that they might engage with content actively, drawing upon their existing identity and surroundings to produce their own interpretations of what senders present to them. The construction of meaning, then, might be seen as a joint project between senders and receivers. Neither does the model refer to the possibility that receivers might directly influence the messages which are sent to them through their provision of different sorts of feedback to senders (Fiske 1990). In the case of interpersonal forms of communication, constant adjustment to the cues and responses of others comprises a critical part of effective interaction. Likewise, mass media are intensely sensitive to audience responses, whether through ratings, market research or direct communication.

Developed specifically as a means to understand the role of communication in society, Lasswell's model has more going for it in this respect than Shannon and Weaver's approach. In specifically inviting us to ask questions about the status of senders and receivers, as well as about content and medium, the model goes further towards the development of a detailed understanding of media processes, something for which it is not always given appropriate credit. Yet the wording and ordering of the model tends to reproduce the linear approach of the Shannon and Weaver model. Although it encourages us to consider the status of the recipient, it is clear that the primary role of the latter is deemed a passive one: to be *affected* in one way or another by what is communicated to them. Later communications models, which drew upon the work of Lasswell and of Shannon and Weaver, did encapsulate feedback loops from recipients back to senders (Westley and Maclean 1957) and/or the potential for audiences to interpret media in different ways (Gerbner 1956), amongst other things. However, many of these adaptations tended still to present communication as a largely one-way process.

Perhaps the most important element of the communications process which is not accounted for in Shannon and Weaver's model is the broader social and cultural environment within which media communication takes place. The model encourages us to think about communication as a process centred upon isolated individuals (Chandler 1994a). Lasswell's approach represents an improvement in this respect because, through encouraging us to think in detail about the identity of the sender and receiver of the message, it allows for some consideration of the context of each. Yet the lack of any explicit emphasis on the role of broader culture and society in the model under-estimates their importance.

ELEMENTS OF MEDIA IN SOCIO-CULTURAL CONTEXT

In this book, we'll draw partially upon the first four parts of Lasswell's question – 'who says what in which channel to whom?' – as valuable early contributions towards the identification of the key elements of the media and communications process. Consistent with the approach of many other contemporary scholars, however, the model I would advocate (see Figure 1.6) specifically focuses upon 'media industry' and 'media users' rather than thinking in terms of 'senders' and 'recipients'. Through these categories, we can specifically emphasise the power and significance of media organisations to mediated communications processes whilst, at the same time, avoiding the portrayal of the millions of people who engage with media as passive individuals whose only role is to receive, absorb or to be affected. The avoidance of a one-way, linear understanding of communication also can be achieved by the representation of a series of multi-directional flows between the different components of the model. And crucially, our understanding of media processes has to incorporate constant flows of influence both to and from a complex broader social and cultural environment, which consists of an established but developing overall world of social relations, ways of life and modes of expression. This broader environment forms an ever-changing context within which industry and users – alongside the technologies and content they use, create and distribute – operate. It should therefore be regarded as integral to the operation of all four of the elements of the media process.

The four elements of media which are represented in the context of broader culture and society in the model above form the basis for the chapters in the first part of this book – entitled *Elements of Media* – and we'll briefly introduce them here.

Equating with the 'in which channel?' part of Lasswell's model, *media technologies* (Chapter 2) refers to the hardware through which media content is created, distributed and used. Crucially, rather than being neutral, technologies such as books, television, online newspapers, social media and music streaming services each offer their own particular sets of possibilities and limitations. For example, books require all of our individual attention and have the capacity to provide extensive depth and detail through the written word, whereas television has greater potential to be enjoyed alongside other activities or with other people and tends to facilitate greater emphasis on what things look and sound like on the surface.

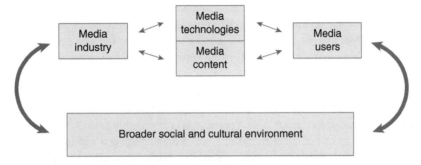

Figure 1.6   Simplified model of the elements of media in socio-cultural context

Rather than simply shaping us, however, technologies are developed and used in ways that relate closely to the social and cultural context of industry and users.

Media industry (Chapter 3) may in some cases be seen as a more specific and contextualised formulation of the 'who?' at the beginning of Lasswell's model. Media and related organisations are far from the only creators of content in the digital age but they continue to dominate its production and distribution. They also play a pivotal role in controlling the development and availability of technologies that enable different forms of communication and, as such connect closely to Lasswell's 'in which channel?' question. An understanding of media processes, then, requires an appreciation of the motivations of these organisations, of the ways they work and their relationships with other organisations, media users and broader social and cultural relations. At the centre of an examination of industry are questions about the large-scale, commercial nature of the most influential media organisations, the implications of their need to generate revenue by attracting advertising and the ways governments and regulators have sought to control their activities.

Media content (Chapter 4) comprises the 'what?' in Lasswell's model and is probably the most talked about element of the media process. We can't hope to understand the role and significance of media by focusing on content alone, but neither should we ignore it. Television programmes, advertisements, music videos, social network profiles, news articles and a plethora of other content all may be seen to represent the world in partial and particular ways and this places limits on the range of likely interpretations or uses of them. This implies that content may have the capacity to influence the thoughts and lives of users and the broader ways of life and social relations of which they are a part. Careful analysis of what is included and excluded and the complex ways meanings are constructed through content remains a key element of the study of media, culture and society.

The notion of *media users* (Chapter 5) is considerably broader than the 'to whom?' in Lasswell's model in that, rather than restricting their role to that of receivers who are affected by media messages, it recognises that those who engage with media play an active role in communications processes. It is crucial, then, to learn about the circumstances in which users engage with different forms of media and the ways they contribute to the generation of meaning through bringing their existing identities, opinions and social position to their encounters with content and technologies. Users also should be understood as small-scale creators and distributors of content, whether through responding to mass media through comments or discussion, sharing via social media or communicating with one another. Some 'users' also engage in the production and distribution of more substantive forms of amateur content in the form of blogs, video, images or music. As we shall see, one of the key complexities of the current media environment is that the distinction between this sort of amateur content creation and more professional forms of media production is not always clear-cut.

The broader social and cultural environment is represented here as feeding, via users and industry, into each of the different elements of the ongoing media process, while at the same time developing and changing as a result of that process. It is impossible to understand the operation and significance of any one of the elements of media without placing it within this socio-cultural context. Because of this, rather than having a separate chapter on the theme, different elements of culture and society are discussed throughout the chapters on technologies, industry, content and users which make up the first part of the book. And the relationship between media processes and the various elements of broader culture and society dominates the second and third parts of the book, which address a range of substantive issues and debates under the themes of *Media, Power and Control* and *Media, Identity and Culture*.

MEDIA, POWER AND CONTROL

The second part of the book focuses on a series of themes connected to the relationship between media and questions of power, influence, regulation and control. We start in Chapter 6 by examining highly influential Marxist approaches which regard media as a form of ideology or, more specifically, a means by which powerful groups manipulate people by reinforcing understandings of the world which serve to legitimate an unequal and exploitative capitalist system. Concerns about ideology also figure, among other perspectives, in Chapter 7, which addresses the specific role of news media as a way of distributing particular representations of the contemporary world to media users. In Chapter 8, our focus shifts to broader questions about what media are for and, specifically, whether their role in society might be improved if governments try to control how they are run. Should we attempt to control media by having subsidised public service broadcasters or restrictions on content, or would we be better served by an unfettered commercial media system? One of the implications of commercial media systems is that they tend to centre upon the incorporation of commercial messages as their key funding source, and Chapter 9 offers a detailed examination of the growth and development of advertising, with a particular emphasis on how strategies and modes of persuasion are transforming in the digital media age. Finally, Chapter 10 addresses the relationship between media, national identity and democracy, focusing in particular upon the possibility that the increasing commercialisation and diversification of media may be contributing to declines in cultural cohesion and socio-political engagement.

MEDIA, IDENTITY AND CULTURE

The third and final part of the book moves us towards questions about the relationship between media and patterns of identity, culture and community. Chapter 11 opens the section through an examination of the implications of media processes for patterns of collective difference and identity in society. In contrast to theories that suggest media tend to erode difference and community, the chapter examines a range of ways that, for better or worse, differences can be amplified and distinct communities strengthened through media. We highlight contrasting examples, from mass media stigmatisation of marginalised groups to the role of niche and participatory media in facilitating a variety of community identities. Chapters 12 and 13 deal with two of the most discussed subjects within the study of media: race and gender. In Chapter 12, we consider intense debates about the exclusion and stereotypical representation of subordinated ethnic and racial groupings within media before examining the implications of the increasing use by such ethnic minorities and migrant groups of specialist and sometimes transnational forms of media. Chapter 13 centres partly on questions about the representation of femininities and masculinities, while also examining debates about the role of audiences and users in the construction of gender. The chapter also examines the link between representations of gender and sexuality, and focuses on developments in the depiction of sexual minorities. The final chapter of the book, Chapter 14, addresses the possibility that, as a result of the rapid and ongoing expansion of media, everyday culture has become so saturated by communication, images and representations that we no longer can hope to know what, if anything, any of it means. Truth, reality and stability all are deemed under threat in a world dominated by fluidity, uncertainty and the loss of meaning.

MAKING CONNECTIONS

These thematic sections of this book offer a useful means of organising and making sense of so large a range of material. However, readers hopefully will identify a range of connections between the issues covered in each part. They may note, for example, that questions of national community clearly relate to identity as well as power and that discussions of gender and race connect to issues of domination and subordination as well as to those of cultural differentiation. And, as one would expect, the issues covered in the chapters of the opening section, on technologies, industry, content and users, will resurface at various points during the discussions of the substantive topics which follow. Equally, a number of particular issues surface at a number of different points in the book. Questions about commercialisation and the quality and depth of media content, for example, appear in all three parts of the book, as do considerations of the relationship between media and advertisers and questions about the increasing specialisation and interactivity of media. Such interconnections are important and readers are encouraged to draw their own links between the various topics covered in the chapters that follow. It is only through making such connections that we can gradually develop a more rounded understanding of the themes and approaches which dominate the study of media, culture and society.

QUESTIONS/EXERCISES

1   Select a piece of media content of your own choice and address the following:

   a) In what ways does the content draw upon elements of existing social relations or ways or life?

   b) In what ways is it selective in doing so?

   c) In what ways might these selective representations influence the future of society?

2   Design your own diagrammatic model of processes of mediated communication and their relationship with the broader social and cultural environment. Think carefully about how you will represent the key elements of the communications process and the nature of the relationships between them.

PART ONE

ELEMENTS OF MEDIA

CHAPTER 2
MEDIA TECHNOLOGIES

FOCAL POINTS

- Theories that suggest that communications technologies influence the social and cultural world
- Arguments about the socio-cultural impacts of print and electronic media
- Criticisms of technological determinism and arguments about the need to study technologies in context
- The growth and properties of digital media and the internet
- Optimistic and pessimistic analyses of the impacts of digital media

INTRODUCTION

When asked to think about media, the first thing to enter many people's minds would probably be an example of media content, whether a film, an advertisement, an audio clip, a music video or a piece of news footage. Similarly, analysis of the social or cultural significance of media often focuses on questions of media content. Is news coverage of current affairs biased? What kinds of things do people disclose about themselves on social media? What do depictions of gender in advertisements tell us about attitudes to masculinity and femininity? Such questions are, of course, of great importance. This chapter, however, is not about content, but about the technologies or hardware through which content is transmitted. It is, in other words, about the significance of media themselves, remembering that media is the plural of medium.

For some commentators, known as *medium theorists*, the properties of communications technologies can have profound social and cultural impacts and the understanding of these impacts should be pivotal to any quest to make sense of media. From the development of newspapers to the growth of different forms of internet platform, the onset of new technologies with distinct capabilities has often been accompanied by intense debate about their likely impact upon power, politics, culture and everyday life. In recent times, debates have raged about the impact of social media, mobile technologies and various facets of the internet, while in the past equally intense discussions took place with respect to newspapers, radio, records, cinema and, of course, television.

This chapter begins by focusing on some of the contrasting conclusions drawn by prominent medium theorists about the development and impacts of print and electronic media technologies. As well as discussing case studies, we will examine criticisms of medium theories, including the claim that such approaches have a tendency to over-estimate the extent to which technologies have inevitable or predictable socio-cultural effects. We will go on to discuss arguments about the significance of more recent digital technologies and the internet.

CLASSIC MEDIUM THEORIES

MCLUHAN: THE MEDIUM IS THE MESSAGE

> …in operational and practical fact, the medium is the message. This is merely to say that the personal and social consequences of any medium – that is, of any extension of ourselves – result from the new scale that is introduced into our affairs by each extension of ourselves, or by any new technology. (McLuhan 2001: 2)

The first of our case studies involves the most well-known medium theorist, Marshall McLuhan, who famously argued in the 1960s that the study of media content was of little significance compared to the analysis of communications technologies. He expresses this through the often-cited slogan 'the medium is the message'. Essentially, he meant that the medium is more important than the message: that it is the capacities of media hardware, rather than the details of particular examples of content, that have real social significance and impact. Debating the specifics of the content of news articles, advertisements or radio broadcasts is regarded by McLuhan as an unnecessary distraction – something liable to result in a failure to see the forest for the trees. To study the social significance of television by focusing on the content of particular programmes is no more useful, from McLuhan's point of view, than trying to learn about the cultural impact of the telephone through reference to the subject matter of a particular conversation between two friends in Toronto or, to take a more recent example, attempting to ascertain the impact of digital tablets by conducting a close analysis of the music listened to on such a device by a particular individual on a Monday morning.

What is important, he argues, is not the detail of the content, but the broader fact that particular modes of communication are made possible. For McLuhan, each media technology enables a different extension of our communicative senses – in both space and time – beyond what was previously possible. Arguing that media should be regarded as 'the extensions of man', he writes that 'after more than a century of electric technology we have extended our central nervous system itself into a global embrace, abolishing both space and time…' (2001: 3). In different ways, then, media technologies expand our physical sphere of communications – we can see, hear, talk or write across greater distances and at greater speed. It is this that leads to McLuhan's most famous pronouncement – that as a result of the ease with which we can communicate across the world through electronic media, we increasingly inhabit a 'global village'.

Crucially, each medium extends our senses in different ways – encouraging certain patterns of communication and preventing others. The central distinction made by McLuhan between different forms of media involves two categories – *hot* and *cool*. Hot media are high definition and data intensive with a large amount of information conveyed – usually to a single one of the human senses. Including books, newspapers and radio, hot media occupy all or most of the attention of an individual and leave few gaps to be completed by the audience. In contrast, cool media are low in information-intensity and high in audience participation – rather like a discussion-based seminar as compared to a lecture. For McLuhan, the cool medium par excellence was television, whose ability to combine sound with what, during the 1950s and 60s, were very low-definition moving pictures, is deemed to have enabled both visual and audio senses to be engaged simultaneously, but each less intensively than in the case of printed literature or radio. As a consequence, television did not spell out every detail, it is argued, leaving audiences able to fill in the gaps. By way of illustration, we might imagine how McLuhan might have compared sports commentaries on radio and television. On the radio extensive detail has to be spelt out by commentators, requiring intense concentration from listeners and strongly shaping their interpretations. In contrast, television commentators are able to provide less detail, allowing viewers to partially interpret moving pictures for themselves.

The most important comparison for McLuhan, though, was between print media, which he regarded as universally hot, and electronic media, which he believed were becoming increasingly cool. Outlining the social significance of the historical development of the printing press, McLuhan (1962) argues that the ability to mass-produce books and, later, newspapers precipitated an end to the age of oral, informal, face-to-face communication and its replacement by a society so dominated by standardised print media that the human senses became fragmented because everything was reduced to and dictated by the format of the written word. The effect of this, he argues, was to standardise dialect, language and culture, dictate particular ordered ways of viewing the world and homogenise societies into hierarchically organised nation states.

Inherently, McLuhan suggests, print media was amenable to such hierarchical arrangements. Isolated, individualised and silent, the reader is dictated to by the one-directional, linear organisation and intense detail of the information in the text, receiving a precise and literal set of messages from a small number of sources and unable to participate or interact with the material. For McLuhan, such technological biases rendered print media responsible for the development of an early capitalist society dominated by rigid cultural hierarchies, standardisation and individual isolation.

In contrast, the ongoing development of electronic media is deemed to have culminated in television, a cool technology, deemed to have liberated audiences from the restrictions of the print age, heralding a return to organic, participatory communicative practices. 'Mechanical, one-way expansion from centres to margins,' he argues, are 'no longer relevant to our electric world' (2001: 39). Whilst print culture served to homogenise language, television's emphasis on cool speech and pictures is deemed to have precipitated a shift away from such centralised officialdom in favour of an emphasis on local dialects and everyday talk. More generally, television is regarded as spontaneous, intimate, informal and incomplete, inviting creative audience participation. Ultimately, the capacities of this cool, informal medium are deemed pivotal to the increasing development of a *global village*, envisaged in the most organic, decentralised of terms. Gone would be the individual isolation and one-way standardised, linear national communication which characterised print culture, to be replaced by a proliferation of multi-directional, decentralised electronic communication across the globe.

KILL YOUR TELEVISION

McLuhan's optimism about the social impact of electronic media was not shared by all commentators. Postman (1987) looks back fondly on the age of print media and describes a range of social ills brought about by developments in electronic and visual communications. From this point of view, early newspapers offered a detailed, localised and relevant source of communication, filled with rich, coherent information of direct significance to the lives of readers. Far from being a disadvantage, as McLuhan saw it, the level of concentration required from readers is deemed by Postman to have encouraged a rational, serious engagement with local issues and to have been important to the development of informed, reasoned critical discussion and political engagement. For Postman, such engagement has gradually been undermined by a series of technological developments, beginning with the telegraph and ending (at the time he was writing) with television.

Developed by Morse in the 1830s and 40s, the telegraph enabled the transmission of coded electric signals across significant geographical distances (see Figure 2.1). Amongst other things, this possibility had a profound impact on newspapers, which became able to report stories from distant places without the inconvenience and time delays associated with physical travel. In Postman's view, however, 'the dazzle of distance and speed' (1987: 67) prompted an increasing emphasis on the superficial reporting of a multitude of enticing stories from elsewhere. When it came to newspaper content, telegraphy is deemed to have been suited only to 'the flashing of messages, each to be quickly replaced by a more up to date message' (1987: 71). Instead of offering coherence, depth and local relevance, each edition would offer an arbitrary mixture of temporary sources of fascination from afar.

Figure 2.1   Telegraph wires ©Robert Hillman

The ability to reproduce photographs as part of newspapers – first developed in the late 1800s – is deemed by Postman to have represented a further step in the direction of superficiality. Where printed text had provided depth and context, encouraging rational engagement and critical thinking, photographs are argued to reduce the complexity of issues to particular observable fragments and encourage emotional, voyeuristic captivation. Worse still, this inherent superficiality is hidden by a veneer of realness and proximity – photographs, then, entice us into the mistaken feeling that we have fully understood the situation depicted. Meanwhile, the desire for image-based journalism is deemed to have affected news priorities themselves, the inclusion of issues increasingly based not on importance but visual appeal. For Postman, this made the photograph the ideal counterpart for the emphasis created by telegraphy on exciting short-lived stories from afar. Together, the two are blamed for a reorientation of mass media towards empty spectacle.

Postman's strongest comments, however, are reserved for the societal impact of television. In contrast to McLuhan's optimism, Postman regards the small screen as having concentrated all the worst tendencies of the alliance of telegraphy and photography, 'raising the interplay of image and instancy to an exquisite and dangerous perfection' (1987: 79) while bringing them to the centre of our domestic lives. Television's emphasis on moving pictures is deemed to have extended the emotionally enticing qualities of the photograph, combined them with sound, and, in so doing, intensified the domination of communications by voyeurism and spectacle. Even more so than photography, moving pictures allow us to imagine that we have seen all there is to know, when in reality we have witnessed only superficial fragments. In place of the depth and coherence once provided by text-based media, the technological properties of television 'suppress the content of ideas in order to accommodate the requirements of visual interest…' (1987: 92).

If television exaggerates the visual biases of photography, then its relentless emphasis on tempo and immediacy may be traced back, according to Postman, to the telegraph. It is no coincidence, argues Postman, that US television news reports each last no more than a minute; that individual programmes rarely last more than 30 minutes; and that rarely is there any sort of link or coherence between one segment of content and another. For Postman, the 'now this!' tendency, whereby content rapidly shifts the attention of the viewer between an array of unrelated subject matter, has resulted from the inherent bias of television as a medium – its 'predisposition toward being used in some ways and not others' (1987: 84). And, as a consequence, audiences are induced into any number of instant emotional responses to the spectacles placed in front of them, but are unlikely to understand or even to remember them:

> There is no murder so brutal, no earthquake so devastating, no political blunder so costly – for that matter, no ball score so tantalising or no weather report so threatening – that it cannot be erased from our minds by a newscaster saying 'now this!'. (1987: 99–100)

The depth of Postman's concern also relates to what he sees as the ubiquity of television – its dominance of lives and imaginations across boundaries of class, age, gender and ethnicity. As a consequence, television's in-built emphasis on superficiality is deemed to have had a profound impact on culture and society off the screen: 'Television is our culture's principal mode of knowing about itself. Therefore... how television stages the world becomes the model for how the world is properly to be staged' (1987: 92–3).

Postman's attack on the social impacts of television shares some features with an earlier polemic entitled *Four Arguments for the Elimination of Television*, in which Mander asserts that the technological biases of television make attempts to regulate its use futile: 'Far from being "neutral", television itself predetermines who shall use it, how they shall use it, what effects it will have on individual lives and... what sort of political forms will inevitably emerge' (1978: 45). And, like Postman, Mander argues that such biases create an emphasis on short, snappy content and a focus on style, presentation and entertainment. Whilst presenting us with all this superficiality, argues Mander, television consumption makes us believe that we understand the world: 'because of television we believe we know more, but we know less' (1978: 349). In contrast to McLuhan's insistence that television would undo the centralised top down culture created by print, Mander also asserts that television is itself inherently a hierarchical, one directional mode of communication which empowers an elite minority, whilst distracting and disorienting a passive mass audience.

TECHNOLOGICAL DETERMINISM

There should be no doubt as to the importance either of McLuhan's highly influential optimistic approach to electronic technologies or of the pessimistic approach taken by Postman. Alongside a range of other medium theorists, including Innes (1951), Ong (1977) and Meyrowitz (1985), they offer a crucial reminder that in order to answer questions about the relationship between media, culture and society we must consider the significance of different media hardware and software. They remind us that questions of power, space and time, as well as patterns of interaction and understanding, can be intimately connected to the dominant means of communication within different societies and eras. Nevertheless, there can also be problems with medium theory, whether it is optimistic, pessimistic or neither. Difficulties vary somewhat from theorist to theorist, but as a whole, the approach has tended to overplay and simplify the role of technologies, regarding them as the primary cause of social change and giving insufficient consideration to the causal significance of the broader context in which they are developed and used.

HOT, COOL OR BOTH?

It should already be clear, not least from the disagreement of Postman, that McLuhan's specific interpretations of the qualities and impacts of media technologies are open to question. His distinction between high intensity low participation (hot) technologies and those that are low intensity and high participation (cool) is confusing, especially when one considers his own categorisation of different examples. In some respects, his interpretation of print media as hot makes sense: books and newspapers do indeed place emphasis on linear textual detail and require intensive engagement from an isolated individual reader. Yet these media surely also have potentially cool characteristics. Is it not the case that reading can generate participation, imagination and critical thought, for example, not least through the construction of our own vivid visual representations of what is being described? Some degree of co-construction is surely taking place here – and arguably more so than in the case of some encounters with television content, where pictures, sounds and sometimes text are each shaped by media producers.

Another dichotomy presented by McLuhan – between cinema which is regarded as hot and television as cool – is even more questionable. McLuhan suggests the way cinema places the viewer in a darkened, silent room in front of an enormous, detailed screen creates a hierarchical and individualising effect similar to the consumption of print media. He contrasts this with the more social, less prescriptive properties of early 1950s and 60s fuzzy black and white television. Now we may agree that, of the two viewer experiences, the cinematic probably was – and is – of higher intensity in McLuhan's terms. Notwithstanding this difference of degree, to categorise two such apparently similar forms of communication at opposite ends of the hot/cool spectrum is curious at best. And McLuhan's emphasis on differences in the quality and detail of the screens in each case has become increasingly redundant as a result of predictable improvements in the resolution of moving pictures and sound on a range of devices, from mobile tablets to large LCD or plasma screens.

The broader point highlighted here is that the very exercise of categorising technologies as inherently 'hot' or 'cool' is hazardous, as is the broader assumption that the inherent properties of technologies predetermine their use and social impact. When I ask students to categorise different media technologies as hot and cool, their most frequent response is to point out that levels of intensity and audience participation are dependent upon both content and the contexts of media users. They surely are right. Listening to a complex play on the radio may require more intense concentration than listening to pop music or light-hearted chat between presenters, something likely to affect, amongst other things, whether listening comprises a primary or secondary activity. The technical capacities of radio are of much importance here but the kind of communication engendered is equally dependent upon content and context of use. Contrary to McLuhan, then, we need to examine the message as well as the medium, and to understand media users too.

GENERALISATION AND REIFICATION

The negative commentaries of Postman and Mander also assume technologies have automatic social effects, regardless of content or context. Both insist deficiencies in television content are an inevitable result of technological bias. Neither entertain the possibility that television content could, through regulation or other means, be made more compatible with a culturally rich, democratic society. Yet both tend to focus on those examples of content that best support their case, making little reference to more in-depth, informative or educational forms of television, for example. Their focus on US television, meanwhile, leaves little space for consideration of television in different cultural contexts or regulatory systems. Many would argue, for example, that early television content in many European countries was significantly different to that of their US equivalents as a result of public service forms of regulation (see Chapter 8). Questions about how media are controlled, then, and about the broader cultural context in which technologies are placed, tend to be brushed aside.

Because they regard technological features as having inevitable and predetermined social consequences, approaches such as those of Postman, Mander and McLuhan can be labelled *technologically determinist*. They assume that the inherent biases of technologies dictate their impact, regardless of who develops and controls them, how they are used and in what socio-cultural context. Technologies, then, are *reified*; that is, they are transformed by the theorists into independent objects, when in reality they are developed, manufactured, controlled and used by people in particular social contexts (Chandler 1995). One of the consequences of this, according to Raymond Williams (1974), is that our attention is distracted away from the human actors and structures responsible for the development and use of technologies and the broader shape taken by society, including with respect to inequalities of power. From this point of view, the techno-optimism of McLuhan plays into the hands of the powerful by offering technology as a magic solution to man-made problems, while the techno-pessimism of Postman and Mander lets powerful interests off the hook by deferring the blame for social problems onto inanimate objects.

TECHNOLOGIES AND SOCIAL CONTEXTS

The opposite view from that held by technological determinists is that, far from having pre-determined socio-cultural impacts, technologies should be regarded as tools whose development and use is dependent on social contexts and human priorities. A garden spade normally is used to help us to dig holes and move soil, but it may also lend itself to various other activities – a support for its user to lean on, a weapon with which to defend oneself, a means to smash windows and break into someone's house and so on. Similarly, it is sometimes noted that a knife may be used to cook, kill or cure. The technology, then, does not determine its use, the latter depending on the physical and social situation of users, on socio-economic conventions, regulations, cultural expectations and a range of other factors. Meanwhile, the very existence of a technology such as the spade – the fact that it was developed and manufactured in the ways it was – is itself reflective of social context. Like other technologies, it is a product of particular human needs, purposes and arrangements (see Williams 1974).

Similarly, communications technologies may be regarded as having been developed as a result of socio-cultural circumstances and open to a variety of possible uses. Often, eventual uses can differ from the purpose for which they were originally envisaged. We tend automatically to regard the gramophone as a piece of equipment oriented to the playing of recorded music, but it was originally intended as a means to record and play back speech. During the initial development of broadcast technology, radio was envisaged not primarily as a mass medium but a wireless form of interpersonal communication – a rival to the telephone. In spite of the extent of their expenditure on market research, those who develop and promote contemporary technologies also are unable fully to predict the ways they are used. That text messaging became one of the most popular uses of the mobile phone, for example, occurred not primarily by industry design but as a result of largely unpredicted consumer enthusiasm for what was originally envisaged as a marginal application (Rettie 2009).

Rather than being predetermined by inherent technological biases, then, the purpose and social role of technologies is dependent upon complex contextual factors, including the interests, capacities and priorities of industry, consumers and a variety of intermediaries. From this point of view, a technology such as television should not be seen as technologically predisposed towards either high participation extensions of the senses or passive short-term escapism. Depending on the context of producers and users – as well as the detail of content – television may, in different circumstances, lend itself to both these types of usage as well as various others; a tool of information and education, for example, or a facilitator of social cohesion and political engagement.

So how do we break-down and study the significance of the contexts in which technologies circulate? Paul Du Gay and colleagues (1997) offer one possible answer, by proposing that, in order to understand the social and cultural significance of technologies we must examine each of a series of interlinked processes – collectively termed the 'circuit of culture' – which all cultural artefacts go through. *Production* refers to the institutional and social circumstances in which a technology is developed, manufactured and distributed, while *representation* concerns media discourse about the technology, which can play a crucial role in developing particular understandings of its purpose and meaning. This might include direct forms of marketing as well as broader popular representations in news, books, fiction or elsewhere. *Regulation* refers to the various forms of control imposed by government or other bodies, which can restrict and shape the ways technologies are used. Meanwhile, *consumption* emphasises the importance of the contexts in which users engage with technologies and *identity* concerns the way in which such consumption practices are intricately connected with the development of individual and collective subjectivities. Du Gay et al. illustrate the examination of these interconnected processes by offering an analysis of the Sony Walkman as a case study, but the model could just as easily be applied to contemporary cultural artefacts or technologies.

CAPACITIES AND CONSTRAINTS

Yet recognition of the importance of the institutional, discursive and consumption contexts in which technologies operate ought not lead us to the conclusion that technologies themselves are neutral. After all, we could list a great many possible uses for the garden spade, but technical constraints relating to size, shape and density prevent it from being a useful means for people to cut grass, apply paint evenly or eat food. Although they are considerably more complicated than spades, communications media, from billboards to social network sites, also do have their own capacities and constraints, sometimes referred to as affordances (Norman 1988), which have implications for the way they are used and their social impacts.

Even though they can under-estimate the significance of context and use, then, we should still learn from medium theorists that technical features matter. While avoiding being over-prescriptive, it remains possible to develop ways of categorising different forms of established media with respect to features that might have social or cultural significance. The extent to which media facilitate communication through text, sound, still image, video or some combination of the four may be a good start, for example. We might then tentatively distinguish *mass* media technologies, which have afforded communication with large groups of people, from *interpersonal* media, more oriented to the facilitation of small-scale interaction between two people or small groups. Likewise we might categorise media with respect to the extent to which they enable *one-directional* or *interactive* communication. *Synchronous* media, which operate in real time could then be identified as distinct from *asynchronous* media, which do not, and so on. Figure 2.2 illustrates the ways in which simple differentiators such as these might work in relation to classic media technologies or what are sometimes termed 'traditional media'.

Through categorising technologies like this we simplify their capacities, but in doing so we may enhance our understanding of their potential significance. For example, the audio-only nature of radio makes it reasonable to propose that, under the right circumstances, it may be better suited than visual media to be used as a secondary activity, which accompanies things like driving or working. Meanwhile, because they are asynchronous physical objects based on printed text and image, we can probably conclude that newspapers are not especially well suited to the communication of live breaking news stories. In contrast, contemporary television, by enabling the instantaneous transfer of moving images and sound, has contributed to a situation in which we can watch and hear live events in real time. The development, use and consequences of this capacity are all dependent upon human priorities and contexts, but the availability of the technology itself still alters what is possible.

Household telephone	Interpersonal medium	Sound	Synchronous	Interactive
Newspaper	Mass medium	Text, still image	Asynchronous	One-directional
Radio	Mass medium	Sound	Synchronous	One-directional
Television	Mass medium	Video, sound, still image, text	Synchronous	One-directional

Figure 2.2   Selected properties of traditional media

INTO THE DIGITAL AGE

For many, recent developments in communications, dominated by the growth of digital and internet technology, have heralded a societal transformation at least as significant as the transitions from oral to print communication and from print to broadcasting. Over the next few pages we explore a number of features of digital media that render their potential impacts significantly different from those associated with the emergence of previous forms of mass media. Most notably, digital media are argued to have brought about the convergence of previously distinct forms of communication; precipitated dramatic shifts in the relationship between media producers and audiences; pluralised, diversified and fragmented the world of media; and enabled users to be connected to media constantly, wherever they are.

CONVERGENCE

Where traditional media each tended to have their own distinct capacities and constraints, digitalisation – alongside the specific development of the internet – entailed the prospect of bringing into a single sphere the technical possibilities of previously separate forms of communication. One of McLuhan's claims was that, whereas print technologies privileged the written word, television served to reunite the human senses by bringing together text, moving images and sound. Processes of digitalisation, however, have enabled the development of media environments even more inclusive and flexible by enabling text, images, music, speech and video all to be converted into a universal system of binary codes (1s and 0s) and then decoded by a single piece of receiving equipment, whether a PC, games console, digital radio, smart phone or digital television set-top box.

Figure 2.3   A digital mobile device © Maksym Protsenko

Depending on content and user priorities, on the internet we consume text, images, speech, audio and video, whether in an integrated fashion on a single site or via a number of different ones. And convergence is not limited to the bringing together of different mass communications processes. Email, instant messaging and Skype, alongside an ever-expanding range of social media platforms, illustrate how seamlessly the internet incorporates interpersonal communication too. While sometimes these modes remain discrete, in other cases mass, niche and interpersonal communication are seamlessly integrated with one another. A typical Facebook newsfeed now combines personal text or image updates between friends with a range of shared content originating from high and medium profile sites – and these may take the form of text, images, speech, music, video or different combinations thereof. To complicate things further, for those users with substantial networks of friends or followers, or those who find their communications shared beyond those initial networks, the boundary between interpersonal and larger-scale communication – and between public and private – is increasingly unclear (boyd 2014). Distinctions such as those in Figure 2.2, then, become rather more difficult to make.

Of course, the internet itself is not the only means through which such convergence is taking place. As well as being increasingly centred on the internet in one form or another, smart phones and larger tablet devices increasingly bring together the telephone with a personal music player, a portable games machine, a diary, a video player and considerably more besides. Because they enable many different media forms to use the same kinds of digital code, then, processes of digitalisation increase cross-compatibility between previously separate technologies. Most of all, the boundary between the internet itself and other forms of digital media is blurring, to the extent that television and radio programmes, as well as newspapers are available to view or listen to via the internet, while the internet is itself becoming an integral part of television services, phones, games consoles and so on.

INTERACTIVITY

As alluded to in some of our discussion under convergence, the *interactivity* of digital media, and particularly the internet, is another socially significant feature. Leaving aside the disagreements between McLuhan and Postman, most agree that broadcasting and print technology afforded a predominantly one-way relationship between a small number of producers and a large audience of readers or viewers. For Bordewijk and Van Kaam (2002), traditional broadcasting took the form of an *allocutionary* medium in the sense that content is distributed in a single direction from a powerful centre, with audiences able only to switch on and off or change channels. The medium allows neither for audience feedback to producers or for mediated communication between different audience members (Spurgeon 2008). The only truly interactive media, prior to the internet, were interpersonal technologies such as the telephone and the postal system. As well as incorporating a range of interpersonal means of communication, the internet for the first time introduced the possibility of interactive group or even mass communication. The capacity for large numbers of people to engage with the same content was combined with a level of interactivity previously only facilitated by interpersonal media. Ordinary people were able to distribute as well as receive content, whether through publishing their own website or blog, sharing and conversing with others on social media, posting messages on public or community forums or producing, uploading and publicising their own multimedia content. While such levels of interactivity were limited to a small minority of intensive users in the early years of the internet, during the course of the first decade of the 2000s, easy to use blogging, social media, video sharing and other facilities had begun to generate extensive levels of participation and user creativity as part of what some referred to as a second phase in the development of web software often termed 'Web 2.0' (Dinucci 1999). Such developments have prompted some to refer to the contemporary web as a medium of 'mass conversation' (Spurgeon 2008).

DIVERSIFICATION

The internet also offers users unprecedented levels of control over what content they interact with. Rather than merely switching on and flicking channels, we are faced with a choice between millions of sites, services and individuals. Similarly, digital television has facilitated a massive growth in the number of different channels on offer, the growth of +1 channels and personal video recording technologies that enable viewers easily to record and view programmes whenever they like. Meanwhile the last few years have seen a rapid expansion of watch-on-demand television and film services based on internet streaming technologies such as Netflix and Amazon Prime that enable people to view content on demand from a wide range of devices. Such technologies increasingly are disconnecting media users from traditional standardised schedules and increasing the range and volume of different forms of content instantly available.

As well as making media more interactive, then, digitalisation has contributed to a substantial diversification and expansion of media content and of the relationships between content and consumers. A previous media system dominated by the simultaneous collective engagement of mass audiences with small quantities of content appears to be fragmenting into a far more complex, disparate and disorganised environment.

MOBILITY

A further feature of the contemporary digital environment is that, rather than being confined to particular fixed locations, more and more of the media outlets we use are mobile, enabling us to communicate from all sorts of locations. Mobile or cell phones enable conversations from wherever we are and smart devices enable us to engage with a vast array of information, content, applications, communities and networks on the move. We can take our entire music collection wherever we go, providing a personalised sound track to our movement through public spaces (Bull 2007) or alternatively stream music, speech or video from online services anywhere we can get access to wifi or a high-speed cellular data network. And we can be in constant contact with what our friends and acquaintances are doing, thinking and feeling – as well as media content they're engaging with – via 'always on' connections to Facebook, Twitter, Tumblr, Instagram, Snapchat and a range of other social network applications. According to a 2013 study by Pew Internet Research, 63% of mobile phone users in the US were using their phone to access the internet and 34% of these 'cell internet users' said they 'mostly' went online using their phone as opposed to another device. For young people these figures were considerably higher, with 50% of 'cell internet users' aged 18–29 'mostly' accessing the internet from their phone rather than another device (Duggan and Smith 2013). Presumably, were the study to have included other mobile devices such as tablets, the overall figure for mobile internet use would have been even higher.

As a result, whether on the train, in the cafe, at work, at home or walking between the two, many of us are drifting towards an 'always on' position when it comes to our engagement with media (Castells et al. 2006). The implications of such constant digital connections are only beginning to be explored.

THE INTERNET AS SOLUTION TO OR CAUSE OF SOCIAL ILLS

Like previous technologies before them, the technological capacities and affordances of the internet and broader digitalisation have been the subject of a range of positive and negative predictions and proclamations with respect to their impact on social and cultural life.

DEMOCRACY AND FREEDOM?

For some techno-enthusiasts, the digital revolution heralded fundamental cultural change and the creation of a better society. The ability of internet users to summon up information or culture on demand and make their own content available to a potential audience of millions, prompted enthusiastic proclamations of a decentralisation of power, a challenge to previously dominant media organisations, a resurgence of political engagement, an enhancement of individual liberty and an improvement in global harmony. Negroponte (1995), for example, predicted that the technology would liberate individuals from the constraints of place, that the operation and control of societies would be decentralised and that community and global relations would be transformed for the better, while Gilder (1992) predicted the transformation of education, the decline of standardised television culture and the draining of power from the established media industry. More recently, John Hartley (2009) celebrates what he regards as the democratisation of television as a result of the capacity on the contemporary internet – specifically via platforms such as YouTube – for ordinary people to become producers and distributors of content. Others have focused on the significance of public conversation and activism via social media and the development of citizen journalism – whereby members of the public document, record and distribute evidence and reports via the internet – as indications of a renewed popular engagement in politics, a challenge to traditionally powerful voices or the enhancement of human freedom, cooperation and participation (see Allan and Thorsen 2009; Jenkins 2008; Papacharissi 2010; Shirky 2008). National governments, meanwhile, have often championed the potential of the internet to enhance political engagement and improve educational achievement.

ISOLATION AND SUPERFICIALITY

For other theorists, however, the technological properties of emerging digital media environments are precipitating problematic social consequences. Concerns have included anxieties about dangers to children online through exposure to inappropriate content or hostile others; arguments about our increasing exposure to online surveillance; and proclamations of social isolation and superficiality. By way of example, we'll explore some contributions to the last of these concerns.

For Sherry Turkle – once regarded as a techno-enthusiast (see Turkle 1995) – the extent of our constant connection to media technologies is having regressive impacts on genuine forms of human interaction and relationship (Turkle 2013). The ability to interact with an infinite range of content or individuals on terms of our choosing is prompting us, she argues, to opt for the convenience of online interactions over the more demanding work of developing deeper forms of relationship centred on physical interaction. We opt, Turkle argues, for the 'illusion of companionship without the demands of friendship' (2012). As a consequence, we find ourselves constantly sharing physical space with others while we each are glued to our individual screens – interacting with a multitude of content and people online whilst ignoring those in our presence. As a consequence we find ourselves increasingly 'alone together', she argues, and entrapped in a vicious circle whereby the more alone we feel, the more we turn to the individualised worlds inside our technological devices (ibid.).

Aspects of Turkle's analysis connect to the writings of other theorists. While her concern is more with the vibrancy, breadth and depth of cultural lives than psychological well-being, Christine Rosen's brief analysis of the individual control afforded to us by digital media devices also speaks to the theme of superficiality. Faced with the possibility, through PVRs, personal music players and other devices, to consume virtually anything we want when we want, we invariably are moved, argues Rosen, to focus on the already familiar and to flick impatiently between different forms of content, quickly rejecting anything without immediate familiarity or appeal (Rosen 2005). For Rosen, this means we're increasingly living in individualised comfort zones: unlikely to be challenged and unable to engage with genuine difference. In some respects, Rosen's point about the impact of limitless individual choice connects to Turkle's focus on the enticing nature of online social worlds, in the sense that every engagement online is selective, partial and fleeting as a result of the constant pull to be somewhere else – a multitude of disparate sips of interaction that never add up to a single gulp, as Turkle puts it (Turkle 2012).

DIGITAL TECHNOLOGIES IN CONTEXT

It is not difficult to see why some theorists have taken an optimistic view of the social impacts of the internet and digital media. On the face of it, such technologies place unprecedented control in the hands of users, freeing them from the structured hierarchical information agenda set by dominant mass media corporations as well as from the broader constraints of space and time. Far more so than broadcast television, digital media tend to be cool, in McLuhan's terms, in that they offer the prospect of engaging a range of senses rather than just one and can involve unprecedented levels of interactive participation. Conversely, there is much that is persuasive in the concerns of Turkle and Rosen, amongst others, who worry about the extent of the domination of contemporary lives by digital technologies. The more of our lives we spend in mediated environments, it might reasonably be argued, the greater the extent to which we are liable to be shaped by their properties and, in that case, the control we are afforded over our online engagements may have negative as well as positive consequences. As with McLuhan and Postman's contrasting interpretations of television, however, some elements of both optimistic and pessimistic discussions of digital media veer towards technological determinism.

At the turn of the millennium, Howard Rheingold expressed scepticism over what he regarded as the blind optimism of theorists such as Negroponte, suggesting that such 'technophilia' replicated the enthusiastic proclamations which accompanied a host of earlier developments in communications technology:

> the same hopes, described in the same words, for a decentralization of power, a deeper and more widespread citizen involvement in matters of state, a great equalizer for ordinary citizens to counter the forces of central control, have been voiced in the popular press for two centuries in reference to steam, electricity, and television (2000: 307).

For Rheingold, we must bear in mind that, although the development of these previous technologies did have a substantial impact on society, 'the utopia of the technological millenarians has not yet materialized' (2000: 307). In other words, if the lofty ideals of techno-enthusiasts, including McLuhan's proclamations about television, have not been fulfilled by any of the succession of technologies on which their hopes have been pinned to date, then we would be wise to exercise caution with respect to their proclamations about the impact of the ever-developing internet.

This is not to say that positive proclamations about the impact of technologies ought to be dismissed outright, or that the transformations brought about by digitalisation are not of great significance. In his criticism of early internet optimists, Rheingold was not saying that the technological capacities of the internet were irrelevant or insubstantial. His point was that the ways the technology is controlled, disseminated and used are liable to reflect the economic, social and cultural relations into which it has become embedded as much as to shape them. From this point of view, it is no great surprise that, just as they exerted control over the railways, the newspapers, radio and television, large-scale commercial organisations and governments have been able to exploit and dominate the internet, using it as a means to consolidate their power (McChesney et al. 2011), even while some ordinary people or grassroots movements may find ways to use the technology to exert their own forms of influence.

There are also hints of technological determinism in the accounts of Turkle and Rosen, even though, in the former case, the conclusions are supported by detailed research. Both lay the blame for the ills they describe squarely onto digital technologies themselves, the inference being that their properties are inherently geared towards the social effects of isolation or individualised cultural superficiality. There is little room here for discussion of whether the negative effects identified might have been present without the technologies in question. Neither is there much emphasis on the variety of different forms of online content or behaviour that may be developing, or the importance of the broader socio-cultural contexts in which different users operate. Might not such contexts – including work patterns, living arrangements, social position amongst other things – have some bearing on the kinds of relationships that individuals develop in contemporary societies? Might they not also prompt different sorts of approaches to the use of digital technologies among different users? Both Turkle and Rosen's critiques are also reliant on particular assumptions about what counts as authentic as opposed to superficial forms of experience. Leaving aside the inherent difficulties with any such judgements, it surely is likely that online interactions give rise to a variety of different sorts of engagement and relationships, with different levels of intensity, meaning and mutual responsibility.

It is also worth noting that, as with optimistic accounts of the internet, some of the fears articulated by Turkle, Rosen and others about the impact of digital media on the individual psyche, quality of human relationships and richness of our engagements with culture do recall earlier anxieties about radio, television and other media. Though the precise arguments are different, the socially isolating and superficial qualities of television have provoked extensive debate and commentary ever since the technology emerged, with many fearing regressive impacts on children's ability to interact effectively with others, for example. That does not necessarily render such fears unfounded but it may be helpful to remember that current digital technologies are not unique in prompting them.

Ultimately, the social impact of internet and digital media use may be especially hard to determine because, especially when combined with the possibility of access from any location, their properties are more varied and flexible than those of previous media. Rather than being a single medium, the internet is better understood as an integrated network of different communicative options: mass and interpersonal, one-directional and interactive, synchronous and asynchronous and image, sound, video and text-based. In combination with the enormous range of content on offer to the user, this means that the range of different uses to which the technology could be put are enormous.

In practice, then, the internet may have as much potential to facilitate high intensity, hot forms of communication, in McLuhan's terms, as low intensity cool ones, and may offer as many opportunities for reinforcement of existing power structures as for their transformation. Marginal political groups might use it as a means to coordinate subversive offline protests; powerful corporations to target consumers with carefully selected advertisements; teenagers to arrange events with long-term friends, or to converse fleetingly with strangers; families to watch mainstream movies; amateur musicians to gain exposure for their work; employers to facilitate communication among employees; and governments and corporations to store and retrieve information on what all of us are doing.

The flexibility and accessibility of internet and digital technologies may in itself suggest particular socio-cultural outcomes, but also make it difficult to predict what their overall impact might be. This doesn't mean that we should give up on trying to assess the implications of how people use the internet and other digital technologies and we'll touch on many such assessments – including some that relate to the arguments above – during the pages that follow. Suffice to say, however, that the technical features of digital technologies are of great importance, but their social outcomes will depend upon the interaction of these with existing relations of culture and power.

CONCLUSION

The development, control and use of communications technologies can have profound implications for everyday lives, individual identities and the broader social and cultural world. Such technologies offer capabilities and limitations that have important implications for how they can be used and their broader socio-cultural significance. The study of media, culture and society, then, must always take into account the implications of the hardware through which media content is distributed. Yet McLuhan's assertion that the 'medium is the message', along with his broader emphasis on media technologies as the primary driver of social change, affords too much power to inanimate objects, failing to recognise the range of uses to which each technology can be put and the extent to which their development and outcomes are shaped by industry and users operating within broader social contexts. This means that, as well as understanding the properties of technologies themselves, we must focus upon the organisations which control them, the details of the content they are used to transmit and the activities and understandings of users.

QUESTIONS/EXERCISES

1   a)   What does McLuhan mean by 'the medium is the message'?

    b)   On what points do McLuhan and Postman disagree in relation to the social impact of print and electronic media?

2   a)   Into which of McLuhan's categories of hot and cool media would you place the following: television; book; news website; radio; games console; social media?

    b)   Are the categories 'hot' and 'cool' useful?

3   a)   What does technological determinism mean and why has it been criticised?

    b)   Apply Du Gay et al.'s 'circuit of culture' model to the technology of the iPad. Consider each of the different processes on the circuit – production, representation, regulation, consumption and identity.

4   In what ways are new digital media different from their analogue predecessors? Why might these differences be socially significant?

5   Are Turkle's fears about the socially isolating impact of digital devices well-founded? Is the suggestion her arguments are technologically determinist justified or unfair?

SUGGESTED FURTHER READING

Du Gay, P., Hall, S., Janes, L., Mackay, J. and Negus, K. (1997) *Doing Cultural Studies: The Story of the Sony Walkman*. London: Sage – Practical illustration of the study of technology in socio-cultural context, via the example of the Sony Walkman.

McLuhan, M. (2001) *Understanding Media*. London: Routledge (originally published 1964) – Classic analysis of media technologies, including elaboration of the author's famous argument that 'the medium is the message'.

Meyrowitz, J. (1985) *No Sense of Place: The Impact of Electronic Media on Social Behaviour*. New York: Oxford University Press – Theoretical discussion of the ways in which television is challenging social boundaries and transforming culture.

Postman, N. (1987) *Amusing Ourselves to Death: Public Discourse in the Age of Show Business*. London: Methuen – Pessimistic account of the socio-impact of electronic media and particularly television.

Turkle, S. (2013) *Alone Together: Why We Expect More from Technology and Less From Each Other*. Philadelphia: Basic Books – Influential recent analysis of the impact of digital and online technologies on social interactions and psychological well-being.

CHAPTER 3
MEDIA INDUSTRY

FOCAL POINTS

- Political economy as a macro approach that emphasises media industry in context
- Concentrations of media ownership, power and influence
- Implications of the imperative to maximise audiences and attract advertisers
- Interventions by government and regulators to control media
- Criticisms of the economic determinism in some political economy perspectives

INTRODUCTION

It was famously asserted in the 1940s by German theorists Adorno and Horkheimer (1997) that, by the twentieth century, music, literature, art, film and other forms of popular culture had become part of a culture industry. Rather than being the product of autonomous artists or grassroots creativity, they argued, cultural goods were increasingly being manufactured and distributed on a huge scale by powerful organisations and had become little different from other industrial products such as food, clothing or motorcars. For Adorno and Horkheimer, this industrial context had profound implications for the kinds of cultural products consumed by the population, as well as for broader socio-cultural relations. Disappointingly, Adorno and Horkheimer did not provide a detailed empirical analysis of the complex ways in which media industries actually work (see Chapter 6). The concept of the culture industry draws valuable attention, however, to the importance of understanding the economic and organisational context in which media production takes place and it is this on which we shall focus in the coming pages.

The study of those who control the production and distribution of media and the broader system in which they operate is vital to contemporary understandings of communication and society. Indeed, for some theorists, such an approach is more important than any other to a broader analysis of media, culture and society. From this *political economic* point of view, media technologies and content, alongside the implications their circulation might have for audiences, ultimately are shaped by the structure of the media industry. And in turn, the media industry itself is regarded as a product of the broader capitalist political economic system in which it operates.

While some political economic media analysts are conservative, many of the most well-known within academic circles take a left wing approach that is critical of the current media system. For Golding and Murdock (1991), what marks out the approach they term *critical political economy* is a specific interest in the ways inequalities of power embedded into broader capitalism play themselves out in the ownership and control of media. Political economic analysis tends to centre on the link between this control of media by the powerful minority and the reinforcement of the unequal system which gave rise to it in the first place. This particular perspective on media draws on Karl Marx's analysis of the unequal, exploitative relations of the capitalist system, something we'll pursue in greater depth in Chapter 6. It also can be regarded as a *macro* perspective, because its primary interest is in the media system as a whole, with the details of different texts, technologies and users regarded as structured by this. As Golding and Murdock suggest, the approach 'always goes beyond situated action to show how particular micro-contexts are shaped by general economic dynamics' (1991: 73).

In what follows, we'll introduce a range of key issues and factors relating to the industrial context of media, before briefly returning to some broader arguments about the place of political economic approaches within the study of media and society.

MEDIA ORGANISATIONS

Rather than referring to a single media industry, it is preferable to speak of a plurality – such is the diversity of media sectors and organisations. For example, we can identify distinct sectors of media, connected to different formats, such as music, television, publishing, advertising, social media and the various sub-sectors within each. Such *horizontal* distinctions, however, are becoming more blurry as a result of processes of media convergence and the development of digital and online communications. We can also note that, within sectors there are a number of different stages of the process of production and distribution, with companies often specialising in one stage or another. Within the film industry, such *vertical* differentiation can be illustrated by the difference between studios, concerned with the development and production of content, and cinemas, which form one of the means through which such content is made available to consumers. The broader distinction between producers of content and those who facilitate its distribution is an increasingly significant one in the digital era, bearing in mind that the latter may include anything from established television networks to interactive content sharing sites such as YouTube.

It is also important to distinguish between profit-making and non-profit-making media organisations. The latter can range from small-scale, voluntary or charitable organisations such as community websites, to all-powerful state-controlled media used by authoritarian governments to distribute propaganda and maintain power within countries like North Korea. The most prominent non-profit media organisations in many developed countries, however, are public service broadcasters such as the UK's British Broadcasting Corporation, which is funded by a licence fee and expected to enrich society through the production of trustworthy, informative and high quality content. Such organisations are important to the history of mass media and remain influential in some countries, but in recent years have found themselves isolated within a media world dominated by corporations whose primary purpose is the pursuit of profit and the satisfaction of shareholders. As Michael Tracey has pointed out, while public media organisations 'acquire money to make programmes', commercial institutions 'make programmes to acquire money' (1998: 18).

COMMERCIAL OWNERSHIP

Although individual companies vary in their size and influence, media industries invariably are *oligopolies*, which means that markets are overwhelmingly dominated by a small number of powerful companies. Concentration of ownership has been a key theme throughout the history of mass media. For example, after an early period dominated by small-scale, independent publications, newspapers became overwhelmingly controlled by large corporations run by so-called newspaper barons. Through a series of take-overs, for example, William Hearst established control over a vast portfolio of titles across the early twentieth century US, with *The San Francisco Examiner*, *The New York Journal* and *The Washington Times* among them. Meanwhile, the UK newspaper market at the time was dominated by three so-called Barons – Viscount Northcliff and his brother Viscount Rothermere, who developed *The Daily Mail* and *The Daily Mirror*, and Baron Beaverbrook, who was responsible for the rise of *The Daily Express*.

McChesney argues, however, that the drive towards expansion and consolidation in the media industry became particularly concentrated towards the end of the twentieth century, making it difficult for small or medium-sized firms to survive as such: 'a firm either gets larger through mergers or acquisitions or it gets swallowed by a more aggressive competitor'

(1999: 20). In some cases expansion would involve the entering of new arenas through the setting up of new subsidiary companies. In the late 1980s, global media giant News Corporation invested heavily in a brand new UK satellite television service called Sky (now BSkyB), providing a substantial stake in the UK television market. In other cases, companies expand by purchasing a controlling stake in other companies. Such take-overs can involve less risk than setting up new operations because one can allow target companies to do the initial ground work and risk-taking, before assuming control of those that are successful.

A constant feature of the media industry, take-overs and mergers can be divided into different types.

1. EXPANSION WITHIN EXISTING SECTOR

Some take-overs and mergers simply involve expansion and/or elimination of competition within a single area of specialism. A local newspaper company might increase its sector dominance by taking over its local rivals or acquiring comparable publications elsewhere. Such consolidation has resulted in the domination of local newspaper markets in many countries by a small number of businesses. For example, Johnson Press PLC owns around 250 local publications across the UK and Ireland. In another example, the ITV television network in the UK originally consisted of a plethora of independent regional companies, but a series of take-overs led to the creation in 2003 of a single company for the whole of England and Wales.

2. EXPANSION ACROSS SECTORS (HORIZONTAL INTEGRATION)

Horizontal integration refers to attempts to take-over other companies in order to broaden one's portfolio across different media sectors. For example, a newspaper company may acquire a stake in the television market by taking control of a broadcasting company. One of the advantages of horizontal integration is the ability to simultaneously market single products across different sectors. Known as media *synergy*, this might involve a company releasing a blockbuster film with an associated CD sound track, computer game, book and television series. The products all promote one another, and the commercial potential of the brand that unites them is exploited to the maximum.

3. EXPANSION UP AND DOWN THE PRODUCTION PROCESS (VERTICAL INTEGRATION)

As well as gaining a stake in different media sectors, media corporations have sometimes sought to control as many different stages of the production process within a sector as possible. A company that owns a music recording label, for example, might buy a controlling stake in an online streaming service, enabling them to control both development and distribution. The achievement of control down the production and distribution chain was a key motivation behind Disney's take-over in 1995 of US television network ABC. To Disney, the television network offered a mass broadcast outlet for the huge amount of content produced by the company's famous studios. This take-over also entailed a horizontal element in that a company with a substantial stake in the film and theme park industries was increasing its stake in the broadcast sector.

Also entailing elements of both horizontal and vertical integration are a series of strategic mergers and take-overs between internet companies and established multimedia corporations at the beginning of the twenty-first century. News Corporation's take-over of social networking site MySpace in 2005 represented, on the one hand, a horizontal expansion from television networks and publishing to the internet and, on the other, a specific attempt to find an effective new outlet for the distribution of News Corporation content, particularly from its Fox studios. A few years earlier, the then dominant internet company America Online (AOL) acquired multimedia giant Time Warner in 2000. Time Warner's extensive portfolio of traditional media content was combined with AOL's potential for online distribution. As with News Corporation and MySpace, it offered greater control of different stages of the production and distribution process (vertical) at the same time as providing a stake for the merged company in a range of traditional and new media sectors (horizontal).

Importantly, mergers are not always successful, and corporations also sometimes split for strategic reasons. Neither of the two deals mentioned in the paragraph above were to prove long-lasting. A sharp decline in the value of internet companies drastically affected the AOL side of AOL-Time-Warner soon after the take-over, forcing a reversal of the merger just two years later in 2002. Meanwhile, having acquired MySpace in 2005, News Corporation presided over a sharp decline in the platform's popularity as compared to competitors such as Facebook and eventually sold it – at a massive loss – in 2011. The last decade also has seen other strategic separations with Viacom splitting in 2006 into CBS Corporation and Viacom Inc. (effectively reversing a previous merger) and, more recently still, News Corporation splitting into 21st Century Fox and a new-look News Corp in 2012.

In spite of such reversals and splits, an overall trend towards consolidation has led to a situation where global media markets remain largely controlled by a small number of transnational corporations whose assets are substantial. Even post-split, 21st Century Fox and News Corp each remain vast in their breadth and reach. The former controls extensive television and film interests around the world, including Twentieth Century Fox and Twentieth Century Fox Television, numerous broadcast, satellite and cable networks, including Fox in the US, BSkyB in the UK and Star TV which operates across Asia. Meanwhile News Corp owns hundreds of newspaper titles across the world as well as global publisher, HarperCollins, over 30 Australian magazine titles and various Australian television interests.

Occasionally, a combination of skill, innovation and new opportunities enable new companies to grow sufficiently strongly that they are able to rival established media corporations. The innovation and adeptness of Google and Facebook, alongside the time it took for existing powerful media corporations to get to grips with the possibilities of the internet, enabled both companies to establish substantial levels of presence, reach and control over their respective sectors and to engage in their own expansions and take-overs. Google quickly managed to virtually monopolise the search-engine market, generating extensive and sustained growth and allowing the brand to diversify into a host of other digital services, including email, online maps, social media, web browsers, office applications, mobile operating systems and much more. As part of this, Google has taken-over numerous other companies, most notably online video site YouTube in 2006 and the mobile phone company Motorola Mobility in 2011, as well as a host of smaller-scale operations. In the longer-term, however, break-throughs such as that of Google appear to represent the exception rather than the rule in a market where the existing power of established transnationals (a category that now includes the likes of Google) offers the competitive advantages that help sustain their dominance. In its early days, for example, Sky television sustained the kind of losses that would have bankrupted smaller companies, but the extent of News Corporation's investment in the service alongside the ability to heavily promote itself in the company's UK newspapers, enabled Sky to increase its subscriber base, acquire its main market rival and, eventually, dominate the UK's subscription television market.

CONCENTRATION OF OWNERSHIP = CONCENTRATION OF IDEAS?

For some, the control of our channels of mass communication by such a small number of commercial organisations has grave implications for the circulation of ideas and culture. Bagdikian (2004: 3), for example, points out that each of the 'Big Five' established media transnationals at the time he was writing, had 'more communications power than was exercised by any despot or dictator in history' and that their tendency to cooperate with one another in the pursuit of mutually beneficial outcomes made their influence over populations, governments and policies around the world immense. Bagdikian's point, arguably, is no less significant today, with many nation states finding themselves dwarfed by the power of giant media corporations and finding it increasingly difficult to control the distribution of culture in their territory.

The concern of some, then, is that the concentration of media ownership leads to a concentration of culture and ideas: that instead of engaging with a diversity of competing perspectives and innovative forms of expression, populations are subject to a narrow and largely monolithic set of messages. 'The significant concern about such patterns of ownership' argues Franklin, 'is that they diminish pluralism and choice, stifle diversity and empower owners to defend and advance their economic interests and political power' (1997: 207). In particular, some argue that the corporate interests of transnationals prompt them to support ultra-capitalist political ideas and that, when taken as a whole, the content they distribute around the world can be expected to reflect this (Bagdikian 2004; Herman and Chomsky 1998).

In Italy the connection between media concentration and the political interests of owners became particularly direct, with media mogul Silvio Berlusconi controlling an estimated 90% of Italian broadcasting during his nine years as the country's president at different periods in the 1990s and 2000s. Having utilised his controlling interest in commercial broadcaster *Mediaset* to assist his electoral ambitions, he then achieved influence over the country's Public Service Broadcaster *RAI* as a result of being Prime Minister (Lane 2005). The links between concentration of media ownership and the dominance of political movements or ideologies is not always quite as direct as this, however. Mostly media owners avoid putting themselves up for election, but their influence can remain considerable. News outlets associated with the News Corp and 21st Century Fox, including UK newspaper *The Sun* and US TV Channel *Fox News*, tend closely to mirror the views of the chairman of both companies and CEO of News Corp, Rupert Murdoch. More generally, even in the context of a diversified and interactive digital media environment, if we consider the range of media content to which we are most often exposed, it is not too difficult to identify common themes, including a general endorsement of capitalism, business and consumerism, as well as to note the relative marginalisation of other ideas, including anti-capitalist perspectives (Herman and Chomsky 1998). We'll explore this further in Chapter 6 on Ideology.

The notion of an automatic or exclusive link between concentration of ownership and concentration of ideas may over-simplify things, however. Although it is true that certain ideas are consistently emphasised and others marginalised, the overall media environment, including books, music and the vast range of content that circulates via the internet, offers a considerable range of perspectives. For all the right wing orientation of its dominant news outlets, News Corporation also owns HarperCollins, a publishing umbrella responsible for books covering a diversity of perspectives including, for example, Naomi Klein's widely read *No Logo* (2000), which offers a wholesale attack on the activities of multinationals. More recently Russell Brand's book *Revolution* (2014), which also amounted to a castigation of corporate power, was published by Random House, which forms part of German-based media conglomerate Bertelsmann. It remains the case that there is a stark imbalance in exposure for different perspectives: for every *Revolution* there are countless books, television programmes and films that reinforce the consumer-capitalist status quo. However, the extent to which such a disparity can be put down to a politically motivated dissemination of the viewpoints of the powerful, rather than, for example, an assumption that audiences are mostly uninterested in anti-establishment views, is a matter for debate. After all, when all else is said and done, the bottom line for commercial media producers is the pursuit of profit.

THE BOTTOM LINE: SOURCES OF REVENUE

The achievement of an effective balance between minimising costs and maximising takings lies at the heart of all that profit-making media corporations do. Understanding how such companies make money is important in appreciating what shapes the services and content they produce.

ADVERTISING REVENUE

Since the early days of US radio, when programmes such as the *Eveready Hour* took the name of their sponsors, advertising has been a pivotal source of revenue for media corporations. It can take various forms, from the purchase of discrete 'space' within publications or between programmes, to product placement within television programmes or film, to carefully targeted text or video ads that respond to our online behaviour. The importance of advertising and sponsorship to media industry profits is such that advertisers, and not audiences or users, often form the primary customers of media corporations. The underlying purpose of most content and services we use, then, is to garner our attention in order that it can be sold to those companies willing to pay the premium. As Baker and Dessart have put it: 'the business of television… is the buying and selling of eyeballs' (1998: 65). Similarly, the ultimate goal of online search engines, content sharing facilities and social media is to make money by bringing advertisers together with suitable consumers (Cohen 2015; Spurgeon 2008). This reliance on advertising means that, in addition to the media organisations themselves, advertisers constitute another set of corporate interests that influence the production and distribution of content as well as the design and orientation of online media services.

DIRECT USER PAYMENT

Another key source of funding for media outlets comes from direct payments from consumers. These include 'per item' payments and longer-term subscriptions to a particular body of content. In the case of print media, direct payments are made in the form of a cover price or subscription. In the world of television, consumers increasingly pay subscription fees for pay TV services and premium channels, or pay-per-view costs for individual films or sporting events. This category of revenue also includes a range of other direct payments; for cinema tickets, books and a variety of downloaded streamed content, for example, or for premium web services. While in some sectors direct payment from audiences is long established, in the case of television it only became possible for companies to control consumer access to different levels of service with the onset of cable and digital set-top boxes in the 1990s. A significant area of debate in recent times relates to whether online news sites should restrict their content to paying subscribers or remain open-access and soley advertiser-funded. In 2013, UK newspaper, *The Sun*, became one of the most high profile newspapers to place all of its content behind a paywall. The result, however, was a drastic reduction in its online readership and, by the end of 2015, content on the site had been made freely available again. Other newspapers, such as the *Guardian*, have had greater success with hybrid models, whereby content is freely available on the internet, but users of mobile devices are charged an annual fee for access to the newspaper via a dedicated app.

PAYMENTS BETWEEN MEDIA COMPANIES

For those involved in the production of content, direct payments from distribution outlets wishing to carry the content are of critical importance. For distributors or retailers of magazines, DVDs, books or their online equivalent, such payments simply take the form of the wholesale price of the goods in question. Where content does not consist of discrete items sold directly to consumers, however, distribution outlets pay content developers or owners for the *right* to screen, broadcast, print, stream or in some other way reproduce the content. Thus, online streaming services such as Spotify pay fees to record labels in return for the right to stream large bodies of content to consumers, as do more traditional music radio stations. And, to take a more established and traditional example, newspapers and magazines pay agencies or individual photographers for the right to print images.

Television services also purchase the rights to broadcast films, dramas and other programmes or events. Often they negotiate exclusive rights deals, which prevent rival companies from being allowed to broadcast the content. Sometimes, rather than paying to broadcast the exact same content, distributors and/or content creators will pay for the rights to a programme idea, format or brand. This enables them to create a new version more suited to the outlet's intended audience. In recent years, numerous programme formats have been sold to a range of territories in this way, including *America's Got Talent*, *Pop Idol* and *The Apprentice*. As well as maximising revenue from existing content by selling goods or rights, producers in the broadcasting sphere are often commissioned to produce brand new programmes by distributors. For broadcasters who produce a proportion of their own content in-house, meanwhile, money is made both from direct distribution via their own outlets and through sale of rights to media companies elsewhere.

MAXIMISING AUDIENCES

Ultimately, what most of these means of revenue point to is an underlying drive to maximise audiences or users and intensify their levels of engagement. Alongside pressures to minimise costs, such pressure can shape the ways commercial media operate and determine the types of content and services generated. The underlying need to serve the wants of audiences may be argued to raise questions about suggestions that media simply act as a direct mouthpiece for the political interests of owners and, consistent with this, some commentators celebrate the importance of the likes and dislikes of ordinary people as a determinant of media content and services.

Others, however, regard audience maximisation pressures as a negative influence that encourages the distribution of whatever content offers the greatest instant stimulation and superficial appeal, to the exclusion of in-depth information and critical forms of expression. Such is the fear that we might lose interest, change channel or turn to another outlet, they argue, producers of content daren't lose momentum and intensity even for a short period (Baker and Dessart 1998; Franklin 1997). The situation is argued to have become particularly bad in recent decades as a result of sharp increases in competition caused by the overwhelming range of content available to consumers to engage with when and where they want. For McChesney, one of the results of this need to keep audiences stimulated and excited is likely to be ever more explicit emphasis, across formats and genres, upon 'the tried and tested formula of sex and violence' (1999: 34).

According to Gitlin (2000), meanwhile, the fear of losing money tends specifically to deter investment in innovative content and encourage imitations of previously successful formats. Sure enough, successful television programmes tend to spawn numerous copycat versions on rival stations because the latter are deemed to represent a safe bet. Such priorities also explain the increasing import of programme formats successful in other countries, where again the risks are lower (Moran 1998). The ever-increasing number of sequels to blockbuster movies and movie adaptions of television series (and vice versa) constitute further examples. Such products offer a particularly risk-free route to commercial success because audiences are familiar with the brand and have already developed attachments to core themes and characters. Generating comparable levels of box-office success for entirely new products can be more difficult and have higher chances of failure, in spite of the well-established practice of generating familiarity through the use of well-known star actors and recognisable plot-lines.

That the profit imperative has often resulted in a tendency to standardise, repeat, copy and instantly gratify is hard to dispute – and a theme to which we shall return at various points during the book. Yet commercial organisations have also developed more innovative forms of content, some of which are undeniably high in their level of detail, complexity, or challenge to audiences. In the realm of television drama, for example, Time Warner's US subscription television network HBO (Home Box Office), has specialised in such premium content, producing a string of critically acclaimed examples, including *The Sopranos*, *Sex and the City*, *The Wire* and *Game of Thrones*. Meanwhile, the more broadly-oriented Fox network, owned by News Corporation, has been responsible for highly respected productions such as *The Walking Dead*, and cable channel AMC produced the critically acclaimed *Breaking Bad* series. For some, such productions represent a golden era for television drama and a vindication of the US's commercial media environment. For others, such premium content still represents the exception rather than the rule, with schedules still dominated by inexpensive, risk-free forms of programming such as panel or talent shows and different forms of 'reality' television.

The ultimate quality or usefulness of these and other different forms of content is, of course, open to considerable debate. As we shall see in Chapter 8, notions of quality are highly contestable. What is clear, however, is that there are a range of commercially produced or distributed forms of media content rather than the simple monolith that some critics emphasise. And this relates, in part, to the increasing diversification of media markets into different niches and segments. In some sectors, the sort of ultra-cheap copy-cat forms of content outlined by critics such as Gitlin and McChesney are indeed becoming more pronounced while, in others, companies respond to demand for content that presents itself to us as more original, in-depth or complex.

THE ROLE OF SPONSORS

Needless to say, the greater one's overall audience, the larger the number of potential advertisers and sponsors and the greater the premium they will pay. In addition to fuelling general competition for audiences, however, advertisers can influence media content in more particular ways. As part of the service they provide to their sponsors, media companies seek not just to offer an audience of appropriate size, but one composed of the particular kinds of consumers advertisers hope to reach. Outlets must ensure they consistently attract consumers of the appropriate demographic composition and lifestyle orientation or demonstrate an ability to differentiate broader overall audiences into segments to which appropriate advertisements are directed. Such targeting is becoming ever-more sophisticated, with online services increasingly differentiating not only between identifiable market segments but also specific individual consumers, on the basis of information generated about their past behaviour or purchases (Cohen 2015).

The range of companies seeking to advertise means that most population groups with disposable income are of interest, but advertisers nevertheless tend to have a preference for so-called 'quality' audiences, which means wealthy, high-spending consumers. It has sometimes been argued that this creates a content bias against marginalised groups such as the poor, the elderly and ethnic minorities (Herman and Chomsky 1998). The scale of this problem may have reduced a little in recent years as a result of expansions in the range of media channels and outlets and the increasing targeting of both advertising and programming towards specialist groups, including those traditionally marginalised such as ethnic minorities.

If they are to continue to advertise, companies will expect a discernable appreciation in sales as a result. It is therefore in the interest of media companies to favour content that is compatible with advertisers' desire to expose their products to willing consumers who are in the mood to spend money. Programmes or copy with a light and cheery feel are particularly valued by some advertisers because people are believed to be more likely to entertain the possibility of buying consumer goods if they are in a positive state of mind. According to Herman and Chomsky (1998), this means that an over-emphasis on detailed, depressing or, worse still, guilt-inducing content about social or global problems may sometimes be deemed unattractive.

In some cases, media will go further still, specifically orienting their content in a manner that encourages audiences to think positively about consuming products of the type being promoted by advertisers. The content of lifestyle magazines and television programmes for example, is often centred on the desirability of purchasing consumer goods in order to enhance one's quality of life. From motoring magazines to make-over television programmes, such content is not only designed to attract a suitable audience, but also to encourage its members to be receptive to advertising by capturing their imagination and enthusiasm for consumption.

Media organisations also have to handle carefully content that could damage the commercial interests of advertisers. Decisions about news items, documentaries, columns, images or storylines that present prominent advertisers in a negative light can be the subject of substantial conflicts of interest. In interview with Jackson et al. (2001: 62), Mike Cones, then editor of *GQ* magazine, referred to his publication's reliance on advertising as 'a marriage of dubious convenience'. To illustrate, he described an incident involving *Blitz*, a unisex style magazine. *Blitz* had published an article focused on the responses of members of the public to perfumes that included a number of highly negative comments about some brands. Subsequently, according to Cones, several fragrance companies withdrew their advertising from the publication, prompting it to go out of business. Cones sums up the lesson from the story:

> And that was it: a very painful, short, sharp lesson of the power of the advertiser. And so we to some degree preserve some editorial integrity. But in the end, if the advertiser looks at what we've put in the magazine and says 'Well this doesn't interest me. I can't see how this is going to enhance my product by being associated with whatever page it happens to be', then they may start looking elsewhere. (Cones, interviewed by Jackson et al. 2001)

While direct advertiser boycotts are unusual, executives and media professionals instinctively know that they must think carefully before biting the hand that feeds them. In 2014 a prominent journalist, Peter Oborne, resigned from UK newspaper *The Daily Telegraph*, claiming the publication had repeatedly sought to bury negative stories about global bank HSBC, which was one of the newspaper's most prominent advertisers. Of course, it is unusual for such specific examples to come to light and, according to Herman and Chomsky (1998), the pressure to avoid damaging advertiser interests can mean shying away both from direct negative coverage of individual companies and from content that might conflict with the broader commercial or political interests of advertisers. Ultimately, according to McChesney and colleagues (2011: 36–7), 'despite the aura of [journalistic] professionalism, s/he who pays the piper ultimately calls the tune' and, as a consequence, 'a privately owned and advertising-supported media system is structurally incapable of providing an honest picture of the economy and is therefore inadequate and unresponsive to the needs of a democratic society'.

The onset of digital media may have further tilted the balance of power between media companies and advertisers in the direction of the latter. Intensified competition and new opportunities for online advertising have left traditional media fighting for a limited pool of advertising revenue, strengthening the bargaining position and expectations of advertisers. According to McChesney and colleagues, advertisers are exerting greater influence over the content of outlets in which their commercials appear, while the distinction between commercials and other content is blurring. An increasing emphasis on content sponsorship, they argue, implies a 'partner' status for advertisers, while elsewhere there has been a growth of wholly advertiser-produced 'branded content' (McChesney et al. 2011). Meanwhile, the more general expansion of product placement, alongside the development of 'hybrid' content such as advertorials (advertisements which have the appearance of editorial content) further illustrate what McChesney (2000) laments as the 'hypercommercialism' of contemporary media. We'll discuss recent developments in advertising in greater detail in Chapter 9.

GOVERNMENTS AND REGULATION

In spite of their overall domination of global communications, corporate media organisations and their sponsors have not had everything their own way. In different ways, national governments have sought to exert their own influence. At the extreme end of such intervention are those situations where governments take on full operational control of core national media outlets. In China, for example, the main television broadcaster, CCTV (China Central Television), forms a part of the communist government and it has regularly been used as a tool for political propaganda. In other cases, such as the UK's BBC, Canada's CBC and Australia's ABC, broadcasters were set up by governments and given statutory objectives and goals, but operated at an arms-length from politicians in order that they could perform an impartial public service role, informing, educating and entertaining the public. The extent to which they are truly independent of government remains the subject of considerable debate (see Chapter 8).

ACCESS RESTRICTIONS

As well as setting up and/or subsidising state or public broadcasters, governments set the parameters under which commercial media operate, controlling who has access to national media networks and on what terms. In the early nineteenth century, the UK government utilised a stamp duty on newspapers, taxes on paper and heavy registration fees in order to prevent the poor from producing and distributing newspapers (Curran and Seaton 2010). Today, the main barriers to running newspapers – or indeed their online equivalents – are commercial ones. Broadcasting, however, has tended to be more tightly controlled. Until 1955, the UK government prevented access to broadcasting to anyone but the BBC and prior to the diffusion of multi-channel delivery platforms in the 1990s, UK homes still only had access to five channels. The BBC's monopoly on radio lasted even longer – until 1973 – after which licences were awarded to a maximum of one Independent Local Radio station per area (Franklin 1997). Even in the 1990s when greater competition was introduced, licences remained restricted and broadcasters had to satisfy a range of criteria to receive one. Part of the reason for such control was that old analogue broadcasting systems were subject to spectrum scarcity – there was only room for a certain number of stations on the airwaves. Yet even in the digital era, governments continue to license broadcasters, albeit with a somewhat lighter touch. In the United States, for example, radio and television channels remain licensed by the national regulator, the Federal Communications Commission (FCC). An increasingly important exception to this, however, is the development of online 'television' or 'radio' services that, like other forms of internet content, require no specific government licence.

OWNERSHIP RESTRICTIONS

Governments also sometimes regulate the amount of a country's communications outlets that any one company can control. Such regulation is designed to maintain competition, prevent individual companies from gaining excessive power across different media and, sometimes, protect key national outlets from being purchased by international companies. Such regulations vary from country to country and can be quite specific. In the UK, for example, the 2003 Communications Act established a 20/20 rule whereby no company controlling a 20% share of the national newspaper market may hold more than a 20% stake in the ITV broadcasting company. It is also possible for the UK government to intervene in other proposed mergers by submitting them to independent review should they be felt to threaten plurality. Such interventions have happened on two occasions, in 2006 in relation to an attempt by BSkyB to purchase shares in ITV, and in 2011 in relation to the then News Corporation's bid to increase its stake in BSkyB. Nevertheless, the direction of travel for the last few decades has been towards deregulation. The 2003 Act, for example, removed a stipulation preventing non-EU companies from acquiring UK broadcasting companies. A comparable relaxation of the rules has also taken place in the US in recent years, although the FCC continues to enforce remaining rules that, among other things, restrict the amount of television 'reach' a single corporate group of television stations can have to 39% of US TV households and prevent a merger between any of the four national television networks.

CONTENT REGULATION

Regulators also take interest in media content, though this varies from country to country and between different media formats, with broadcasters often subject to stricter rules than publishers. Most countries require minimum standards of broadcasters with respect to taste and decency and restrictions are often placed on graphic violence, swearing and sexual explicitness. Even in the US, which often prides itself on the lack of interference in media content, strict rules exist when it comes to decency and sexual content. Over the last decade or so, the FCC has attempted to underline its role as protector of decency, fining a number of networks for fleeting indiscretions during live broadcasts, although many of these were subsequently challenged. The most well-publicised was the eventual overturning by the court of appeal of a huge fine of $550,000 for CBS after Janet Jackson's bare breast was inadvertently revealed during the half time show of the 2004 prime-time Super Bowl broadcast. In spite of such challenges, the FCC has continued to act against broadcasters. In 2015 it recommended a fine of £325,000 for television station WBDJ for a broadcast containing imagery from an explicit porn website as part of a news piece on a former porn star. WBDJ is in the process of an appeal. Regulators also regularly implement age classification systems in order to inform consumers about the levels of adult content in films, DVDs, music and other forms of content.

Sometimes, regulation of broadcast content goes further than minimum standards relating to decency, however. All broadcast news or current affairs content in the UK, for example, is required to show 'due impartiality', effectively banning news providers from favouring any particular viewpoint. Meanwhile, the country's commercially funded terrestrial broadcasters, ITV, Channel 4 and FIVE, have to fulfil what amount to quotas for particular kinds of content, such as news, current affairs and children's programmes. Such 'positive' regulation is intended to improve the overall quality and value of television to the public, on the assumption that, if left to their own devices, commercial media will tend to favour immediate stimulation and superficial entertainment (see Chapter 8).

In some countries, a further role for positive content regulation is the development or protection of national culture. In Canada, broadcasters must adhere to a quota system in order to nurture Canadian culture and prevent the nation's media from being dominated by imported content from the powerful US media industry. Content is measured against a complex points system and can be designated as Canadian according to a number of different criteria. In the case of Canadian radio, for example, music is designated as Canadian content if at least two of the following are Canadian: the composer, the artist, the place of production/performance or the writer of the lyrics. Overall, at least 35% of the music played on Canadian radio stations must be deemed Canadian content in order for them to comply. When it comes to television, in order to be designated as Canadian content, productions must achieve at least six out of a possible ten Canadian content points, based on factors such as the nationality of writers, directors, lead actors and others. Required quotas of Canadian content for television vary according to type of station. The quota system has been the subject of intense debate (Edwardson 2008). Supporters argue that quotas have served as a vital way to protect and nurture Canadian identity, creativity and expression in the face of US cultural and financial dominance. Opponents, however, criticise the scheme for excessive bureaucracy and for effectively forcing viewers to watch or listen to certain forms of content, rather than allowing them to decide what they would prefer in an open market place. Collins sums up the dilemma between community and individual freedom:

> Organized and self-conscious protective activity is necessary for a community to survive when… exogenous culture [i.e. US popular culture in this case] is so attractive to community members that the boundary markers between communities are elided. In the latter case, the collective right of the community to continued existence may conflict with the individual right of its members to enjoy access and consumption of exogenous information. (Collins 1990: 252)

Recently, Canadian content rules for television stations have been relaxed somewhat, with regulator the CRTC announcing in 2015 that local TV stations would be freed from all quota requirements during day-time hours. A 50% Canadian content quota remains during prime-time, however.

DEREGULATION

There is also considerable debate about the broader issue of how much governments should interfere with the operation of media companies, involving fundamental questions relating to power and influence, freedom of speech and the overall purpose of media. And it is increasingly clear that, in most countries, regulation is gradually becoming more relaxed, with the possible exception of restrictions relating to extreme violence, sexual content or bad language. Even in communist China, there are some signs of deregulation. Government subsidies to CCTV, for example, now are combined with advertising revenue, forcing CCTV to compete for audiences in a commercial market place with local television companies and pan-regional satellite networks such as News Corporation's Star Television.

In part, the trend towards deregulation is due to the development of new technologies. Highly restrictive licensing regimes were often justified on the basis that there was only a certain amount of broadcast bandwidth available and that this scarce resource had to be protected in the best interests of the public. This shortage of bandwidth was brought to an end by the onset of digital broadcasting, which enabled the simultaneous transmission of a multiplicity of channels. Meanwhile, the internet, by massively expanding the amount of content available to users from around the world, has made national regulation a more complicated undertaking. The bringing together of previously separate media onto the same platform exacerbates the problem by making the application of different sets of rules for different media types increasingly unworkable. If an online 'newspaper' includes text, video and audio clips, should it be subject to relaxed newspaper guidelines or tougher broadcasting codes?

The boundaries between private and public communication are also blurring on a medium that brings together anything from individual interactions on social networking sites to the core online content of huge media corporations. It might not be easy to impose restrictions on the latter without also impinging on the former. Experience so far suggests that, with some exceptions, regulators will fall back on lighter touch approaches, or leave the task of content regulation to global commercial platforms, including the likes of Facebook and Twitter, something with its own complex implications. China's extensive attempts to control use of the internet by blocking access to various sites and monitoring users demonstrates that regulation by national governments can be possible, but this case is probably not representative of broader trends. The move towards deregulation in most countries cannot just be attributed to new technologies however. It also reflects the broader ascendency of free market political ideologies which regard government interference as an impediment to business and consumer choice. We'll examine such arguments, alongside those of advocates of regulation in Chapter 8.

REGULATION TO SUPPORT INDUSTRY: COPYRIGHT

Not all forms of government intervention work to constrain the money-making potential of large media corporations. Copyright laws, which establish the right to claim legal ownership of and exclusively publish and distribute original ideas and culture, are essential to the ability of the producers or publishers of such works to make money. Without copyright laws, films, television programmes, pieces of music, images or other works could be used or sold by any individual or company without acknowledgement or payment to those who produced them. The prospect of having no control over who can use or sell their finished product would render it virtually impossible for those who invest in the production of original content to profit from doing so. Not surprisingly, then, while they strongly oppose most forms of regulation, media corporations have exerted all their power and influence to lobby for the consolidation, enforcement and expansion of copyright law. In particular, transnational companies have acted together to pressurise governments to try to ensure such law is standardised and watertight across the globe and that governments prioritise its enforcement.

In particular, media content industries have worked tirelessly to ensure their profits are protected in a digital age where copying and distributing content is seemingly easier than ever. High on the list of industry concerns were so-called peer-to-peer file sharing sites, pioneered by Napster in 1999, which facilitated the transfer of digital files, including music tracks, television programmes, movies and computer games, between the computers of users around the world. The music industry responded, under the auspices of the Recording Industry Association of America (RIAA), by lobbying for amendments and clarifications to copyright law and the establishment by governments of effective ways of policing transgressions. Napster was successfully sued for facilitating the infringement of copyright, forcing it to shut down in 2001 and several other sites suffered a similar fate. Some individual users were also taken to court. The industry also has developed additional strategies, including lobbying of governments to pressurise internet service providers (ISPs) to freeze the accounts of users repeatedly found to be participating in the illegal distribution of content. In 2008, the UK's six largest ISPs signed a memorandum of understanding, brokered by the government, in which they undertook to send warning letters to users whose accounts had been used for illegal file sharing. Needless to say, arguments rage over the legitimacy of such tactics and over the ethics and morality of file sharing itself (Rojek 2005). Ultimately, however, the RIAA's tactics relating to enforcement may have been less effective in reducing levels of illegal file sharing than the eventual establishment and growth of legitimate means by which consumers can freely access and listen to vast catalogues of music via streaming services such as Spotify, which pay royalties to the recording industry and artists. Though such services are themselves controversial, particularly in relation to the amount of royalties they pay, they appear to have largely nullified mass demand for illegal file sharing.

CONCLUSION: ECONOMIC DETERMINISM?

An understanding of media as an industry – or a set of industries – is of the utmost importance to any broader analysis of the relationships between media and society. By asking questions about how media are controlled, by whom, and under what circumstances, political economic approaches to media not only rectify some of the problems with the technologically determinist accounts we encountered in the previous chapter, but also provide a corrective to approaches that focus narrowly on the study of media content or audiences. The answers to political economic questions tell us a great deal about why the media content and technologies we use take the form and character that they do and are essential to discussions about the ways media could be changed or improved. As a consequence, we shall return to these macro questions of media production and regulation at a number of points in the rest of the book.

Nevertheless, it is important that the emphasis placed by some theorists on the primacy of political economic contexts of production does not result in other aspects of the media process, including technologies, content and audience activities, being simply regarded as automatic effects of this. In the same way that those who over-emphasise the impact of technologies are referred to as technological determinists, some political economists are criticised for being economic or material determinists. This means that they sometimes are prone to assume, on the basis of a broad-brush analysis of the way media industries work, that the details of media content and its impact on audiences are largely predictable and prescribed in advance. As we have seen, it is sometimes assumed, for example, that media are standardised as a result of the profit imperative or that concentration of ownership leads to the concentration of ideas, without much real analysis of content itself or the ways audiences engage with it.

The notion that media are largely determined by their political-economic context remains a position worthy of consideration and readers should make up their own minds in this respect. Before doing so, however, they should also consider the approaches to media analysis outlined in the following chapters, which deal with the ways in which scholars have sought to understand the detail of media content and how audiences use and interpret media.

QUESTIONS/EXERCISES

1 a) What is the difference between vertical and horizontal integration?

   b) Does the concentration of media ownership lead to the concentration of ideas?

2 a) Why are critics concerned about the pressure on commercial media organisations to maximise audiences?

   b) Are their concerns well placed?

3 a) What can we learn about the influence of advertisers on media content from Peter Oborne's allegations against *The Daily Telegraph* in respect of its treatment of negative stories about HSBC?

   b) What sorts of media content or services are liable to be most appealing to advertisers?

4 a) Is it right that the Canadian government should seek to influence the cultural identities of its citizens by imposing Canadian content quotas? How could we justify such an approach?

   b) Should governments and internet service providers assist the recording industry by cracking down on online sharing of music?

5 Given that media are dominated by powerful corporate organisations, to what extent is it inevitable that the content and services they provide will reinforce the powerful interests they represent?

SUGGESTED FURTHER READING

Bagdikian, B. (2004) *The New Media Monopoly*. Boston: Beacon Press – Critical discussion of the implications of the concentration of media in the hands of powerful corporations.

Doyle, G. (2013) *Understanding Media Economics – Second Edition*. London: Sage – Comprehensive and up-to-date introduction to the workings of contemporary media industries.

Edwardson, R. (2008) *Canadian Content: Culture and the Quest for Nationhood*. Toronto: University of Toronto Press – Outline of the ways in which the Canadian state has sought to regulate media content in order to protect and nurture national identity.

Gitlin, T. (2000) *Inside Prime-Time: Revised Edition*. London: Routledge – Detailed account of the workings of the US television industry, uncovering the institutional priorities which underlie programming decisions.

Golding, P. and Murdock, G. (1991) 'Culture, Communications and Political Economy', in Curran, J. and Gurevitch, M. (eds) *Mass Media and Society – Third Edition*. London: Arnold, pp. 70–92 – Theoretical outline of critical political economy as a perspective on media centred upon industry and its broader capitalist context.

CHAPTER 4
MEDIA CONTENT

FOCAL POINTS

- Semiology as an approach that regards media texts as arrangements of signs
- Narrative, genre and discourse analysis as related approaches to textual analysis
- Differences between qualitative and quantitative forms of media analysis
- Content analysis as a systematic, quantitative approach
- The need to understand texts in their broader context

INTRODUCTION

In the last two chapters, we have examined the technologies via which media communication is transmitted and the industry which controls them. In spite of the importance of both these elements of the media process, a substantial amount of academic analysis has involved the detailed study of media 'messages' themselves – the very content which McLuhan regarded as so irrelevant. Whether they take the form of novels, newspaper articles, pieces of music, television programmes or the words, images or videos users post on social network sites, the units of content that carry such 'messages' are referred to as *texts*. This chapter is about how scholars have sought to analyse media texts, the motivations for their approaches and the kinds of conclusions they have drawn. We'll examine a number of different approaches, focusing particularly on two contrasting case studies: semiology and content analysis.

Although oriented towards media products themselves, the analysis of texts is not concerned with an understanding of content for its own sake. Rather, theorists seek to understand the broader social and cultural significance of media messages: their relationship with the social relations and cultural identities of the world in which they operate. This involves an appreciation of the way that, rather than either reflecting society neutrally or shaping it through content invented out of thin air, media offer us selective representations of the world which have some capacity to influence or shape the future. This circular understanding of content as representation helps to illustrate the potential importance of textual analysis. It shows that, in some cases, we might be able to come to tentative understandings of aspects of 'real' social relations through studying their representation in media. A study of changing representations of men and women in adverts over the last 50 years, for example, might tell us a great deal about shifting attitudes in broader society. More often, however, textual analysis tends to be used as a way of drawing attention to the ways media content selects and constructs the world, and the ways such representations might influence the future.

MEDIA TEXTS AS ARRANGEMENTS OF SIGNS

One of the best known approaches to the study of media texts is *semiology*. Pioneered in the writings of Ferdinand de Saussure (1974) and Charles Peirce (1931–48), and developed in relation to mass media texts by European structuralist theorists such as Roland Barthes (1968), semiology regards all communication, from speech to images to television programmes, as made up of signs. The role of the semiologist is to decipher the ways different arrangements of signs generate meaning. According to de Saussure, all signs are made up of two core elements – a *signifier*, which is the means of representation, and a *signified*, which is a concept which is represented. For example, a smile acts as a signifier: its signified is the concept of the happiness or amusement of its bearer. Particular forms of music have also acquired the role of signifiers in certain contexts: for emotional concepts such as fear, anger or joy. Importantly, the word 'sign' should not be taken to mean the same as the term 'signifier'. Rather, 'sign' refers to the duality of signifier and signified – the relationship between the two. Equally important is that the signified in de Saussure's approach is not, as Barthes (1968) puts it, 'a thing' but a concept – an idea. Thus smoke signifies not fire itself as an external object, but the human concept of fire.

The most underlying system of signs in society is language. In writing this chapter, I hope to convey meaning (signified) through particular arrangements of letters and words (signifiers) drawn from language, which is an ever-developing sign system. Successful communication requires a socially learned agreement, between myself as author and you as reader, as to the meaning of the signifiers I am deploying. Semiological analysis, then, can be carried out upon written texts or speech, through deconstruction of the way arrangements of words generate meaning.

The premises and techniques of the approach are also used, however, to make sense of the construction of meaning in other forms of text: images, songs, websites, films, adverts, news reports, magazine covers and so on. Written texts involve arrangements of letters and words, images involve compositions of shapes and colours and music involves compositions of sound, but ultimately, they all may be regarded as amalgamations of signs. And just as the communication of messages through speech (*parole*) requires the establishment and learning of a shared language (*langue*), so the conveyance of meaning via image, music or film is reliant upon the development and shared understanding of their own conventions. We understand particular arrangements of music, lighting, camera shot and so on in films, then, because we have learned and accepted the semiotic conventions through which this media format operates.

SIGNS AS ARBITRARY?

The successful communication of meaning, then, is reliant upon shared societal systems of understanding because, rather than being universal, the relationship between signifier and signified is culturally specific. In many societies we have become used to equating black with the concept of evil and white with good, but this is based upon a historically established convention and it is possible that in a different society with a different history, the associations between signifier and signified could be reversed, or even that there would be no semiotic connection at all between colour and morality. Nevertheless, signs are not necessarily entirely neutral. Often there is some initial 'relative analogy' (de Saussure 1974) or 'motivation' (Barthes 1968), behind the relationship between signifiers and signifieds. Peirce (1931–48) elaborates on this through a distinction between icons, indexes and symbols.

Icons, he argues, are signs in which there is a physical resemblance between signifier and signified (or, as he put it, the sign and its object). Words such as 'splash' or 'crack' are iconic because their sound imitates the phenomenon they signify. In representing people, objects or events with analogous sets of shapes and colours, photographs also can work on an iconic level. The most well-known use of the word icon today is probably in relation to symbols on the screens of tablets, phones and computers. Only some of these, though, are consistent with Peirce's sense of the term. A printer symbol that consists of an image of a printer is iconic, but some of the so-called icons used to open commercially branded pieces of software are not.

Indexes, Peirce's second type of sign, also involve a connection between signifier and signified, but rather than being a physical resemblance, the correspondence relates to a prior association between them of a sensory or causal kind. The most commonly cited example here is the use of smoke to signify fire. The two always accompany one another and this makes the use of the former to signify the latter far from random. Similarly, we could think about the use of images of dark clouds to signify rain or the use of tears to signify sadness. In each case, the culturally learned relationship between signifier and signified is based on an existing association.

In contrast to icons and indexes, Peirce's third type, *symbols*, are entirely arbitrary and there is no obvious initial connection. Because of this, such 'unmotivated' signs, as Barthes (1968) referred to them, are also liable to vary more between one culture and another. With the exception of words that imitate their object, language works on a symbolic, rather than iconic or indexical level, because there is no logical connection between the appearance or sound of words and the concepts to which they refer. The connection between the arrangement of letters 'fire' and concept to which it refers, is reliant upon an arbitrary historical agreement between English speakers to associate the two with one another. There are also all sorts of symbols outside the realm of language. The use of a green light to signify 'go' may have become commonplace across the globe as a result of cultural influence, but it is symbolic because there is no particular reason for it.

LEVELS OF MEANING

Whether arbitrary or not, when it comes to texts that consist of complex arrangements of signs, the connection between signifier and signified may not always be simple or one-dimensional. Through development of a distinction between *denotation* and *connotation*, Barthes (1968) elaborated the notion that signifiers may simultaneously convey meaning on different levels. Denotation refers to the most immediate level of meaning – the interpretation of what is represented at its most basic level of intelligibility. A photograph of a woman's face and body on a fashion and beauty magazine (see Figure 4.1) may refer, in the first instance, to the individual represented or significance of individual elements or features of the face, body and their decoration: the concepts of hair, eyes, skin, jewellery, make-up and different clothing, for example. It is important to remember here that denotation is not the same as signifier, even if sometimes the difference between the two seems negligible. Rather, denotation is the signified in its most immediate, literal and obvious sense. Because of its immediacy, denotation, particularly in the case of visual images, has a strong chance of being recognised across cultures.

Of greater ultimate interest to mass media semiologists, though, are *connotations*, which Barthes refers to as second order or 'associative' meanings. Here we are in the territory of cultural inference and implication. Under the right cultural circumstances, the image on our magazine cover may convey not only the immediate meanings outlined above, but also broader concepts that are further removed from what is immediately represented. The expression on the face, the identity of its owner (Kylie Jenner) and the way it has been made-up and photographed, alongside bodily posture, clothing and other features of the woman in question, may be taken to signify more abstract concepts such as beauty, sexiness, satisfaction, confidence, success or being fashionable, for example, or the notion of a connection between these qualities and broader concepts of femininity. Because they are further removed than denotations from the signifier itself, connotations are, it is argued, more likely to be culturally specific – their communication is unlikely to be successful unless the audience is well versed in the particular cultural conventions through which they operate. Connotations, then, are more *polysemic*, or open to different possible meanings, than are denotations.

Figure 4.1   *Cosmopolitan* front cover, February 2015 © Hearst Magazines UK

For some, the distinction between denotation and connotation is an ambiguous one (Hall 1993). When one considers that even fairly immediate concepts such as 'face', 'woman' and 'make-up' are themselves socially constructed, then arguably there is no such thing as a 'literal' or absolute meaning. Even Barthes (1968) himself recognised that denotation might plausibly be regarded as the first and most immediate level of connotation. Nevertheless, for Hall (1993), once the culturally constructed nature of all meaning is recognised, the denotation/connotation distinction remains analytically useful in distinguishing between immediate and relatively uncontested meanings (denotations) and broader, more malleable inferences (connotations).

SIGNS AS RELATIONAL

Rather than operating in isolation from one another, signifiers generate meaning as a result of their relationships with other signifiers. We cannot understand the cover of a fashion/ beauty magazine through an isolated examination of the image in the middle of it and neither can we make sense of an online news article by focusing only on the words in the headline. To analyse the ways meaning is conveyed, we have to understand the working of signs in relation to one another. For semiologists there are two relational axes on which to focus – paradigmatic and syntagmatic.

The *paradigmatic* axis concerns the relationship of each individual signifier in a text, with a set of alternative signifiers that could have been used instead. The set of alternatives is known as a paradigm. Paradigmatic analysis, then, involves breaking up the text into its components and assessing the significance of each element by considering how the meaning would have been different if alternative signifiers had been used instead. The idea is to compare what was selected by the producer of the text with what was not selected. Barthes illustrates the point with reference to the garment system (1968). We can identify a number of different paradigms or types under headings such as headwear, footwear, above waist garments, below waist garments, underwear and so on. Having identified these, we can then analyse the significance of the choices a person makes by comparing them with alternatives within their paradigm. We can understand the significance of a long flowing skirt, for example, by imagining if it was substituted with a PVC mini-skirt, or a pair of jeans.

The use of colour also provides plenty of opportunities for paradigmatic analysis. A predominance of red in a media text is liable to create a different impression than a predominance of green, blue or yellow. And colour can have specific impacts on meaning in particular situations. In order to demonstrate the absorbency of products such as nappies, adverts sometimes have shown blue liquid being absorbed by their products. Paradigmatic analysis may help us to understand why blue might be used rather than, for example, yellow, green, purple, red, black or clear. Meanwhile, in the case of the female image on the front cover of a beauty magazine we might identify a number of paradigms, including choice of model, use of lighting, categories of clothing, hair style, direction of gaze, categories of facial expression, bodily posture and so on.

While paradigmatic analysis concerns the comparison between what is present and what is absent, *syntagmatic* analysis asks us to consider how the different signs present in a text interact with one another. Having divided the text into pieces, then, we then need to examine how its components fit together. The paradigmatic comparison of individual items of clothing with absent alternatives may be valuable but we cannot understand the significance of each component, or the overall impression conveyed by the outfit they form, unless we examine their relationship with one another. A pair of jeans may convey a different message if worn with a sports T-shirt and trainers, than if combined with a stylish, sparkling designer jacket, as in the case of our *Cosmopolitan* example.

Until they are placed into a particular semantic context, individual signifiers can be particularly polysemic, or open to interpretation. Red could signify danger, fire, heat, horror or sex, while yellow might imply heat, summer, happiness, cowardice or illness. The meaning is only clarified by the relationship between the colour and the other signifiers against which it is placed. In the context of a traffic light or warning sign, red conveys danger, but when used as the backdrop for footage of a silhouetted couple gazing at one another it may connote sexual desire. For Barthes, images tend to be particularly polysemic, making it especially important to study the ways their meaning is *anchored* by other signifiers – particularly verbal headlines, captions or voice-overs, but also sound, music and various other features.

In the case of our fashion/beauty magazine example, the image of a smiling female celebrity, holding a confident, active bodily pose and gazing at the reader, is anchored by the title of the magazine, *Cosmopolitan*, as well as a series of snappy textual references to looking sexy, tips for 'hot' lips, skin and nails, weight-loss and sex and relationships with men. The reader, we might argue, is prompted to regard the flawless, relaxed, gazing Kylie Jenner as a sexy, sophisticated, confident and successful ideal of femininity, and encouraged, via the various references to self-improvement, to regard this image as something to be strived for, through taking heed of tips inside about how to keep in shape, enhance one's body and, presumably, achieve a 'sexy' look through acquiring and assembling suitable outfits. Amongst all this, references to Jenner as a 'mogul' and to '1-2-3 steps to figure out your future' entail connotations of career and success that, among other things, reinforce the association of this particular version of glamorous femininity with independence and control. Finally, references to relationships with men, in the form of encouragement to 'make men obsessed' with you through looking sexy, male testimonials about relationship regrets and a story seemingly about BDSM experimentation all serve to connect the cosmopolitan femininity on offer with the achievement of male attention, sex or intimate companionship.

In theory, the process of semiology involves the sequential completion of paradigmatic and syntagmatic analysis: 'What has to be done is to cut up the "endless" message… into minimal significant units… then to group these units into paradigmatic classes, and finally to classify the syntagmatic relations which link these units' (Barthes 1968). In practice, however, it is difficult to fully separate the two stages because of the extent to which they both inform one another. To understand why red was used rather than blue or yellow (paradigmatic), I need to take into account the context in which the colour appears (syntagmatic).

UNCOVERING MYTHOLOGY

In addition to denotation and connotation, Barthes (1972) spoke of a third order of meaning: *mythology* – or *myth*. Myths are broader sets of cultural assumptions and beliefs evoked and reinforced by media texts. They help to shape the way in which we interpret denotations and connotations in media messages, but are themselves further developed and reinforced every time they are evoked. Barthes illustrates this relationship in his analysis of a cover of the French current affairs magazine *Paris Match*. The cover depicts a young black man in French military uniform looking up proudly – probably at a Tricolour flag. The connotations of this, argues Barthes, relate to the proudness of members of France's colonies to represent, identify with and defend the country. In turn, this taps into and develops a broader existing myth about the greatness of French imperialism: 'I see very well what it signifies to me: that France is a great Empire, that all her sons, without any colour discrimination, faithfully serve under her flag, and that there is no better answer to the detractors of alleged colonialism than the zeal shown by this negro in serving his so-called oppressors' (Barthes 1972: 116).

Although his notion of mythology does not necessarily infer something false, Barthes is critical of the operation of myths, suggesting that they invariably serve powerful interests by making dominant ways of thinking appear natural and obvious. The primary purpose of semiology, for Barthes, is to deconstruct and expose the operation of myth through media content and numerous cultural analysts have followed his lead in this respect. Studies of advertising, for example, have placed emphasis upon the cumulative establishment of the myth that happiness is commensurate with the acquisition of consumer goods (Kellner 1995; Williamson 1978. Such themes also pervade our example of the beauty magazine cover. The connotations of the text, which emphasise feminine fulfilment through fashion, style, cosmetics, self-confidence and sexiness, activate broader cultural myths: about the equation of happiness with particular kinds of individual consumerism and bodily enhancement, for example, and the association of even the most active, relaxed and assertive forms of femininity with physical attractiveness to, and sexual relationships with men (see McCracken 1992).

LIMITATIONS OF SEMIOLOGY

Various criticisms have been raised about semiology as an approach to media analysis. Although he questions de Saussure's claim that semiology is a science, Barthes (1968) nevertheless asks us to accept that, if used properly, the approach can reveal the definitive meanings of media texts within a given societal context. But how do we know that semiological readings of adverts, films or images are accurate in their 'revelations' of meaning? The problem, for some critics, is that, for all its technical-sounding terminology, semiology tends to be unsystematic (Strinati 2004). Rather than comprising a clear and orderly set of step-by-step procedures which would result in similar conclusions if repeated by another analyst, the interpretation of meaning tends to be a messy undertaking centred on individual interpretation. It is, in other words, *unreliable*.

Sometimes semiological readings lack even minimal levels of systematisation. For example, in emphasising his casual observance of the *Paris Match* cover and stating that 'I see very well what it signifies to me', Barthes (1972: 116) indicates that, far from emerging through the careful application of procedures, his conclusions apparently have emanated from some sort of intuition on his part – something presumably lacking in 'ordinary' readers. As well as making semiology unreliable, such emphasis upon the subjective interpretation raises question about *validity*. Are semiologists measuring what they purport to be measuring – the definitive meaning constructed by a message – or are they in fact revealing their own unique personal response to it? And, as Strinati (2004) asks, how are we to know the difference between one and the other?

More fundamentally, perhaps, semiology risks reifying media content, implying that particular arrangements of signs, operating within particular language systems, generate definitive meaning all by themselves. Questions about the specific motivations and operation of media industries and regulators are bypassed, then, by a form of textual determinism. In fairness, Barthes recognises the importance of media industries in his emphasis on the role of a 'deciding group' in the development of mass media sign systems, which unlike language itself, are liable to be shaped by the few rather than the many (1968). However, he offers no means or prospect of analysing the media industry, prompting Chandler (1994b) to argue that semiology may be of some value in understanding *what* meanings are generated and *how*, but is not able to show *why* or what we can do about it.

Meanwhile, in assuming that there is such a thing as a definitive meaning which can be discerned by appropriately skilled analysts, semiology neglects the engagement between media content and users. It is assumed that the connotations identified by the semiotician are definitive and hence liable to be 'received' by audiences. Yet research suggests that the range of different audience interpretations and responses to media texts can be considerable, something which has led some to suggest that there is no such thing as a fixed or pre-given meaning and that meaning is produced only through the interaction of text and audience (Morley 1992).

For Fiske (1991a; 1991b), texts not only need to be understood in relation to the ways audiences engage with them, but also in the context of their relationship with other texts and broader culture and society. From this point of view, the signs within an individual text have a syntagmatic relationship not only with one another but also a range of other texts circulating in the present and past. The front cover of *Cosmopolitan*, then, needs to be understood in relation to the way its meaning systems connect with a host of other representations in television, film, advertising, social media and websites. These *intertextual* relationships make it potentially hazardous to separate off any particular text. Texts, then, 'need to be understood not for and by themselves but in their interrelationships with other texts and with social life...' (Fiske 1991b: 4).

It would be unwise, however, to dismiss semiology entirely. The approach remains influential and continues to inform crucial debates about the kinds of meanings predominant within media and the ways they are constructed. In particular, we should be wary of rejecting it on the grounds that it is unsystematic. Over-reliance upon personal interpretation may be hazardous, but, as we shall see, this can be a feature of more systematic approaches too. It is important to recognise, meanwhile, that a flexible, unsystematic approach may provide the only means through which we can hope to make detailed, contextualised sense of textual meaning. Through focusing on such detail, semiology shows us how every element of a text is of significance, that no part of a message is coincidental or neutral and, most of all, that it is the complex relationships between signifiers which generate meaning, rather than any individual elements in isolation. Sometimes people suggest that semiologists read too much into apparently simple texts. Perhaps, but it is worth bearing in mind that every detail of each media text has been painstakingly selected and positioned for a particular reason: very little is accidental or inconsequential.

NARRATIVE, GENRE AND DISCOURSE ANALYSIS

Semiology is not the only means by which scholars have sought to conduct in-depth or qualitative analysis of the content of media texts. A number of related approaches have emerged which each develop the analysis of texts in different ways. Importantly, rather than being mutually exclusive, particular elements of such approaches, together with semiology itself, are often combined in different ways.

NARRATIVE ANALYSIS

Narrative analysis treats media texts as diverse as films, adverts, blogs, documentaries and news columns, as composed of different forms of story-telling and seeks to identify the conventions and devices with which such narratives are constructed (Fulton et al. 2006; Gillespie 2006). Semiology is of great importance here because many of the devices used by story-tellers are reliant upon the successful communication of meaning through signs – the use of music to infer emotion or to hint at what may happen next, or the use of clothing or accent to signify particular character traits, for example. Narrative analysis is particularly concerned with understanding the narrative conventions on which stories draw and, in doing so, deconstructing the ways audiences are being asked to make sense of content. One of the key focal points here is the order in which events are represented. For example, according to Todorov (1978), story-telling often activates a standard plot structure, in which a state of *equilibrium* or normality is established at the beginning which is *disrupted* in some way by a causal event and eventually *re-instated* in a slightly different form at the end as a result of corrective action. Films and novels often work in this way and so does the construction of plot in many documentaries or news stories. Many of the accounts of the World Trade Center attacks of September 11th 2001 drew upon this sort of disruption of normality structure, and anticipated, in one way or another, a return to normality after America had taken appropriate corrective action.

Narratives also involve standard character types. Propp (1968), for example, identified seven character types which operated within Russian folk tales as follows:

1. the villain (who disrupts normality)
2. the donor (who gives the hero a gift to enable normality to be restored)
3. the helper (who accompanies the hero)
4. the princess (in need of rescue from the villain)
5. the dispatcher (who initiates the hero's journey)
6. the hero (who restores normality)
7. the false hero (who promises to restore normality but ends up abandoning or betraying the cause).

While, to some extent, these are specific to the type of tales that Propp studied, they are also familiar in various different sorts of stories. If we take the original *Star Wars* (Episode 4) film, for example, we have a clear villain and hero in Darth Vader and Luke Skywalker, a combined donor and dispatcher in the form of Obi Wan Kenobi, a princess in need of rescue (Leia) and a number of helpers (Han Solo, Chewbacca, C3PO and R2D2). The only one of Propp's characters which is absent is the false hero, something that becomes a key theme in the film's sequels (and eventual prequels), which focus on the fall from grace of Luke's father Anakin. Of course, the basic conventions and character types identified here barely scratch the surface of narrative analysis, which aims to understand in extensive detail the ways different stories are structured, the explicit and implicit devices used to convey different events and the ways emotional responses are generated.

GENRE ANALYSIS

A further variant, which relates closely both to narrative analysis and semiology itself, is *genre analysis*. Here, the curiosity of analysts is focused acutely upon the relationship of different texts to one another and the ways they are clustered into particular types or genres (see Solomon 1976). Examples of genres include romance, comedy, science fiction, news and soap opera and genres can also be thought of in terms of hierarchies, so that the genre of comedy, for example, might be divided into stand-up, sitcom, romantic comedy, panel show and so on. Genre analysis is concerned with the establishment and operation of distinct conventions within each genre or sub-genre – conventions that relate to audience expectations about narrative structure, subject matter, setting, editing, music, visual features and so on.

For example, soap operas typically involve a series of overlapping and ongoing narratives about different members of a community which continue from episode to episode. They also seek to generate a broadly credible and mostly serious set of representations of relationships, dilemmas and personal crises. In contrast, sitcoms usually are centred on a particular family, friendship group or workplace and focus on representations that are exaggerated for comedic value. They also tend to utilise a simple beginning-middle-end narrative form in which, consistent with Todorov's standard structure, each episode begins and ends with a state of normalcy. Generic conventions also apply to informational programming. 24-hour news, for example, has developed a somewhat unique set of conventions of its own: the emphasis on fast moving live-ness, breaking stories, graphics, logos, on-screen tickers and two-way question and answer sessions between anchors and reporters 'at the scene'.

As well as being concerned with the characteristics of established genres, the ways they are constructed and their orientation to different sorts of consumers, genre analysts have taken a particular interest in the ways in which genres draw from and overlap with one another, something which in some cases results in the development of entirely new genres. Particular attention has been focused in recent years upon the apparent merging of information-oriented genres with those associated more with fiction and entertainment. The now well-known genres of the docusoap and scripted reality show are examples, the conventions of which are drawn from a mixture of drama, soap opera and sometimes even game show. Meanwhile documentaries and news programmes themselves make increasing use of narrative devices and techniques associated with drama, including the use of reconstructions, graphic and emotive footage, dramatic music and allusions to traditionally fictional roles such as hero and villain.

DISCOURSE ANALYSIS

Although semiology has its roots in linguistics, the former is probably more often associated with the study of image-based media than the in-depth examination of the minutia of language-use. Subsequently, there has been a growth of interest among some theorists in the specific construction of meaning through the arrangement of words and sentences in media. Commonly used in analysis of news in its various formats but equally useful for other kinds of media, *discourse analysis* (Fairclough 1995; Kress and Hodge 1979; Talbot 2007) is concerned with the ways broader beliefs, worldviews and social structures are embedded in and reinforced through the use of verbal or written communication. The approach draws upon linguistics and also on the post-structuralist theory of Michel Foucault (Hesmondhalgh 2006). Foucault repeatedly emphasised that the realities that we experience are constructed by the discourses through which we describe and understand them and, crucially, that such discourses are closely intertwined with relations of power.

Critical approaches to discourse analysis, as outlined by Norman Fairclough (1995), bring together Foucault's emphasis on discourse and power with a specific focus on the use of language in media. They are typically concerned with analysing how dominant ways of thinking and structures of inequality inflect and are reproduced through speech and writing. The approach aims to explore the fine detail of both the content and structure of language-use in media – something that involves both paradigmatic and syntagmatic dimensions. Focusing on various elements of vocabulary, grammar and syntax, analysts ask how the particular formulations used position the speaker and the audience, what they include and exclude and how they invite audiences to understand events, individuals, groups and identities.

One example of a point of interest in discourse analysis has been the way different forms of words can attribute or obscure responsibility for events, emotions or reactions. The hypothetical headline 'Anger as Refugees Flood Britain' places the critical spotlight squarely on the actions of refugees, who are the sole active agent in the formulation and thereby implied to be responsible. In contrast the word 'anger' is not connected with any active agent; instead of telling us who is angry using a verb (to be angry) and an actor, my hypothetical headline de-personalises and passifies this aspect of the story by nominalising the verb (turning it into a noun), so that those responsible for the anger are absolved of scrutiny and the anger itself legitimated as a sort of universal (and natural) reaction among right-thinking people. Another example of a common focal point for discourse analysis is the construction of communities through formulations of language and the positioning of speaker and audience in relation to these. Billig (1995), for example, carried out a classic study of the construction of national identity in UK newspapers through the repeated use of words such as 'us', 'our' and 'we' in headline and article phrasing (see Chapter 9).

Crucially, rather than understanding individual texts in isolation, discourse analysis attempts to place them in context. One simple example of this is that if one places my example on refugees into the context of the broader newspaper construction of a national 'us' which Billig identifies, then we might suggest that the 'anger' in the first example is implicitly being constructed as a natural emotion associated with this national 'us', which is implied to include both the journalists and their readers, but not the refugees.

FROM QUALITY TO QUANTITY: CONTENT ANALYSIS

Semiology, alongside related approaches such as narrative, genre and discourse analysis, is focused upon providing an in-depth or *qualitative* explanation of the content of media texts and the implications of that content. As well as being the primary strength of such approaches, this emphasis connects to the lack of systematisation regarded as problematic by some critics. The tradition that most contrasts with semiology and other qualitative approaches in this respect is *content analysis*. Rather than focusing upon qualitative interpretations and detail, content analysts are concerned with the identification of broad empirical trends across a range of texts. Proponents claim that, through the use of rigorous and systematic *quantitative* methodology, they can produce findings that are empirically verifiable: capable of being proven or unproven by unbiased evidence.

'OBJECTIVE, SYSTEMATIC AND QUANTITATIVE'

According to one of its early proponents, content analysis can be understood as an 'objective, systematic and quantitative' approach to the measurement of media content (Berelson 1952: 18, cited in Gunter 2000). More or less repeated in the definitions proposed by more recent theorists (e.g. Kerlinger 1986), this threesome is worthy of explanation.

The notion of *objectivity* suggests that, rather than coming about as a result of the biases of researchers or their methods, findings and conclusions should accurately reflect the reality of the phenomenon being studied. Results should be *valid*, then, in that they measure what they claim to measure and *reliable* in that a repeat of the procedures followed by a different research team would yield the same findings. This emphasis upon the achievement of objectivity through the application of systematic methods reflects the grounding of content analysis in *positivism*, an epistemology (or theory of knowledge) that regards social research as analogous to the natural sciences and, as a consequence, prescribes the replication in the social sciences of scientific rigour and standards of proof.

The positivist emphasis on objectivity often is associated with research methodologies that seek to *quantify* the frequency with which particular phenomena occur. Consistent with this, content analysis involves the prior identification of particular types of content and the counting of their number of occurrences across a sample of texts. Rather than analysing the detailed semiological construction of particular versions of masculinity in a particular advertising campaign, then, I might count the number of times male characters are presented doing designated activities. These might include stereotypically masculine activities – such as participating in sport, doing physical work, driving cars or drinking beer – and those traditionally associated with women, such as housework or childcare. The idea would be that, if I follow the appropriate procedures, such an approach would enable me confidently to generalise my results – to come to a definitive conclusion as to what proportion of television adverts present men in traditionally masculine roles, for example. I may then be able to compare my conclusion with earlier studies, or comparable work in different countries. If my study is designed with sufficient care, I may even seek out actual data about the distribution of men's time in society in order to compare this with my results and ascertain how 'accurate' media representations of masculinity are.

It is through being *systematic* that, according to proponents of content analysis, we can produce findings that are objective, generalisable and comparable with other studies. Systematisation means that we reduce the potential for bias through the rigorous application of a carefully devised set of parameters, definitions, techniques and procedures. The idea is to leave as little as possible to chance or to the subjective judgements of researchers. Systematisation also creates the possibility for studies to be repeated by other research teams, either for purposes of direct verification or to enable meaningful comparison from place-to-place or time-to-time. There are various examples of systematisation in content analysis and we'll illustrate here by focusing upon some of the most important.

CATEGORIES AND CODING

Rather than beginning with a media text and describing it in whatever way the analyst deems most appropriate, content analysts code content into pre-defined categories. Such categories, alongside the systems of classification of which they are a part, must be defined precisely and applied consistently. If I want to measure the number of 'acts of violence' within a sample of content, then I must first define what counts as an act of violence for the purpose of the study. Does a gentle push count, for example, does someone need to be visibly hurt, and do I include or exclude verbal intimidation? Also, what will count as an individual unit of violence? In the case of a prolonged gang fight, do I count every individual blow struck or do I record the whole encounter as a single unit? Such decisions make a radical difference to findings and therefore must be prescribed and systematised in order to ensure rigour. I may wish to further categorise acts of violence recorded – whether according to descriptive types (kicking, punching, striking with a weapon, etc.), levels of extremity or other factors.

Wimmer and Dominick (2006) stress that, in order to avoid confusion, categories must be *mutually exclusive*, in that they should not overlap with one another, and *exhaustive*, in that they should cover the full range of possibilities. If we wanted to measure the frequency of different story types on news websites, the following category set would not get us very far: 'international stories', 'crime stories', 'sports stories', 'celebrity stories' and 'other'. Firstly, the international stories category clearly has the potential to overlap with the other three, and secondly the category set as a whole is far from exhaustive. Where would I place a story about a local politician or one about a lost cat, for example? These and many others would have to be coded within the 'other' category, which means they would effectively be excluded from the analysis.

POPULATION AND SAMPLE

Another crucial area for systematisation is defining the sample of content on which analysis is to be carried out. Qualitative approaches such as semiology are often unsystematic here, because there is a tendency for analysts to focus on examples of content that happen to interest them or to illustrate trends they already believe to be taking place. Although there may be some advantages to such *purposive* approaches to sampling, it means that we cannot know how typical or widespread the outcomes of the analysis are. In content analysis, this would be unacceptable: samples are expected to be generated according to a consistently applied set of principles designed to ensure *representativeness*. To be representative, the make-up of a sample must be such that it can accurately and fairly stand in for the broader *population* of content that a study is trying to draw conclusions about. Examples of populations might be 'advertisements on Canadian local television', 'French news websites' or 'Russian social networking site profiles'. It is by having a sample likely to be typical of its population that content analysts are able to generalise their findings.

Content analysis sampling often takes a multi-stage form. A study of UK printed newspapers may establish rules for including first a set of publications, second, a series of dates, and third a selection of content from each edition. Such parameters must be carefully designed in order to avoid sample bias. If my sample consists of the front page content of *The Times*, the *Guardian* and *The Daily Telegraph* every Saturday during the period 15th December to 2nd January, for example, then it would be far from typical of its population: it would exclude all non-front-page and weekday content, it would favour 'quality' newspapers over the popular press and it would over-represent a non-typical time of year dominated by Christmas. To avoid such biases, I might include a greater range of newspaper types, days of the week and content from each edition as well as a more usual period of the news year. I could also consider introducing an element of randomisation into the selection of dates, newspapers, pages and so on.

CASE STUDY: GERBNER AND TELEVISION VIOLENCE

George Gerbner and colleagues' classic annual studies of US television violence from 1967 onwards provide a particularly well-known and influential example of content analysis in action (Gerbner and Gross 1976). The population for the studies was limited to 'dramatic programming', with non-fiction such as sports, game shows and news excluded. The sample consisted of drama transmitted during every weekday evening and weekend morning for a single week during each year the study was carried out. Violence was defined as 'the overt expression of physical force (with or without a weapon) against self or other, compelling action against one's will on pain of being hurt or killed, or actually hurting or killing' with a single unit defined as 'a scene of some violence confined to the same parties' (1976: 184). The studies placed emphasis on the level and type of violence in each individual programme; the involvement in violence of individual major and minor characters; and the coding of each specific violent act. The approach enabled the categorisation of violence into different types as well as analysis of factors such as the kinds of characters involved and the consequences of violence as part of the plot.

The studies demonstrated that a high proportion of dramatic programming contained violence. In 1975, for example, 78% of the programmes analysed contained violent episodes and 64% of lead characters were involved in an episode of violence. An average hour of viewing contained eight violent episodes, a figure that rose to 16 in children's weekend daytime television. Over the years, findings also illustrated consistent patterns relating to types of violence and, fascinatingly, the profile of those involved. For example, violence was committed as often by characters with a 'happy fate' as those with an 'unhappy' one, but the former – who tended to be young, white, American males – were killed and injured less, their violence presented as more efficient and their character as more attractive (Fiske and Hartley 1988). Young male characters were most likely to be perpetrators of violence while women and the elderly were more likely to be its victims. Female characters, for example, were as likely to be killed as to be a killer, while males were almost twice as likely to be a killer than to be killed. This effect was concentrated even further if gender was combined with ethnicity and other factors: 'old, poor and black women,' it is pointed out, 'were shown only as killed and never as killers' (Gerbner and Gross 1976: 190).

Through focusing upon the profile of characters, Gerbner and colleagues' work measured not only violence itself but also how different social groups are represented in media. It also illustrates a range of comparative ways that content analysis can be used. As well as comparing results from one year to the next in order to illustrate changes over time, Gerbner compared his findings with statistics on crime within society itself, something that led him to argue that television representations exaggerated and distorted the level of crime and violence in society.

LIMITATIONS OF CONTENT ANALYSIS

Among the various ways scholars have sought to study media texts, content analysis has possibly been the most influential with respect to the public, the media industry and policy-makers. The approach has clear potential value as a means of facilitating broad assessments of the quantitative character of media representations and, in particular, enabling meaningful comparisons, whether across time and space, between media outlets or between media and 'real' society. In spite of the tendency of its proponents to emphasise the superiority of their systematic numerical approach over qualitative approaches such as semiology, however, content analysis has significant weaknesses of its own.

While it carries advantages with respect to reliability and the ability to generalise, content analysis can lead to findings that are simplistic and lacking in depth. Rather than being carefully understood as part of the particular context in which they present themselves to viewers, selected segments of media texts are extracted and simplified into instances of abstract categories such as 'episodes of violence' or 'representations of men in traditionally masculine roles'. Attempts usually are made to incorporate fragments of context through the recording of certain aspects of the characters or narrative, but these are inevitably superficial. Gerbner is able to differentiate between violent episodes committed by characters with 'happy' and 'unhappy' outcomes, for example, but such categories are themselves simplified abstractions and barely scratch the surface with respect to the complexity of the contexts in which violence is given meaning for real audiences. Such contextualising variables as do exist also have a tendency to be ignored in the headline figures of studies. Gerbner makes a great deal, for example, of figures such as the number of violent episodes per hour of viewing, which take no account of context at all. Appreciation of the relationship between the parts and the whole in the construction of meaning is largely bypassed in content analysis, then, as a result of an overriding emphasis on reducing, categorising and quantifying.

The claims to objectivity of some proponents of content analysis are highly questionable, meanwhile. For all the emphasis upon being systematic and reliable, outcomes and conclusions are still shaped by subjective agendas and judgements. The formulation of research questions, design of samples, devising of categories and identification of units of analysis are all reliant upon human judgements and all liable to affect results. In defining a single unit of violence in his 1970s studies, for example, Gerbner stipulates that if a new agent of violence enters into an existing violent episode, then this moment should be recorded by his team as a separate violent episode – in other words, what could conceivably be construed as a single fight would be recorded as two separate violent episodes (Gerbner and Gross 1976). Whether we think this approach sensible or not, it is a subjective judgement call liable to have had a substantial impact upon the quantity of violent acts recorded by the studies. While they do not invalidate such studies, such decisions ensure that findings can reflect the particular approach the researchers chose to take as much as the 'reality' they are seeking to shed light upon.

As with other approaches to the analysis of media texts, content analysis also is subject to the limitation that the context in which such texts are produced and consumed is neglected. There is a danger that role and motivation of producers in selecting and emphasising particular kinds of content may be overlooked, and also that it will be assumed, without evidence, that the prevalence of particular forms of content will shape the outlook or behaviour of audiences.

In fairness, some content analysts, including Gerbner, have recognised this and sought to combine their analysis of media content with direct research on media audiences – something to which we shall return in Chapter 5.

CONCLUSION: PUTTING TEXTS INTO CONTEXT

The approaches outlined in this chapter are united in their focus upon the details of media content as a means of learning about the relationship between media, culture and society. Yet, as we have seen, such approaches can differ significantly in their motivation, focus and methodology. In particular, it has been illustrated via our two main case studies of semiology and content analysis that there is a stark contrast between qualitative and quantitative approaches, the former offering detailed analysis of the ways meaning is produced in a handful of examples and the latter taking a large-scale systematic approach in order to ascertain broader trends. While both have their specific weaknesses, both have also provided those seeking to understand the role of media in society with useful tools and insights. Likewise, the range of related approaches to the analysis of content, including narrative and genre analysis, each have the potential to offer valuable clues as to the connections between the forms of culture we consume via media and the broader socio-economic context in which we live. There may be a case, then, for the development of dual or multi-method studies, which combine elements from different qualitative or quantitative approaches in order to maximise the benefits of each.

The notion that media selectively represent the broader social and cultural world – and in so doing offer the prospect of influencing the future of that world – provides a broad framework within which we can make sense of the role of media content. It also illustrates the importance of observing and understanding what media content consists of and how meaning is constructed. However, only as part of an overall analysis that includes an understanding of the role of technologies, institutions and media users, can the analysis of media texts provide a truly effective contribution to our understanding of the relationships between media, culture and society. In particular, we cannot hope to gauge the ultimate significance of what we may observe within the content of media texts without the development of an understanding of what real audiences and users do with such texts. It is this that we turn to in the next chapter.

QUESTIONS/EXERCISES

1 Distinguish between the following terms associated with semiology:

   a) signifier and signified

   b) icon, index and symbol

(Continued)

(Continued)

   c) denotation, connotation and myth

   d) paradigmatic and syntagmatic analysis

2 Select an example of a magazine, newspaper or web banner advertisement and carry out a detailed semiological analysis of the ways it conveys meaning. Try to break the text of the ad down into its components, focusing on each element individually as well as the relationship between them.

3 a) In respect of their approach to narrative, what are the differences and similarities between the conventions of news stories, Hollywood films and soap operas?

   b) Think of a recent Hollywood film and explore how closely Propp's character types can be applied to it.

4 a) What are the strengths and limitations of Gerbner's use of content analysis as a means to tell us about violence on television?

   b) Would a qualitative approach to the study of violence on television be more or less useful do you think? What approach might such a study take?

5 In what ways might qualitative or qualitative forms of textual analysis be used to study interactive forms of communication such as those that take place on social media?

SUGGESTED FURTHER READING

Barthes, R. (1968) *Elements of Semiology.* London: Cape (first published 1964) – Detailed account of the workings and significance of semiology by the theorist with whom it became most associated.

Fairclough, N. (1995) *Critical Discourse Analysis: The Critical Study of Language.* Harlow: Longman – Influential outline of critical discourse analysis as an approach to the study of media content.

Fulton, H., Huisman, R., Morphet, J. and Dunn, A, (2005) (eds) *Narrative and Media.* Cambridge: Cambridge University Press – Collection of chapters focused upon the role of narrative in different genres of film, broadcasting and print media.

Gerbner, G. and Gross, L. (1976) 'Living with Television: The Violence Profile', *Journal of Communication*, 26: 173–99 – Presents results and conclusions from Gerbner and colleagues' annual measure of television violence using content analysis.

Williamson, J. (1995) *Decoding Advertisements: Ideology and Meaning in Advertising.* London: Marian Boyars (originally published 1978) – One of the most well-known critical applications of semiology to the study of media texts.

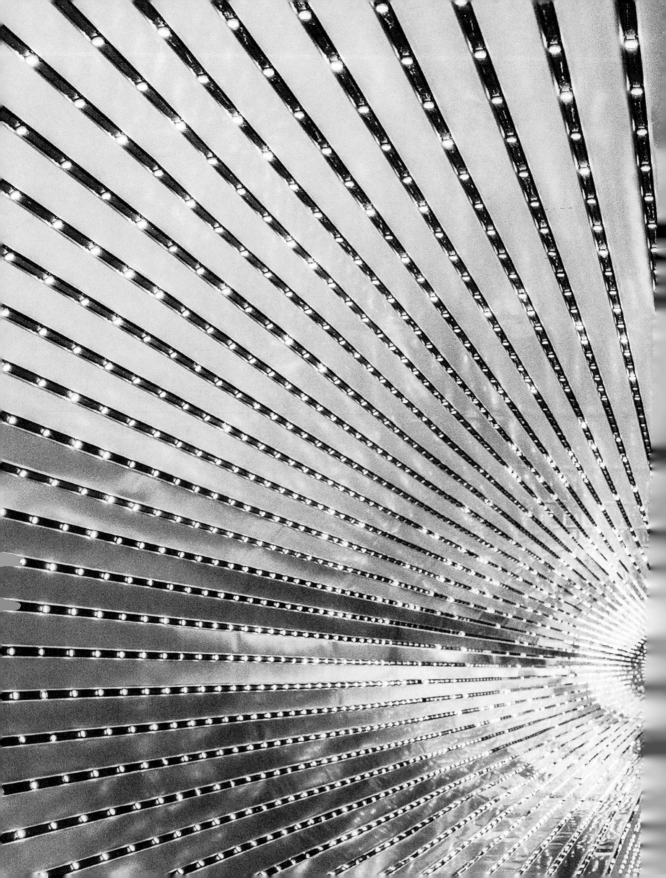

CHAPTER 5
MEDIA USERS

FOCAL POINTS

- Attempts to measure the effects of media on individual attitudes and behaviour
- Studies focused on the personal uses and functions of media
- Developing understandings of media users as active, oppositional or subversive
- Ethnographies of audiences, fans and users
- Levels and types of user engagement in digital environments

INTRODUCTION

Analysis of the habits, practices and identities of those who use media forms a vital part of the development of an understanding of the relationships between media and the broader social and cultural world. As we have seen, technological, industry-oriented and content approaches have faced the criticism that they attribute too much power to the medium, the producer or the text, respectively, in determining the significance and impact of media. Such approaches all can sometimes assume that media users form a passive element of the communications process whose role is limited to receiving pre-existing meanings and being affected by pre-determined outcomes.

In contrast, other media researchers have sought to understand what happens when individuals, families or communities engage with media texts and technologies. These approaches to what traditionally was called 'audience research' have varied considerably in terms of their methodology and theoretical approach. Most notably, perhaps, while some have sought to analyse how media audiences are affected by pre-existing media meanings or stimuli, others have attributed to them a more active role in the selection, use and even creation of media for their own purposes. Although there are considerable points of overlap between the two, the history of user and audience studies also can usefully be divided between approaches originating from US empiricist research traditions and those emerging from European cultural studies.

US EMPIRICAL TRADITIONS OF AUDIENCE RESEARCH

Systematic research on media audiences was initiated by researchers in the United States in the first half of the twentieth century. It was prompted by a variety of factors, not least the increasing use of media by politicians, advertisers and others as a means to influence people and a sense among researchers that existing approaches to media influence were inadequate. Theories emanating from the neo-Marxist Frankfurt School (whose prominent members had emigrated to the US during the Nazi era – see Chapter 6) and from US mass society theorists such as Reisman (1953) presented what subsequently has been labelled a 'hyperdermic syringe' model of media, whereby standardised messages were assumed to be automatically injected into a passive audience, resulting in a culture of mass ignorance and manipulation. Existing empirical studies of influence, meanwhile, had been largely confined to 'audience measurement' approaches, which evaluated the effectiveness of advertising or political campaigns by establishing how many people they had reached (Nightingale and Ross 2003). Alongside the lack of empirical basis for the pessimistic claims of the Frankfurt School and others, the deficiencies of such existing research prompted a drive for specific analysis of the influence or 'effects' of media. From the 1940s, extensive audience research began to be carried out, leading to intense debate about the influence of media on audience attitudes and behaviour.

EFFECTS RESEARCH

As its name suggests, effects research is concerned with attempting to measure the influence or impact of media. It has been particularly concerned with the influence of political propaganda and anxieties about negative impacts of media on individual behaviour. We'll start with the latter area, in which interest has been particularly focused on the relationship between media consumption and violence. Analysis of media influence in this respect became particularly prominent among US researchers during the 1960s and remains a key point of research and debate today.

BOBO DOLLS AND SHORT-TERM BEHAVIOURAL EFFECTS

Speculation among newspapers, campaigners and academics about the negative impacts of media violence on consumers – and children in particular – has dominated discussions about media influence for decades. As part of this, researchers have sought to measure empirically the extent of any negative influence. Much of this research has taken the form of laboratory experiments carried out by behavioural psychologists. The most well-known of these were a series of so-called 'bobo doll' experiments led by Albert Bandura during the early 1960s (e.g. 1961; 1963). Influenced by social learning theory, which focuses on the capacity of individuals to develop behaviours through their observation of others, Bandura and colleagues explored the circumstances in which children might be prone to imitate the violent behaviour of adult role-models. Some of these experiments focused specifically on the role of television.

In one experiment, Bandura et al. (1963) divided a sample of young children into three experimental groups and one control group. Each of the experimental groups were exposed to an individual violently attacking an inflatable 'bobo doll'. The doll was hit with a toy mallet, punched, kicked and sat on, all of which was accompanied by shouts such as 'sock him in the nose!' and 'hit him down!' For the first group this was performed by an adult in the same room as the children, while for Groups 2 and 3 the events were viewed on television; Group 2 watched a film of an adult attacking the bobo doll, whilst for Group 3 the violence was perpetrated by an adult dressed as a cartoon-style cat. In the second stage of the experiment, all the groups were subjected to 'aggression arousal' by being refused permission to play with toys, in order to recreate the kind of circumstances in which violence might occur. Finally, the children were placed into a room containing a variety of toys, including a bobo doll and a mallet and, this time, allowed to play. The children's play was carefully observed, particularly with respect to levels of aggression and imitative aggression, the latter referring to the similarity between acts of aggression exhibited and those they had observed earlier.

All three experimental groups exhibited higher levels of aggression and imitative aggression than the control group. The group exposed to the adult attacking the doll on television exhibited the highest levels on both measures, while the group exposed to the violent cat character exhibited the lowest among the experimental groups. Bandura claimed to have demonstrated not only that children had exhibited clear social learning, through imitating the behaviour of role-models, but that this was particularly concentrated if the behaviour was viewed on television. Meanwhile, the lower aggression scores for the group exposed to the violent cat was taken to indicate greater propensity to imitate realistic rather than unrealistic role-models.

Bandura, Ross and Ross' influential work forms part of a much broader and ongoing body of experiments designed to measure immediate media effects. Such experiments vary with respect to their precise structure. While the Bandura experiment described above took a *post-test-only* format (the behaviour of subjects was tested only after exposure to the stimulant), for example, other work has tested subject behaviour both before and after exposure (Gunter 2000). The idea of such *pre-test-post-test* designs is to further isolate the stimulant as the sole cause of behavioural or attitudinal change, though there is a danger that exposure to the pre-test could, in itself, affect post-test responses (Wimmer and Dominick 2006). While many experiments are laboratory-based, others take the form of field experiments whereby researchers measure the response of individuals to particular stimuli within their own environments, often over a period of days or weeks rather than hours. Importantly the results of these various experiments are not consistent. And in one early post-test-only experiment, Feshbach (1961) claimed to have demonstrated that the watching of violent media had a cathartic effect on angry subjects, making them less rather than more hostile.

Nevertheless, meta-studies, which review the findings of numerous studies during a particular period, suggest that many experimental studies of media violence have indicated an association between consumption of violent media and aggressive behaviour. In 2015, a review of studies of video-game violence concluded that exposure to such violence was indeed a risk factor for aggression, though it cautioned that there was insufficient evidence to link such exposure to criminal violence. Amongst other things, the study found that 12 of 14 recent studies had identified a link between video-game use and aggressive behaviour, while 12 of 13 had found that video-game use increased aggressive affect (feelings, emotions) (American Psychological Association Task Force on Violent Media 2015).

LONG-TERM 'CULTIVATION' EFFECTS

In contrast to the emphasis on short-term behavioural effects in most experimental studies, other researchers have focused upon the longer-term impact of media use on people's overall attitudes and outlook. George Gerbner argues that television dominates the symbolic environment of those who view it, becoming central to the milieu in which they form their understandings of the world. As a consequence, television is deemed to gradually cultivate attitudes to the real world based on the distorted version of society it presents to us. Gerbner was particularly concerned about this because, as we saw in Chapter 4, content analysis studies he had carried out demonstrated that this 'television world' was thoroughly dominated by crime and violence. Not satisfied with measuring content alone, Gerbner sought to assess the long-term impact on viewers of repeated engagement with the violent world of television.

In a series of surveys in the late 1970s, representative population samples were categorised as light, medium or heavy television viewers. Their answers to a series of questions about attitudes towards crime and violence were then analysed. Many questions related to general opinions, personal experiences and fears, while others were factual – relating to the prevalence of crime within society, for example. The studies consistently found that those respondents categorised as heavy viewers were more likely to respond with 'TV answers', which means responses commensurate with the bleak, violent view of society presented by television. Heavy viewers, for example, were more fearful of becoming the victim of crime, and more likely to have an exaggerated view of the proportion of reported crime that is violent (Gerbner et al. 1977). Gerbner's conclusion was that heavy television viewing cultivates a fearful attitude to the world, something that may induce 'second order effects' such as supporting political parties that campaign on a 'tough on crime' platform, distrusting one's neighbours or refusing to allow children to play outside. Gerbner summarises:

if you are growing up in a home where there is more than say three hours of television per day, for all practical purposes you live in a meaner world – and act accordingly – than your next-door neighbor who lives in the same world but watches less television. (1994: 41).

METHODOLOGICAL PROBLEMS

Studies that appear to demonstrate significant short- or long-term effects of media violence on viewers have been enormously influential, not only within academia but also broader public discourse. Yet there are doubts about the methodological approaches used to demonstrate such 'effects'. Laboratory experiments allow researchers directly to isolate and assess the impact of the factor in which they are interested (in this case exposure to particular forms of media) by engineering situations in which the circumstances of subject groups are identical in all other respects. Bandura and colleagues, then, could conclude that it was exposure to different forms of aggressive activity that prompted the behavioural differences between their groups because everything else about the way they had been treated was identical.

Yet the artificiality that enables this manipulation of variables is also the biggest weakness of experiments. While they may offer useful clues, they cannot prove that children actually will imitate television violence or be prompted to behave aggressively by video games when placed in the context of their normal everyday lives. Furthermore, there is a substantial conceptual difference between seriously attacking a fellow human being and the kinds of proxies experimental researchers use for aggressive feelings or behaviour – which include anything from respondents' verbal responses to images placed in front of them, to their willingness to deliver bursts of noise to consenting opponents (Ferguson 2015). A further issue is that laboratory experiments are only capable of measuring the short-term effects of a small number of brief stimuli, whereas in everyday life, media influence must surely relate to the cumulative impact of multitudes of content. Field experiments move a step closer to studying people within everyday contexts but they too place people into situations that are artificially engineered.

By focusing on the long-term cultivation of attitudes through measuring self-reported attitudes via surveys, Gerbner avoids the short-termism and artificiality of behavioural experiments. Yet there are difficulties with aspects of his approach also. Although he identified *correlations* between heavy television viewing and the expression of fearful attitudes about crime and violence, he did not prove that the television viewing was the *cause* of these attitudes. It is also possible that a fearful outlook contributed to a tendency to stay in and watch lots of television, or that a different variable relating to the characteristics of heavy television viewers might have explained the correlation. Although Gerbner employed statistical controls to show that the correlation had not been caused by sex, age, class or education levels, Gunter (2000) notes that the impact of other factors, including ethnicity, income and working hours were not tested. We should be cautious, then, before drawing too many conclusions about causality from this sort of survey research.

LIMITED EFFECTS AND TWO-STEP FLOW

The style of effects research pioneered by Bandura and colleagues and taken forward by others can be described as employing a reasonably straight-forward stimulus–response model of learning, not entirely dissimilar to what some have described as the hypodermic syringe model. In contrast, effects researchers at the University of Columbia were sceptical about the notion of a direct chain of influence between media and individual attitudes or behaviour. Research they carried out on media and voting behaviour during a US presidential election found that exposure to newspaper- and radio-based political campaigning had little direct impact on audiences (Lazarsfeld et al. 1944). The study, which involved repeated interviews with a panel of individuals and one-off interviews with members of their local community, concluded that political allegiances were more strongly influenced by religion, social class, family ties and local social networks than by mass media. Most displayed little knowledge of candidates or issues, let alone any indication their voting behaviour might be altered by exposure to media. The role of media, then, seemed mostly limited to the reinforcement of existing intentions rooted in tradition and community (Berelson et al. 1954).

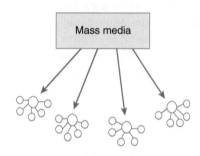

= Opinion leader

= Individuals in social contact with opinion leader

Figure 5.1   Two-step flow model (Katz and Lazarsfeld 1955)

The possibility of media influence was not entirely ruled out, however. It was argued that media coverage and campaigns were liable to have some influence on a relatively small number of politically engaged and influential individuals within each community. These individuals, it was argued, would then pass on their opinions to those around them, creating an indirect form of media influence that the researchers called the 'two-step flow'. Influence was only possible, then, because it was transmitted via interpersonal contact within trusted social networks. Paul Lazarsfeld further developed the two-step flow model of media influence in his subsequent collaborations with Elihu Katz (1955). This included examination of the significance of interpersonal networks as an intermediary of media use and influence in relation to popular culture. In a survey-based study of young women's habits and opinions relating to movie-going, for example, they identified certain respondents as discerning 'movie leaders', who were looked to by others as a source of expertise in the selection and interpretation of such media.

USES AND GRATIFICATIONS

Having worked with Lazarsfeld on the two-step flow model, Katz later became a key exponent of an alternative approach to the relationship between media and audiences. Instead of focusing on whether audiences are or are not affected by media messages, the *uses and gratifications* approach sought to understand how audiences actively select and utilise media for their own purposes. The difference between this 'uses' perspective and effects work is summed up nicely by UK theorist Halloran (1970), who asserted that 'we must get away from the habit of thinking in terms of what the media do to people and substitute it for the idea of what people do with the media'. Uses and gratifications reversed traditional communications models such as that of Lasswell (see Chapter 1) which started with media encoders and ended with audience reception and effects. The varied needs and uses of audiences were now deemed pivotal features and media content was relegated to a set of resources that gratified such audience goals. The model is essentially a *functionalist* one, in the sense that it regards mass communications content as a resource that emerges to fulfil individual needs and goals and, in turn, enables society as a whole to function more effectively.

Uses and gratifications research typically involved surveys or interviews with individuals in order to ascertain the functions different forms of media had for them. Reliant upon 'self-reporting' by consumers themselves, such research resulted in the development of elaborate typologies of needs and uses. Distinctions often were made between short-term escapist gratifications such as immediate relief or entertainment, and longer-term educational functions, which related to lasting forms of knowledge and understanding. Katz et al. (1973) identified 14 needs under five different categories, while an alternative model developed by McQuail et al. (1972) distinguished between the following:

- 'Diversion': a short-term escape or emotional release, enabling suspension of everyday routines and problems.
- 'Personal relationships': a substitute for face-to-face social companionship, a facilitator of relationships or a source of community belonging.
- 'Personal identity': a resource for the development or reinforcement of personal values, meanings and a sense of one's place in the world.
- 'Surveillance': a source of knowledge, information and engagement with the world.

There remains an unresolved question about the extent to which particular kinds of content or medium are differentially suited to particular needs. In other words, to what extent does the structure or content of media prescribe that it can only result in particular outcomes? Rosengren and Windahl (1972: 27) suggested that there had emerged 'a growing consensus that almost any type of content may serve practically any type of function', while Katz, Blumler and Gurevitch (2003: 42) were not so sure, calling for greater investigation of 'the attributes that render some media more conducive than others to satisfying specific needs'.

FUNCTIONALIST AND COMPLACENT?

Having pioneered the detailed study of media influence, researchers associated with the University of Columbia and others played a significant role in a shift away from the study of direct media effects and towards an interest in the place of media within individual lives and identities. Lazarsfeld and colleagues' conclusions on political influence showed that we couldn't begin to understand people's relationship with mass communications without an awareness of their broader social context. In focusing on the purposes of active media users, uses and gratifications perhaps represented a logical development from this. Both models remain influential. Uses and gratifications research, for example, has proven popular with some researchers of internet use (Ruggiero 2000) while it is not difficult to see how we might apply two-step flow, or at least some variant thereof, to a contemporary digital context in which our consumption of media content is increasingly filtered through our social networks on Facebook, Twitter and other software (see Bakshy et al. 2011). Yet, while they may help us think through the relationship between media and users, neither approach is without its problems.

The research of Lazarsfeld and colleagues was based only on the issue of media influence on voting behaviour itself. Subsequent research, which focused not on voting but on which political issues voters thought were the most important, demonstrated a close correlation between respondent answers and the issues most strongly emphasised in newspaper coverage, suggesting that media might play a role in setting the public agenda (McCombs and Shaw 1972). More importantly, Lazarsfeld et al.'s research was unable to provide an understanding of the long-term influences with which Gerbner has been concerned. In the short-term, an individual may resist or ignore particular media messages, but it remains possible that over a longer period both they and those around them may incorporate greater amounts of knowledge and experience derived from media. Lazarsfeld's conclusions also rest on the observation that individuals were subject to the comparatively stronger influence of religion, local communities and families. Many theorists believe that, in recent times, individuals have become less firmly rooted within such tight-knit localised communities, while social class affiliations have become more fragile, families more complex and religious participation less universal (Bauman 2001). With the weakening of these alternative sources of influence, might the influence of media become more substantial?

Uses and gratifications, meanwhile, can be criticised for assuming that individuals always have a clear rationale for their media consumption. In some cases clear motivations or functions may be of less importance than factors such as the force of habit. The reliance of researchers on surveys that require audiences to self-report the purpose of their media use may contribute to an exaggeration of the importance of active, rational choices. This is because people may be unlikely to admit to being mindless couch potatoes or having no particular reason for their actions. The focus of uses and gratifications research on individual psychological needs, meanwhile, prompts David Morley to argue that the approach neglects the role of sociological categories such as class, ethnicity, locality and gender in patterns of media use and interpretation. As Morley puts it: 'Uses and gratifications is an essentially psychologistic problematic, relying as it does on mental states, needs and processes abstracted from the social situation of the individuals concerned' (1992: 48). In this respect, some 1970s uses and gratifications work represented a move away from the more sociological orientation of earlier University of Columbia research.

Finally, the functionalist premise of uses and gratifications theory results in an overall perspective that comes across as complacent and uncritical. It is assumed that media exist to satisfy the demands and needs of audiences and that media consumption is an active process which, with the exception of occasional 'dysfunctional' uses, is beneficial to individual everyday life and the smooth functioning of a pluralist society. This rosy picture omits the possibility of manipulation or propaganda and in so doing risks rendering media beyond serious critique, whether in respect of the kinds of content from which audiences can choose, or of the structures of ownership, funding and control. Theories of mass culture may have overestimated the passivity of audiences (see Chapter 6), but uses and gratifications risks taking things too far in the opposite direction.

CULTURAL STUDIES: DOMINANT
AND OPPOSITIONAL READINGS AND BEYOND

ENCODING, DECODING AND PREFERRED MEANINGS

Counter-posed to the US tradition, with its emphasis on behavioural effects research and functionalist audience models, is an audience perspective rooted partially in European cultural theory and centred upon questions of discourse, meaning and power. Pivotal here is Stuart Hall's work at the University of Birmingham's Centre for Contemporary Cultural Studies (CCCS). Drawing upon semiology, Hall places emphasis on the 'encoding' of meaning into media texts by producers. 'The discursive form of the message', he argues, 'has a privileged position in the communicative exchange' (1993: 98). A neo-Marxist thinker influenced by the work of Antonio Gramsci, Hall also argues that these encoded meanings 'have the institutional/political/ideological order imprinted in them' and are liable to reinforce the dominant order by reinforcing dominant or *hegemonic* ideas (ibid.: 93).

Yet at the same time as recognising the role of media encoders in influencing audiences, Hall's model, which was developed in the 1970s, broke away from semiology by recognising that what he termed the 'preferred meanings' encoded into media texts would only be realised if they were 'decoded' appropriately by audiences. The possibility was entertained, then, that audiences could actively challenge the meanings of media messages. And rather than understanding such active interpretations as the manifestation of individual psychological needs, as uses and gratifications theory would, Hall argues that audience responses to media are related to socio-economic context and clustered within three categories:

- The *dominant-hegemonic* position refers to audience interpretations that are commensurate with the meaning encoded into the text and, hence, with the dominant cultural order within which the media industry is assumed to operate.
- The *negotiated* position refers to acceptance of the overall view encoded into a text, but disagreement with specifics. Dominant premises are largely accepted but specific 'exceptions to the rule' may be insisted upon (ibid.: 102). Audiences might, argues Hall, accept the broad premise of a media report that suggests workers' wages must be frozen to control inflation, but may insist that certain sets of workers deserve higher pay.
- The *oppositional* position occurs when the preferred meaning is identified and rejected by audience members. Here, a news report about the need to reduce wages might be rejected as a distorted message that serves to reinforce dominant interests and perpetuate inequalities. For Hall, such oppositional readings act as a crucial site for contestation of the dominant order.

In spite of continuing to emphasise the role of preferred meanings and dominant interpretations, Hall's discussion of differential audience responses helped to precipitate a shift of European approaches away from semiological interpretations of texts and towards an interest in the decoding of meaning and, specifically, the possibility of subversive audience interpretations.

SOCIAL CONTEXT AND DIFFERENTIAL READINGS

Also a member of the CCCS, David Morley shared Hall's view that semiology under-estimated the importance of audiences, arguing that Barthes and others were guilty of 'an endless quest for a mythical object – the "real" or "ultimate" meaning of the message' (Morley 1992: 76). Morley also rejected the individualistic audience-centred approach of uses and gratifications, preferring to draw on Hall's emphasis on dominant, negotiated and oppositional readings and the role of socio-economic context as their primary arbiter. What was important was 'the differences between the cultural frameworks available to different individuals,' he argued, 'so that I, say, as a Durham coal miner, interpret a message about government economic policy differently from you, say, as an East Anglian bank manager – that is not a difference which is simply attributable to our different psychologies' (1992: 80).

Morley investigated such differences through research on the 1970s' UK current affairs television programme, *Nationwide*. Having identified what were regarded as right-wing, pro-establishment preferred meanings of the programme through textual analysis (Brunsden and Morley 1978), Morley showed episodes to 29 different audience groups representing different segments of society (Morley 1980). Each group was invited to discuss the programme and their perspectives were mapped in relation to Hall's dominant, negotiated, oppositional typology. The study concluded that responses to media content were not determined by social class alone but connected to understandings people had access to as a result of more particular social and occupational positions. A group of politically conservative bank managers were deemed to have exhibited a dominant reading because they barely noticed *Nationwide*'s perspective on current affairs, accepting its dominant premises without question. In contrast, a group of left-wing shop stewards formed a highly critical appraisal of the programme, which they deemed guilty of presenting a façade of inclusivity while promoting middle-class, right-wing perspectives.

LIMITATIONS OF HALL'S MODEL

Morley's study also highlighted limitations with Hall's typology, however, as not all the groups proved easy to classify. A group of inner-city college students refused to engage with the discourse of the programme at all, on the basis that it was of no interest to them. Although he tentatively identifies this as an oppositional reading, Morley recognises that such disengagement is distinct from conscious opposition and not really accounted for by Hall. There were also difficulties categorising the responses of a group of print management trainees, who were sharply critical of what they regarded as the *left-wing* bias of *Nationwide*. This was classed as a dominant reading, on the basis that the group had not identified the right-wing, middle-class bias that Brunsden and Morley's analysis of the programme had pointed to. But how do we know that Brunsden and Morley's interpretation was 'right' and the print manager trainees' interpretation 'wrong'? In spite of his criticisms of semiology, had Morley placed too much emphasis on what he and Brunsden – from their own particular social position – took to be the 'real' meaning of the text?

Even if we accept that it is possible for analysts to identify the preferred meanings encoded into individual media texts, the case of Morley's print manager trainees highlights an ambiguity with Hall's dominant, negotiated and oppositional typology. The model seems to attempt simultaneously to classify *both* a) the extent to which an audience accepts the coding of a particular media text *and* b) the positioning of the audience's response vis-à-vis broader dominant meaning systems. The implication is that the preferred meaning of media content automatically embodies broader dominant understandings of the world and that acceptance of the former automatically equates to acceptance of the latter. But what about audience interpretations of oppositional texts? If I view a series of blogs encoded with an anti-capitalist view of the world and interpret them favourably, then is my interpretation dominant, because I accepted the preferred meaning, or oppositional, because, in doing so, I took a resistant stance towards capitalist ideology?

Partly as a result of this, Hall's model remains rather too inflexible to enable a detailed understanding of a range of audience responses to different media texts. More fundamentally, although it acknowledges the potential for different readings and responses, it continues to focus on audiences as receivers or decoders of messages. The value of this in enabling Hall to retain an emphasis on the ideological role of media ought not to be under-estimated (see Chapter 6), but such an approach does not get us particularly far with respect to what it is that audiences and users actually do with media.

AUDIENCES AS PRODUCERS OF MEANING

If Hall and Morley raised the possibility of audiences developing subversive interpretations, then many of those who followed in their footsteps ended up dispensing with the notion of audiences as receivers of meanings altogether, preferring to see everyday media users as active, creative and productive. As was the case with uses and gratifications approaches, but with greater emphasis on the social and political significance of consumption, one-way transmissions models were turned on their head and audiences afforded the role of central instigators rather than passive recipients.

Of particular note here is John Fiske. Though he draws on neo-Marxist theory in emphasising the inequalities of power, social control and homogenisation within which contemporary communication takes place, his primary focus is on how such forces are resisted by the everyday cultural practices of ordinary consumers. The economic power of the culture industry may be great, argues Fiske (1991a; 1991b), but its cultural influence is limited to an ability to provide a variety of texts from which consumers will actively choose. Products are successful or unsuccessful, according to this view, not because of economic muscle or manipulation, but depending on whether they offer a suitable range of potential meanings and uses for the lives of consumers. And crucially, contrary to Hall's semiology-derived model, such products do not have fixed, a priori meanings waiting to be 'decoded'. Rather, meaning is produced by consumers themselves in their interaction with texts. This prompts Fiske to proclaim that 'popular culture is made by the people, not produced by the culture industry' (Fiske 1991a: 24).

Such is the importance of user creativity, according to Fiske, that texts only become popular if they offer a suitable 'excess' of potential meaning for audiences to develop their own understandings. The global popularity of pop stars such as Madonna, then, can be explained through the capacity of such texts to be generated into a range of meanings of significance to different groups of consumers. The product is sufficiently flexible that it allows itself to be transformed into both repressive and empowering sets of symbolic meanings: 'Madonna is circulated among some feminists as a reinscription of patriarchal values, among some men as an object of voyeuristic pleasure, and among many girl fans as an agent of empowerment and liberation' (1991a: 124). We might add that Madonna became a significant symbol of affection in many gay and queer communities.

In emphasising the political significance of creative acts of consumption, Fiske draws upon de Certeau's notion of cultural 'guerrilla warfare' to describe the everyday refusal of consumers to submit to powerful structuring forces (1984). Forces of homogenising power are met, it is argued, with ongoing grassroots cultural resistance, through small-scale 'poaching' and 'trickery' (ibid.). Fiske illustrates using the example of 1980s consumers ripping their jeans to generate a new set of distinctive grassroots meanings for a popular, standardised commodity: 'it is a refusal of commodification', he argues, 'and an assertion of one's right to make one's own culture out of the resources provided by the commodity system' (Fiske 1991a: 15). For Fiske, what can be applied to jeans can also be applied to newspaper articles, television programmes, films and popular music. Such products all are continually 'ripped' or adapted by consumers and such adaptations amount to small-scale challenges to the forces of power and control.

ETHNOGRAPHIES OF AUDIENCES, FANS AND USERS

For all his emphasis on the importance of audiences as producers of meaning, Fiske's analysis of examples is disappointingly reliant upon his own readings of textual content rather than detailed research of audience or consumer practices (Stevenson 2002). Fortunately, the development of an ethnographic tradition of research, centred upon in-depth interviews with and observations of media users already was well underway by the time his most well-known pronouncements were made and has continued to develop since. Studies of romance readers (Radway 1987), soap opera fans (Ang 1985) and magazine readers (Hermes 1995), alongside elaborations of the use of domestic media technologies by an increasingly audience-focused Morley (1988) and Ann Gray (1992), were among a plethora of pioneering projects offering qualitative accounts of how media fit into the everyday worlds of audiences. Such studies placed front and centre the contexts, competences, choices, interpretations and understandings of ordinary readers and viewers.

In a further example, Paul Willis (1990) places emphasis on the control and 'symbolic creativity' exerted by a group of young respondents over their media use, whether in the form of creative engagements with adverts, the incorporation of soap plots into real-life dilemmas or critical readings of magazine advice columns. Emphasis also is placed on the productive social activities of consumers, including the creation and exchange of popular music mix tapes (which we might compare to contemporary swapping of playlists), whereby individuals would appoint themselves grassroots filters and manipulators of the music world. On the basis of the detailed accounts of young people themselves, the study concludes that ordinary cultural consumption tends to be discriminating, skilled, active and creative.

While Willis and Fiske celebrate the creativity of consumption across the board, studies of 'fan cultures' have tended to focus upon the intense engagement of particular groups of consumers (see Hills 2002). Henry Jenkins' (1992) seminal ethnographic study of a community of sci-fi film and television fans shows how participants integrated cultural narratives into their individual everyday contexts and reflected on content through exchanges with other enthusiasts. Such reflective engagement frequently would extend towards production of their own DIY texts, in the form of stories or videos that offered alternative versions of the official product, for example. Jenkins makes sense of such activities through an extension of de Certeau's notion of 'poaching'. The sci-fi fan cultures he studied are deemed to have appropriated those sections of media products that interested them, transformed them for their own interests and used them as the basis for the development of an active, autonomous community. And such communities also entailed an activist element, attempting, for example, to influence official versions of the products they enjoyed by mounting campaigns for the inclusion of new character types or the revival of favoured series.

The ability easily to connect, converse and share ideas on the internet is deemed by Jenkins (2002) to have begun to transform fan cultures, with individual fans able instantaneously to engage with a vast range of individuals and interpretations before, during and after consumption of their favourite texts. In an ethnographic study of an early online forum for soap opera fans, Nancy Baym (2000) describes the facilitation by this online space of extensive interpersonal relationships centred upon mutual enthusiasm for soaps as a shared fan-object. For Baym, the internet had substantially enhanced the possibility for participation in such fan communities and made the perspectives and creations of fans more visible, to the extent that the boundary between producers and audiences was blurring.

One criticism of early fan culture studies is that there was a tendency to focus disproportionate attention on the activities of unusually committed or 'spectacular' groups of fans who actively attended conventions, produced DIY media or participated intensively in community forums, something that left the identities of more ordinary media fans largely invisible. For Jonathon Gray and colleagues (2007: 3–4; also see Sandvoss 2005) this carries the risk of reinforcing stereotypes of fandom as a marginal activity, while excluding fans who 'merely love a show, watch it religiously, talk about it and yet engage in no other fan practices or activities'. The shifting orientation of media in digital environments, they argue, has rendered emphasis only on the most spectacular or committed fans particularly inadequate, given the increasing positive emphasis on cultivating fans and fandom by the producers of media content and the extensive opportunities for ordinary fans to consume intensively through niche and on-demand services and casually converse with one another via a range of social media spaces.

DIGITAL PARTICIPATORY CULTURE?

In some of his more recent work, Jenkins (2006; 2008) draws somewhat broader conclusions about possibilities offered by contemporary digital environments for the development of widespread forms of participatory culture. In a *convergence culture* where the boundaries between different forms of mass and interpersonal media are breaking down, a variety of media users and fans are contributing to and shaping media environments in which the grassroots creation, adaptation, circulation and spreading of content are pivotal, he argues. While accepting that large-scale media producers and distributors remain powerful, Jenkins suggests that distinctions between production and consumption are blurring as fans increasingly influence the form and distribution of content through their networked online creativity, interactions and, sometimes, activism. Increasingly, theorists have sought to capture this apparent merging of production and consumption through the use of terms such as produser or produsage (Bruns 2008).

We might add that, as well as becoming increasingly able to create, distribute or share content via blogs, social media, YouTube and so on, users also enjoy greater levels of control in their capacity as consumers of content. Multi-channel and on-demand television, mobile technologies and the internet offer the capacity to actively select between a seemingly infinite range of content and shape the time, place, format and order in which they consume it. Ethnographic work on uses of the iPod by Michael Bull (2005; 2007), for example, emphasises the ability to have one's entire, hand-picked music collection, complete with customised playlists, on instant demand as one traverses the city. Individuals are able to transform the public environments they travel in, developing their own personalised soundtrack through the ongoing selection and ordering of music suitable for their mood or environment.

AN AUDIENCE CONTINUUM

While early fan culture studies may have singled out and differentiated the practice of small communities of exceptionally committed fans from those of 'ordinary audiences', proclamations about the broader possibilities of participatory culture sometimes have been argued to over-estimate the power of media users. For Christian Fuchs, although Jenkins recognises the continuing power of large-scale media corporations, the implications of this are understated in an account most notable for its emphasis on the active participation of users and fans (Fuchs 2014). We might add that, in spite of Jenkins' relatively broad conclusions about the possibilities of participatory culture, his account relies for much of its evidence on case studies of what seem like particularly intensive user groups. In spite of acknowledging at one point that 'some consumers have greater abilities to participate in [participatory culture] than others', Jenkins might have elaborated further with respect to the varied implications of convergence for different sorts of media users.

Others have sought to explicitly identify and make sense of identifiable levels and types of media use through the development of typologies of user engagement. The most well-known and often-cited such typology was developed by Abercrombie and Longhurst (1998) prior to the onset of the kinds of digital participatory cultures described by Jenkins, as part of what they termed the Spectacle and Performance audience paradigm. Centred on the shifting and overlapping audience types and the integration of audience processes within everyday life and identity, this perspective also focused on identifying different audience types on the basis of intensity of consumption patterns, connections with other consumers and levels of productive activity. The 'audience continuum' (Abercrombie and Longhurst 1998) consists of the following categories:

- *Consumers*, whose media use is relatively generalised and unfocused with productive activity limited to everyday talk about texts with friends;
- *Fans*, who are understood to be heavy general media users liable to develop strong attachment and interest in certain widely circulated genres, stars or texts but without this

leading to intense or organised contact with other fans or productive activities beyond everyday conversation;

- *Cultists*, who develop particularly concentrated specialist attachment to certain genres or texts, regularly communicate with discrete yet informal networks of other fans and consume, create and circulate specialist 'fannish' literature or media specific to such communities;
- *Enthusiasts*, who intensively consume, produce and share specialist small-scale media produced by and for organised networks of highly intensive fans, including art, poetry, criticism or fiction based on the characters or scenarios of the mass circulated fan-object;
- *Petty Producers*, whose enthusiasm goes beyond amateur appropriations and creativity towards their own professional or semi-professional forms of cultural production that are organised through the market rather than via groups of enthusiasts, whether as musicians, writers, film-makers and so on.

Importantly, no typology or 'continuum' is perfect or can possibly incorporate all the different variables or types of media consumption into its schema. Abercrombie and Longhurst's categories are debateable in some respects and may also benefit from some updating were we to adapt them to the contemporary digital media environments described by Jenkins. For example, it isn't clear whether the first two categories – which presumably account for the majority of users – can fully capture the impact of social media on the reach or significance of the online conversations and sharing such ordinary *consumers* or *fans* might engage in, or the extent to which basic level social media activity may constitute an important form of user differentiation in itself.

Nevertheless, the audience continuum was in some respects ahead of its time in attempting to bring together different levels of consumption and production into a single spectrum. By doing so, Abercrombie and Longhurst are able to resist simple all-powerful producer versus passive audience binaries at the same time as steering clear of the universalisal application of notions such as participatory culture. Instead they illustrate a spectrum of different forms and intensities of user-engagement, recognising as part of this the potential for individuals to move from one type of engagement to another and, indeed, for any identifiable audience or fan community to contain more than one of the positions identified (Longhurst and Bogdanovic 2014).

CONCLUSION: AN UNCRITICAL CELEBRATION?

In placing the microscope squarely on the ways people use and understand media as part of their existing social backgrounds and contexts, the development of ethnographic approaches to fans, audiences and users has helped shift the focus away from the notion of media users as receivers who are passively affected by media to a greater or lesser degree. Meanwhile, the attempt in Fiske, de Certeau, Jenkins and others, to explore the political significance of the activities of users as acts of cultural subversion represents a substantial break from the functionalist and individual-oriented uses and gratification approach.

In spite of the tendency to emphasise cultural struggle rather than cosy consensus, however, such perspectives may sometimes have over-celebrated the power of consumers as part of media processes.

Although it makes regular mention of forces of power, control and homogenisation, Fiske's account, by attributing the production of meaning to audiences, seems to afford little real influence to industry or broader structures of dominance – less of a struggle between consumers and the culture industry than an inevitable series of triumphs by the former. For Golding and Murdock (1991: 86), such a version of events constitutes a 'populist romance in which the downtrodden victims caricatured by economic determinists [i.e. theorists who assume audiences are manipulated] are revealed as heroic resistance fighters in the war against cultural deception'. The possibility of media industries acting as an (effective) instrument of ideology is largely foreclosed by such an approach (Stevenson 2002), as is the notion that its operations are responsible for any substantive influence or impact.

Jenkins' more guarded celebration of user participation and power in digital media worlds recognises though arguably underplays how such activities and consumers themselves are shaped, constrained and exploited by the corporations that control high circulation content and the platforms through which users engage with one another. Important, here, is an argument that at least some aspects of the empowering consumer behaviour lauded by Jenkins could, from a different point of view, be regarded as a form of commodified, unpaid labour. According to this view, through enthusing, discussing, sharing, appropriating and creating, participatory fan cultures ultimately tend to serve the interests of established media companies through helping promote, distribute and authenticate their products (Fuchs 2014).

Some ethnographies of users have been more cautious and specific in the power and agency they afford to consumers. Morley, for example, balances his emphasis on audience activities and understandings with recognition of the influence of the media industry and broader social structures. Meanwhile early fan culture studies, including those of Jenkins, tend more clearly to confine claims about audience productivity and subversiveness to groups of unusually committed audiences (Jenkins 1992). The implied distinction here between creative fans and passive ordinary consumers has sometimes itself been criticised (Hills 2002). While they tend to be more inclusive and nuanced, a similar point could possibly be made about user typologies such as those of Abercrombie and Longhurst. For better or worse, their continuum is unable to avoid coming across as, essentially, a hierarchy of user intensity, skill and productivity. Yet, while the model may benefit from further refinement and updating, its attempt to recognise the presence of different forms of media use, whether across audiences as a whole or within particular groups, may be preferable to universalised notions of users as either active or passive, participants or receivers.

Most importantly, the study of audiences and users has rightly established itself as a core and essential component in the study of media and society and the evolution of such work in the age of interactive digital, online and mobile media technologies is of the utmost importance. Understandings of the activities, identities and lives of audiences and users, though, must be placed in the context of the constraints and limitations on media use that are built into the structure of texts, systems and technologies and the role of industry and power relations in shaping such constraints.

QUESTIONS/EXERCISES

1 a) Can a laboratory experiment involving the hitting of an inflatable doll tell us anything about the social impact of media violence? What are the strengths and weaknesses of Bandura et al.'s approach?

   b) Did Gerbner's combination of content analysis and survey research prove that media cultivates a fearful attitude to crime and violence?

2 a) Is the 'two-step flow' approach a useful way of understanding questions about media influence? How might such an approach be adapted to understand the role of social network sites as part of media processes?

   b) Produce your own uses and gratifications typology by identifying as many motivations and functions of media use as you can think of and arranging them into categories.

3 In what ways did Morley's *Nationwide* project develop Hall's dominant, negotiated and oppositional model of audience interpretations? What are the strengths and weaknesses of Hall's approach?

4 a) What does Fiske mean when he says that 'popular culture is made by the people, not produced by the culture industry'? And is he right?

   b) What is the difference between Fiske's approach and the uses and gratifications perspective?

5 a) In what ways, according to Jenkins, have contemporary digital environments, including social media, led to transformations in the power and influence of media users and fans? Is he right?

   b) Taking Abercrombie and Longhurst's audience continuum as a starting point, construct your own typology of contemporary media users with respect to levels and/or types of engagement.

SUGGESTED FURTHER READING

Fiske, J. (1991a) *Understanding Popular Culture*. London: Routledge – Classic analysis of popular culture that argues that consumers produce active and sometimes subversive meanings in their interactions with cultural texts.

Gunter, B. (2000) *Media Research Methods*. London: Sage – Outline of approaches to the study of media impact, oriented particularly to psychological and effects approaches.

Hall, S. (1993) 'Encoding, Decoding', in During, S. (ed.) *The Cultural Studies Reader*. London: Routledge, pp. 90–103 (article originally published 1980) – Develops a model of the media process, which emphasises industry as encoders of meaning as well as outlining different forms of audience responses.

Jenkins, H. (2008) *Convergence Culture: Where Old and New Media Collide*. New York: New York University Press – Widely discussed analysis of participatory culture, fandom and media users in the age of interactive digital technologies.

Katz, E., Blumler, J. and Gurevich, M. (2003) 'Utilization of Mass Communication By the Individual', in Nightingale, K. and Ross, A. (eds) *Critical Readings: Media and Audiences*. Maidenhead: Open University Press (article originally published 1974) – Reflective outline on the uses and gratifications perspective from authors involved in the development of the perspective.

PART TWO

MEDIA, POWER AND CONTROL

CHAPTER 6
MEDIA AS MANIPULATION?
MARXISM AND IDEOLOGY

FOCAL POINTS

- Arguments about media as a purveyor of mass ignorance and distraction
- Identification and critique of dominant meanings in media content
- Case study of ideologies of consumerism in media
- Cultural imperialism theories and the global circulation of ideology
- Distinctions between cultural and political economic approaches to Marxism

INTRODUCTION

Marxist approaches to questions of media and society argue that the prevailing socio-economic order is exploitative and that media form an integral part of this system, both reflecting and bolstering the agendas of established powerful interests through systems and content saturated with establishment ideology. This chapter examines such critical approaches to media in greater detail, focusing in particular upon Marxist notions of media as ideology. We begin with an introduction to Marx himself, before examining key neo-Marxist approaches, including the early Frankfurt School, European cultural studies perspectives and critical political economy. We also will consider arguments between different Marxist approaches and broader criticisms of assumptions they share.

Importantly, Marxist approaches contrast with some of the perspectives on the question of media users examined in Chapter 5. In particular, functionalist uses and gratifications perspectives and notions of subversive fans and audiences both place users – rather reassuringly – as active agents in control of their own destinies. Even those strands of effects research which endorse the notion that media could shape audiences have tended to focus either on measuring the immediate influence of particular stimuli (adverts, political campaigns) or on identifying longer-term effects of selected 'problematic' features (e.g. violence). According to Stuart Hall (1982), such perspectives are pluralist, in the sense that they focus on particular forms of influence but fail to address broader questions of media control or offer a critical analysis of the prevailing system of power. Such approaches have largely assumed, in other words, that the current socio-economic system is basically a good thing and that, with the exception of certain problematic aberrations, media form a valuable component in its efficient operation. In contrast, Marxist approaches, including that of Hall himself, reject the broader capitalist system and regard media as purveyors of dominant ideology.

MARXISM AND IDEOLOGY: BASICS

It is not possible to capture the sophistication of Karl Marx's complex broader theory here but a reminder of some basic tenets of his critique of capitalism is useful in order to understand subsequent developments of the approach as a means to understand media. For Marx, capitalism is characterised by the ownership of wealth and property by a small but all-powerful class group, the *bourgeoisie*, and the exploitation of the non-wealth-owning majority, or *proletariat*. The capitalist system perpetuates the power of the bourgeoisie, who control the means of production (factories, machinery, raw materials), and ensures the subversion of the proletariat, whose labour is hired in order to produce objects that generate wealth. Such workers are alienated, argued Marx, because they put most of their life into the production of objects, only to see such objects appropriated and sold by their bourgeois employers. Lacking control over the purpose or product of their labour, workers are reduced to a commodity object themselves, their labour sold to the bourgeoisie in order that the latter might profit from it. The only way the proletariat can own any of the objects they have devoted their life to produce is to buy them by paying their wages back to the bourgeoisie. For Marx, capitalism is defined by this class relationship – the power of the bourgeoisie depends on their exploitation of the proletariat and the more the proletariat sell their labour to the bourgeoisie, the greater their alienation and subordination.

So why would the proletariat majority put up with such exploitation? Marx's answer reflects his materialist approach to the relationship between dominant economic relations – which he refers to as the mode of production – and the realm of culture, politics and ideas. For Marx, the dominant ways of thinking in a society always will reflect the prevailing mode of production and the interests of the ruling class. Writing in 1859, he put it in the following way: 'the mode of production of material life determines the general character of the social, political and spiritual processes of life' (2000: 67). What this suggests is that capitalist economic relations are accompanied by a corresponding set of dominant cultural values, ideas and beliefs – ideology in other words. The circulation of this dominant ideology, via institutions such as the family, the political system and religion, acts as a support for the material situation from which it emerged by making the proletariat happier to accept the situation in which they find themselves. More specifically, ideology promotes false-consciousness, blinding workers to the true nature of their exploited position by inverting capitalist arrangements so that they appear natural and inevitable rather than historically specific and changeable. Religion, for example is deemed to act as 'the opiate of the people' (1844: preface), a sedative which numbs the pain of workers through presenting their man-made and historically specific situation as inevitable and induced by God's will.

Marx famously had predicted that the proletariat eventually would overcome their false-consciousness and overthrow the capitalist system. The failure in much of the world for such a proletariat revolution to take place was a significant point of debate for a range of variants of neo-Marxism which were to emerge within the twentieth century. Another key focus for such neo-Marxists was the massive growth of mass media and popular culture, which increasingly were attributed a role as significant as that which religion had afforded for Marx in the nineteenth century.

THE CULTURE INDUSTRY AS MASS DECEPTION

Of great importance to neo-Marxist analyses of media are a group of theorists collectively known as the Frankfurt School, whose work was mostly completed in the United States after an escape from Nazi Germany in the 1930s. The rise of fascism was to influence the work of scholars such as Theodor Adorno, Max Horkheimer and Herbert Marcuse, but their primary concern was with the apparent triumph, within the West, of capitalism, which had apparently seen off a range of destabilising moments, not least the Russian revolution, world wars, general strikes and the great depression of the 1930s. In spite of all these, capitalism had managed to develop and thrive, its logic so firmly embedded that the prospect of significant working-class opposition in countries such as the United States appeared to have faded.

The result of this continual growth of the system Marx had predicted would be overthrown, was that the ability of individuals to think and act freely, imaginatively and creatively – to be human as the Frankfurt theorists saw it – was being crushed by a relentless all-encompassing capitalist machine. People were *reified*, they argued, or reduced to objects: cogs and pulleys of the system. Lofty enlightenment ideals about expansion of mind and enhancement of the human condition had failed to materialise, it was argued. Instead of liberating humans, the project of reason and rationality had been incorporated into capitalist economic relations, taking on a pragmatic, *instrumental* logic focused upon maximising efficiency, profit and control, something that was suffocating critical thought, creativity and human subjectivity.

In seeking to understand how the population had been induced to accept such objectification, the Frankfurt School turned to the ideological role of consumerism and mass media. While Marx regarded ideology as a discernable set of ideas which emerged from capitalist relations, the Frankfurt School's analysis of the ideological role of media and culture envisages something more all-pervasive. Describing the rise of what they term *the culture industry*, Adorno and Horkheimer (1997) argue that, like everything else, human expression and creativity had been subsumed into the capitalist logic and surrendered to its relentless processes of instrumentality and rationalisation.

From their point of view, art in its pure form represented everything important about human subjectivity, including creativity, freedom and independent critical thought. Under capitalism, however, art had become a mass commodity, little different from the range of other industrial products on the market. For Adorno, culture ceases to be a creative social relationship between artist and audience, then, and becomes reified into a set of anonymous consumer objects exchanged for money. This emphasis is developed further by Marcuse (1964), who argues that the superficial lure of such objects generates 'false needs' in the minds of workers. The attractions of meaningless, superficial consumption, then, provide motivation to work ever harder for the system, while distracting people from their true needs, which, for the Frankfurt School, involve their release from oppression and their ability to develop and flourish as individuals. In contrast, the momentary release provided by cultural consumption serves to incorporate consumers further into the capitalist machine:

> We may distinguish between true and false needs. 'False' are those which are superimposed upon the individual by particular social interests in his repression... Their satisfaction might be most gratifying to the individual but this happiness... serves to arrest the development of the ability... to recognize the disease of the whole and grasp the chances of curing the disease. The result then is euphoria in unhappiness. (Marcuse 1964: 4–5)

The Frankfurt School also specifically criticise the content of culture industry products which, as a result of profit maximisation are deemed to be wholly standardised. Rather than challenging, inducing creativity or stimulating independent thought, the predictability of such products makes the process of consumption simple, repetitive and effortless. Pre-digested in order to slip down easily with minimum fuss, such products can be compared to baby food, argues Adorno (1991). 'No independent thinking must be expected from the audience', he and Horkheimer explain, 'the product prescribes every reaction' (1997: 137). In his best-known case study Adorno argues that popular jazz hits of the 1930s and 40s were structurally indistinguishable from one another – to the extent that sections or components of one tune could be transferred into the equivalent position within another. Like the listeners who consumed them, such components are deemed little more than interchangeable cogs in a system, lacking any significance or consequence: 'Complications have no consequences' argues Adorno, for 'regardless of what aberrations occur, the hit will lead back to the same familiar experience and nothing fundamentally novel will be introduced' (1990: 256). The result of this standardisation, according to Adorno, is the inducement of mindless modes of listening, dominated by enslavement to rhythm or escapist forms of emotional identification.

What is true of music is deemed equally true for other media. If in popular music, 'the whole is pre-given and pre-accepted before the actual experience of the music starts' (ibid.: 257), then so in the Hollywood film, 'as soon as the film begins, it is quite clear how it will end, and who will be rewarded, punished, or forgotten' (Adorno and Horkheimer 1997: 125). Another key phenomenon identified across media content is *pseudo-individualisation* whereby standardised commodity objects are presented with an illusory veil of difference and diversity. This veil might take the form of unexpected twists within standardised film plots, or passages of apparent originality within formulaic songs. Pseudo-individualisation might also relate to the construction of apparently distinctive stylistic identities for artists through the cultivation of image and identity – or what we would now term celebrity. For Adorno it is this appearance of difference that makes standardisation acceptable to people: 'concentration and control in our culture hide themselves in their very manifestation. Unhidden they would provoke resistance' (1990: 307).

The Frankfurt School's contention, then, is that media and culture have been incorporated into an all-encompassing socio-economic system dominated by instrumentalism, rationality and objectification. The result is an industrialised version of cultural expression, whose enticing, standardised form numbs the minds of the population, crushing their capacity for independent thought and distracting them from the development of real solutions to their alienation. The culture industry acts as a conduit for the incorporation of the masses themselves into the system and helps to bring about an end to any realistic prospect of mass opposition.

UNSUPPORTED ELITISM?

The immediate response of many who first encounter their writings is to reject the Frankfurt School's approach and, in particular, its implication that they themselves are among the mindless consumers, stupefied and blinded by pre-digested cultural texts. Many theorists, too, find uncomfortable what they regard as a patronising attack on the cultural tastes and interests of ordinary people. The approach ought not to be dismissed too quickly, however, not least because many of the arguments have a quite remarkable level of fit with elements of contemporary media and culture. In fact, many would accept that the commodification of culture identified by the Frankfurt theorists has expanded beyond measure since the time of their writing. And there surely is no shortage of contemporary examples of cultural artefacts to which we might plausibly apply Frankfurt School style cultural critique.

It is hard to dispute, for example, that most contemporary popular music takes a predictable, standardised structure, or that lyrical themes, the cultivation of stars and the format of performance are often formulaic. The notion of pseudo-individualisation also has potential application. We watch countless television programmes and films whose basic narrative and structure are extremely similar, yet often think and speak of such texts as though they were substantively distinct or original. The same might be argued about news stories and some other forms of 'factual' content, whether audio-visual or written. Similarly, we argue vehemently about the merits of the different songs, bands or genres in our music listening in spite of the most striking similarities in song structure, lyrical themes and performance convention. The Frankfurt School's broader emphasis upon the lure of cultural consumerism and its provision of temporary, superficial forms of enjoyment also seems at least as applicable now as over half a century ago. If theories sometimes go rapidly out of date as society changes, then in this case, we might plausibly suggest that the opposite is true.

This does not mean, however, that the work of the School is without significant problems. Much of the approach rests upon a belief that the essential condition of humanity revolves around a particular version of individual self-determination, imagination and creativity. Distinct from Marx's (also questionable) materialist emphasis upon the human importance of meaningful labour, this idealist Frankfurt School assumption is debateable and rather ill-defined. How do we know self-determination and creative subjectivity as they envisage these are indeed what is most naturally human, and who decides what counts as creative or human and what does not? On what basis does Marcuse, for example, know that certain 'needs' or experiences of enjoyment are more legitimate or genuine than others? We cannot accept the Frankfurt School's critique of capitalism in its entirety unless we are sure about their very particular understanding of how human life *should* be.

In spite of its relevance to examples across media cultures today, the Frankfurt School's dismissal of mass culture was probably over-generalised at the time and would certainly be too sweeping if applied across the board to the more complex, fragmented and interactive digital media system of today. In labelling *every* cultural industry product as standardised and dismissing *all* apparent variants as pseudo-individualisation, the Frankfurt scholars underestimate the possibility that the pursuit of profit might in certain circumstances encourage innovation and difference. In a digital culture characterised by on-demand access to a seemingly limitless array of content distributed in a multitude of ways, their work does provide a valuable reminder that more does not necessarily mean different. Yet it is difficult to accept that there are no meaningful distinctions at all between cultural industry products.

For all their emphasis on the industrialisation of culture, the Frankfurt School theorists carried out little analysis of how the institutions which produce and distribute culture actually work (Thompson 1990). Such analysis may have confirmed some of the trends they allude to, but would probably have revealed a set of motivations, decision-making procedures and ways of working rather more complex than they allow for. The Frankfurt School also fail to provide evidence for their claims about the negative impact of mass culture on audiences. Their appraisal of mass cultural content may have been detailed at times, but it is a significant leap to infer, from such textual analysis, confident conclusions about how audiences respond. As Thompson puts it, 'Horkheimer and Adorno try to read off the consequences of cultural products from the products themselves' (1990: 105).

Moreover, their certainty about the universally passifying impacts of mass culture sits uncomfortably with the ability they bestow on themselves to criticise it. On the one hand they insist that the whole population has been incorporated by the all-encompassing pragmatic-rationalist machinery of the capitalist system and its culture industry, crushing any capacity for independent thought or critique, but on the other they claim for themselves the unique ability to see how the system works and respond to its cultural products in a different way to everyone else. This has prompted some to claim that the Frankfurt School are essentially elitist: they assign to themselves a penetrating discernment and taste deemed to be lacking among ordinary people.

IDEOLOGICAL MEANINGS

For Thompson (1990), the Frankfurt School present a 'social cement' version of the concept of ideology. Rather than persuading people to support the status quo by propagating a particular set of dominant ideas, the culture industry directly binds or cements people to the system by crushing their capacity to think critically or independently at all. Other theorists, however, have focused greater attention on identifying the propagation via media texts of specific viewpoints, meanings and modes of representation that are deemed to serve ideological purposes.

BEYOND MARX'S MATERIALISM

Importantly, the development of attempts to critique the presence of such ideological messages within media content rested on challenges to Marx's materialist insistence that the realm of ideas automatically mirrors the material situation of a given society. Marx's position afforded little possibility that the proletariat could escape false consciousness through the exposure of ideology by theorists, or indeed through any sort of struggle confined to the realm of ideas. For Marx, in order to change dominant ideas, you had to change the economic system, not the other way around. This deterministic stance was softened in the theory of Louis Althusser (1971), who suggested that although an economic base determines culture and ideas 'in the last instance', the latter nevertheless have 'relative autonomy'. For Althusser, in order to survive and reproduce itself, the economic system relies on control of dominant thinking through *ideological state apparatus*, a category that includes media alongside religion, schools and the family among other institutions. But the principle of relative autonomy introduces the possibility that there might be some diversity, disagreement and struggle within these spheres and that dominant ideology might be challenged. Under the right circumstances, then, culture and ideas may have the capacity to be changed independently of the underlying material or economic system.

Antonio Gramsci (1971), writing some years earlier, had gone further still in emphasising the importance of independent struggle and change within the realm of culture and ideas. Gramsci coined the term *hegemony* to refer to the predominance of taken-for-granted ways of understanding the world that strengthen the interests of the dominant political group. In order to maintain their position of economic and political power, argued Gramsci, the dominant group must achieve hegemony by dominating the realm of ideas and culture. Yet, rather than automatically submitting to dominant interests, civil society is characterised by an ongoing struggle between hegemonic and counter-hegemonic ideas. The dominant group may have significant advantages given the resources at its disposal, but the maintenance of hegemony, in Gramsci's view, is constantly subject to challenge. Rather than being pre-determined by the economic or material situation, struggles for influence over the everyday common-sense understandings held by the population are deemed pivotal to the conservation or overthrow of a prevailing system. And, in Gramsci's account, intellectuals, broadly defined, play a crucial role in these ideological struggles. Taken together, Gramsci and Althusser open up the possibility that, through exposing and challenging the operation of dominant sets of ideas within media content, social theorists might, themselves, play a role in social change.

For Stuart Hall, media constitute the primary site for the playing out of the kinds of struggles over meaning outlined by Gramsci. As we saw in Chapter 5, Hall recognises that some audience groups may not fully accept the messages encoded into media texts. This did not prevent him, however, from regarding media as a highly effective means through which hegemony was established. Television was deemed particularly powerful because of the way it presented itself as an impartial 'window on the world' for viewers, making ideological representations look objective and natural (1982: 75). For Hall, whether it emitted deliberate bias or not, media discourse rarely stepped outside of a set of underlying, unquestioned frameworks and assumptions that served dominant interests. 'Broadcasters', he said, 'may not be aware of the fact that the frameworks and classifications they were drawing on reproduced the ideological inventories of society' (Hall 1982: 72).

In spite of the best intentions of news providers, then, the regular reporting of economic crises or industrial disputes as damaging to the economy or to 'the national interest' activated common-sense, ideological assumptions: that the strengthening of capitalism was a good thing, that the effective functioning and survival of this system was in our best interests and that we should all identify with our country. Drawing heavily on Gramsci, Hall also focuses on the ways the dominant system would respond and adapt in the face of challenges. In *Policing the Crisis* (1978) he and colleagues argued that sensationalised and racialised coverage of violent crime during the 1970s functioned as part of a re-establishment of hegemony in the face of a variety of threats to the system, including the rise of rebellious youth subcultures and increasing moral permissiveness. Focused upon 'muggings', the coverage stigmatised racial minorities and evoked more general themes of a society out of control; something that paved the way for new forms of political authority and repression. Through adapting and responding to challenges, then, hegemony was restored.

Barthes, whose contributions to the development of semiology were examined in Chapter 4, is also of great importance to the development of a tradition focused on the deconstruction of ideological messages within media texts. Through his emphasis upon 'mythology', he emphasised that semiology should not be limited to the isolated analysis of particular texts but should identify the repeated activation and reinforcement in such texts of broader prevailing ways of understanding the world. Like Hall, on whom he had been an important influence, Barthes suggests that ideology 'transforms history into nature' (1972: 129). The circulation of myths, in other words, serves to make assumptions that are historically specific appear to be natural and inevitable. One of the primary focuses in Barthes' work and that of more recent critics of ideological media content has been the operation of myths relating to consumerism. Using this theme as a case study to illustrate the way some theorists have sought to uncover the operation of ideological meanings within media, we'll briefly elaborate.

CASE STUDY: CONSUMERIST MYTHS

Contemporary culture is saturated with messages that promote consumerism and the desirability of commodities. Not only are we surrounded by a multitude of different forms of direct advertising, but the broader promotion of consumerism extends to a wide range of media content that centres on or endorses consumption as a primary focus and goal in contemporary life. Academic critics with Marxist or neo-Marxist sympathies often have sought to identify the operation of such meanings through textual analysis that aims to deconstruct the ideological significance of media texts. For Douglas Kellner (1995), media increasingly subject us to a basic ideological premise that buying or consuming is to be aspired to, that the identity of each of us is, first and foremost, as a consumer and that in order to achieve happiness, status and fulfilment we should strive to maximise and/or refine our consumption. Because of the relentlessness of this underlying message, a questionable premise about the status of members of society and the means to human fulfilment begins to seem natural and taken-for-granted. In turn, this works in the interests of the prevailing capitalist social order, by encouraging the population to work hard to enhance their capacity to consume while enabling capitalists to maximise their wealth accumulation and material dominance.

It is for this reason that Kellner, alongside other analysts (e.g. Williamson 1978), has subjected advertisements to ideology-critique, elucidating in particular how such texts establish products as symbols for culturally desirable concepts related to identity, fulfilment, happiness or freedom. Such ideals are often filtered through the lens of gender, he argues. Thus, Marlboro's historic use of the symbol of the cowboy associates smoking its cigarettes with tradition, independence and rugged masculinity, while Virginia Slims' 'you've come a long way baby' campaigns have associated smoking the brand's cigarettes with a modern, glamorous femininity, liberated from old stereotypes of passivity (Kellner 1995: 336). Profound human concepts such as freedom and independence, then, as well as fundamental understandings of what it is to be male and female, become traits to be acquired primarily through consumption (see Chapter 9 for more on advertising).

As Kellner emphasises, however, ideologies of consumerism go far beyond the messages to be uncovered in direct advertising. Partly because of their own interest in attracting advertisers, magazines, news, television programmes, films, popular music and various other media forms often valorise consumption. Make-over programmes, for example, present the transformation of individual appearances, homes, vehicles or gardens, through the discerning purchase and combination of appropriate goods. Narratives typically connect such transformations with the prospect of improvements in the happiness and fulfilment of individuals featured. We're not necessarily supposed to agree with the approach taken by the 'experts', and debating such details is part of the appeal, but underlying it all is a reinforcement of the notion that we should all, at regular intervals, look to transform our individual lives and identities through attention to our consumer practices (Redden 2007).

Consumer magazine formats, whether online, in print or on television, are often centred on reviewing and enthusing about particular categories of consumer goods associated with niche lifestyle groups, from gamers, to health and fitness enthusiasts to car fanatics. Ideological deconstruction of women's fashion and beauty magazines by Ellen McCracken (1992) in the early 1990s established how such publications reinforced versions of successful femininity that revolved around discerning consumption of clothes, beauty products and other goods. It is not difficult to draw comparable conclusions in relation to a range of magazine content today. Such programmes and publications *may* be scrupulous in their care to treat different products with scrutiny and fairness, but the broader reinforcement of consumerism as an unquestioned solution to life's problems proceeds largely unquestioned.

Cross-cutting many different media genres and formats, the celebrity industry comprises a particularly pervasive source of consumerist ideology. Celebrities, it might be argued, present us with idealistic consumerist fantasies in the form of attractive, wealthy and popular individuals whose clothes, accessories, make-up, cars, houses and broader lifestyles are the subject of mass fascination (Marshall 1997). This level of public interest is frequently used as a direct means to sell consumer products to us through endorsements of particular products. For Ellis Cashmore (2014: 183), however, such direct forms of advertising are less important than the status of celebrities as 'adverts… for the culture in which these products have value and the golden life those products yield'. Not all coverage of celebrities is positive, of course, and we're often invited to take enjoyment from wardrobe failures, questionable tastes and aberrant behaviour. Far from dampening enthusiasm for the consumerist myth, however, such individual 'failures' illustrate the importance, both for celebrities and for the rest of us, of consuming as effectively as possible.

For neo-Marxist critics, in the course of presenting the consumption of objects as the primary means to happiness and liberation, media distract us from the possibility of achieving such goals through radical social change. And they also mask how the production of consumer goods themselves is premised on capitalist exploitation. In his analysis of the cultural construction of wine in France as a blissful substance whose consumption symbolises belonging to a great nation, Barthes (1972: 61) reminds us that such a myth masks the alienative relations of production on which the consumption of wine is dependent. Part of the ideological message then, is the promotion of *commodity fetishism*: the symbolic separation of commodities from the social conditions in which they were produced. Naomi Klein's (2000) analysis of the global cultivation of consumer brands highlights various instances of this, not least the huge investment by Nike in the construction of an image associated with individual human achievement and excellence. While consumers in the West were persuaded to pay a premium for Nike products in order to buy into such symbolism, Klein argues, the exploitative conditions in which many such items were produced – often in poor developing countries – were rendered invisible.

POLITICAL ECONOMY AND IDEOLOGY

While the approach of some ideology critics has been to expose the operation of dominant meanings in media content, others have placed greater emphasis upon the commercial structures of media ownership and control. As we saw in Chapter 3, critical political economy seeks to carry out the kind of detailed analysis of the workings of the culture industry the Frankfurt School failed to provide. To a degree, the approach bypasses the Frankfurt School's variant of neo-Marxism, and indeed those of Althusser and Gramsci, preferring the more materialist emphasis in Marx's own work. Proponents are critical of what they regard as culturalist approaches to Marxism which, from their point of view, over-estimate the autonomy of the sphere of culture and ideas and too frequently study media content in isolation from the economic and material relations in which it is produced (Golding and Murdock 1991).

In contrast, critical political economists concentrate on the economic dominance of the wealthy and powerful and the way this translates into ownership, influence and control over the dissemination of ideas (Murdock and Golding 1995). They replace the culturalist emphasis on meaning as a site of intellectual struggle, then, with a materialist stance that locates ideology as something centred on the context of media production and control.

MANUFACTURING CONSENT

Alongside the writings of Murdock and Golding, the best-known example of this approach is perhaps Herman and Chomsky's book, *Manufacturing Consent* (1998) in which it is argued that the extent of corporate control over communications leaves little possibility of any sustained critique of the prevailing capitalist order. Five institutional 'filters' in the set up of the media system are identified, each of which serving to make counter-ideological forms of content less likely.

Filter one is the ownership and profit orientation of media and cultural institutions. Media are overwhelmingly controlled by a small number of highly powerful corporate institutions and although these corporations often compete with one another, they also have common political interests because of their shared corporate status. Notably, they each stand to benefit from global capitalism itself and from government policies conducive to open markets and profit maximisation. They therefore are likely, according to Herman and Chomsky, to oppose regulations that constrain their commercial operations and dislike media content that criticises contemporary capitalism.

Filter two relates to the imperative to attract and retain advertisers, most of whom also constitute large-scale money-making corporations who share the interest of media companies in the promotion of deregulated global capitalism. Such advertisers are also unlikely to be enthusiastic about content that is critical of the capitalist status quo or that exposes problematic corporate activities, for example, providing media companies with a further incentive to filter out such content. More generally, advertisers are deemed to have a preference for light, entertaining and superficial forms of content because these are deemed most conducive to the positive reception of commercials by audiences.

Filter three concerns the extensive influence on media of a range of other wealthy and powerful groups. Including governments, mainstream political parties, high profile pressure groups and large-scale corporate interests, such groups are able to use their wealth and power to manipulate flows of information to media through carefully orchestrated and expensive public relations strategies. The organisation of press conferences, the stage-managed release of information, comment, images or footage and the cultivation of beneficial relationships with journalists, enables such groups to wield disproportionate influence on media organisations only too pleased to be provided with regular sources of inexpensive content.

Filter four, 'flak', refers to the negative consequences liable to result from any substantial coverage by a media organisation of counter-ideological messages. In the unlikely event that any such messages should manage to make it through filters one, two and three, the media organisation/s responsible can expect a barrage of high profile criticism and labelling, alongside legal challenges and/or the withdrawal of advertisers.

Linked closely to this is the fifth and final filter, which comprises a broader ideology of anti-communism deemed to dominate US society. An atmosphere that associates critical content with the US' (now former) cold war enemies, they argue, serves as a further barrier to the media exposure of such content. In recent years, a broader rhetoric around notions of 'anti-Americanism' has also been of significance, with the charge regularly levelled against opponents of the Bush administration in the years following the attack on the World Trade Center in 2001, for example. Nevertheless, perceived socialist or communist values are often constructed as part of what anti-Americanism entails.

The cumulative effect of the five filters operating together, according to Herman and Chomsky, is to ensure that media are thoroughly dominated by ideological forms of culture that serve the interests of the status quo.

CULTURAL IMPERIALISM AS GLOBALISATION OF IDEOLOGY

Approaches associated with critical political economy have been particularly evident in the development of Marxist critiques of the globalisation of media and culture in the last decades of the twentieth century and beyond. In contrast to McLuhan's optimistic discussion of a technologically driven global village which would foster mutual understanding between previously unconnected cultures (see Chapter 2), *cultural imperialism* theories focused on the globalisation of culture as a highly unequal process dominated by powerful capitalist interests based in wealthy countries. The drive to minimise costs and maximise profits is deemed to have prompted media and culture industries, with the help of global communications technologies, to operate in a thoroughly international manner.

Operating globally enables large, integrated corporations to maximise the *supply* of materials and labour available to them and, thereby, to minimise costs by sourcing the cheapest. Why produce branded clothing in the US when you can contract a company in Haiti to do it for you with cheaper labour (Klein 2000)? And, even more importantly, from the point of view of cultural imperialism theorists, companies maximise *demand* for their products and services by turning the whole world into their market. Such is the importance of maximum exploitation of global markets to the success of companies that most media products – from television series to popular music – are now produced with global appeal in mind. This is sometimes deemed to have encouraged an emphasis upon simplicity, standardisation and the erosion of local distinctiveness.

Having first emerged in the 1970s, cultural imperialism theories contend that the globalisation of media and culture involves the systematic exploitation and cultural domination of small countries by powerful transnational companies based in wealthy parts of the world (Boyd-Barrett 1977; Schiller 1976; 1992). Standardised forms of international media culture are distributed by transnational companies to as many countries as possible. Unable to compete with the wealth, influence and market dominance of the transnationals, domestic media in smaller countries are forced to rely on cheap imported products centred on Anglo-American culture and ideology rather than developing their own distinctive home-produced cultural spheres. Reliance on such imported content and systems also means that, rather than being invested in local economies, money is transferred out of such countries and into the coffers of the transnationals (see Figure 6.1).

In another facet of cultural imperialism, cultural resources are sometimes also appropriated from smaller countries by transnationals. For example, some have noted the appropriation and packaging of selected local musicians around the world by the international recording industry as part of the construction and development of the World Music genre oriented to niche middle-class white audiences in the West (Taylor 1997; 2007). Individual artists may achieve substantial success as a result, it is argued, but often relinquish control over their art and how it is packaged to record labels oriented to the expectations of Western audiences. Often, argues Taylor, this means packaging and

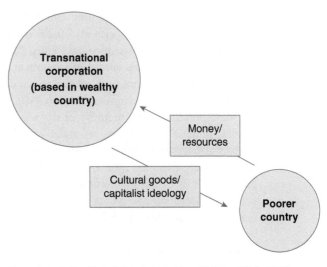

Figure 6.1   Cultural imperialism (adapted from Malm and Wallis 1993)

coding the work of such artists as exotic, different or 'other' on the basis of simplistic understandings of their country of origin rather than including them in established genres such as rock, dance and so on (Taylor 2007). Meanwhile, rather than benefiting local industry or economies, the money earned by the work of such artists largely goes to corporations based in wealthy countries.

Cultural imperialism theorists liken the exploitative and hierarchical relationship between what they refer to as core and peripheral countries to the exploitation and cultural indoctrination of colonised populations by Western imperial powers in the nineteenth and early twentieth century. The difference is that, instead of being imposed through military rule, cultural domination is attributable to overwhelming financial muscle and the use of communication technologies. Either way, one of the most striking results, it is sometimes argued, is the swamping of indigenous cultures by an increasingly monolithic global mass culture originating in powerful countries. What the Frankfurt School referred to as the culture industry, then, is deemed to have gone global. For Peet, previous global diversities are fast disappearing as an entertainment-oriented mass culture originating in the West comes to dominate ways of life around the world:

> The tendency is towards the production of one world mind, one world culture and the consequent disappearance of regional consciousness flowing from the local specificities of the human past… the new gods of entertainment are worshipped around the globe in one big fan-club. (Peet 1989: 195–6)

To take an obvious example of such homogenisation, the domination of popular music industries around the world by English language music, particularly from the UK and North America, has led to a situation in which, as well as often listening primarily to English-language music, musicians around the world increasingly sing in English too, whether or not it is their native language (Crystal 2003).

While part of the criticism for cultural imperialism theories is of the process of homogenisation per se, such theories also focus on the specific role of global mass culture as a form of Western, capitalist ideology. Thus, for Peet, the export of mass culture is intrinsically linked to the global spread of capitalism itself as a material and social system: 'mass production and consumption have meant standardised, programmed ways of thinking with little room for regional variation... global capitalism evolves as a single way of life gradually incorporating... the majority of the world's population' (Peet 1989: 193). And while cultural imperialism theories are usually centred on a macro political economic analysis, support also has come from theorists using textual analysis to identify ideological messages within widely exported media texts. In the 1970s, Dorfman and Mattelart (1971) carried out an analysis of Disney comics, which, at the time, had been sold in some 47 different countries. Dorfman and Mattelart's analysis suggested that the narratives in the comics, featuring characters such as Donald Duck, were riddled with dominant American capitalist meanings. Characters, for example, are deemed to have exhibited a constant obsession with making money, becoming rich and indulging in compulsive consumerism. Narratives also demonstrate regular engagement in ruthless competition in order to achieve such goals. There are even references to imperialism itself, in the form of stories where characters compete to exploit oil and gold in far-away lands. Dorfman and Mattelart conclude that the global circulation of products such as Disney comics is a vehicle for the spreading of ideologies that normalise Western capitalism and consumerism.

ARGUMENTS AND CRITICISMS

POLITICAL ECONOMIC VERSUS CULTURAL APPROACHES

As we have seen in the cultural imperialism case above, sometimes textual analysis and political economic approaches to media are used in support of one another in the development of arguments about the role and impact of ideological communications. Nevertheless, there continues to exist something of a schism between the two approaches. Ideology critique via textual analysis is often associated with a culturalist or cultural studies approach to Marxism, influenced by the emphasis upon relative autonomy of the cultural sphere in the work of theorists such as Althusser, Gramsci, and Hall, while critical political economy takes a materialist approach closer to that in much of Marx's own work.

Political economists have often criticised the likes of Barthes, Hall and others for focusing their attentions on the detailed ways dominant meanings are conveyed via media texts, without providing any substantive understanding of material structures of media ownership and control (Garnham 1995). This, it is argued, relates to an over-estimation of the autonomy of the sphere of ideas and culture from forces of material determination. For political economists such as Nicolas Garnham, the cultural sphere is subject to 'ultimate determination by the economic' (ibid.: 219), something which means that it is the operation of the structures of ownership and control which provides the most fruitful site for analysis. For their part, those associated with the culturalist approach criticise what they regard as the deterministic stance of political economists who, from their point of view, too often draw simplistic conclusions about the content and ideological impact of media on the basis of macro-analysis of structures of control. Herman and Chomsky, for example, assume that oppositional messages inevitably are filtered out of media by the systems and structures they describe, but provide little detailed analysis of media content to demonstrate the operation of such ideological bias in practice.

Likewise, in spite of exceptions such as Dorfman and Mattelart, theories of cultural imperialism tend to draw bold conclusions about the swamping of local cultures by standardised, ideological mass cultural products from the West, largely on the basis of a macro analysis of the functioning of the media industry and global capitalism (Tomlinson 1991). In contrast, culturalist perspectives suggest that, even if communications are materially dominated by powerful, globalised capitalist interests, the dominant ideas that this is liable to give rise to will always be accompanied by the potential for marginal forms of culture to emerge. From this point of view, even if hegemonic meanings tend to predominate, academic analysis and intervention should be focused, in detail, on the ways that struggles over meaning are played out.

COMPLEX COMMUNICATION FLOWS AND CONSUMER RESISTANCE

Whilst the notion of the cultural sphere as relatively autonomous and a site of struggle initially was deployed as part of a project dominated by exposing the workings of ideology or hegemony within media texts, culturalist perspectives have in recent times become associated with greater doubts about the value of Marxist approaches to ideology. Such doubts relate both to the diversity and multi-directional flow of meanings within modern culture, particularly in relation to the growth of interactive digital cultures, and to the general capacity of media users to develop active and subversive uses for media.

For many, the sheer range of ideas circulating in the contemporary cultural sphere renders an exclusive emphasis on mind-numbing mass culture or dominant meanings, over-simplistic. Just as the Frankfurt School over-generalise their critique of the culture industry, so theorists like Hall are sometimes criticised for their implication that, in spite of the occasional presence of counter-discourses, ideological or hegemonic meanings pervade the vast majority of media content. Likewise, in focusing on the global circulation of a monolithic mass culture, theories of cultural imperialism arguably under-estimate the range and complexity of cultural products that are transferred around the globe (Tomlinson 1991). For every Star Wars or Beyoncé, there are numerous smaller-scale, more narrowly targeted global products, from marginal music genres to independent film, to DIY blogs or YouTube videos. Cultural imperialism theory is also ill-equipped to account for the resilience against global imports of strong local media industries in countries such as Mexico, Brazil and India, less still the emergence of such countries as powerful media exporters who create counter-flows of culture to populations based in North America and Western Europe (Hesmondhalgh 2007).

Emphasis on the diversity and multi-directionality of cultural flows has become particularly influential in light of recent shifts towards a digital media climate with a vastly increasing range of content and services, increasing interactivity and blurring distinctions between consumers and producers (Jenkins 2006). As we shall see in Chapter 10, however, we should be cautious of assuming that an increase in the number of different messages, channels and 'senders' automatically renders the world of communications plural or demo-cratic and Marxist understandings of power irrelevant. Firstly, an increase in the quantity of content does not automatically equate to an increase in the pervasiveness of counter-hegemonic forms of expression. The Frankfurt School's notion of pseudo-individualisation may retain some use in reminding us of this. Secondly, powerful media organisations continue to control substantial proportions of the culture most of us consume. The capa-city to influence the distribution of existing content or circulate our own ideas and culture undoubtedly are significant, but the most influential forms of content remain controlled by powerful corporations, as do the various social media platforms via which so many of us interact, share and circulate content. Indeed, for some commentators, the work media users engage in through discussing, adapting, sharing and distributing media content constitutes a new digital form of exploitation. Such work, they argue, constitutes unpaid labour – a free resource being appropriated by powerful commercial interests to promote their prod-ucts through word-of-mouth and to harvest information about us for marketing purposes (Cohen 2013). We will elaborate further on this idea in the coming chapters.

Perhaps the biggest and most sustained challenge to Marxist theories of ideology, however, has come from emphasis on the capacity of consumers of both traditional and contemporary media forms to produce their own meanings and uses from existing content. The implication of such arguments is that, even if media are dominated by large-scale profit-making interests and/or by standardised or ideological content, we ought not assume that users necessarily will be manipulated or homogenised. In response to criticism of the global ideological impact of US soap *Dallas* among cultural imperialism theorists, a classic audience study by Katz and Liebes (1985), illustrated that, rather than having their culture and ideas swamped by US ide-ology, audiences in different countries each drew upon different sets of local understandings in their responses to it. As we saw in Chapter 5, a plethora of other studies and theories about media users (e.g. Fiske 1991a; Jenkins 1992; 2006) have raised equally strong questions about the implicit assumption in many Marxist approaches that media users are passive victims of media manipulation.

CONCLUSION: AVOIDING EASY DISMISSALS

The arguments against Marxist notions of media, power and ideology are enticing, persua-sive and often difficult to disagree with. It is heartening to think of members of society, ourselves included, as active, critical users, drawing creatively from a vast range of content, influencing how it is distributed through our online sharing and even producing some of our own. In contrast it can be profoundly uncomfortable to suggest that ordinary people are manipulated, ignorant or suffering from false-consciousness. Such an approach is often labelled as patronising and elitist, sometimes justifiably so. Yet there is a danger that the desire to avoid being regarded as patronising, together with the convenience of legitimating our own popular cultural tastes, might lead us towards a complacent celebration of a status quo in which media remain thoroughly dominated by powerful corporate interests. Marxist approaches may be open to criticism, then, but we would be well advised not to dismiss their critical approach to questions of media, power and control too easily.

QUESTIONS/EXERCISES

1 a) To what extent can Adorno and Horkheimer's criticisms of popular cultural products be applied to contemporary media content? Are there any examples of contemporary music, film or television which you would argue are **not** standardised and could **not** be construed as pseudo-individualisation?

   b) In what ways might Marcuse's notion of 'false needs' be applied to the example of contemporary make-over shows?

2 a) In what ways do Althusser and Gramsci move away from Marx's deterministic approach to the relationship between material relations and dominant ideas?

   b) Why is this important to the development of a tradition focused on identifying and critiquing ideological meanings in media content?

3 Select an example of a media text (e.g. a website, television programme, image or film) and subject its structure and content to ideology critique: in what ways might it reinforce dominant understandings of the world?

4 Should we regard the transnational circulation of media and consumer goods today as cultural imperialism? List the strengths and weaknesses of such an interpretation.

5 a) What is the difference between culturalist and political economic versions of Marxism when it comes to questions of media and ideology?

   b) Are Marxist approaches to media rendered entirely redundant by i) assertions that audiences are active or ii) the diverse and interactive form taken by contemporary digital media environments?

SUGGESTED FURTHER READING

Adorno, T. (1990) 'On Popular Music', in S. Frith and A. Goodwin (eds) *On Record: Rock, Pop and the Written Word*. London: Routledge (article first published 1941) – Famous critique of the standardised structure of popular jazz music, deemed to induce passivity and conformity in listeners.

Fuchs, C. (2014) *Social Media: A Critical Introduction*. London: Sage – Introduction to a variety of different forms of social and interactive digital media that takes a clear Marxist stance centred on critical theory.

Hall, S. (1982) 'The Rediscovery of "Ideology": Return of the Repressed in Media Studies', in Gurevitch, M., Bennett, T., Curran, J. and Woollacott, J. (eds) *Culture, Society and The Media*. London:

Routledge – Criticises pluralist approaches to media and sets out a critical cultural studies approach to the question of ideology.

Herman, E. and Chomsky, N. (1998) *Manufacturing Consent: The Political Economy of the Mass Media.* London: Vintage (originally published 1988) – Political-economic analysis of the filtering of media content by structures of ownership and control.

Tomlinson, J. (1991) *Cultural Imperialism: A Critical Introduction.* London: Pinter – Offers a strongly critical account of theories of cultural imperialism as an approach to the globalisation of media.

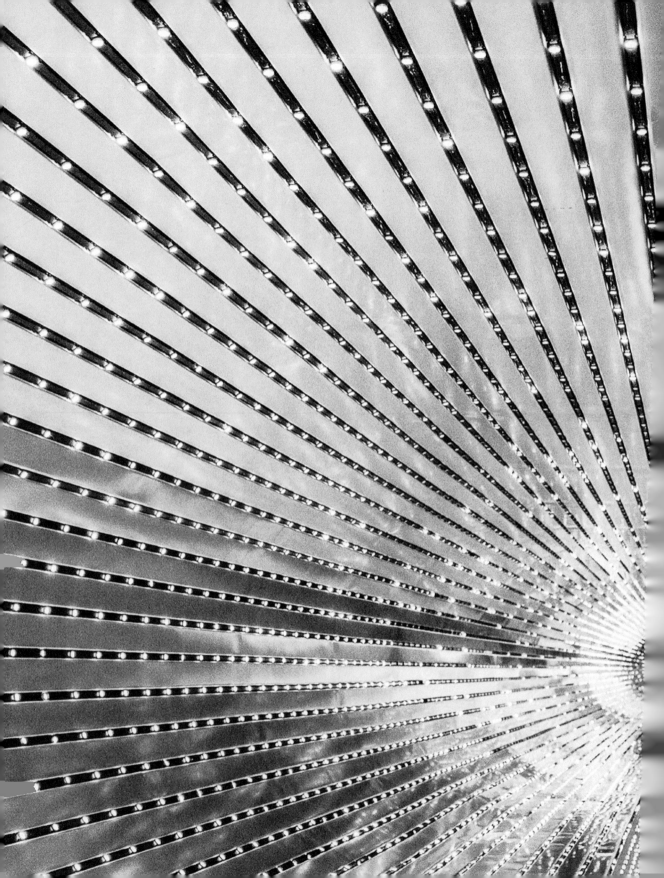

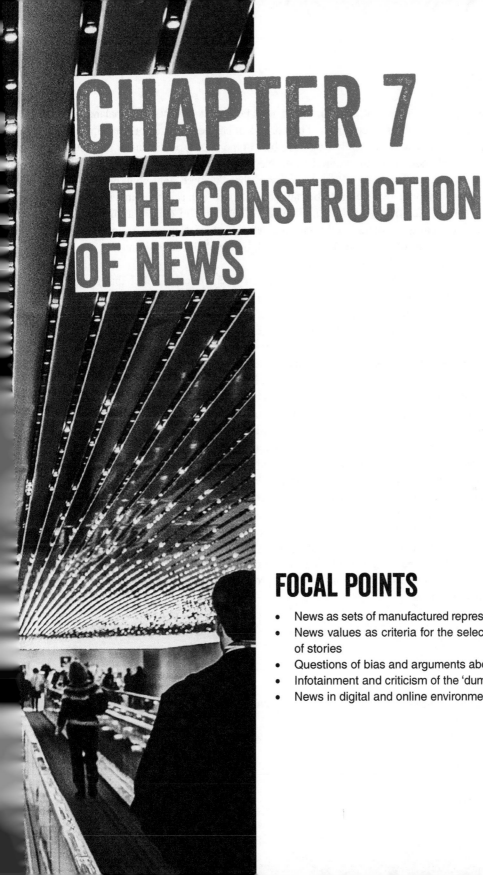

CHAPTER 7
THE CONSTRUCTION OF NEWS

FOCAL POINTS

- News as sets of manufactured representations of the world
- News values as criteria for the selection and construction of stories
- Questions of bias and arguments about news as ideology
- Infotainment and criticism of the 'dumbing down' of news
- News in digital and online environments

INTRODUCTION

Most people would probably agree that, sometimes, the news falls short of presenting a balanced and truthful reflection of the world. Accusations of bias or lack of balance in coverage sometimes come from academics, but just as frequently from members of the public, politicians or interest groups. Over the last decade or so, for example, Fox News has been subject to particularly frequent criticism that its coverage of a wide range of issues has favoured right-wing perspectives and failed to live up to its own claims to be 'fair and balanced'. During the same period, the BBC, whose charter specifically requires impartiality in coverage of current affairs, has found itself subject to accusations of both right-wing and left-wing bias. Newspapers are also a regular target for accusations of unbalanced coverage, with 'red-top' UK tabloids such as *The Sun* and *The Mirror* often singled out for criticism.

Annoyance about perceived bias in news coverage can often reflect a belief that such instances constitute a betrayal of what news can and should be. Here, biased news is contrasted with ideals of news as a vital public service that provides neutral information and truthful facts. Consistent with notions of media as mirror, this view suggests that news should offer an undistorted reflection of the world. It also informs the way some forms of news are regulated. While bias is permitted and expected in UK newspapers and online news sites, for example, television broadcasters are subject to a statutory public interest requirement to 'ensure that news, in whatever form, is reported with due accuracy and presented with due impartiality' (Ofcom 2016). The qualifier 'due' here recognises the impossibility of covering 'every argument and every facet of every argument', but the aspiration for essentially unbiased news is clear.

It will become apparent in this chapter, however, that news can *never* constitute an unbiased mirror on the world. Although based upon real events and controversies, the content of newspapers and bulletins is manufactured and constructed in particular ways according to prevailing cultural values, audience expectations and institutional priorities. What we read, view or listen to comprises not a neutral account of the world, but one or more versions or *representations* of that world. Some may be more detailed, better substantiated, faithful in intentions and inclusive of different viewpoints than others – and we may well wish to support and encourage these. But none are unbiased. The content of news, therefore, tells us as much about the practices, values and structures of those who produce and consume it, as about the world it purports to represent.

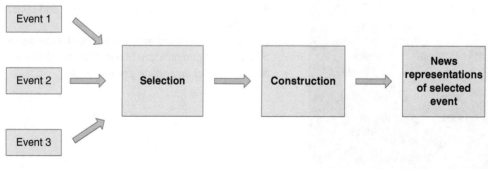

Figure 7.1   News filtering

When considering the ways news is manufactured, it is valuable to envisage a filtering process to illustrate how the plethora of events, issues or viewpoints that could be covered on a given day are streamlined into the content of a news website, broadcast bulletin or printed newspaper (see Figure 7.1). The processes involved are complex but we can usefully distinguish between two sequential stages: the *selection* of events and issues on which to base stories; and the subsequent *construction* of such stories.

SELECTION, GATE-KEEPING AND AGENDA SETTING

Discussions about bias often focus on the way stories are told by news providers. Before deciding how to tell a given story, however, outlets must select which events, topics or controversies to cover. Through taking such decisions, news organisations act as *gate-keepers* with the capacity to affect what we know, care and talk about and, conversely, what passes under our collective radar. This apparent power to shape public priorities is known as *agenda setting*, a term associated with research by McCombs and Shaw (1972), who identified a correlation between the amount of news coverage devoted to an issue and the importance attributed to it by the public. Such findings may suggest that news gate-keeping determines what people think is important, though we should note that the empirical direction of causality here is ambiguous – it is not clear, in other words, whether stories included by media shape or reflect public priorities.

So what factors influence whether an event will be included in the news? My writing this paragraph is an event, as is your reading it. Yet, none of us would expect these things or most of the other events in our daily lives to be reported on by professional journalists. But what is it about such events that is unsuitable compared with the kinds of stories which regularly are included? Detailed consideration of the criteria used by journalists and editors in evaluating newsworthiness can provide greater understanding of the priorities of news media. As well as excluding a host of undeniably trivial events, these criteria, which are known as *news values*, also can result in selections and exclusions that are more controversial.

NEWS VALUES

As we shall see later, there are differences of priority and emphasis between news outlets in terms of the blend of stories covered by each at a given time. Yet analysis suggests such outlets also tend to share a number of core criteria, or news values, which determine story selection. The best-known attempt to outline these shared news values is provided by Galtung and Ruge (1973), who identify 12 criteria that are intended to be cumulative rather than independent of one another: the more that apply and the greater the extent to which they apply, the more likely an event is to be covered.

1. FREQUENCY (AND IMMEDIACY)

For an event to make a news story, argue Galtung and Ruge, it helps if its time-span is compatible with the frequency with which news is published or broadcast. Criminal or violent incidents tend to be ideal because they play themselves out in a short time-span between one edition of a newspaper or bulletin and the next. In contrast, gradual improvements in a country's education system are unlikely to make the news unless highlighted by a discrete event such as the release of a report or a school visit by a member of government. Similarly, the slow process of repairing a war-torn country may receive less coverage than the discrete event of the bombing which damaged it. More recently, some have connected this notion of frequency with an increasingly prominent specific role for *immediacy* or *recency*, which refers to the particular emphasis placed by news providers on breaking new stories (e.g. Bell 1991).

2. AMPLITUDE

Amplitude refers to a threshold of noticeability. The more extreme or dramatic an event is within its category, the more likely it is to receive prominent coverage. And in the age of television and online news, many argue that the specific role of spectacle and drama in the selection of news stories is becoming pivotal (Baker and Dessart 1998). A story is particularly likely to be covered if the drama is captured directly through sound, image or film (Harrison 2006). A dramatic police car chase is more likely to be covered if it was caught on video, for example.

3. CLARITY

The propensity for an event to be presented in a clear or one-dimensional manner can increase its chances of receiving coverage. Events make good news copy, it is argued, when ambiguities about cause, meaning or significance are at a minimum. Stories that can involve clear attribution of right and wrong and obvious victims and villains fit well within this category – and replicate the kinds of moral clarity and simplicity we are presented with in much fictional media. Acts of criminal violence, for example, can easily be centred on blameworthy individual perpetrator/s and individual victim/s with whom audiences can empathise. In contrast, arguments about the detail of political policy tend to be complex, messy and uncertain.

4. CULTURAL PROXIMITY

News providers tend to favour stories that involve practices, places or people that are culturally familiar to their audience. News is ethnocentric, argue Galtung and Ruge, in that it is biased towards that which seems closest to us. Thus, among Canadian news providers, disasters in Canada itself or in countries regarded as culturally similar to Canada, receive greater coverage than similar events in other parts of the world. Nevertheless, events in culturally and geographically distant places may still sometimes be newsworthy if they have some other form of relevance. A disaster in South Africa may receive more news coverage in Japan if Japanese citizens were among the casualties.

5. PREDICTABILITY

Newsworthy stories tend to connect to our expectations about how the world works. Sometimes this may relate to specific anticipated events. Media speculation about the possibility of violence at protest marches can create expectations that then lead to the prioritisation of coverage of any actual violence. In other cases, stories can become newsworthy because they confirm broader social expectations or stereotypes. News stories about young people getting into trouble, for example, can activate stereotypical expectations about youth delinquency.

6. UNEXPECTEDNESS

Crucially, however, Galtung and Ruge argue that predictability works alongside a tendency to emphasise events that are extraordinary or unusual as compared to the normal events of most of our everyday lives. A story about the disappearance of a child may be liable to fit with certain established expectations (about the danger of paedophiles, for example) at the same time as attaining its newsworthiness primarily because of the rarity of such an event. It is often the way elements of predictability work together with unexpectedness that is critical then.

7. CONTINUITY

Once a story has entered the news agenda, it may gain sufficient public interest to give it the momentum to continue to be newsworthy. This can prompt news providers to allocate significant space to ongoing stories even if there have been few developments. In 2007, the disappearance of a young child, Madeleine McCann, dominated headlines across the UK for several months. Even in the absence of major developments in the case, news providers continued to prioritise the story by focusing on the behaviour and public statements of McCann's parents and a mixture of speculation and hearsay. The level of interest generated by the initial coverage made it imperative for outlets to continue to find something to say about the story.

Variations on this news value have been emphasised by other commentators. Rock (1973) emphasises that, once a story has been ratified as news through inclusion by one provider, it often will be picked up by other outlets, reflecting the professional influence of journalists on one another and the desire not to miss out on a story that has momentum. The point arguably has become even more important today, with online and television news providers often influenced by one another throughout the day as well as by the morning's newspaper front pages. And in the digital age, particular stories can gain or retain newsworthiness through the visible momentum they develop through mentions on social media too (Grzywinska and Borden 2012).

8. COMPOSITION

The notion of composition emphasises the need for bulletins or newspapers to fit together as a whole. Providers may seek to complement stories with others that connect to the same theme or, conversely, to achieve a balance of types of story, which may mean giving prominence to some domestic stories on a heavy foreign news day, for example, or slotting in something light and trivial on the day of a big political story.

9. ELITE NATIONS

Quite simply, it is suggested that events that relate to the most powerful nations in the world are more likely to be covered than those taking place in poorer, less influential places.

10. ELITE PEOPLE

Similarly, stories about powerful or famous people are more newsworthy, on the whole, than those who are poor or unknown because the actions of the former are liable to be of greater consequence or interest. Celebrity stories have become particularly valuable because they encapsulate extraordinary levels of wealth, power and influence at the same time as having proximity and relevance to the lives of ordinary people (from relationships to babies to weight loss, for example), engendering identification and empathy (see Cashmore 2014).

11. PERSONIFICATION

Personification refers to the extent to which a story can be represented through a focus on the intentions, actions or emotions of individuals. Rather than emphasising the determination of life by structural forces outside people's control, news tends to present a world dominated by individual morals, decisions and behaviour. Such a focus is felt to engender identification and emotional engagement from users in a way that emphasis on broader societal structures cannot. The notion of personification helps explain the increasing emphasis on human interest stories, including those about crime, celebrities, disasters and the over-coming of adversity – as well as the tendency to tell stories about structures or policies through an emphasis on individuals.

12. NEGATIVITY

Finally, Galtung and Ruge argue that negative news stories dominate the news agenda because they tend to fit well with other news values. Negative stories, they argue, often concern discrete short-term events, are easier to present in an unambiguous manner and tend to involve rare or unexpected phenomena. A fall in a nation's crime figures may well receive less coverage than a particular one-off criminal incident on the same day. As well as being a negative rather than a positive crime story, such an incident is likely to fit better with established expectations, offer greater potential with respect to personalisation and form a self-contained story with clear villains and victims.

OUT OF DATE?

Since Galtung and Ruge developed their explanation, other theorists have sought to adapt or expand on their schema (e.g. Harcup and O'Neil 2001) while some have dismissed their work as unsuited to the analysis of twentieth century news (Brighton and Foy 2007). Amalgamating the categories developed by a range of scholars, including Galtung and Ruge, Harrison (2006) identifies the following largely self-explanatory categories as of particular importance to story selection: availability of pictures or film; short dramatic occurrences; novelty value; capable of simple reporting; grand scale; negative; unexpected; expected; relevance/meaning; similar events already in news; balanced programme; elite people/ nations; personal or human interest framing.

The value of more recent work in clarifying existing themes and identifying the importance to contemporary news of criteria such as visual imagery and recency/immediacy is clear. We might also want to consider adding the theme of *sexual appeal or intrigue* as a distinct category in itself, particularly in light of the orientation and content of click-driven online news sites. Nevertheless, it is striking how closely compatible Harrison's amalgamated list is with the original Galtung and Ruge model, something that arguably renders suggestions that the latter is entirely unsuited to contemporary news wide of the mark.

CASE STUDY: MAJOR TERRORIST ATTACK STORIES

The biggest news story around the world in the last few decades was the terrorist attacks on New York and Washington on September 11th, 2001. The newsworthiness of the story may seem obvious, but it serves as a valuable case study with which to illustrate the continuing usefulness of much of Galtung and Ruge's model. A clear set of events unfolded in a manner compatible with the frequency of publication of newspapers and the desire for immediacy that characterises online and television news coverage. The amplitude and unexpected-ness of the events was enormous, as was their potential for negativity – the tallest buildings in the world were destroyed, the most powerful country in the world was being attacked, the explosions, fires and falling buildings were as dramatic and spectacular as one could imagine and the human costs were extensive. The event had the potential to be presented in simple, unambiguous terms and also had a clear personal angle, with respect to the presen-tation of violent, destructive attackers and helpless, distraught victims. The event involved an elite nation, a variety of elite people and offered cultural proximity for some nations and relevance for others. The story also involved elements of predictability, cohering with some Western stereotypes of extremist Muslim fanatics, for example. And it offered a clear dem-onstration of *continuity*, the slightest new development or speculation dominating the news agenda for days, weeks and months afterwards. Perhaps the only factor it failed to satisfy is *composition*, as the story was so big that its relationship to other stories was of little con-sequence. It became what Liebes (1998) terms a 'disaster marathon', in that real-time news devoted most if not all of their time to a single unfolding story for several days.

More recently, the terrorist attacks on Paris in November 2015 gave rise to prominent and ongoing coverage that often took 'disaster marathon' form. Although the attacks were smaller in scale and less visibly spectacular than the September 11th attacks, they satisfied many of the same news values. Interestingly, however, the coverage of the Paris attacks also generated public debate about the priorities of Western news providers. Of particular concern to some critics was the stark contrast between wall-to-wall coverage of Paris and minimal coverage of a terrorist bomb attack orchestrated by the same group in Lebanon a day earlier. Both attacks had claimed scores of lives and tapped into similar news values, but the stark difference in levels of coverage illustrated the extent to which news agendas can be determined by a combination of perceived cultural proximity and the elite status of nations such as France. The disparity also demonstrated the importance of unexpected-ness as a news value in that, for complex reasons, in much Western public perception, a deadly terrorist attack in France felt more unusual, surprising and arresting than an attack on Lebanon.

CONSTRUCTING STORIES

According to Bell, journalists are 'the professional story tellers of our age' (1991: 147). Having selected particular events on the basis of their story-potential, they and their editors make a series of decisions about how to turn them into a good story, arranging headline, commentary text, images, illustrations and/or film and/or audio footage accordingly. Each element will connect to the broader *angle* on the story the outlet is seeking to achieve. As well as determining what will make a good story in the first place, news values influence the version of events constructed. An event selected on the basis of its potential as a human interest story will be represented with particular emphasis on this angle. Conversely, a story which fits awkwardly with some news values may be constructed in a manner which attempts to compensate for this. Consider the increasing focus on individual personalities in political news stories, for example.

Semiology and discourse analysis (see Chapter 4) can help us understand how different elements of news stories work together to create a particular angle or impression. Headlines, images, footage, music and commentary all can be viewed as sets of signifiers that invoke particular connotations, while the written or spoken language used can be analysed with respect to vocabulary, syntax, grammar and other features. It can be particularly helpful to think about news content as sets of paradigmatic selections and syntagmatic combinations (Hartley 1982).

Focused on comparing each element of a news report with alternatives that might have been used, paradigmatic analysis reminds us that, for every headline, caption, photo or interview quote included, others were rejected. Let's take the example of images. One of the best-known media clichés is that the camera never lies. Yet each image captures a selective viewpoint and editors often select one or two images from a range of possibles. Paradigmatic analysis helps us understand such decisions and their impact on the interpretations readers are being invited to make. If a murder story includes a large black and white close-up of the scowling face of the perpetrator, we might ask why a close-up rather than a medium or distanced shot, why a scowling face rather than a smiling one, why black and white reproduction rather than colour and, indeed, why an image of the perpetrator rather than, say, the head of the police investigation.

The use of language in news stories is equally important. Headlines identify the outlet's main angle and influence our interpretation of the story. They can also be analysed using a paradigmatic approach to discourse analysis focused on the selection of words. If presented with the hypothetical headline 'Terrorist Killed by US Drone Strike' we might seek to better understand the likely connotations by comparing the words present with possible alternatives. Why not 'bomb' instead of 'strike' for example, why 'terrorist' rather than 'father' or 'residents', and why 'killed' rather than 'assassinated'? The idea here is not necessarily to infer that the words used are 'wrong' but rather to understand what impact the choices made have upon preferred meanings.

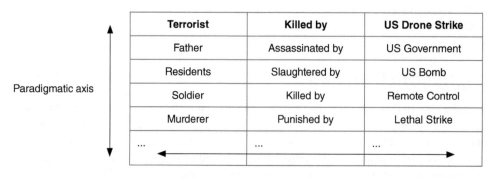

Terrorist	Killed by	US Drone Strike
Father	Assassinated by	US Government
Residents	Slaughtered by	US Bomb
Soldier	Killed by	Remote Control
Murderer	Punished by	Lethal Strike
...	...	...

Paradigmatic axis

Syntagmatic axis

Figure 7.2   Simplified illustration of syntagmatic and paradigmatic news analysis

Syntagmatic analysis, meanwhile, involves an assessment of the semantic impact of the way story components have been arranged and combined. Therefore, having examined each of the words in our headline separately, we then need to consider how they work together (see Figure 7.2). The term 'strike', it could be argued, implies a clean, precise attack, something reinforced by the emphasis on the single 'terrorist' who has been killed, rather than, for example, any other people who happened to be in the vehicle, building or area. As well as inferring a single casualty, the emphasis on 'terrorist' serves to dehumanise the person identified, reduce them to the status of inhuman enemy and protect the audience from mixed feelings about the event. The decision to use 'killed' rather than 'assassinated', meanwhile, avoids connotations of possible illegality. Taken together, it could be argued the headline infers a precisely targeted attack with a single casualty whose terrorist status justifies the attack. The audience, it could be argued, is protected from worrying about who else might have been hurt, injured or otherwise affected and reassured as to the precision, cleanliness and, perhaps, justified nature of contemporary warfare as carried out by the US. This example is a hypothetical one and it is, of course, vital to understand that such interpretations are to an extent subjective. Nevertheless, it is reflective of numerous recent media stories involving US interventions in Iraq and Syria and also connects to academic analyses of previous wars, including the Gulf Wars of 1990 and 2003, in which US and UK authorities sought to promote the use of terminology such as 'surgical strikes' that inferred the cleanliness and precision of contemporary military technologies as a means to maintain public support (Allen and Zelizer 2004).

On a broader scale, syntagmatic analysis emphasises the context into which individual components are placed. A piece of video footage may be open to a range of interpretations, but simultaneous audio commentary or on-screen text often serves to clarify. The presence of on-screen captions such as 'Striking Back' and 'War on Terror' which accompanied footage of post-September 11th US military action in Afghanistan in 2001 helped frame such pictures as depicting a just response to terrorist provocation rather than, for example, an attack on a sovereign nation. And if a black and white mug-shot of a perpetrator of violent crime is juxtaposed with a colour picture of the victim smiling with her family, then the combination may contribute to a powerful narrative involving an innocent, family-oriented victim slain by a ruthless, heartless villain.

Because news representations of events revolve around story-telling, narrative analysis can also be valuable in making sense of them. News stories often approximate elements of the characters and structure of fictional stories (Lule 2001). When reporting crime stories, media often strive to construct idyllic representations of victims, whose normal, happy family life is cruelly disrupted or ended by an inherently cruel, villainous perpetrator. Such a depiction activates news values of clarity and predictability through drawing on deeply embedded conventions of fiction running through countless fairy tales, children's cartoons and movies. The ability to replicate elements of familiar fictional plots is part of what makes stories attractive to media as well as an influence on the version of such stories we are presented with. In addition to the victim and the villain, the hero is another favoured character, part of what makes rescue stories – particularly if they involve women, children or cute animals – particularly newsworthy.

DIFFERENCES BETWEEN OUTLETS

One of the criticisms of attempts to develop universal sets of news values is that they can gloss over potentially significant differences between one outlet and another that affect both the selection and construction of stories.

MEDIUM

News on outlets that allow greater frequency of update tends to be dominated by recency and immediacy. Covering breaking stories faster than one's competitors and continually updating content is an increasing priority for online news sites and television news channels. Both seek to generate an emphasis on fast-moving real-time coverage, the increasing use of regularly updated live-blogs on some news sites replicating the continuous coverage that characterises news channels. In contrast, print newspapers provide a more structured, tightly prepared presentation, with particular emphasis, where possible, on carefully planned exclusives. As a result of not being confined to a serial real-time stream, both newspapers and their online siblings also can cover a far larger overall number of stories and features than television or radio news and many have responded to declining print circulation by increasing their overall quantity and range of content.

News coverage on outlets that enable effective visual communication, meanwhile, tends to place particular emphasis on this (Harrison 2006). In particular, the availability of enticing footage of dramatic or emotional events often results in prioritisation of a story and, particularly on television news, journalists will prioritise visual angles on stories they cover. Visual emphasis on sexualised female images of one form or another is a further notable feature driving story selection and construction on some online news sites, including – though not limited to – *Mail Online*, whose highly successful business model relies at least in part on the display on the right hand side of the site of regularly updated images of conventionally attractive celebrities and other women in revealing clothes. While also a feature of some offline outlets, such imagery has become of particular importance online, acting as effective 'click-bait' on a medium that is saturated with content and that allows precise measurement of numbers of views for each unit of content.

STYLE AND MARKET POSITION

News outlets of the same medium also can differ in respect of their style and approach. In the UK, distinctions often are drawn between populist 'red-top' newspapers like *The Sun* and *The Daily Mirror* and highbrow or 'quality' publications like *The Daily Telegraph*. The former adopt an informal, opinionated style, place strong emphasis on enticing illustrations and are oriented to personalised human interest stories, celebrity gossip, sports and the construction of sensation and emotion. Arguably this amounts to a particularly strict and intensive application of the kind of news values outlined earlier. In contrast 'quality' newspapers have been able to apply at least some of these news values somewhat more loosely, placing emphasis – at least some of the time – on in-depth coverage of complex politics, financial and international stories and adopting a somewhat less individualised tone.

Such distinctions with respect to style and approach reflect the need to deliver consistent, clearly defined and loyal audiences to advertisers. Broadly speaking, more populist news providers tend to be associated with audiences of a lower social class position on average and, consistent with this, go out of their way to orient their presentation, style and subject matter to 'ordinary' people. Importantly, though, readers of popular formats also tend to be more demographically diverse than those of high-brow providers, which are dominated by highly educated professionals. Curran and Seaton (2010: 96) explain that this reflects long-standing differences in funding, with quality papers reliant on delivering narrow, high-spending, elite audiences to advertisers willing to pay a premium, and the popular press more focused on attracting advertisers through quantity of readers.

POLITICAL STANCE

With the exception of those operating under statutory requirements to be balanced (UK television news, for example), news providers are often associated with a particular political orientation and this too affects news values. A pro-Republican outlet in the US may devote greater space to a story about a Democrat political scandal than a Republican one, for example. Editorial positioning forms an additional element of the targeting of a loyal readership, but it can also be influenced by the views and interests of proprietors. Few would regularly adopt a position at odds with their readers, but as we saw in Chapter 3, a succession of media 'barons', from William Hearst to Rupert Murdoch, have used their newspapers as a means to promote their own political agendas (Eldridge et al. 1997).

SIMILARITIES: BACK TO BIAS AND IDEOLOGY?

In spite of the importance of such differences, if we consider the range of conceivable versions of news at a given time, then arguably it is the similarities between outlets that are more noteworthy. For this reason, the efforts of Galtung and Ruge and others retain value in seeking to map out the priorities that underlie so much journalism. Such approaches, however, do not go as far as some Marxist thinkers, who argue, not only that news collectively presents a monolithic and selective version of the world, but that this representation is systematically oriented towards a bourgeois, neo-liberal perspective. Whilst they do lament the 'distorted' view of the world created by news media, Galtung and Ruge interpret this as a complex set of biases attributable to journalistic procedures and priorities. For Stuart Hall (1973: 182), such identification of what he terms 'the formal elements in news making' is a useful step, but one that fails to identify the ways news values trigger, reinforce or 'index' the circulation of dominant ways of thinking about the world.

News values, from this viewpoint, are rooted in ideology: they emanate from and reinforce an existing consensus controlled by the powerful (see Chapter 6). We might argue, for example, that an emphasis on personalisation in news is rooted in pro-establishment, neo-liberal ideas about individual choice, sovereignty and responsibility that serve to obscure the ways structures of inequality constrain individual lives. Likewise, dominant ideas may be strengthened by a tendency to prioritise cultural proximity, to tap into what confirms existing expectations and indeed to focus on celebrity gossip, sex or spectacular negative events. Our engagement with extraordinary murders, explosions and disasters, alongside our addiction to the spectacular intrigue of the lives of the rich and famous, serves to reinforce the normality and desirability of the everyday status quo within our living rooms, it might be argued, and to distract us from the policies or agendas that constrain our lives.

CLASS BIAS

Marxists, then, argue that the selection and construction of stories reflects systematic political and class bias as much as it does formal news values. In the 1970s and 80s, the Glasgow University Media Group (GUMG) claimed through a series of powerful content analysis studies that UK news consistently favoured capitalist, middle-class messages that reinforced the existing political order (1976a; 1976b; 1982). Television coverage of a series of industrial disputes was accused of bias in favour of employers and against striking workers. Greater attention is deemed to have been afforded, for example, to the negative impacts of strikes on the economy or consumers, than to the poor pay and working conditions against which workers were protesting. Also, while striking workers were typically depicted in the context of the 'event' imagery of picket lines and protests, employers appeared as part of what were deemed 'factual' sequences, through footage of them working in offices. Employers and government ministers, meanwhile, are deemed to have been given an easier time by interviewers than trade union representatives. For the GUMG, this represented just one example of the exclusion of working-class viewpoints by middle-class journalists who had little connection with or understanding of them (1982). Given this inevitable class bias, as the GUMG saw it, the aspirations of the country's then television news providers to impartiality are regarded as an ideological mask – a means of parading subjective class ideology as objective reporting.

Having carried out his own analysis during the same period, however, Harrison (1985) rejects the GUMG's accusations of class bias, arguing that such assertions were themselves biased by the group's Marxist understandings of the world. The GUMG's content analysis is deemed to have been selective and its criticisms questionable. While it is far from easy to arbitrate between such competing versions of the same coverage, there are also some other criticisms of the GUMG that are worthy of consideration. Nick Stevenson (2002), for example, questions what he deems an ambiguous position on the question of objectivity, whereby news was seemingly attacked by the GUMG both for its lack of objectivity and its quest for objectivity. Absolute neutrality may indeed be unattainable, argues Stevenson, but an aspiration to treat issues in a fair-minded, balanced way may be preferable to the abandonment of such goals. A further problem with the GUMG's analysis, identified by Stevenson (2002), is their emphasis on the personal middle-class background of journalists as the primary explanation for biased coverage. While personal background may indeed have been of some significance, the extent of the emphasis on it appears to neglect the role of the institutional environment, working practices and priorities under which journalists operate. If Galtung and Ruge underestimated the connection between news values and broader ideology, then the Glasgow group's approach to ideology and bias may have benefitted from greater attention to the kind of operational factors that drive news priorities.

INSTITUTIONAL BIAS

Other theorists *have* attributed biased or ideological meanings to the way news providers are owned, financed, controlled and operated. As we have seen, Herman and Chomsky's analysis of the filtering of media by powerful owners, advertisers and interest groups focuses especially on news and 'factual' content (see Chapter 6). According to this view, subordinate or oppositional events, issues and voices are excluded because the news production system is controlled by, paid for, fed by and centred upon vested interests.

Sure enough, news is overwhelmingly controlled by large-scale and increasingly concentrated corporate interests. In 2008, two thirds of UK national newspaper sales were controlled by just three corporations (Curran and Seaton 2010). In turn, news providers themselves are reliant for much of their content upon a small number of news agencies, or 'wire services' that make money through generating and providing content to subscribing outlets. The majority of international news originates from just three of these: Reuters, Associated Press and Agence France Presse, who each have numerous local branches around the world. A UK study by Lewis and colleagues (2008) found that 49% of press stories had originated from copy supplied by news agencies.

A further vital source of news copy is provided by press releases and other activities engineered by public relations (PR) organisations seeking to promote the interests of their clients, who include individuals, corporations, politicians or other organisations. The objective of press releases is to feed ready-made stories to journalists in the hope of getting good publicity for their client. By writing-up events, product launches, announcements or research findings in a length and style suited to news, PR professionals make it as simple as possible for journalists to complete and file the story. In a scenario in which it is becoming harder to make news profitable and where journalists are expected to produce 'more and more with fewer and fewer resources' (Davis 2013: 96), the number of stories that originate from press releases and other PR activities has sharply increased. Lewis and colleagues' aforementioned UK study (2008) found that 19% of press and 17% of broadcast news consisted of entirely or mainly reproduced public relations material, while McChesney and Nichols (2010) suggest that 50% of US news originates from press releases. That so much of the news we read is originating from the paid-for marketing materials of vested interests has significant implications for notions of journalistic independence and implies further concentration of news agendas in the hands of the powerful (Davis 2013).

The impacts of reliance on advertising, meanwhile, look set to become more stark as news shifts further away from direct consumer payment and towards online open access. It isn't only that '"don't bite the hand that feeds you" is written on every newsroom wall', as Bob Franklin (1997: 95) puts it, but also that advertiser funding has a broader influence on the kinds of news that are profitable. In the print newspaper market, the rewards for delivering high-spending premium consumers to advertisers has created a market-bias towards bourgeois-oriented political news. Curran and Seaton (2010) point out that, in 2009, half the UK's daily newspapers were competing for just 25% of newspaper readers, such is the premium paid by advertisers for access to this affluent minority. The situation appears to be similar for online news where, in 2012, the published cost per thousand readers of a mid-page banner advertisement on the *Financial Times'* online site was over eight times higher than that of *The Mirror* and four times that of the highly successful *Mail Online* site (Jackson 2012). For Curran and Seaton, such patterns lead to reinforcement of inequalities of power. Serious, detailed coverage of politics is largely confined to publications oriented to elite consumers who, as a consequence, are more informed and influential than the majority of readers, who are left with populist journalism whose financial model requires audience maximisation through sensationalised coverage of crime, celebrity, sex, sport and personalised forms of politics (Curran and Seaton 2010: 91).

THE POWERFUL INFLUENCING THE POWERFUL

Importantly, the ideological influence of news organisations not only involves the possibility of directly influencing audiences. Every bit as important is the direct influence they can have over politicians and other powerful figures as a result of their *perceived* ability to affect public opinion. In the UK, the perceived power of *The Sun* to influence voting behaviour, for example, has prompted politicians to go to considerable lengths to secure its support. *The Sun*'s decision to support David Cameron's Conservative Party in the 2010 General Election was accompanied by extensive interaction between Cameron and senior figures in the then News International both before and after he became Prime Minister in 2010 (Gaber 2012). In particular, Cameron developed close relationships with Rebekah Brooks, then Chief Executive of News International, and Andy Coulson, former editor of *The News of the World*, who became Cameron's Communications Director. Such a situation renders it hard to dismiss the notion that news can serve powerful interests.

In the UK, the links between news organisations and powerful political and public figures have been illuminated by the Leveson Inquiry, set up in 2011 following revelations of widespread illegal phone-hacking by major newspapers, including *The Sun*'s then sister paper *The News of the World*. For several years, the newspaper had been hacking the phones of politicians, celebrities and members of the public as a means to get exclusive stories. More significantly, politicians, police and others had failed to speak out or properly investigate this, in spite of clear evidence as to the scale of illegal activity. What apparently amounted to a collective cover-up appears to have reflected a culture of carefully cultivated personal relationships between News International staff and high ranking police and politicians – alongside an intense concern among the latter two groups to manage press coverage of themselves and their organisations by maximising positive stories and minimising negative ones.

For, as well as proving invaluable friends, powerful newspaper groups can make career-threatening enemies for public figures, not least if they have access to private phone records. The perception that newspapers can make or break political parties, institutional reputations and individual careers, then, had apparently enabled the country's most powerful newspaper group to wield the most extensive influence (Gaber 2012). Ultimately, the phone-hacking scandal resulted in the resignations of Andy Coulson, Rebekah Brooks and others, the closure of the *News of the World* and substantial embarrassment for its parent company. There was also much talk of tighter regulation of newspapers, with the Leveson Report eventually recommending in 2013 a form of self-regulation underpinned by the state. A few years later, however, public interest in the case has died down, attempts to create tighter regulation have foundered and few believe anything to have substantially changed in the relationship between newspapers and politicians.

INFOTAINMENT AND THE PERSUIT OF CLICKS

For some commentators, concern relates as much to the notion that news is becoming increasingly superficial as to the identification of explicit bias or ideology (Gans 2004). There has for some decades been concern about the light, entertainment-oriented approach of overtly populist outlets such as the UK's 'red-top' newspapers, but more recently concern has focused on the apparent drift of *all* news outlets towards such an agenda. 'Quality' newspapers, for example, have been accused of responding to declining circulation figures by placing greater and greater emphasis upon sports coverage, entertainment news and a range of consumer and lifestyle issues (Barnett 1998; Temple 2006).

Similar concerns have been expressed in relation to what is sometimes deemed a populist shift in television news in recent decades (Dahlgren 1995; Langer 1998). The special status afforded by US networks to news as a subsidised flagship of brand prestige was diluted by the intensification of competition brought about by multi-channel television in the 1990s. Increased pressure for news to be profitable in its own right prompted a transformation towards so-called *infotainment*. Informing audiences about world events in a thorough, trustworthy, fair-minded manner was no longer sufficient – they also needed to be entertained. Emphasis shifted towards those serious stories with the greatest immediate visual, emotional and human interest potential, alongside an increasing proportion of lighter content such as sports and entertainment. According to Postman and Powers (1992), the underlying concern of news producers increasingly was to try to 'grab you before you zap away to another news show' (cited in Langer 1998: 4). A few years later Bob Franklin explored the extent to which the minutiae of television news was becoming driven by viewing figures, quoting a senior UK news executive as follows:

> I know on a minute by minute basis what time people turn off and on during the previous night's news. I'm having that developed into a schematic analysis for the production team to see, so we are more and more focused on the maximization of the audience ratings. (cited in Franklin 1997: 256)

There can be little doubt that, since that time, such pressures have intensified. An emphasis on presentation and tempo has become particularly paramount, with pre-recorded reports as concise and fast-moving as possible and snappy exchanges between presenters and reporters preceding rapid movement onto the next story. The sense of urgency is further strengthened by a focus on live, breaking news. Bold 'LIVE' captions, rolling on-screen tickers summarising latest developments and speculative two-ways with a range of reporters, witnesses or commentators at the scene are intended to captivate audiences into the feeling of watching events as they happen, alongside dramatic, spectacular and emotional footage wherever possible.

In recent years, audience-maximisation pressures are becoming particularly acute in the case of online news sites, where the availability of precise information on the number of clicks, likes and social media mentions generated by each image, video or article is beginning to drive news agendas as never before. As part of what Anderson (2011) refers to as the 'culture of the click', homepages are constantly updated and reorganised, while new stories are commissioned according to data about what audiences are viewing and sharing. Such data are becoming integral to newsroom cultures and priorities, leading to increasing pressure to balance existing journalistic values with the relentless pursuit of clicks (Lee et al. 2014). Alongside a broader pressure on journalists to produce more content and on outlets to deliver stories relating to audience trends as fast as possible, such pressures are argued to be contributing to a climate in which journalistic originality, depth, care and quality are being sacrificed in favour of content that is quick, inexpensive, new and immediately appealing (Davies 2008).

Perhaps unsurprisingly, meanwhile, studies indicate that most-clicked stories tend frequently to fall within what some term 'soft news', which does not address public affairs or politics (Bokzkovski and Peer 2011). In the case of *Mail Online*'s site, the formula for success has centred, amongst other things, on a stream of constantly updated celebrity stories accompanied by images of attractive, largely uncovered female bodies on a right hand panel, something that contrasts at least in some respects with sister paper, *The Daily Mail*'s more conservative agenda. And although much of their emphasis remains on more weighty stories, even more 'serious' providers such as the *Guardian* usually feature a substantial number of images of celebrities and sports personalities on their main home pages designed to attract attention and clicks – and the effectiveness of these in generating views is clear from the outlet's constantly updated list of 'most viewed' stories.

The difficulty with all this, for some critics, is that, much though they may enjoy being entertained by this fast-paced emphasis on spectacle, personality, entertainment, sex and emotion, audiences may be unlikely to develop from such infotainment a useful critical understanding of the social and political world. As well as becoming increasingly distracted by trivial matters emanating from lifestyle, celebrity and sports journalism, people's understanding of those serious issues touched on may increasingly centre on the immediate emotion and spectacle of incidents, rather than the broader picture of which they are a part, or so it is feared. As Peter Dahlgren (1995: 56) put it in relation to television news two decades ago: 'these production values of rawness and immediacy… do not necessarily enhance our understanding: the close-ups on trees may obscure the forest.'

CONCLUSION: SIGNS OF HOPE?

There are some important criticisms we might make of those who bemoan the ideological role of news or the perceived drift towards infotainment. Notions of news and news values as rooted in ideology are subject to the criticisms of broader Marxist approaches to ideology outlined in Chapter 6. Not only can they treat viewers as largely passive dupes, manipulated by dominant meanings, but they also may under-estimate the increasing diversity of versions of news on offer to contemporary consumers. The overall differences between the editorial stances of mainstream outlets may not amount to as much as we might hope, but especially if one takes into account the increasing range of columnists who contribute to the online versions of some newspapers, it would be wrong to say that the version of the world we are presented with is entirely monolithic.

Meanwhile, contemporary digital and online environments are playing host to a massive increase in the range of alternative sources of news and comment available, from sites oriented towards the perspectives of ethnic or sexual minority populations to individual bloggers focusing on a range of issues and concerns. Bringing together news making and dissemination technologies, mobile media such as phones and tablets, alongside other digital devices, increasingly are enabling ordinary members of the public to contribute to, produce, disseminate or analyse news in a range of ways. From distributing eye-witness images to news organisations, to publishing DIY video or blog reports on events, such activities are sometimes referred to as *citizen journalism* and they play an increasing role in the range of versions of world events available to us (Allan and Thorsen 2009; Gillmor 2006).

Particular attention in recent years has been focused upon the role of the exchange of comments, images, stories and footage on social media as an influence on various stages of the news process. Not only do newspapers closely gauge and respond to social media mentions of stories, but it is also increasingly common for stories to develop independently via a combination of citizen journalism and social media sharing – and for news organisations to cover such stories only once they have gained grassroots momentum. In 2014, news outlets across the world ended up covering a story about prominent UK scientist Tim Hunt making apparently derogatory comments about female scientists at a conference. The story had come to light as a result of one of the delegates at the conference tweeting about what he had said and subsequent retweeting and discussion on Twitter, Facebook and other platforms on a massive scale. As it happens, there are ongoing controversies surrounding the accuracy and impact of this particular story – something that perhaps draws attention to potential difficulties with the notion of news generated from social media. Nevertheless, the propensity for the public to distribute stories and exert collective influence over the news agendas of major providers is viewed by some as a form of democratisation (Shirky 2008).

It is equally important to remember that, on occasion, mainstream media outlets, themselves, have brought about change through holding those in power to account, something which sits uneasily with more deterministic models of ideology. *The Washington Post* and *New York Times*, among other publications, played a key role in the exposure of a US political scandal known as Watergate, which ultimately prompted the Republican president, Richard Nixon, to resign. Meanwhile, although the episode demonstrated plenty that was wrong about the power of news providers, the UK phone-hacking scandal was itself exposed as a result of ongoing investigative journalism from the *Guardian* newspaper. That newspaper was also involved, alongside the *New York Times*, in reporting an incendiary series of revelations about the surveillance activities of US and UK intelligence agencies originating from whistle-blower and fugitive Edward Snowden in 2013. Those who subscribe to notions of news as ideology may claim, with some justification, that such instances relate to the exposure of selected excesses, while leaving broader systems of power unscathed. Nevertheless, they illustrate that the relations between news providers and other powerful groups can sometimes be far from cosy or amiable.

Though there is some merit in their observations, those who criticise the perceived 'dumbing down' of television news, meanwhile, sometimes appear to assume that news either was, could or should ever be an untarnished source of objective, rational information (Langer 1998). As we have seen, news is always partial and biased as a result of the circumstances in which it is produced. This includes the version of news often longed for by critics of dumbing down, which tend to represent a particular rationalist, dispassionate and, some would argue, bourgeois approach to the world (Temple 2006). In implicitly lusting after this elite form of news, Temple argues, such critics fail to recognise the potential for contemporary news formats to engage members of the population who would otherwise be excluded.

Some years earlier, Fiske (1991b) argued that if ordinary people are to engage with news and think about events then producers must find ways to appeal to their tastes and sensibilities, something that may include rejecting out-dated paternalist approaches. According to this view, popular news may sometimes amount not to 'dumbing down' but 'reaching out' (Barnett 1998). Rather than dismissing popular news altogether, commentators such as Fiske, Temple and Dahlgren call for such providers to balance their emphasis on popular appeal with responsible, informative coverage of matters of importance (Dahlgren 2009).

None of this means that the concerns of critics of ideology or of infotainment are illusory or insignificant, however. The news values that govern the selection and construction of stories do result in the overall dominance of a restricted set of understandings of the world and, for better or worse, tend to be supportive of existing structures of power. Likewise, it is hard to dispute that the increasing focus of various news outlets on keeping audiences entertained and maximising clicks has resulted in an emphasis on immediacy and instant appeal and, at least sometimes, a reduction in depth and detail. It is important that academics continue to subject news to critical analysis in these and other respects. Such criticism should ask how representations are selected and constructed, hold the versions of the world with which we are presented to account and contribute to our ability to distinguish between more and less useful versions of news. As well as being subject to controversy and debate, however, such judgements will always be relative ones, for ultimately all news is borne of selection, manufacture and bias.

QUESTIONS/EXERCISES

1   How do the following terms relate to the process of news construction: gate-keeping; agenda setting; news values; selection; construction?

2   Visit the homepage of a major news outlet and assess the way the most prominent stories are positioned and covered in relation to Galtung and Ruge's list of news values. Which news values are particularly important for each story and are there any that appear particularly consistently?

3   Find an example of a crime story in a newspaper or on a news website. In what ways does the way the story is constructed draw upon familiar narrative structures or character types?

4   a) What is Hall's criticism of Galtung and Ruge's approach to news values?

    b) What criticisms can be made of Marxist approaches to news?

    c) Why should the increasing shift of news towards infotainment be the cause of concern? Are such concerns justified?

5   Does the increasing relationship between news and social media represent a positive or a negative development do you think? Why?

SUGGESTED FURTHER READING

Allan, S. and Thorsen, E. (eds) (2009) *Citizen Journalism: Global Perspectives*. New York: Peter Lang – Collection of chapters focused upon different manifestations of 'citizen journalism'.

Cohen, S. and Young, J. (eds) (1973) *The Manufacture of News: Social Problems, Deviance and The Mass Media*. London: Constable – Classic collection on news, including crucial contributions by Galtung and Ruge and by Hall.

Glasgow University Media Group (1976a) *Bad News*. London: Routledge and Kegan Paul – Famous content analysis of UK news coverage which accused the country's main broadcasters of systematic class bias.

Lee, A., Lewis, S. and Powers, M. (2014) 'Audience Clicks and News Placement: A Study of Time-Lagged Influence in Online Journalism', *Communication Research,* 41(4): 505–30 – Recent quantitative analysis of the significance of the measurement of clicks in the placement and prioritisation of news stories.

Temple, M. (2006) 'Dumbing Down is Good For You', *British Politics,* 1(2): 257–73. URL: www.palgrave-journals.com/bp/journal/v1/n2/pdf/4200018a.pdf – Defends the popularisation of news on the basis that contemporary formats are more inclusive and less elitist than traditional approaches.

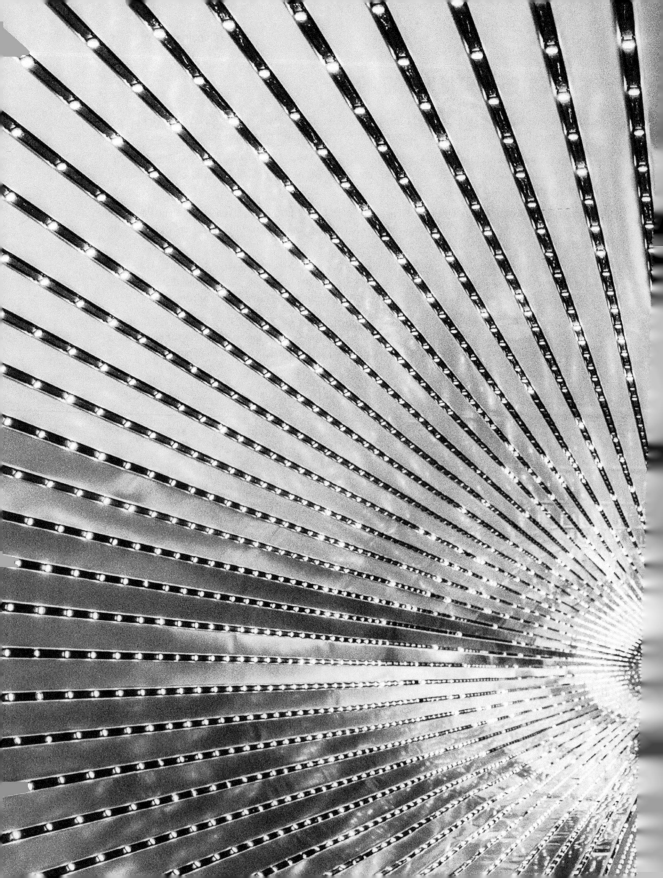

CHAPTER 8

PUBLIC SERVICE OR PERSONAL ENTERTAINMENT? CONTROLLING MEDIA ORIENTATION

FOCAL POINTS

- Competing views on what media are for and how they should be controlled
- History and principles of public service broadcasting
- Arguments about government influence, elitism and questions of quality
- Debates about censorship of offensive/harmful content, including sex and violence
- The dominance of free market approaches to media in digital environments

INTRODUCTION

As media become ever-more integrated into our lives, fundamental questions about what they are for and how societies should use them are of paramount importance. With a particular focus on broadcasting and its evolution into the digital era, this chapter addresses contrasting perspectives on the purpose of media and the principles that should guide how they are controlled. We'll contrast public service models, which endorse government intervention to ensure media are used as a resource for the collective well-being of society, with consumerist approaches that place emphasis on individual choice and corporate profit. We'll also examine a distinct but related set of arguments about the extent to which controversial forms of media content should be censored in order to prevent harm to society. As well as closely examining such arguments, the chapter draws on examples to illustrate the way such perspectives have influenced the operation of media in the past and present.

PUBLIC SERVICE BROADCASTING

Advocates of public service models of media argue that mass communication systems are crucial resources that should be used in a manner which benefits society as a whole. From this point of view, governments should increase the prospects of media being used for the public good, rather than leaving control of such technologies solely in the hands of profit-driven corporations. The approach has its roots in a mixture of moral conservative and social democratic ideals. For its conservative supporters, what initially was known as public service broadcasting implied controlling radio and television to protect the moral fibre of society. For the majority of contemporary advocates, however, the emphasis is on the designation of television and radio, alongside newer forms of digital mass communication, as vital collective resources whose potential benefits to society cannot be realised by free market approaches. We would not leave our national education system in the unfettered control of the commercial sector, goes this social democratic argument, so neither should we surrender the operation of mass media to such interests (Webster 2002).

REITH AND THE BBC

Public service broadcasting (hereafter PSB) was pioneered in the UK where, after a brief period of commercial control, the BBC became a public corporation charged with informing, educating and entertaining the public. The personal vision of the corporation's first director general, John Reith, played an important part in the development of an approach to broadcasting oriented to improving the knowledge, taste and moral awareness of audiences and enhancing the collective well-being and cohesion of the nation. The notion of universality was key: in order to foster national unity and enlightenment, the BBC should have a monopoly on broadcasting and its mix of programming should be available identically across the nation. Reith was equally adamant that the BBC must be protected from commercial involvement or competition which, in his view, would result in an unprincipled quest to maximise audiences. To have consigned an invention so extraordinary as radio to the pursuit of profit and cheap entertainment 'would have been a prostitution of its powers and an insult to the character and intelligence of the people' (1925, cited in Franklin 1997: 119).

Crucially, Reith sought to challenge his audience, providing them with what was beneficial rather than pandering to the easier entertainment they might have chosen for themselves. 'It is occasionally indicated to us', he proclaimed, 'that we are apparently setting out to give the public what we think they need – and not what they want, but few know what they want and very few what they need' (1924, cited in McDonnell 1991). Reith's opposition to commercial involvement was supported in 1923 by the Sykes Committee, which recommended that the then British Broadcasting Company should be funded by a licence fee, payable by every household in possession of a radio. By 1927, on the basis of these conclusions and those of the 1926 Crawford Committee, the BBC had been established by royal charter as a licence-fee funded organisation with exclusive rights to the UK's airwaves. In order to protect its independence, the BBC would be answerable not directly to the state, but to an independent Board of Governors (which later became The BBC Trust and was abolished in favour of an external regulator in 2016).

Figure 8.1   Original façade of BBC Broadcasting House, London © Nick Hawkes

CONTRASTING PSB ARRANGEMENTS

Reith's BBC offered a diet of programming more mixed than critics sometimes give it credit for (Franklin 1997), but one that placed emphasis on news, high culture, patriotism and Christian morality. Often accused of overt paternalism, the approach reflected Reith's moral principles and his ruthless control over the organisation. Yet the broader principles of the BBC served as a model for countries around the world. Across Western Europe, as well as in countries as far apart as Japan, Canada and Australia, comparable PSB organisations emerged, each of which intended to develop content that was high in quality and beneficial to the national public. Organisational and funding arrangements varied, however. While in many European examples and Japan, a licence fee comparable to the UK's was used, others, such as the Australian Broadcasting Commission (now Corporation), have been funded by direct government subsidy, raising concerns for some as to the level of independence of the broadcaster from the politicians who directly allocate its resources. Meanwhile the Canadian Broadcasting Corporation, from its conception in 1936, relied upon a mixture of direct government subsidy and revenue from the selling of advertising, bringing in a degree of commercial pressure.

While in some countries public service broadcasters competed with commercial rivals from an early point, in the UK Reith was insistent that this would undermine the remit of the BBC by forcing it to chase audiences. Yet, after extensive debate, the BBC's monopoly was broken in 1955, with the setting up of a commercial form of public service broadcasting, provided by an amalgam of regional companies under the Independent Television (ITV) network. The move embraced the notion, pioneered in Canada, that broadcasting for the public interest could be provided within an environment subject to commercial pressures. ITV's commercial network was (and still is) regarded as a public service broadcaster, subject to specific requirements with respect to the kinds of content distributed. Today, the UK also has two further public service broadcasters in the form of Channel 4 and FIVE, both funded by advertising, the latter with fully commercial status and the former a public corporation.

DEVELOPING PSB PRINCIPLES

In spite of the variations in the approach to PSB in different countries and across time, many of Reith's initial principles have remained constant. In 2004 and 2005, Ofcom, the current UK media and communications regulator, undertook a detailed consultation on the future of PSB, the outcome of which was the identification of four broad social purposes:

- To inform ourselves and others and to increase our understanding of the world, through news, information and analysis of current events and ideas.
- To reflect and strengthen our cultural identity, through high quality UK national and regional programming.
- To stimulate our interest in and knowledge of arts, science, history and other topics, through content that is accessible, encourages personal development and promotes participation in society.
- To support a tolerant and inclusive society, through the availability of programmes which reflect the lives of different people and communities within the UK, encourage a better understanding of different cultures and perspectives and, on occasion, bring the nation together for shared experiences. (Ofcom 2004)

Some of the specifics in these elaborations which continue to develop over time, differ from the days of Reith. Yet the emphasis on enlightening and focus on encouragement of national cohesion are consistent themes even if, in the case of the latter, an emphasis on inclusion and diversity has replaced the monolithic Reithian vision of national identity. These themes also predominate in Michael Tracey's outline of eight principles of PSB, which, amongst other things, cover the provision of education and information, the nurturing of a national sense of togetherness, provision for minorities, a commitment to quality programming and the liberation of programme makers from commercial or establishment restraints (Tracey 1998). A further important theme identified by Tracey – and by a UNESCO report on public service broadcasting around the world (Banerjee and Seneviratne 2005) – is the facilitation of public engagement and participation, something that entails societal belonging and involvement in public life and debate (see Chapter 10). In this respect, the PSB approach is a model of media that regards individuals not as isolated consumers but citizens – members of a national public or community with a commitment to one another and a stake in the improvement of society (Murdock 1992). Sure enough, wherever and whenever it has existed, PSB perhaps can best be summarised by the principle that mass media should be used collectively to 'make us better than we are' (Tracey 1998: 19).

ENABLING OR IMPOSING?

Those whose licence fees or taxes are used to pay for public service broadcasters sometimes resent the drain on their money that such institutions appear to represent. Some argue that content is insufficiently distinct from that of commercial competitors, others regard them as out of touch with audiences, while many want to be allowed to choose whether to pay for such services. 'Why should I pay so much for the BBC...', the complaint sometimes goes, '...when I don't even watch its programmes?' Justifications for PSB, however, ask us to look beyond the individual, short-term preferences each of us may choose to exercise and instead ask what would be most beneficial to all of us in the longer term. Entertainment and popularity are central to the PSB agenda, not only because collective enjoyment fosters cultural bonds, but also because of the importance of catering for the whole of society rather than an elite few. Yet public service broadcasters seek to combine this with loftier goals such as challenging, enlightening and empowering audiences: making popular content high in quality and quality content popular (Tracey 1998). This is a tall order, of course and they may not always have been successful in striking the balance. There also are some broader difficulties with public service models of media that we should consider.

THE LIMITS TO INDEPENDENCE

The first difficulty with public service models of media is the ongoing issue of government influence. This is a particular concern for broadcasters reliant upon the continuation of direct funding from the state but also affects licence-fee-funded organisations, who rely on government support for the continuation of their funding arrangements. The BBC's history is littered with episodes in which its independence has been tested. The first was the general strike in 1926 in which Reith fended off government calls for the corporation to become an instrument of state propaganda (Briggs 1961). His success in doing so was a significant victory for independence, but this did not prevent the BBC from coming under the control of a government Ministry of Information during the Second World War (Curran and Seaton 2010). It has never since been so directly controlled, but the corporation's independence has continued to come under pressure, particularly during times of national crisis and war. In 2003, it was the subject of high profile attacks from government officials for a news item that suggested politicians had 'sexed up' the case for invading Iraq. Intense pressure, alongside a public inquiry, resulted in the resignation of the BBC's Director General and the Chair of its Board of Governors. Meanwhile, in 2016, concerns have been expressed about the implications for BBC independence of a proposal for government to appoint several members of a new unitary board responsible for operational control of the corporation.

QUESTIONS OF QUALITY

While their relationship with governments have always led to tensions, however, a more substantial difficulty for public service models of media relates to the question of who decides what sorts of media content are good or bad for us. Reith's belief was that people did not know what was good for them and that the BBC should decide for them. For all his intentions about making cultural excellence available to all, the approach was a highly undemocratic one. We rarely hear such blunt dismissals of public taste today and the range of public service content on offer is also more diverse. Yet justifications of public service media continue to rest upon an apparent distrust of the choices the public might make if left to themselves in an unfettered commercial marketplace.

This paternalist position is apparent in the constant references made by regulators and public service broadcasters to the importance of maintaining 'quality'. The UK regulator Ofcom, for example, has stated that 'as a society we clearly demand a wider range of high quality UK content than would be provided by the market' (2005) while in 2016 the UK government included prominent reference to 'high quality' as part of its proposed new mission statement for the BBC. At face value, most would accept that quality and excellence are worthy goals. Yet, rarely is much elaboration provided on what, exactly, is meant by them, or by whose standards they should be measured. A recent Ofcom statement (2015) that reaffirmed the centrality of 'high quality' to public service broadcasting elaborated only with 'well-funded and well produced', but for many the notion of quality implies considerably more than this. According to David Elstein (1986), quality actually serves as a byword for an elitist agenda that privileges establishment values. Media mogul Rupert Murdoch takes a similar view, suggesting that, 'much of what is claimed to be quality television here [in the UK] is no more than the parading of the prejudices and interests of the like-minded people who currently control British television… producing a TV output which is so often obsessed with class, dominated by anti-commercial attitudes and with a tendency to hark back to the past' (R. Murdoch 2001: 39).

Murdoch's dismissal may have been self-serving, but he is not alone in connecting notions of quality to the agendas of established powerful groups. For sociologist Pierre Bourdieu (1984), the concepts of aesthetic quality and good taste reflect and reinforce deep-seated class divisions. Essentially, the bourgeoisie construct a distinction between their own high or pure aesthetic and a diametrically opposed vulgar aesthetic, consisting of what are regarded as the naïve and superficial enjoyments of the working class. This cultural distinction serves to reinforce class differences because entry into elite social worlds is restricted to those with the requisite *cultural capital* – in other words, those in possession of the appropriate cultural tastes, knowledge and experience. From owning the right pictures to showing knowledge of suitable literature, cultural capital provides a route to social acceptance and, in turn, economic benefits such as elite forms of education or employment.

Proponents of public service media may argue, with some justification, that their versions of quality are less restricted than those associated with Bourdieu's high aesthetic, and that, in attempting to distribute it to the masses, they are seeking to challenge rather than reinforce class distinctions. Yet Bourdieu's broader emphasis on the culturally constructed nature of taste serves as an important reminder that notions of quality will always reflect the particular cultural context, or habitus as he would call it, of those who invoke them. To put it much more simply, quality is, to some degree, subjective: one person's quality may be another person's dross. In requiring particular elite individuals or organisations to produce or ensure quality programming, then, we may be endorsing the imposition of a very particular set of aesthetic and social priorities.

Yet perhaps, if it is justified, this position is not so untenable as it may seem. After all, do any of us, of whatever class background, feel that our everyday choices of what content to view or share are necessarily the most beneficial for society? We may strongly defend our right to make them, but this ought not to be taken to mean we want our personal choices, and the kinds of market demand they create, to be the sole determinant of our collective cultural future. It goes without saying that the public service agenda is born of a particular set of ideals with their roots in particular sections of society. Yet the pursuit of such ideals may still be powerfully justified, not because the tastes of one class group are inherently superior, but because certain kinds of content may be shown to have greater collective benefit than others. Perhaps we might, as John Mepham (1990) has suggested, define quality not as inherent aesthetic purity, but as something determined by the social usefulness of different forms of media. Arguments will rage about what is useful and what is not, argues Mepham, and this is how things should be in an inclusive, accountable public service system. They may not always have been effective at doing so, but public service media should serve and be accountable to the public – offering the population a permanent stake in ongoing debates about which kinds of programming are valuable and which are not.

CENSORSHIP: PREVENTING HARM AND OFFENCE

Supporters of public service approaches to media endorse what sometimes is termed 'positive' media regulation. That is, they believe that broadcasting or other media systems should be set up and controlled in a way that encourages the production of desirable content or services. A distinct, but equally important set of arguments emphasise the need for 'negative' forms of regulation, often in the form of censorship, to prevent or limit problematic or harmful content. Pro-censorship arguments are somewhat distinct from arguments in favour of PSB and it should not be assumed that those who support the former will necessarily support the latter. What connects the two positions, however, is the belief that media should be subject to regulation in the best interests of society.

AVOIDING OFFENCE

Arguments in favour of media censorship sometimes have drawn on ideas developed by Patrick Devlin (1963), who argued that, in order to maintain an orderly and functional society, it was necessary to nurture a moral consensus. For Devlin, if deviant moral behaviour was permitted or encouraged, then it might proliferate, causing the shared bonds of moral consensus to fragment and society to break-down: 'If men and women try to create a society in which there is no fundamental agreement about good and evil, they will fail', he said, and 'if, having based it on common agreement, the agreement goes, the society will disintegrate' (Devlin 1963: 10). For Devlin, in order to prevent such disintegration, society had the right to restrict the freedom of individuals. If the majority found a particular form of behaviour offensive or immoral, then in the interests of social cohesion, such an act should be restricted. Devlin's arguments also had implications for media depictions of opinions, behaviour or ways of life offensive to the majority. In short, the logic was that such expressions should be controlled or censored.

Devlin's emphasis, he claimed, was on the importance of moral consensus itself, rather than the inherent rightness or wrongness of any particular behaviour, but other conservatives took a more absolutist approach, campaigning for censorship on the grounds that certain forms of media content were, quite simply, immoral. In 1961, attempts were made to ban the paper-back publication of D.H. Lawrence's *Lady Chatterley's Lover* on the grounds that its sexual content, explicit language and depiction of adultery were obscene and depraved. While bans of the book were implemented in some countries, a landmark UK trial ended with a not guilty verdict, the jury deciding that the literary merit of the work justified its publication. In spite of this pivotal victory for liberalism, calls for the censorship of content deemed immoral and religiously offensive persisted.

Notably, campaigner Mary Whitehouse launched a 'Clean Up TV' campaign, calling for action to curb the increasingly explicit depiction of sex. She also used a dormant blasphemy law to successfully prosecute *Gay News* for its publication of a James Kirkup poem which fantasised about sexual contact with a recently deceased Jesus Christ. During the same decade, Monty Python's *Life of Brian*, which offered a satirical parallel to the story of Jesus, was subject to protests and local bans in the UK, the US and elsewhere, having been accused of blasphemy. More recently, the BBC's decision to screen satirical musical, *Gerry Springer The Opera* in 2006 prompted extensive protests led by evangelical Christian groups, who argued that its satirical depiction of Jesus and the Devil as Springer's guests was blasphemous and offensive. By this point, however, such groups probably did not speak for most of the UK population, making their campaigns incompatible with Devlin's argument about protection of the morals of the majority. As with campaigns from some European Muslim groups and others against the publication of Salman Rushdie's *The Satanic Verses* in 1989, and of newspaper cartoons depicting the prophet Mohammad, they were perhaps more compatible with the notion of censorship to prevent offence or hurt to religious groups who formed a minority within the countries in question.

For some commentators, as well as leading to offence, forms of speech that attack the beliefs of minority groups have the potential to reinforce their sense of exclusion from society or even encourage religious or racial hatred. Such arguments were heard regularly as part of the extensive debates that followed the 2015 terrorist attack on the offices of French satirical magazine *Charlie Hebdo* – which had frequently published images of Mohammad, to the dismay of many Muslims (Khan and Mythen 2015). They also have sometimes been used to justify calls to prevent certain speakers from being given a plat-form at universities. In 2015 the University of Cardiff was subject to a petition to cancel a talk by veteran feminist campaigner Germaine Greer on the basis that she held views that were offensive and hostile to people with transgender identities. Such views constituted a form of hate speech, it was argued, and allowing her to speak would therefore violate the university's obligation to foster a safe space for all students. Amongst other things, such arguments have illustrated how the boundary between offence and more tangible forms of harm can be blurry.

PORNOGRAPHY

Campaigns to restrict or censor what are regarded as hate speech also illustrate that pro-censorship arguments are not confined to those with conservative agendas. A further example of this is provided by campaigns to censor pornography, which bring together an unlikely pairing of conservative defenders of religious values and left-wing feminists concerned about female exploitation. The conservative case centres on the argument that porn undermines family values and heterosexual monogamy, threatening traditional understandings of sex as a dignified expression of love within marriage and inducing social consequences such as rising divorce rates, teenage pregnancies and sexual diseases. Campaign group, Mediawatch UK, puts it in the following way:

> We believe that pornography, because of its casual, immoral and responsibility-free approach to sexuality, contributes significantly to the social problems of sexual dysfunction, the continually rising rates of sexually transmitted infections, the increasing rate of marital breakdown and the annually rising sexual crime rate. (2005: online)

More recently organisations such as Safetynet and Safermedia have deployed similar arguments as part of a campaign to protect children from online pornography. According to Safermedia (2013), 'viewing pornography leads to an acceptance of violent and unhealthy notions of sex and relationships; it objectifies women and normalises aggressive sexual behaviour'.

The final points here, on female objectification and sexual crime, provide a connection between the arguments of such groups and those of radical feminists such as Dworkin (1981) and MacKinnon (1988), who campaigned to ban pornography in Minneapolis and Indianapolis on the basis that it violated women's civil rights. Far from threatening existing values, for Dworkin and MacKinnon, pornography is entirely consistent with a patriarchal society which for centuries has treated women as sexual objects. In porn, it is argued, women's sexuality is controlled and violated by men: by the male-controlled porn industry which makes money out of subjecting women to humiliating, degrading and sometimes violent sexual acts; by the men who consume women's sexuality by watching porn; and by the male actors depicted in pornographic texts. For this reason, there is little substantive difference, for Dworkin, between porn and prostitution, both of which involve men selling women's bodies to other men. Rape too, is deemed consistent with the status porn establishes of women as sexual commodities, except that here, they are stolen instead of paid for. At one with Morgan's (1980: 128) assertion that 'pornography is the theory, rape is the practice', Dworkin is clear that the two legitimise one another:

> Pornography as a genre says that the stealing and buying and selling of women are not acts of force of abuse because women want to be raped and prostituted because that is the nature of women and the nature of female sexuality. (Dworkin 1995: 240)

Although Dworkin and MacKinnon's work is now fairly old, many of their arguments inform contemporary debates about pornography and sexual content. In the UK substantial support was recently gathered by an online feminist campaign against the daily publication in *The Sun* newspaper of bare-chested women on page 3 of its print-edition. The campaign's arguments reference the general objectification of women and possible links to sexual violence, as here:

The page 3 girl image is there for no other reason than the sexual gratification of men. She's a sex object. But when figures range from 300,000 women being sexually assaulted and 60,000 raped each year, to 1 in 4 who have been sexually assaulted, is it wise to be repeatedly perpetuating a notion that women are sexual objects? (Holmes 2012)

In 2015 the newspaper did remove topless models from its print edition, though it is unclear whether this represented a response to the campaign or a broader reassessment of what readers expected.

VIOLENCE

Media violence has been another focal point for censorship campaigns. Certainly, there can be little doubt as to the quantity of violence consumed by media audiences. Referring to the US, Gerber argues that:

> The average viewer of prime-time television drama… sees in a typical week an average of 21 criminals arrayed against an army of 41 public and private law enforcers… An average of 150 acts of violence and about 15 murders entertain them and their children every week, and that does not count cartoons and the news… (Gerbner 2002)

The notion that such on-screen violence may be harmful is frequently supported by media campaigns focused upon its connection to high profile murders. In the UK, the presence of a *Childs Play 3* video in the house of one of the teenagers who in 1993 killed toddler James Bulger prompted calls for the film and others like it to be banned, while in 1999 US media partially blamed the content of computer game *Doom 2* and the music and imagery of Marilyn Manson for the 1999 Columbine school shootings. In 2007, meanwhile, the video game *Manhunt 2* was banned in several countries and given restricted classifications in others on the basis of what was deemed a gratuitous approach to violence. Separately, following the murder of Jane Longhurst by a man who had been a heavy consumer of violent pornography, in 2008, the UK government made it a criminal offence for individuals to possess what it defined as 'extreme pornography'.

Often drawing upon experimental studies from behavioural psychology (see Chapter 5), campaigners argue that vulnerable individuals such as children may be liable to directly imitate media violence or to become more likely to respond to stressful situations in an aggressive manner (American Psychological Association Task Force on Violent Media 2015; Berkowitz 1984). Others have argued that over a longer period of time, violence may be rendered normal by our repeated exposure to it, either desensitising us to its negative impacts (Drabman and Thomas 1974) or leading to an excessively fearful understanding of the world (Gerbner and Gross 1976). Even if it doesn't prompt imitative behaviour or increased aggression, on-screen violence may seriously frighten, disturb or upset audience members and this, itself, may be seen as a significant social harm.

PREVENTING HARM OR INHIBITING FREEDOM?

Pro-censorship arguments offer useful reminders of the potential for media content to upset, offend, or harm. The question of whether, and in what circumstances, regulators should restrict or remove offending content is a complex one, however. Devlin's approach, in particular, is hard to justify in the context of contemporary multicultural societies where the banning of otherwise harmless forms of minority behaviour and expression in the name of social cohesion seems unrealistic and counterproductive. The nineteenth-century ideas of John Stuart Mill – against whom Devlin pitched parts of his argument – arguably have retained greater application. Specifically warning against the tyranny of the majority, Mill argues that individual freedom of behaviour and expression ought to be a key foundation of enlightened societies. Majority opinion at any moment in time, he argued, is potentially fallible and must be allowed to be tested against opposing ideas – even if they may offend – in order for societies to progress:

> The peculiar evil of silencing the expression of an opinion is that it is robbing the human race... If the opinion is right, they are deprived of the opportunity of exchanging error for truth: if wrong, they lose what is almost as great a benefit, the clearer perception and livelier impression of truth, produced by its collision with error. (Mill 1975: 24)

Society should only have the right to restrict individual freedom, according to Mill, if specific and clear harm is caused to others. The law should not seek to protect society from the offence or hurt feelings that minority practices or beliefs may cause, and neither should it protect individuals from themselves by forcing them to behave in a way which society deems good for them. Beyond this, however, Mill's 'harm principle' leaves plenty of scope for discussion. After all, many of the arguments in favour of censorship assert that, in one way or another, harm *is* caused by such material. The problem is that many of these claims are controversial.

In the case of accusations about the harmful effects of exposure to media violence, evidence is inconsistent and questionable. Speculation about the causal impact of media in relation to isolated murder cases can offer no sustainable basis for censorship, however shocking the headlines. When it comes to broader evidence, many studies claim to have demonstrated some sort of impact on audiences, while others are less clear. But as we have seen, the experimental approaches of most such studies have been subject to criticism (Ferguson 2015), making it difficult to know how much credence to give their findings (see Chapter 5). Most commentators agree, that even if media violence may have potential impacts on user aggression, it is only liable to lead to harmful consequences in the case of a small minority of individuals whose propensity for violence is largely attributable to other factors. The attentions of policy-makers, then, may be far better focused on the unusual factors at work in the lives of these extraordinary individuals rather than the impacts on everyone else of media content viewed by millions of them every day (Gauntlett 1998).

The degree of harm caused by pornography is also the subject of contention. Although many sex offenders have a history of pornography use, it is far from clear that the latter contribute to their criminal behaviour. Overall levels of sex crime in particular countries, meanwhile, do not seem to be correlated with levels of pornography use (Segal 1992). It remains likely that mainstream forms of pornography contribute to a broader media portrayal of women centred on sexual objectification and the achievement of sexual attractiveness to men (see Chapter 11). Yet recognition of this more general problem renders the singling out of pornography puzzling. Some might find them less edifying, but are we sure that the explicit portrayals of sex in porn are any more harmful in terms of their representation of femininity than portrayals in fashion and beauty magazines, romantic fiction, television crime drama or Hollywood blockbusters?

One of the factors emphasised by those feminists who do single out porn is that it is specifically demeaning or harmful to the actresses involved in its production. Yet other feminists have questioned the implicit suggestion here that sex workers are automatically passive, manipulated and unable to make choices for themselves:

> We are exhorted to save our sisters… but of course most sex workers are not looking for feminist salvation. On the contrary they complain bitterly about the stigmatization of women who work in the sex industry by anti-pornography feminists. (Segal 1992: 9)

It is also important to remember that, in spite of an overall bias towards the selling of female bodies to heterosexual male audiences, men's bodies feature in porn too and there are substantial and growing audiences for specialist forms of porn among both heterosexual women and LGBT people.

There is sufficient doubt about the evidence presented by those who regard violence and pornography as the cause of specific social harms, that the restrictions on freedom that heavy forms of censorship would impose seem hard to justify. This does not mean that all such forms of expression should be uncritically celebrated or that attempts to regulate should be entirely abandoned. It is of great importance that we continue to study the consequences of media use and are prepared to intervene where it can be demonstrated that significant harm is likely to be caused. The most obvious example, perhaps, is the managing of how children consume different forms of media content – and here the use of legally enforceable classification systems and child-friendly digital and online filters offer ways to help parents – and sometimes young people themselves – to establish their own boundaries. Questions remain, however, as to who determines the criteria to be used by such filters.

There are also opportunities to vary levels of restriction and control according to the public accessibility of content. Collins and Murroni (1996), propose that the more private a channel of communication is, the less it should be subject to censorship. The implication is that a conversation between a group of friends should be largely free of censorship, but that restrictions may sometimes be justified in the case of free to air or network television, whose audience consists of a large cross-section of the population. In between these extremes, Collins and Murroni place media consumed by a committed and specialist 'volunteer audience'. Including subscription-based television channels, websites or specialist magazines – such media are argued to require less stringent controls because there is less chance of their accidentally being stumbled upon by those liable to find them offensive or upsetting. As we shall see later, however, notions such as public, private and even volunteer audience are becoming increasingly blurred in contemporary digital and online environments.

COMMERCIAL COMPETITION AND CONSUMER CHOICE

So far the chapter has focused upon the merits and problems with the arguments of those who believe that governments should seek to achieve benefits for society by exerting controls on media. Our discussion now turns to those who believe it is wrong for governments to interfere significantly with media in the interests of social goals. Opposed especially to the PSB approach, this position draws upon *neo-liberal* political ideology. Influenced by the eighteenth-century economic theory of Adam Smith, its primary concern is not with individual political or moral freedom, though these can feature in the approach, but with market freedom: the freedom to buy, to sell and to make money.

Smith's doctrine called for a free market, or 'laissez-faire' (leave to do) economic system in which government interventions are reduced to a minimum, allowing businesses to compete freely in a quest to maximise profits, without barriers such as trade tariffs, state subsidies or regulations. Instead of trying to manipulate markets in order to achieve particular financial or social outcomes, governments should loosen their grip and allow economic and social outcomes to be determined by the 'invisible hand' of the market (Smith 1904). The success or failure of products, services or ideas should be determined primarily by the laws of supply and demand, not by government meddling. If there is a need for something scarce, it will become profitable for someone to provide it, if there is too much of something or it ceases to be useful, then those in search of profit will move elsewhere. After a decline in the influence of laissez-faire economics during the mid-twentieth century, so-called neo-liberal approaches became dominant during and after the 1980s, with the relaxation in many countries of regulations on businesses, reductions in taxation and government spending and the selling of state-owned utilities to the private sector.

NEO-LIBERAL APPROACHES

When it comes to media, neo-liberals believe it is wrong for governments to shape how they are used. Instead, they argue, commercial organisations should be free to provide media products and services and to succeed or fail on the basis of supply, demand and market competition. The invisible hand of the market, it is argued, will most effectively ensure provision of those products and services that are useful, because consumer demand will make their provision profitable. Free competition between companies, meanwhile, will force each to improve quality, innovate ideas and reduce prices. In contrast, the guaranteed income streams provided by government subsidies, licence fees and restricted market places are deemed to promote complacency and stagnation. Rather than being forced to consume a diet of media content deemed to be good for them by government-appointed bodies, consumers in a free market system would be trusted to make their own choices.

Calling for the deregulation of the UK broadcasting market dominated at the time by the BBC and its commercial rival ITV, media mogul Rupert Murdoch summed up the neo-liberal approach to broadcasting, in a lecture at the end of the 1980s entitled 'Freedom in Broadcasting':

> Competition lets consumers decide what they want to buy: monopoly or duopoly forces them to take whatever the seller puts on offer. Competition forces suppliers to innovate products, lest they lose business to rivals offering better; monopoly permits a seller to force outdated goods onto captive consumers. Competition keeps prices low and quality high; monopoly does the opposite. Why should television be exempt from these laws of supply and demand? (R. Murdoch 2001: 38)

Redefining the notion of a public service broadcaster as 'anybody who… provides a service which the public wants at a price it can afford' (2001: 39), Murdoch asserts that it is competitive commercial companies, in an open market place with minimal restrictions and controls, which can deliver such services most effectively.

Murdoch's wholesale rejection of PSB, except in the sense of 'providing a service the public wants' goes to the root of the argument. It is the satisfaction and enjoyment of individual consumers which should be the primary purpose of broadcasting according to this view. For Murdoch, the profitability of providing such satisfaction acts as guarantor that the market will deliver it. Rather than focusing upon the long-term needs of society as a whole, the neo-liberal approach casts us all, first and foremost, as individual consumers, and prioritises the need to satisfy each of us in this role.

In the same Edinburgh International Television Festival lecture slot in 2009, Murdoch's son, James – by then Chairman and Chief Executive of News Corporation – made a similar argument, attacking the 'authoritarianism' and 'lack of trust' of government attempts to regulate media and asserting that an unconstrained commercial system is the only way to maximise creativity and innovation, create a plurality of voices and provide effective choice. Public service broadcasting, he argued, was analogous to a form of creationism, whereby governments and regulators artificially design and plan everything in advance. In contrast, the free market was deemed to represent the natural, competitive process of evolution that allows content, services and technologies to continually develop according to demand (J. Murdoch 2009).

US BROADCASTING: A FREE MARKET MODEL

In the US, a long-established embrace of free markets, together with the specific protection afforded to freedom of the press in the first amendment to the country's constitution, has contributed to a history of broadcasting largely centred upon profit. From its earliest days, the US radio system was dominated by a competitive market place and commercial sponsorship. Some regulation was deemed necessary in order to protect limited bandwidth: the Federal Radio Commission (later the Federal Communications Commission or FCC) was set up in 1927 to allocate broadcasting licences and it was even established that licensees should serve 'public convenience, interest and necessity', but the industry was largely left to decide for itself what this meant (Baker and Dessart 1998). Meanwhile, competition for listeners was assured by the number of licences awarded in each area. While regulators elsewhere were acting to restrict competition, the FCC's most notable early interventions in the market were designed to protect it through avoiding the establishment of monopolies. Meanwhile, the audiences whose attention broadcasting companies coveted acted as the means to attain their primary goal, which was the attraction of commercial sponsors.

The US system did allow some space for 'public broadcasting'. In the early years, local educational radio and television stations were run by colleges, universities and charitable organisations such as the Ford Foundation. A more coordinated public system, complete with modest state funding was developed in the 1960s, with the creation of the Corporation for Public Broadcasting, responsible for distributing government money to public stations, and eventually the Public Broadcasting Service which acted as a connecting organisation for a plethora of local broadcasters (Baker and Dessart 1998). PBS enjoyed moderate successes, notably in children's educational programming but the paucity of government funding has resulted in reliance on donations, viewer contributions and, increasingly, advertising, as well as an inability to seriously compete with powerful commercial networks. Isolated attempts were also made to impose public service regulation on the content of commercial stations, the most notable of which was the Fairness Doctrine which, in 1949, imposed on all FCC licensees a requirement to broadcast programmes on matters of public importance and to offset any particular viewpoints covered with opposing perspectives. A principle was established that broadcasters had a responsibility to provide balanced coverage of matters of politics and controversy.

DIGITALISATION AND THE DECLINE OF REGULATION

From the 1980s onwards, however, much of the regulation that did exist in the US system has been relaxed in a climate dominated by neo-liberal voices, some of whom have argued that, rather than being regarded as a unique societal resource, broadcasting should be treated no differently to any other commercial goods or services. 'TV', said Mark Fowler, chairman of the FCC from 1981 to 1987, 'is a toaster with pictures' (cited in Baker and Dessart 1998: 27). Against the background of the onset of multi-channel cable television, Fowler oversaw the relaxation of a variety of rules, including the withdrawal of the Fairness Doctrine in 1987. The impact of the neo-liberal political climate that Fowler represented, combined with the development of cable, digital and the internet was to have an even more dramatic impact, however, on those countries that, unlike the US, had broadcasting histories dominated by powerful public service broadcasters.

Digitalisation and convergence have offered the perfect partner for neo-liberal voices because, by bringing spectrum scarcity to an end, they created the technical possibility for an open marketplace. Viewers could be offered such extensive choice of what content to engage with and when, it was argued, that they would no longer need governments to intervene. If viewers felt offended by content on one channel, then infinite alternatives would be available. Likewise, if they felt insufficiently challenged or informed by reality TV or talent contests, then they would be able to watch news, complex dramas or documentaries on a different channel, via on-demand systems or on the internet. The demand for such products would mean that a market unfettered by technological or government limitations would supply them. Instead of a smallish number of heavily regulated channels expected to cater for the needs of everyone, then, we would each choose from a plethora of specialist content. In James Murdoch's (2009) view, for governments to continue to try to control things from above in such a context would amount to the imposition of 'analogue attitudes' in a 'digital present'.

For all James Murdoch's complaints about continuing regulation, the relationship between multi-channel television and the neo-liberal revival has resulted in a substantial decline in the dominance of public service broadcasting in many countries (Tracey 1998). In the UK, the multitude of digital channels awarded licences since the 1990s have been able to operate free from the public service obligations expected of the country's terrestrial broadcasters, as have more recent on-demand services such as Netflix, Amazon Prime and, of course, a plethora of online sources of content. As a result, commercially funded public service broadcasters have found themselves subject to particularly intense competition from opponents who, unlike themselves, are subject to minimal regulation. Such competition has created huge pressure to reduce costs and chase audiences, something increasingly hard to square with their public service obligations. The provision of digital television services and set-top boxes, meanwhile, has also been largely entrusted to commercial organisations, giving them considerable influence over which channels are made available to the public and how they are displayed or ordered.

The future of non-commercial funding of public service broadcasters is also in doubt. The ability to easily enable or disable access has prompted many to propose funding organisations like the BBC or CBC by viewer subscription and/or payment on-demand. Instead of being forced to pay regardless of their engagement with content or services, consumers would voluntarily subscribe – or not – bringing an end to the principle of universality so important to proponents of public service media around the world (see Banerjee and Seneviratne 2005). This would also force such broadcasters to orient themselves to an appropriate market and compete for subscribers rather than receiving funds automatically. A recent UK government White Paper backed retention of the licence fee for another ten years, but encouraged 'the first moves towards a more sustainable funding model in the longer term', identifying subscription as the likely option. The paper also called for 'distinctiveness' and 'high quality' to be placed at the core of the corporation's mission statement, a move regarded by some as an attempt to turn it into a niche, high-brow provider, rather than one with universal appeal (DCMS 2016).

DIGITAL CENSORSHIP

In some respects, censorship has also been in relative decline in many countries since the second half of the twentieth century although, as we shall see, the thirst for controls on media in respect of moral decency remains strong. In part, the decline of certain forms of censorship has reflected a relentless pushing at the boundaries of acceptability by artists, broadcasters and others as part of increasingly competitive market environments that can encourage the challenging of boundaries and taboos. Technological developments, meanwhile, have emboldened anti-censorship campaigners by strengthening the case that those offended by particular forms of content can easily avoid it.

Censorship also is more complex in digital and particularly online environments. As a result of convergence, the boundaries between previously distinct media formats have broken down and, in particular, differences between interpersonal private communication and public mass media content are becoming blurry (boyd 2014). In an age where an individual tweet from a hitherto unknown individual can be shared to the extent it is viewed by millions of people, is it any longer feasible to enforce different standards for recognised media corporations than we do for what 'private' individuals say or share on social network sites? A further problem is that, because of the massive proliferation of content from different sources, and the inherently international nature of the way the internet operates, enforcing standards on content at a national level is far from simple.

Nevertheless, censorship persists in various places and is becoming increasingly commonplace on the internet. The UK, for example, passed laws in 2006 against the 'glorification' of terrorism and 'incitement to religious hatred' and in 2008 against ownership of 'extreme pornography', all of which were labelled by opponents as attacks on freedom of expression. Meanwhile, in 2014 attempts to clamp down on pornography were taken further still in the form of a ban on the depiction of a seemingly arbitrary list of specified sex acts (including spanking, face-sitting and female ejaculation) by UK pornography producers. Counter-intuitively, meanwhile, the otherwise 'laissez-faire' US television environment continues to have strict negative regulations on broadcasters relating to decency. Programming which is deemed 'obscene' is banned outright, while 'indecent' or 'profane' content is only permitted during hours when children are less likely to be watching (Federal Communications Commission 2016). The recent recommendation of a fine of $325,000 for television station WBDJ for a news broadcast containing imagery from an explicit porn website illustrates a continuing zeal to intervene when it comes to sexual decency in a country seemingly dominated by a mixture of neo-liberal economic thinking and conservative moral values (see Chapter 3).

The international nature of the internet, meanwhile, has not prevented China from imposing extensive filtering and censorship, blocking access to many foreign websites and services and particularly content regarded by the government as politically sensitive. On a smaller-scale both France and Germany block content related to Holocaust denial and Naziism and measures are taken to block child pornography in most countries. And, in addition to broader bans on particular kinds of pornography in some countries, the importance of so-called adult filters online also appears to be increasing. Following extensive campaigning by a number of groups concerned about the potential exposure of children to sexual content, in 2013 the UK government secured the agreement of commercial Internet Service Providers to turn adult filters on by default so that, unless consumers actively decide to turn them off, any content deemed unsuitable for children would be blocked.

While for some this development constituted a valuable protective measure, others have expressed concerns at the power the move gave to unelected commercial technology companies to act as society's moral arbiters. Complex moral decisions as to what content should be blocked from millions of devices or households, they argue, are being left to commercial technology companies, whose algorithms block or allow content on the basis of criteria that are largely hidden. In this respect, the increasing importance of ISP filters forms just one example of a broader trend towards what we might term the privatisation of online censorship. As Julie Adler (2011: 237) has put it, 'in a capitalistic society, in which private companies own and maintain the Internet's infrastructure, the gatekeeping role of non-governmental actors goes largely unchallenged'.

According to Adler, a trend has emerged for various organisations whose platforms act as conduit for the communication of content to take an over-compliant, safety-first, over-censorious approach with respect to legal requirements or pressure from politicians. Thus, YouTube, she argues, tends to delete apparent copyright violations without checking whether they might be allowable under fair use while other platforms, from Apple to US classified site Craigslist, have removed content as a result of political pressure or public campaigns. Meanwhile, Facebook has found its criteria for deleting content subject to extensive scrutiny and controversy and has now developed a detailed community standards page that sets out its content rules. Arguments about the details of such rules, whether on Facebook or elsewhere, are difficult to resolve. Should images that depict bare female nipples be allowed? What about male nipples? Should extreme or potentially offensive political imagery or commentary be allowed? And what counts as extreme or offensive? The complexity of such questions makes it all the more important to question who the arbiters of such dilemmas are, how transparent their decision-making is and how accountable they are for the decisions they make. Notably, are we entirely content that the moral codes and criteria by which media content is or is not allowed – and even by which our everyday online conversations are policed – are increasingly determined by commercial tech companies?

CONCLUSION: A ROSY COMMERCIAL FUTURE?

In spite of the continuing significance of censorship, deregulation and the proliferation of free markets seems liable in other respects to continue in the coming years. The competitive commercial environment called for by the Murdochs and others have been unleashed in many of the countries which had originally embraced restricted public service approaches to broadcasting. And if the funding and structure of public service broadcasters eventually is reformed consistent with free market principles, it is hard to envisage such arrangements being re-implemented. So should public service approaches be defended or should we regard the increasing marketisation of media in digital environments as inevitable or even desirable?

Competition and markets, alongside the proliferation of content, undoubtedly have enhanced viewer choice and fuelled all manner of technical and creative innovations. No longer do people have to accept the agenda or scheduling of one or two national broadcasters or regulatory bodies. Rather, they are increasingly free, subject to payments of one kind or another, to select their own cultural path from the plethora of content made available by competing commercial providers. And, in turn, the choices that individuals make will influence the future commissioning and scheduling decisions of broadcasters. It would be unrealistic to deny, then, that competition has placed greater pressure on media organisations to ensure that they remain in touch with viewers. It is also becoming clear that in the new media environment, markets increasingly are catering for at least some specialist minority groups, some of whom report a preference for such services over national public service broadcasters (see Chapter 12).

There remain substantial disadvantages with a fully free-market approach to media, however. Rather than replacing powerful public broadcasters with an open marketplace comprising a plethora of competing independent companies, deregulation tends to reinforce trends towards the domination of communications by a small number of transnational corporations (McChesney 2000). Increasingly, such corporations dominate our symbolic worlds, shape our understandings of current events, host our interactions with one another and, as we have seen, decide what we can and cannot say. Intensified competition for advertising revenue, meanwhile, has prompted a ruthless emphasis on audience maximisation, as well as a bias towards those content and services most compatible with marketing and consumer culture. And while specialisation, innovation and quality undoubtedly account for elements of the commercial picture, a substantial amount of commercial content, across a variety of channels, continues to consist of repeated, standardised formulas and centred upon the minimisation of costs and risks.

'So what?', free marketers may say, 'the consumer gets what the consumer wants'. Leaving aside whether this is true, the key question, perhaps, is whether we want the future of our mass communications to be quite so enslaved to the immediate and sometimes lazy decisions we all make with our tablets and remote controls when flicking between content at the end of a tiring day. Do we want such choices to be our only influence on the future of our media? Or would it be valuable also to have the opportunity to influence – in a more considered and collective fashion – the broader, longer-term priorities and principles through which at least some parts of media systems are operated. Ultimately, are we content to be temporarily amused individual consumers or should we continue to strive for at least some media content and services we believe truly improve and empower us individually and collectively and which address us as active, engaged members of society?

QUESTIONS/EXERCISES

1　Compile a list of arguments for and against the funding of public service broadcasters by voluntary subscription instead of by licence fee or government subsidy.

2　a)　Try to produce a definition of quality, which could be used to judge television programmes.

　　b)　Is it feasible for regulators to fairly judge the quality of broadcasting output?

3　a)　In what circumstances, if any, is the censorship of media content beneficial to society?

　　b)　What is the difference between moral conservative arguments in favour of the censorship of pornography and those of feminist campaigners such as Dworkin and MacKinnon? Are either set of arguments convincing?

(Continued)

(Continued)

   c) In what ways, in online environments, is the regulation of content being left in the hands of commercial platforms? Should we be concerned about such a development?

4 a) Is James Murdoch right to say that attempts by government to regulate media demonstrate a lack of trust in consumers?

   b) In light of such claims, how might public service approaches be defended?

5 What are media for? What ought to be their role in society?

SUGGESTED FURTHER READING

Baker, W. and Dessart, G. (1998) *Down the Tube: An Inside Account of the Failure of US Television*. New York: Basic Books – Critical history of the development of the commercial television system in the US.

Banerjee, I. and Seneviratne, K. (eds) (2005) *Public Service Broadcasting: A Best Practices Sourcebook*, UNESCO. URL: http://unesdoc.unesco.org/images/0014/001415/141584e.pdf – United Nations review of public service broadcasting that sets out contemporary definitions and outlines its continuing importance in countries around the world, including in the digital age.

Dworkin, A. (1981) *Pornography: Men Possessing Women*. London: Women's Press – Feminist attack on pornography as a manifestation of the objectification and exploitation of women by men.

Mill, J.S. (1975) 'On Liberty', in *Three Essays: 'On Liberty', 'Representative Government', 'The Subjection of Women'*. London: Oxford University Press (essay first published 1859 and reprinted in various collections) – Classic liberal defence of freedom of expression.

Murdoch, J. (2009) 'The Absence of Trust', MacTaggart Memorial Lecture, Edinburgh International Television Festival, URL: http://image.guardian.co.uk/sys-files/Media/documents/2009/08/28/James MurdochMacTaggartLecture.pdf – An attack on UK media regulation and the BBC by the Chief Executive of News International Europe and Asia, and son of Rupert Murdoch.

CHAPTER 9
ADVERTISING: EMERGENCE, EXPANSION AND TRANSFORMATION

FOCAL POINTS

- The emergence and development of advertising as an industry
- Changing approaches to the construction of symbolic value in advertising content
- Arguments about the adaption of advertising to changing cultural sensibilities
- Ultra-targeting, responsiveness and interactivity in digital advertising
- Arguments about the role and significance of advertising in contemporary societies

INTRODUCTION

Everyday life in late capitalist societies is saturated with advertising. An average trip around town will involve encounters with commercials via billboards, shop fronts, in-store television and the inside and outside of buses, trains and taxis. And we should expect no respite if we enter a leisure centre, cinema, café or bar. Commercials have even become a feature of many workplaces and educational establishments. Back in the 'private' sphere of our homes, we are bombarded by commercials via television, radio, games consoles and, of course, the internet, in which advertising forms an integral part of engagement with content and everyday interactions with others. And as a result of the increasing ubiquity of mobile digital devices, these advertising-centred online cultures accompany many of us everywhere we go.

As part of this, advertising plays a particularly pivotal role in contemporary media worlds, comprising one of the most pervasive forms of media content as well as the primary funding source for contemporary media and, as part of this, a direct and indirect influence on content, format and affordances. As such, the operation of advertising, the nature of its content and practices and impact on broader media environments warrant detailed scrutiny. As we shall see, there is nothing especially new about advertising, per se, or its substantial influence on media and broader cultural life. In recent years, however, there have been profound and rapid changes to advertising as it has adapted to challenges and moved to harness new sets of opportunities within fast-changing interactive digital media environments.

THE DEVELOPMENT OF ADVERTISING

EMERGENCE

For Raymond Williams (1980: 170) advertising in its broadest sense, or 'the process of taking or giving notice of something', is as old as humanity itself and distinct from the specific development of 'an institutionalised system of commercial information and persuasion'. The first signs of the latter emerged, according to Williams, with the development and growth of newspapers, though for much of the nineteenth century, commercial messages were confined to specific parts of newspapers and typically consisted of 'simple, basically factual' notices – what we now tend to refer to as classifieds. Gradually, however, more distinctive and 'persuasive' advertising techniques emerged, including via media such as fly-posters, and trade-cards included in boxes of coffee or cigarettes, which bypassed the constraints of the press (Cross 2013; Williams 1980). The end of the nineteenth century saw the development by mainstream corporations of now familiar persuasive techniques, including memorable slogans such as Pears' Soap's 'Good morning, have you used Pears' Soap?' (see Figure 9.1) (Williams 1980). As advertisers sought to inspire the imagination of consumers, illustrations, imagery, distinctive logos and distinct characters began to accompany such slogans and increasingly were visible in newspapers as well as early mass distribution magazines (ibid.; Cross 2013). Amongst others, patented food and drinks (including Kelloggs, Cadbury, Hovis, Campbell's Soup, Coca Cola) were leading this revolution, establishing brand enthusiasm and loyalty through coordinated approaches to advertising and package design (Cross 2013; Williams 1980). And as the twentieth century developed, manufacturers of new household technologies, from the gramophone to the camera, invested heavily in advertising's potential to combine specific branding with persuasion as to the uses of unfamiliar products.

GROWTH AND PROFESSIONALISATION

For Williams (1980), then, it was the half-century from 1880–1930 that saw advertising develop into a fully-fledged, organised and influential industry of persuasion. Williams connects this transformation with the emergence of a new phase of corporate capitalism characterised by attempts to exert control over markets by increasingly dominant large companies. Advertising comprised an example of such control, allowing corporations to avoid costly price wars and manipulate demand for their goods instead (McChesney et al. 2011). Advertising, it is argued, offered the only means – aside from price – for companies to differentiate their product from the similar

Figure 9.1   Early Pears Soap advertisement

offerings of competitors. Competition persisted, then, but its primary site was the stimulation of demand through effective advertising and the establishment of brand identities (ibid.).

Corporations also were assisted by a gradual rise in disposable income among ordinary workers during the first half of the twentieth century in established capitalist societies, precipitating the development of working-class disposable income and purchasing power (Miles 1998). This partly reflected long-term economic growth but also the predominance of economic policies centred upon stimulating economic demand through investment and seeking to keep employment and wages high. It was further stimulated by *Fordist* approaches to industrial production, whereby high quantities of low-cost, standardised goods were produced using assembly-line techniques and workers were paid wages sufficiently high to enable the possibility of their purchasing such commodities. As a consequence, according to Steve Miles, 'a whole new world of consumerism was on offer to the working majority' (1998: 9).

By the post-war years of the 1950s and 60s, then, consumer industries, and the advertisers so important to them, found themselves in a socio-economic environment well-suited to their needs and this precipitated further growth. Advertising and marketing had become organised, discrete and powerful industries, staking a claim for themselves as legitimate professions, complete with scholarship, textbooks, training, research methods, research, awards, professional associations, regulatory bodies and codes of ethics (Davis 2013). 'Dubious, ad hoc and questionable occupations' had evolved, argues Aeron Davis, 'to become "respectable" pillars of business and society' (ibid.: 19). This consolidation also had involved evolution of the role of ad agencies themselves from simple buyers and sellers of ad slots to the providers of a full range of research-based, creative advertising services for clients.

POST-FORDISM, NICHE MARKETS AND BRANDING

An increasing emphasis on sophisticated forms of market research meant that, during the latter half of the twentieth century, advertising became better at responding to the particular concerns and wants of different consumers. Identification of niche markets and the tailoring of messages based on demographic and other characteristics accompanied a broader expansion of the range of goods produced. Gradually the standardisation of Fordism was giving way to a more flexible post-Fordist system dominated by the selling of wave after wave of specialist products to market segments (Miles 1998). At the same time, marketing concerns were encroaching further into the initial design and orientation of products themselves. No longer were advertising and marketing limited to developing messages about existing products. Rather, they were playing an increasingly pivotal role across the post-Fordist commercial process from conception onwards. Advertising and marketing also encroached into non-commercial sectors, including charities, political parties and pressure groups, educational establishments and others. Image-management and advertising became increasingly important, as did the marketing directors, ad agencies and others who accompanied them (Davis 2013).

As the twentieth century became the twenty-first, the subservience of product design and selection to marketing concerns had become striking. Initially developed as a way to give meaning and appeal to products, brands have expanded to become broader sets of conceptual meanings with which companies wish to associate themselves (Danesi 2006). While in some cases (such as Coca Cola) the brand remains associated with its product, in others (such as Virgin) it enables the association of a range of products and services with the conceptual meanings the brand conveys (Lury 2011). At this point, the clarity and meaning of the brand becomes the primary source of value for companies and its needs dictate many corporate decisions, including those related to product development. As Aeron Davis (2013: 78–9) puts it, 'In many cases, perfumes, shirts and tracksuits, cups, fast-food packaging and toys are not produced to smell nice, wear, consume food in or play with. They are constructed because they are most simply transformed in the service of the wider brand.' In industry terms, then, advertising came a long way in the twentieth century, coming to dominate commercial decision-making at the same time as establishing itself as the primary funding source for media.

MODES OF PERSUASION: FROM INFORMATION AND USE TO SYMBOLS AND IDENTITY

Just as the orientation of the advertising industry changed across the course of the twentieth century, so did the content of advertising itself. In particular, many have identified a shift from 'informational' and product-oriented advertising centred upon *use value* – what objects do, why they might be useful, how they might fit into consumers' everyday lives – towards an increasing emphasis on different forms of *symbolic value* that seeks to equate objects with associative meanings usually connected to the identity of those who consume them. In other words, advertisements gradually focused more on what products might *mean* and *say* about their consumers, rather than the practicalities of what they could *do*. Here, the material product itself, as Raymond Williams suggests, 'is never enough' as advertising transforms the significance of objects so that they are 'validated... by association with social and personal meanings' (1980: 185). Similarly, Judith Williamson (1978) argues that commercials were bringing together things and humans in such a way that they became interchangeable. Through inviting us to affirm, enhance or transform our identities through consumer choices, advertisers were, effectively, selling us ourselves, she argues. For many theorists, this intertwining of consumption and identity constitutes a core facet of the broader *consumer culture* that emerged alongside the development of advertising (Miles 1998; Lury 2011).

DEVELOPING FRAMES

Research by William Leiss and colleagues (1997) has sought to explore how advertising has historically framed the relationship between people and consumer objects, positing (initially) four distinct phases stretching across the twentieth century. The first of their proposed frames, *idolatry*, consists of a 'strong tone of veneration about products' – a rational, denotative (direct, literal) attempt to persuade consumers to purchase on the basis of the qualities of the product. Associated mostly with print media in the early twentieth century, this frame centres on use-value and depictions of 'the object itself and its image' (ibid.: 330). The second cultural frame, *iconography*, coincides with the rise of radio advertising and sees the rational-utilitarian emphasis on goods themselves beginning to give way to connotative (implicit or associative) sets of symbolic meanings centred upon the status of consumers. 'Automobiles were expressions of a modern outlook' argue Leiss et al., 'soaps of family integrity and caring, shoes of sobriety or status' (1997: 334). However, there remained an emphasis on the object itself and, rather than representing fully-fledged individuals, images of people functioned as broader symbols of social status, morals or values.

The post-war years of the 1950s and 60s, in which television becomes the dominant medium for advertising, play host to a new phase, *narcissism*, in which advertising centres on an emotional appeal to the individual personality or psyche of the consumer. Through what Leiss et al. term, 'black magic', advertisements offer consumers personal emotional fulfilment as well as the chance to cultivate and project personality. Particularly notable, they suggest, were 'mirror ads', featuring a face gazing out at the audience, creating emotional identification that, in turn, becomes associated with the product. A further feature was the representation of social interactions, whether in the form of romance (often as a proxy for sex) or family bonds, establishing the importance of consumer goods as part of relationships. This interpersonal emphasis is taken further in Leiss et al.'s final cultural frame, *totemism*, associated with the post-Fordist years of the 1970s and 80s. Alongside broader market segmentation and niche targeting, the dominant advertising approach shifts to an association of products with lifestyles and communities. Here, advertisements cultivate the notion of goods as overt badges (or totems) of collective identity.

While Leiss et al.'s original analysis ends during the 1980s and charts a seemingly unstoppable development in the cultivation of specific individual and social symbolic value, a more recent study by Barry Richards and colleagues (2000) suggests things may not be quite so simple. Richards et al.'s analysis, which includes the 1990s, indicates a return to prominence of more rational forms of address centred upon the pragmatic use-value of the product itself during this decade and connects this with an equally important shift away from the lifestyle groupings of Leiss et al.'s totemism stage and towards an emphasis on the unique individual consumer:

> Since it is in the actual use of the product that people will be most aware of their unique configuration of need and desire, a return to the product and its features could be consistent with the intense individualisation of the late modern consumer. (2000: 247)

This focus on the sovereignty of the individual consumer is taken further in an updated version of Leiss et al.'s earlier schema (2005) that includes a fifth cultural frame, *mise-en-scene*, in which fixed depictions oriented to pre-defined lifestyle groups are replaced by a focus on the agency and shifting orientations of individualised consumers, encouraging them to craft their own identity through consumption. Life is presented, they argue, as an individual 'script-writing exercise' (ibid.: 568), a postulation that connects to broader suggestions in social theory that contemporary individuals increasingly are charged with constructing their own identities, including through consumption (Bauman 2000; Beck and Beck-Gernsheim 2001). For example Leiss et al. refer to a 2000 NextMonet advert imploring consumers to 'FIGHT SAMENESS' through purchasing 'art with a point of view: yours'. Crucially, the ad does not explicitly prescribe specific meanings or identities but invites consumers to build their own distinctiveness through consumption on their own terms.

For a more recent example, we might consider a recent campaign by make-up company MAC (see Figure 9.2). Against a dark background, the campaign's central ad features the strikingly made-up faces and, sometimes, upper bodies, of six winners of a competition run by the brand, who between them include different ethnicities, body sizes, hairstyles and (particularly unusual for a make-up ad) genders – a heavily made-up young man with punkish hair featuring alongside five women. Working together, the images clearly are intended to symbolise diversity and individuality, the latter anchored by the twitter hashtag '#MACnificent Me' in the centre and 'celebrate your style, heart and soul' at the bottom. Aligned with the images and their context – a competition for 'real' users of the brand's make-up – the core words here are 'me' and 'your' in emphasising that MAC as a brand and product-range frees people to express their inner-selves. Yet, whether ads like this end up prescribing specific forms of meaning, even whilst explicitly emphasising individuality, is open to debate. For all its symbolic emphasis on diversity, for example, there is much about the individuals depicted in the MAC ad that remains similar, not least their largely youthful appearances, styles of make-up, familiar model-like poses and contextualisation within an ad with a sophisticated, high-fashion identity.

Figure 9.2   MAC advertisement, 2015 © Make Up Art Cosmetics

CULTIVATING COOL

There are some facets of advertising messages that are not fully fleshed out within Leiss et al.'s scheme. An example is the development of broader attempts among advertisers at the end of the twentieth century to associate their brands with what some have termed 'cool' (McGuigan 2009). A difficult concept to pin down, 'cool' has come to encapsulate a range of symbolic qualities, including being confident, self-assured, genuine but also up-to-date, youthful, discerning and active and innovative with respect to cultural taste. It has come to be a key facet of the kinds of symbolic value many advertisers hope to cultivate, providing a means to appeal to new generations of consumers and to older groups that aspire to be youthful (Klein 2000). For Jim McGuigan (2009), in their quest for cool, advertisers have often borrowed from the creativity of grassroots cultures, particularly those associated with groups of young people regarded as subversive or edgy. Hip hop and various other forms of black youth and music culture form primary examples here, as do a variety of other music and style related subcultures and movements. Advertisers came to recognise that it was the very grassroots, spontaneous nature of such cultures, as well as their subversion of certain establishment norms – including those associated with dominant forms of consumer culture – that offered the possibility for them to be coded as cool.

In order to incorporate such versions of 'cool' into their branding, parts of the industry invested heavily in so-called insider marketing or 'cool-hunting' – often conducted by young employees connected to such cultures (McGuigan 2009). The idea, argues Naomi Klein (2000: 72), was that cool-hunters 'would search out pockets of cutting-edge lifestyle, capture them on video-tape and return to clients like Reebok, Absolute Vodka and Levi's…' with advice as to the kinds of sensibilities or imagery with which they should be associating themselves. As well as incorporating such symbols into advertising itself, marketers also sometimes sought to integrate brands directly within 'cool' youth cultures in order that the product or brand could appear to emerge as an organic part of cool culture rather than a subsequent co-opter (ibid.). Brands such as Adidas and Nike have worked hard to exploit and cultivate ongoing association of their brands with hip hop and black urban youth cultures through sponsorship and provision of clothing to rap stars, bringing prototypes of new trainers to show young people in urban areas and sponsoring neighbourhood sports programmes (Arvidsson 2005; Klein 2000).

A further aspect of attempts to identify and deploy cool is an emphasis on irony, parody and self-critique. Conscious of increasingly critically-minded consumers who distrust and mock established advertising techniques and keen to co-opt this, advertising increasingly generates and deploys cool through holding itself and its products up to ironic forms of critique. They need to, argues Klein, 'self-mock, talk back to themselves while they are talking' (ibid.: 78). Klein gives the example of a campaign to promote the movie *Show Girls*, six months after it had initially flopped in cinemas. The campaign responded to an emerging grassroots trend to throw Show Girls parties centred upon ironic hilarity at the show's 'implausibly poor screenplay and… aerobic sexual encounters' through a series of newspaper ads that quoted negative reviews of the film, seeking to rebrand it as a 'rich, sleazy kitch fest' (ibid.).

SHIFTING YET MIXED APPROACHES

In spite of their significance in some respects, it is important not to assume that all or most advertising is deploying coolness and ironic critique in the ways described above. More generally, it is important to remember that, rather than being a simple linear development, the development of advertising content has, in practice, been somewhat messy and diverse. While certain modes of address may have predominated in one period or another, most were characterised by a mixture of styles and approaches. Likewise, as Richards and colleagues' (2000) contribution illustrates, while an increasing emphasis on symbolism comprises a clear ongoing development, we ought not forget that more rational product-oriented forms of persuasion continue to play a role. Equally, while Leiss et al. may be right to emphasise a shift towards advertisements inviting consumers to construct their own personalised meanings, this tendency too is partial, with many ads continuing to cultivate more specific associations, identities and meanings. For every NextMonet 'FIGHT SAMENESS' and 'MACnificent Me', there are plenty of other campaigns appealing to lifestyle identities, emotional attachments or practical benefits that are more prescribed.

ADVERTISING IN THE DIGITAL AGE

If the development of advertising in the twentieth century was striking, then the extent of its transformation in the first two decades of the twenty-first century may be no less remarkable. For Matthew McCallister and Emily West, when it comes to contemporary advertising and promotional culture, 'everywhere we look, boundaries and categories that once seemed fixed and knowable are blurring and destabilizing' (2013: 1).

CHALLENGES TO 'TRADITIONAL' ADVERTISING

Prior to the turn of the century, the predominant model for media advertising involved the delivery of clearly demarcated commercial messages via discrete advertising slots. Still visible today, these take the form of space on the printed (or electronic) page or breaks within scheduled radio or television content. In recent years, however, the effectiveness of 'spot' advertising has declined, prompting the development of new approaches. In the sphere of broadcasting, the increasing level of control audiences have over what exactly they view and when is making it easier and easier to avoid commercial breaks (Spurgeon 2008), something pushed a stage further by online content services that present subscribers with a library of advertising-free content to view when they please. At the same time, broader declines in the popularity of broadcast and print media as compared to online communications have contributed to a decline in their effectiveness for advertisers. According to Pew Research, circulation of US daily newspapers declined in every year but one during the decade from 2004 and 2014, while ad revenue across US newspapers fell from $44.9 billion to $16.4 billion between 2005 to 2014 (Barthel 2015). Advertising, then, is increasingly orienting itself away from traditional mass media and towards flexible, interactive digital environments.

A NEW ERA OF ADVERTISING?

Accompanying the declining effectiveness of discrete spot advertising in broadcast and print media, has been the development of a range of new opportunities and strategies for advertisers in the emerging digital media environment. In the discussion below, we'll examine some of the ways advertisers – and those aiming to benefit from their revenue – have responded to this shifting scenario.

MERGING WITH CONTENT

One response to the challenges to traditional spot advertising has been to reduce the separation between advertising and primary media content (McChesney et al. 2011). The most obvious example is product placement, whereby branded products – from iPhones to Coke cans – are integrated into the environments or storylines of television programmes, films or video games. While the tactic is hardly new, there are signs that in an era where discrete advertising can more easily be avoided by consumers, the ability of placement to integrate advertising with the content consumers choose to engage with has prompted an 'explosion' in its importance (Homer 2009).

Another 'covert' approach takes the form of the advertorial, whereby paid-for promotional content has the appearance of independent copy. Advertorials became increasingly commonplace within magazines from the 1990s onwards and the drift towards such hybrid content has intensified on the internet. An even more effective 'covert' tactic, however, is to bypass direct advertising and instead encourage journalists to write about one's brand or product for free through providing them with easily accessible stories at a time where pressure to produce copy is unprecedented. As we saw in Chapter 7, this encouragement may take the form of general press releases, publicity stunts or product launches aimed at attracting journalists' attention, or the offer of exclusive interviews or free samples in the hope they will be reviewed or mentioned in some way (Davis 2013). Strictly speaking, such activities come under the title *public relations* rather than advertising.

A more up-front way to close the gap between advertising and media content has been the expansion of direct sponsorship of programmes or series, something first pioneered in early 1920s' US radio, with the 'Eveready Hour', a variety entertainment programme that took the name of its sponsor (Baker and Dessart 1998). Today, most programmes on commercial networks carry the brief messages of a dedicated sponsor at the opening and closing credits and the start and end of commercial breaks. There also have been moves towards sponsorship of segments within programmes. Sky News in the UK includes distinct sponsorship – complete with brief commercial messages – of its weather forecasts and sports bulletins as well as having apparently devised discrete pollen and destinations reports with sponsorship opportunities specifically in mind. As well as making mentions of the sponsor difficult for audiences to avoid, direct sponsorship also associates the brand directly with the content itself, the reputation of its producers and its popularity with audiences. Advertising becomes integral to content consumers have actively sought out, then, rather than 'being a cause of irritation and interruption' (Spurgeon 2008: 28).

Some advertisers have gone a step further by creating their own forms of 'branded-content' intended to attract the active, willing attention of consumers through their level of appeal (Arvidsson 2005; Baltruschat 2011; Spurgeon 2008). A well-known early example was a series of short, high production-value films made by BMW in the early 2000s featuring a well-known director and multi-star casts, including Clive Owen as a professional driver involved in a series of driving-related scenarios (involving a BMW of course). The perceived quality of the films and the nature of the celebrities involved ensured they were viewed extensively, written about by journalists and part of millions of everyday conversations, generating extensive publicity for BMW. More recently, retailer John Lewis have invested heavily in extended and high profile Christmas advertisements every year. Rather than having the look of a traditional advert, the ads depict a short story related to Christmas, accompanied by carefully chosen music, with the brand itself only indicated at the end. As well as being shown on television, the 2015 advert, entitled 'Man on the Moon', featured prominently across UK news outlets and was shared extensively across social media. What had been created, then, was less a traditional advertisement than a prominent media event.

ULTRA-TARGETING

A further theme of digital advertising is the increasingly precise targeting of those consumers most likely to be interested in hearing about a product or service. While the last quarter of the twentieth century saw the targeting of specialist groups through appropriately targeted niche media, the internet has made it possible to target messages directly to individuals through precise information about their interests harvested from their online activities and interactions. As Nicole Cohen (2013: 179) has put it, 'as we spend time online, we generate information that is instantly collected, analysed, sold and then presented back to us in the form of targeted advertisements that reflect our online behaviour and consumption patterns'. For Christine Rosen (2005) this shift towards personalisation in advertising forms part of a broader cultural shift from 'narrowcasting' oriented to distinct communities, to 'ego-casting' oriented to the individual.

While sometimes individual targeting draws on accumulated information about long-term tastes and activities – as in the case of recommendations from online retailers on the basis of past purchases – in other cases, it can tap into immediate moods or desires. If I use a search engine, for instance, the search results are often prefaced with advertisements for products related to my keywords. Google's 'adwords' system enables advertisers to purchase particular search terms and have a simple classified-style ad for their product appear when users enter the term. Not only does this enable advertisers to 'be seen by customers at the very moment that they're searching… for the things you offer', as Google (2015) boasts, but it also enables payment on the basis of results because Google only charges when an ad is actually clicked. Elsewhere, 'action-based' pricing is being taken further, with providers exploring models for charging only when ads lead to subscriptions or purchases (Spurgeon 2008). The availability of precise information on the effectiveness of advertising through measures such as click-throughs, subscriptions and purchases, meanwhile, enables advertisers to hone their approach ever-more precisely.

Search-based advertising is not limited to general search engines, extending to any site with a search facility, including the likes of YouTube and social media platforms. And such platforms also display adverts to us on the basis of sophisticated profiling on the basis of the content we create or share, the people we're connected to and the things we 'like'. Meanwhile, it is increasingly common for advertisements triggered by our online behaviour to 'follow' us, across different online platforms and spaces. Spend time perusing an item on an online retail site, and we can expect in the coming days to see repeated adverts for it, whether we're brows-ing an online news site or engaging with friends on social media. Known as 'retargeting' this approach uses information collected through web cookies that connect particular activities to an individual IP address to try to convert 'window-shopping' into purchases (Cohen 2013; Dwyer 2011). The notion of targeted advertising following us around wherever we go may also be beginning to extend to physical locations, with the development of GPS-based forms of advertising that target us via our mobile devices on the basis of our location and/or profile.

INTERACTIVITY

As well as being more precisely targeted, a further feature of digital advertising is its responsiveness to our actions. In contrast to so-called 'push' advertising, where advertisers place messages in front of large groups of people in an allocutionary, or one-way, manner, advertisers increasingly are seeking to interact with us individually, taking our actions as their cue. It could be argued that the development of branded entertainment takes a simi-lar approach in seeking deliberately to engage with consumers who have actively sought out branded content rather than to 'push' it to less willing audiences. And the notion of responding rather than pushing advertisements at consumers forms only one of the ways in which advertisers are seeking to harness the interactivity of digital environments.

In particular, advertisers increasingly are attempting to utilise everyday online interactions between users as a means to build and publicise brand identity. Keen to enter into the often private and intimate worlds that play themselves out in social media environments, advertisers are increasingly conscious of the effectiveness of users liking, sharing and talking about their brands as a means to build corporate identity. If it is advantageous to persuade journalists to write about one's brand, then, it may be doubly helpful if, through 'viral marketing', one can encourage ordinary consumers to collectively enthuse about it to one another. Harnessing the power of word-of-mouth on a massive scale, then, is what many advertisers are attempting to achieve via social media.

There are various mechanisms for this. Setting up brand or product profiles on sites such as Facebook or Twitter and cultivating likes or followers is a simple one, enabling the advertiser to benefit from what amount to friend-to-friend endorsements. Tools that automatically publicise on social media what commercial goods an individual has listened to, read, subscribed to or bought elsewhere on the internet take this one step further. As MacRury (2013) suggests, such mechanisms amount to a more precise, intimate digital equivalent of store-branded carrier bags, communicating on a consumer-to-consumer level a personal endorsement of the product or brand. Returning to an earlier theme, advertisers increasingly are seeking to combine the viral possibilities of social media with forms of branded entertainment as a means to harness collective enthusiasm and grassroots forms of publicity. Pepsi Max's 'Test Drive' video, featuring a reality TV style prank, in which a race driver in disguise goes for an eventful test drive with an unsuspecting car salesman, generated extensive retweets, shares and likes, enabling the video, designed to publicise Pepsi Max as 'a zero calorie drink in disguise' to achieve almost 45 million views on YouTube to date.

Sometimes advertisers are seeking to harness not just the likes and shares of users but also their creativity. According to Spurgeon (2008), a watershed moment in this respect was provided by a series of amateur videos posted in 2005 and 2006 featuring spectacular chemical reactions between Diet Coke and Mentos mints. The videos went viral, promoting thousands to replicate the experiments and millions of others to share them. Following initial uncertainty, both companies eventually exploited the mood. Coke, for example, set up a 'Poetry in Motion' competition challenging consumers to show what extraordinary things they could do with everyday objects (Spurgeon 2008). More generally, the publicity generated by the Coke Mentos experiments alerted the advertising industry to the commercial potential of user-generated content, providing an 'iconic illustration of how and why advertisers, media and advertising industries are increasingly compelled to think about new media consumers as key creative participants in advertising, media and marketing processes' (ibid.: 2). There is also a connection here with ongoing attempts to associate brands with 'coolness' through embedding them in grassroots culture. The difference on social media, perhaps, is the speed with which messages and imagery can organically spread and the simplicity with which they can be monitored, measured and harvested.

A word of caution, however. While the digital era has indeed seen extraordinary developments in advertising strategies and practices, we ought not assume that all advertising is now highly interactive, responsive, individually targeted and so on. It is not necessary to look far – on the internet, throughout the city and on more traditional media such as television or magazines – to see that for every innovative viral branded-content campaign, there also are plenty of more familiar, long-standing advertising formats and techniques to be found, not least of which are spot advertisements, whether they appear in traditional ad breaks, the beginning of YouTube videos or as banner ads on web pages. Just as we should be cautious in assuming an all-encompassing linear development with respect to the meanings conveyed in advertising content, we should recognise considerable and perhaps unprecedented diversity in the formats and operation of advertising. Similarly, when we put our discussions of content and format together, we find interesting combinations and contradictions. While in the most basic terms, the spike in individually targeted online advertising seems to cohere with Leiss et al.'s emphasis on sophisticated individualised symbolic approaches to meaning, in many cases and particularly on search engines, ultra-targeted online advertisements take the form of direct, text-based classifieds – a rejuvenation of relatively simple, text-based object- or service-oriented messages focused on use-value.

CRITICAL PERSPECTIVES ON ADVERTISING

For advocates, advertising and associated industries have come to comprise an important part of a pluralist circulation of information and meaning in contemporary democracies, offering consumers a wide range of choices with which they can engage or disengage as they see fit. Many also emphasise that recent shifts to more interactive, individually targeted and responsive forms of advertising indicate an increase in advertising's usefulness and a democratisation of how the industry works. It might be added that the advertising industry has provided the funding to enable the flourishing of a wide range of independent media services. As industry representative, the Advertising Association puts it, 'without the funding that advertising provides, much of what people value could face a significant decline in quality; much else would require fees and charges beyond what millions would be able to pay' (2015). For many critical commentators, however, advertising represents a particularly pervasive form of ideology, both in the content of advertising culture itself and the implications that reliance on commercial funding has for the orientation of media and culture. Marxist critics argue that media – and everyday lives – have become saturated with commercial culture to the extent that there is little alternative to its logic. For McChesney and colleagues (2011: 40), advertising comprises 'expensive and privileged communication conducted primarily by a small number of corporations to change the behaviour of the vast majority of the population'.

MANIPULATIVE MAGIC

For Raymond Williams (1980), advertising has come to constitute 'the official art of modern capitalist society', reflecting and reinforcing the dominance of corporate capitalism. Advertising's emphasis on the construction of symbolic meanings for consumer objects prompts Williams to understand it as a 'highly organized and professional system of magical inducements and satisfactions' (ibid.). For Williams, to infer that genuine meaning can be achieved through the purchase of objects amounts to a distortion both of the real purpose of consumer goods and the conditions required for human fulfilment. Rather than being marketed on the basis of imaginary meanings, objects, in his view, should be sold and used for their practical benefits. Williams imagines a world free from advertising's 'magic' in which 'beer would be enough for us, without the additional premise that in drinking it we show ourselves to be manly, young in heart or neighbourly', or where 'a washing-machine would be a useful machine to wash clothes, rather than an indication that we are forward-looking or an object of envy to our neighbours' (1980: 185). Meanwhile, through offering us personal symbolic fulfilments through individualised consumption, advertising obscures the collective, social and longer-term means to authentically achieve such goals. For Williams, then, advertising is a self-interested industrial system of manipulation that distorts relations between humans and objects in a manner damaging to our well-being.

A further charge is that advertising's 'magical' emphasis on consumerism obscures the conditions in which objects are produced. Here critics draw on Marx's concept of *commodity fetishism*, whereby objects become expropriated from the (unequal and exploitative) social relations of their production and acquire an independent existence centred on their exchange-value. While Marx's development of the term far preceded the saturation of society by advertising, neo-Marxists suggest advertising enhances and concentrates such fetishisation, taking the veneration of goods as discrete entities to new levels, while removing them further from the exploitative social relations in which they were produced (Williamson 1978). As a consequence, it might be argued that advertising distorts, but also distracts. We have all become so allured by the symbolic meanings of consumption constructed by advertising that these increasingly dominate our existence, distracting us from the broader ills that underlie consumer society and the possibility of radical social change. Amongst other things, such ills include extensions in the exploitation of ourselves and/or others in our role as workers, for, as Davis puts it, 'consumer freedoms and choices often impose considerable restraints on working conditions', which means that '"sovereign consumers", unless born into wealth, must also be subaltern employees' (2013: 46).

Inspired by the structural semiology of Roland Barthes and others (see Chapter 6), Judith Williamson (1978) connects a Marxist meta-analysis with a detailed examination of the construction of symbolic meaning in advertising. Drawing on Lacan's psychoanalytic notion of the mirror-phase, whereby the young child experiences their mirror image as an external, idealised version of themselves, Williamson argues that advertising often works through presenting consumers with such idealised versions of self, compelling them to a narcissistic and alienative form of identification and desire in relation to the identities represented and the objects with which they are associated (ibid.). For Williamson, then, advertising is alienative on a psychoanalytic level, through estranging us from ourselves – suggesting we literally lose ourselves within the ad – at the same time as contributing to a broader form of commodity-fetishism and hyper-consumerism (also see Chapter 6).

SUBVERSIVE CONSUMERS?

Some analysts have criticised what they see as determinist elements of Marxist analyses of advertising such as those of Williams and Williamson. Richards and colleagues (2000), for example, question the rather simplistic dualism posited by Williams between the 'imaginary' symbolic values pervaded through advertising and what he deems the authentic purposes of objects centred only on rational use-value (also see Miller 1995). Is the notion that objects have no significance other than their most basic use-value either a realistic or a desirable one, it might be asked, and is advertising uniquely responsible for the invention of non-utilitarian meanings? Questions also have been raised about the Marxist dualism between production and consumption that underlies the notion of commodity fetishism, whereby the former is regarded as the only natural source of human identity and all symbolic meanings associated with the latter are automatically false, passive and superficial (Miller 1995). On what basis can it be asserted that symbolic pleasures and identities experienced by consumers as genuine are in fact fake?

This last argument leads to the most consistent criticism of Marxist approaches, which is that they under-estimate the potential for consumers to respond to advertising in active, critical ways and develop their own meanings for the objects they consume. In fairness, Williamson does recognise scepticism among consumers to some ad messages, noting a tendency towards sentiments such as 'It's a pack of lies' or 'just after your money', but implies that such criticism is restricted to distrust of denotative claims relating to use-value, with symbolic, connotative meanings regarded as harder to resist. Thus, 'a mother may not believe that brand X really washes brighter than brand Y but she may unconsciously absorb the message of the signifier, which offers a mirror relationship with her and her children' (Williamson 1978: 175). More fundamentally, little to no consideration is given to the notion that audiences may actively contribute to the meanings of consumption. Ultimately, argue Richards et al. (2000: 91), the consumer in this formulation 'has no meaningful input into the way that objects around him or her are known'.

In contrast, for theorists such as Daniel Miller (1995), the construction of consumer meaning consists of a complex set of relationships between producers and consumers and Marxist approaches are in danger of failing to appreciate the variety of purposes to which consumers may put consumer goods. Earlier, Paul Willis (1990) had argued more starkly still that, rather than prescribing particular meanings, advertisements provide an open set of symbolic resources for young consumers to engage with creatively on their own terms. On the basis of detailed ethnographic research he identifies active discernment and criticism in young people's talk about ads as well as marked differences in their response to different commercials, prompting Willis to lament what he refers to as '"anti-mass" blunderbuss arguments' (ibid.: 52). As we saw in Chapter 5, others, including John Fiske (1990), draw attention to the broader creativity of consumers in adapting commercial goods to purposes of their own. Here, the meaning of objects represents a complex interaction or struggle between advertisers on one side and the grassroots meaning-making of consumers on the other.

Arguments about the active involvement of consumers in advertising processes have become particularly important in relation to the development of interactive digital technologies. For Christine Spurgeon (2008), digital technologies are presenting advertisers with interactive 'mass conversational' environments in which consumers are exhibiting unprecedented levels of agency in selecting what they engage with, share and converse about and, sometimes, in transforming ads or commodities into their own forms of creativity, whether via images, DIY videos, music or blogging. In an age of so-called convergence cultures (Jenkins 2008), such consumers – or *prosumers*, as some refer to them – increasingly have 'direct involvement in the selection and distribution of media content, the appropriation and transformation of media content to create new media content, and the generation and circulation of original content' (Spurgeon 2008: 7) confirming 'the passive receiver of mass media to be as much a fiction as the compliant consumer of mass markets' (ibid.: 10).

While the notion of an interactive relationship with advertising partly concerns claims about the agentic nature of consumers, it also relates to the ways advertising has adapted to shifting consumer sensibilities. As market research became more sophisticated, branching into cool-hunting and the like, advertisers learned that to maximise their effectiveness they needed to resonate with ephemeral sensibilities. As we have seen, such adaptation includes the direct incorporation of grassroots meanings, movements or identities into advertising. A circular set of processes takes place, then, whereby consumers develop their own appropriations of commodities and, in turn, advertisers adapt to and re-embrace such appropriations.

For Spurgeon, nowhere is this more true than in the 'mass conversational' environments of the internet. As well as relentlessly scouring the digital footprints left by consumers for information and ideas to inform their campaigns, advertisers increasingly seek to engage the creativity and interactiveness of users, creating stimuli for them to interact with, share, discuss, or respond to. As a consequence, it is not uncommon in parts of the industry to hear references to contemporary advertising as 'collaboration' or 'co-creation' whereby advertisers encourage users to willingly contribute to campaigns on terms of their own choosing – a situation in which, as Cohen (2013: 180) puts it, 'everyone seems to win'.

INTERACTIVE OR CO-OPTIVE?

While advocates may regard advertising's embrace of changing consumer sensibilities and interactive engagements with users as evidence of a democratic transformation of their industry, others regard such trends as evidence of its manipulative power (McGuigan 2009). For Robert Goldman (1992), although agentic audiences have developed ways to resist advertising, the co-option of these critical discourses by advertisers for their own uses represents not an egalitarian meeting of minds, but the nullification of that which is co-opted. Active and critical forms of grassroots culture, then, are reduced to another set of signifiers for advertisers to use in the service of long-standing commercial goals. Similarly for Williamson (1978), advertising's pervasiveness comes partly from its ability to exploit and recuperate critique: 'advertisements will always recuperate by using criticisms of themselves as frames of reference which will finally enhance, rather than destroy, their "real" status' (ibid.: 174). For Williamson too, this represents an indication of advertisers' power and influence rather than some sort of subservience to consumers. And, as well as incorporating criticism of themselves, advertisers also, it is pointed out, frequently draw upon broader notions of resistance, subversion and radicalism, whether in a political or cultural sense. In 2001, for example, magazine adverts for Shiseido make-up depicted elaborately made-up female faces, juxtaposed with the caption 'Be Radical' in one case and 'Empowering' in another, associating the brand with the notion of difference, boldness and female independence. The effect of this, it might be argued, is to transform the notion of liberation from a substantive and ongoing set of political goals into an empty form of symbolism to be achieved by using the right make-up.

At the same time as harvesting grassroots cultures and oppositional discourses for useful symbolic meanings, marketers, it is argued, have become specifically exploitative of the unpaid, creative labour of consumers. The idea of audiences as unpaid workers was first introduced by Smythe (1981) in relation to the relationship between mass media, consumers and advertising but has since increased in its usefulness as a concept. Whether in the form of young people in inner city ghettos giving credence to Nike trainers, or users of Facebook contributing through their interactions to ever-richer marketing profiles, advertisers – along with the media companies who court their business – have managed to put us all to work for their own ends, it is argued. For Cohen (2013) the exploitation of consumers on social media represents a 'double-commodification'. First, the digital footprint created by our everyday interactions is sold to advertisers as an effective means for them to target the ads to appropriate consumers. Second, social media need not even invest in media content of their own, as do traditional media platforms, since they rely upon user-generated content, which Cohen understands as a further instance of 'outsourcing unpaid labour to users'. In both senses, then, our everyday interactions, shares and likes are being commodified – put to commercial use. As Cohen puts it, 'social media, free from strictures of time and place, have pushed the work of the audience to the extreme: these sites still package audiences into demographics for advertisers, but the audience also provides the content that is the very constitution of these sites' (ibid. 180). Cohen's explanation of dual commodification arguably omits a third form of unpaid labour whereby advertisers rely on users to distribute their content through shares, adaptations and likes and, sometimes, provide ideas and creativity for their campaigns. Once again, what some regard as a democratisation of advertising represents, for others, the manipulative co-optation of the everyday lives and interactions of consumers into the self-interested agendas of commercial corporations.

CONCLUSION: UBIQUITOUS COMMERCIALISM

The pervasiveness of commercial advertising on interactive media platforms also draws attention to the lengths to which the saturation of everyday life by advertising and commercial culture has gone (Dwyer 2011). Though there are differences between platforms, social media often bring 'private' lives and intimate interactions into what are essentially commercialised settings whose parameters are defined by the interests of advertisers. As such, they convert our everyday interactions into commodities and intersperse them with commercial messages (MacRury 2013). We may have a significant degree of control over our 'social privacy', through determining which of our friends, colleagues, acquaintances or others have access to what we say (Hodkinson 2015; Marwick and boyd 2014) but when it comes to 'institutional privacy' – our ability to control access to us by large-scale organisations – social media offer few such possibilities. Effectively, Cohen argues, everyday social relationships themselves have been commodified: 'people must consent to being watched – and to the commercialisation of more and more aspects of our lives… including activities we may pursue precisely because we are seeking non-commodified spaces or social relations' (ibid.: 186). Put this together with the commodification of the various other on and offline spaces and it's easy to see why some suggest that advertising and consumer culture have become ever-present to the extent of being unnoticed. We may indeed have developed the skills and discernment to view ads critically and have undoubtedly been afforded a degree of control with respect to whether we share, contribute to or like commercial messages. Yet the extent to which we are surrounded, together with the capacity of advertisers to incorporate us into their agendas, makes avoidance of the broader consumerist ideology they collectively promote less likely.

This is particularly so because the ubiquity of this ideology reflects not just the pervasiveness of direct, identifiable advertising but also its impact on content, delivery systems or platforms that rely upon advertisements for funding (Dwyer 2011). Such funding may enable such organisations to operate (mostly) free from government interference but only at the cost of a degree of subservience to the needs of their corporate clients, whether in respect of the kinds of content delivered by television services, the selection and construction of stories by online news or the design of search engines and social media platforms. Sometimes this can be particularly direct, in the form of avoidance or even self-censorship of content that might run counter to the commercial interests of advertisers (see Chapter 3) but more common – and pervasive – is a broader bias towards consumer-friendly formats and content (see Chapter 6). For Baltruschat (2011: 57), as well as pervading the content of TV formats such as reality television and make-over shows, this consumerist ideology can also be seen in the orientation of social media towards individual identity-construction and performance – or what Baltruschat calls the branding of the self.

That does not mean that all content in these commercial worlds is shaped by sponsors or explicitly focused on consumption. At times, advertisers are happy just to associate themselves with cultural phenomena venerated by consumers and critics, as in the case of some of the 'quality' television dramas produced by studios such as HBO, even if the stories, settings and characters have little obvious connection to them. Similarly, the move away from direct sponsorship or commercials by platforms such as Netflix may be regarded as a form of de-commercialisation of culture in these particular environments, at least with respect to direct advertising. The broader picture, though, is of a media sphere dominated in one way or another by the needs and interests of its commercial partners. And as advertisers move further towards integrating their messages with different forms of content and with our everyday interactions, there are few signs their commercial influence over the realm of culture is liable to dissipate.

QUESTIONS/EXERCISES

1   a) Go through each one of Leiss et al.'s advertising frames, establishing the key time-period and characteristics of each. For each one, see if it is possible to identify either a historical or contemporary advertisement that serves as an example.

b) On the basis of what you were able to find, what would you conclude about Leiss et al.'s designation of different advertising frames to particular historical periods? Is there a dominant advertising frame at present, do you think?

2   a) In what ways have advertisers sought to draw on youth cultures as part of their construction of meanings? Think of some contemporary examples.

b) Why do advertisers do this?

3   What does Raymond Williams mean when he interprets advertising's emphasis on symbolic value as a form of magic? Is his perspective persuasive?

4   In what ways has advertising been transformed in relation to the emergence of new digital media environments? Should these be celebrated as a democratisation of advertising processes?

5   a) Identify some examples of how the concept of unpaid labour might be applied to the relationship between digital media users and advertising.

    b) How valid is the use of this concept as a critique of advertising in digital and online environments?

SUGGESTED FURTHER READING

Cohen, N. (2013) 'Commodifying Free Labor Online: Social Media, Audiences, and Advertising', in McAllister, A. and West, E. (eds) *The Routledge Companion to Advertising and Promotional Culture*, Abingdon: Routledge – Provides a useful critique of the exploitation of users' free labour on social network sites by advertisers.

Leiss, W., Klein, S., Jhally, S. and Botterill, J. (2005) *Social Communication in Advertising: Communication in the Mediated Marketplace – Third Edition*. New York: Routledge – Influential historical analysis of advertising content, including identification of different phases of representation of the relationship between objects and consumers.

McGuigan, J. (2009) *Cool Capitalism*. London: Pluto Press – Critical discussion of attempts to capture and deploy 'cool' by contemporary corporations, including reference to marketing and advertising.

Spurgeon, C. (2008) *Advertising and New Media*. Abingdon: Routledge – Detailed introduction to the transformations being undergone by advertising in digital media environments.

Williams, R. (1980) 'Advertising: The Magic System', in *Problems in Materialism and Culture*. London: Verso, pp. 170–95 – Seminal piece outlining the emergence of advertising as an industrialised system of commercial persuasion and attacking its generation of magical or imaginary meanings for consumer goods.

CHAPTER 10
MEDIA AND THE PUBLIC SPHERE: DIGITALISATION, COMMERCIALISATION AND FRAGMENTATION

FOCAL POINTS

- Understandings of media as potential facilitators for a participatory public sphere
- The role of media in the construction of national identity and culture
- Arguments that commercialised media distort and discourage public engagement
- The impact of digitalisation on public participation, engagement and cohesion
- Criticisms of attempts to nurture the public sphere and national identity

INTRODUCTION

What role do contemporary media play in people's ability to identify with and participate in their society? Do social media, news sites, games or television enable us to engage with the broader culture and politics of our nation or do they facilitate a mass 'opting-out' into fragmented digital environments centred on consumption? Building on some of the arguments discussed in previous chapters, the forthcoming pages address the complex relationship between media, public culture and democracy. We begin by focusing on the theme of citizenship and the role of media in facilitating what is known as the public sphere, with particular attention to the influential work of Jürgen Habermas. The chapter goes on to discuss the ways media construct national community and the implications of this for belonging and engagement. The second half of the chapter focuses on the impact of recent changes in the world of media on the cohesion of societies and on political and cultural participation. This will involve a consideration of the implications of an increasingly interactive and fragmented media environment.

MEDIA AND THE PUBLIC SPHERE

HABERMAS' PUBLIC SPHERE

Discussions about the role of media as facilitator for citizenship and the public sphere often revolve around the early work of Jürgen Habermas, a contemporary German theorist who emerged from the Frankfurt School. Habermas argues that the ongoing project of human emancipation is dependent on the ability of publics to participate in ongoing rational communication about matters of significance to their society and its future. According to his idealistic vision, societies should collectively progress and improve on the basis of public agreement reached through inclusive rational discussion, free from the corrupting influence of pragmatism, money and power. Writing in the 1960s, Habermas (1992) discusses, as a model for his vision, the development of the eighteenth and early nineteenth century bourgeois public sphere in Europe. The public sphere, he argues, consisted of a space for the development of shared culture and ideas, located between the realm of 'public authority' (government) and the private realm of 'civil society'. Private individuals would come together into a shared space and public opinion would be developed through discussion of ideas, values and events. These ongoing discussions would feed into government and the commercial sector, guiding their direction and holding them to account.

The primary physical setting for this eighteenth century public sphere, argued Habermas, consisted of coffee houses within major European cities and the educated, bourgeois clientele of such establishments. Equally important to the process, however, was the development of a critical, politically-oriented newspaper industry, which fed into, represented and responded to the public discussion and opinion that took place in such spaces. Whilst he accepts this eighteenth century culture of elite gentlemen was far from inclusive, for Habermas, this ought not obscure the broader possibilities highlighted by what took place. It offered a model for the notion that private individuals might come together to form a rational, participatory public sphere and that the private interests of individuals and commerce would be balanced with those of the greater good.

Habermas argues that during the heyday of the coffee house era, a productive equilibrium was achieved between the state, business, family and the public sphere itself. Yet, as capitalism expanded, public culture is deemed to have found itself increasingly squeezed out by an expanding state and a drastic growth in the power of industry and commerce. Referred to as the *system*, these 'steering mechanisms' of society, including administration and the market, are dominated by instrumentalism and, specifically, an emphasis on ensuring their own reproduction and expansion. The gradual saturation of the system's influence into the realm of everyday culture, or the *lifeworld*, is argued to have resulted in the proliferation throughout that sphere of an instrumentalist, pragmatic logic and a distortion of the once independent, free and critical public sphere (Habermas 1987). The open, rational public culture on which Habermas focused so much attention, then, had been choked by the increasing domination of all aspects of society by hierarchical, instrumentalist ways of thinking that centred upon pragmatism and organisational self-interest. Over the course of the rest of the chapter, we'll focus on how these abstract elements of Habermas' account of the decline of the public sphere relate to the practicalities of media within contemporary societies.

MEDIA AND PUBLIC ENGAGEMENT

Many have adopted the public sphere ideal sketched out by Habermas as a vision for societies to strive for, and have focused particularly on the role of media in such a project. They envisage a democratic situation in which, rather than being confined to occasional elections, public engagement in politics and society takes the form of an informal, open culture of everyday micro-cultural interaction, where values, ideas, culture and opinions are constantly shared, exchanged and debated. The developing outcomes of such public interactions would then feed back into governing bodies in a substantive and ongoing manner. Such theorists believe media and communications have a substantial role to play in the development and/or survival of such a public culture. Let's examine why.

STIMULATING AND INFORMING DEBATE

The first role of media in the facilitation of the public sphere is the provision of a detailed and reliable appraisal of events, ideas and discussions of public interest, not least those relating to the activities of governments and other powerful institutions. In other words, news, documentaries and other forms of media content should act as trustworthy stimulators of public debate and reliable providers of the knowledge necessary to participate in an informed manner. One can hardly engage in meaningful, rational discussion without being strongly acquainted with subject matter, existing viewpoints and forms of evidence. As we have seen, it is not conceivable for media to be entirely neutral, 'factual' or unbiased (Chapter 7), but for proponents of the public sphere this does not mean we ought to regard all versions of the world as equally valid or useful. An effective, empowered public sphere, it is argued, requires journalism, in particular, to be trustworthy, rational, reliable, honest and thorough, as well as accessible to the whole population.

REPRESENTING PUBLIC OPINION

In an effective public sphere the developing outcomes of micro-debates across society would also be relayed back via media channels to everyone else, both to facilitate the further development of discussion and enable influence on powerful institutions such as commercial corporations and government. In the ongoing provision of information and relaying of viewpoints, then, media must be responsive, reflecting the range of developments in public culture and opinion rather than imposing an elite agenda. A circular process of stimulating and relaying should take place, continually feeding and being fed by society's ongoing conversation with itself while enabling a two-way interaction between the public and powerful institutions.

ACTING AS AN INCLUSIVE FORUM FOR CONVERSATION AND DISCUSSION

As well as relaying public culture and opinion back into media through the intermediary of journalists, writers, actors and others, media can act as forums for the direct expression of ideas, opinions and information by people themselves. Media should set themselves up as virtual spaces in which members of society directly interact and engage with one another. Letters pages, phone-in shows and comments facilities on news websites all constitute potential examples of this, but arguably are in the process of being replaced by more all-inclusive forms of social media.

NURTURING PUBLIC BELONGING AND COMMUNITY

For many commentators, the public sphere also implies participation in a broader public culture and the nurturing of a sense of cohesiveness, common identity and belonging. The political functions of the public sphere, it is argued, cannot be fulfilled unless people are sufficiently engaged in society in a broader sense. For Garnham (1993: 369), this implies a need to nurture some sort of common identity or values: 'it is impossible to conceive of a viable democratic polity without at the same time conceiving of at least some common normative dimension'. Such an emphasis on the generation of community draws on use of the notion of *fraternity* by French philosopher Rousseau to refer to the importance of developing a cohesive national brotherhood characterised by strong bonds of attachment and mutual obligation and responsibility.

Consistent with Rousseau, the sense of belonging and community evoked by many advocates of the public sphere tends to centre on the nation. After all, Habermas' account of the bourgeois public sphere is, as Stevenson (2002: 61) puts it, 'explicitly connected to the nation state' rather than anything more local or international. Interestingly, in his later work Habermas questions the need for political engagement to be rooted in normative cohesion or community and rejects the automatic centring of the public sphere on the nation state itself (1996; 2001). For many of those influenced by his early work, however, the facilitation by media of national identity and community comprised a key component of connecting private individuals with a culture of public participation (Garnham 1993; Scannell 1989). And it so happens that media and national identity do have a long-standing historical relationship with one another, the former often being credited with a key role in the development of the latter.

NATION AS IMAGINED COMMUNITY

The notion of national belonging and community relates to cultural convention rather than natural affinity. 'Nationalism is not the awakening of nations to self-consciousness; it invents nations where they do not exist', argues Gellner (1983: 169). And there is little doubt about the pivotal role of communications technologies here. From the mass publishing of books and newspapers to the development of the telegraph and eventually the telephone, communication created greater links and commonalities between localities, the distinctiveness and separation of each becoming gradually less significant than the larger entities of which they were a part.

For Anderson (1991), the combination of mass printing technology and the early stages of European capitalism enabled the mass distribution of books across national territories, creating large-scale, geographically distributed reading publics. The gradual standardisation of print languages across national markets contributed to a concurrent homogenisation of everyday language. Equally important, common printed materials generated shared cultural agendas and experiences, making it possible for people across each nation to read and engage with the same literature. The development of newspapers amplified this by providing a time-symmetry to the shared experience of the nation: whole countries would engage with the same set of controversies and events at the same time. Media were partly responsible, therefore, for the development of a sense among disparate people that they had something in common and belonged to one another. Anderson (1991: 6) terms this media-induced sense of sameness 'imagined community'. 'It is imagined', he argues, 'because the members of even the smallest nation will never know most of their fellow members, meet them, or even hear of them, yet in the minds of each lives the image of their communion'.

If the distribution of print media was heavily responsible for the construction of national identity prior to the twentieth century, then the responsibility was taken up by radio and then television in the years that followed. In geographically small or medium-sized countries, the most prominent broadcasters tended to reach the whole nation simultaneously and even in larger places such as the US, independent local or state broadcasters soon were rivalled by national networks which replicated content throughout the country. The combination of spectrum scarcity and regulation ensured only a limited number of channels and programmes were available, which enabled the collective engagement of substantial proportions of the national population with a shared set of cultural experiences. It became possible, then, for the entire nation to sit down 'together', digesting the same stories, ideas, art or music often at the same time. This had profound implications for citizens' everyday awareness of one another and the distinct national culture they formed.

As we saw in Chapter 8, the fostering of national identity has also been a central element of public service broadcasting since the early days of Reith's BBC. And while much has changed since the 1920s, theorists have continually emphasised the importance of public service broadcasting in bringing national publics together. Arguing that 'broadcasting has brought into being a culture in common to whole populations and a shared public life of a quite new kind...', Paddy Scannell (1989: 138) highlights the construction by television of a shared sense of time – in the form of daily schedules and of a collective annual calendar, the latter enabling populations to come together at regular intervals to experience key symbolic events, from sports finals to political ceremonies, major national charity events and seasonal messages from the head of state. One-off events, of course, can be equally important, not least funerals, weddings, anniversaries and births related to royal families or other nationally important figures. Importantly, Scannell argues that the continued nurturing of shared public culture – which he explicitly connects to broader public participation and citizenship – depends on there being common media experiences across the population, something he links to the continued promotion of a limited number of national mixed programming television channels for everyone:

> …equal access for all to a wide and varied range of common informational, entertainment and cultural programmes… must be thought of as an important citizenship right in mass democratic societies. It is… perhaps the only means at present – whereby common knowledges and pleasures in a shared public life are maintained as a social good for the whole population. (1990: 26)

For Michael Billig (1995), as well as bringing members of populations together, news media provide regular reminders to audiences about national identity. Overt expressions of national sentiment, he argues, can often be found within coverage of national sports teams, immigration and wars. Yet under the surface of such overt expressions, he argues, lie a multitude of mundane and barely noticeable everyday references. Illustrating the point with his own discourse analysis of UK daily newspapers, he demonstrates that nation was evoked repeatedly as a means of framing the most everyday and ordinary of stories: 'Britain's best cartoons', 'Worst places in Britain to be without a job', 'Britain basked in 79 degree temperatures yesterday' were among countless examples. The use of 'we', 'us' and 'our' as universal, unspoken code for nation is even more prevalent, he claims, whether in headlines, captions and article text: 'Europe taking *our* money', for example, or 'Time *we* changed Government.' 'We' could in theory have a variety of meanings, but no one needs telling that in these contexts it refers to the nation. It is this barely noticeable 'banal nationalism', argues Billig, that makes more overt expressions so resonant.

Media, then, have enabled shared national spaces that enable the imagining of broader publics; provided shared experiences and agendas to connect geographically separated people; and repeatedly flagged our allegiance to country and one another through representations of the national 'us'. For much of the twentieth century, it might be argued, national media tended to operate in a *centripetal* manner, drawing geographically and sometimes culturally disparate people into shared spaces and binding them together. And, for theorists such as Garnham and Scannell, the facilitation of such public cohesion forms an important component of the development of inclusive forms of *political* engagement and citizenship such as those envisaged by Habermas'. As we shall see, however, both Habermas and those influenced by his work accept that the bourgeois public sphere he described declined alongside the continued rise of capitalism and commercial mass media, and that contemporary conditions are far from ideal for the generation of a contemporary version. In Habermas' original account, the role of media in this failure relates to the inability of a commercialised communications system to facilitate democratic participation.

DECLINE OF THE PUBLIC SPHERE

In spite of the importance of media as facilitator of shared national experience and identity during the twentieth century, the public sphere itself had already failed by this point according to Habermas. The increasing domination of society by markets, the state and instrumental reason were deemed to have undermined his vision of a genuinely free, critical and inclusive space characterised by informed and rational public discussion. As part of this, he identifies a number of specific failures of media. The theme that unites these is commercialisation, something that coheres with his emphasis, in common with earlier Frankfurt School theorists, on the rise of instrumentalism.

FROM FACILITATORS TO SHAPERS

The range of small-scale newspapers and pamphlets in operation during the eighteenth and early nineteenth centuries was regarded by Habermas as suitable to the task of facilitating public discussions by feeding and absorbing a range of ideas, observations and viewpoints. Subsequently, he argues, the intensification of capitalism precipitated a concentration of media power. As greater control of the press – and subsequently broadcasting – fell into the hands of a small number of companies, the impact of media is deemed to have shifted from facilitator to shaper: 'Whereas previously the press was able to limit itself to the transmission and amplification of the rational-critical debate of private people assembled in a public, now conversely this debate gets shaped by the mass media to begin with' (1992: 188). And this influence is deemed to have been used by corporate media to promote whatever set of political arrangements would best facilitate the consolidation of their profit and power. Rather than empowering the people by holding dominant institutions to account, media themselves became synonymous with the powerful, having been colonised by the system, as Habermas would have it.

The situation was exacerbated by the increasing significance of public relations, or what Habermas calls 'opinion management', to the shaping of news agendas in the twentieth century. Not only were media owned by powerful interests, but other powerful interests were using their wealth to hire professionals to enhance their image and promote their ideas by influencing journalists and news agendas. As we saw in Chapter 7, studies indicate that press releases and other PR activities account for a substantial and increasing proportion of contemporary news content. This, for Habermas, amounted to the hijacking of the public sphere and distortion of public communication and debate by techniques normally associated with consumer advertising. Alongside concentrations of media control and ownership, the broader control over discourse exercised by the powerful via public relations and advertising are understood to have centralised power and shaped agendas rather than assisting in their devolvement to the public.

COMMERCIALLY DRIVEN CONTENT

A further consequence of the colonisation of media by commercialism is, according to Habermas, a concentrated emphasis on profitability. Rather than being an end in itself the communication of culture and discourse becomes a means to attract audiences and advertising revenue. Following in the footsteps of earlier Frankfurt School theorists such as Adorno and Horkheimer, Habermas blames this profit orientation for an emphasis on immediately stimulating but superficial forms of culture. An emphasis on trivia, sensation, emotion and personalisation, he argues, distracts the public from political engagement while ensuring debate that does take place is superficial, misinformed and centred on simplistic emotional response rather than critical reasoning. In particular, Habermas laments the corrosive impact of consumerist ideology across media content – a theme explored in Chapters 6 and 9 – arguing that audiences are lulled into believing their contribution to society lies in short-term decisions over the purchase of goods, rather than collective commitment to participation in democracy: '…private enterprises evoke in their customers the idea that in their consumption decisions they act in their capacity as citizens…' (1992: 162).

Addressed in relation to news in Chapter 7, the theme of media 'dumbing down' is often closely connected to arguments about media and the public sphere. Michael Tracey (1998: 264), for example, castigates 'the corrosive influence of the main currents of popular culture', which he blames for 'the trivialization of public discourse, an evangelism of the ephemeral, the celebration of the insignificant and the marginalization of the important'. Tracey connects this trend not just to deregulation in general but the decline of public service broadcasting and of the emphasis placed therein on facilitating public knowledge and participation through reliable, in-depth coverage of matters of public controversy.

The circulation of culture, ideas and opinion, then, is argued by Habermas, and some of those influenced by his ideas, to have become an increasingly one-way process dominated by a media-driven agenda of superficial distractions, consumerism, public relations and self-serving current affairs coverage. Rather than enabling public culture to influence and hold to account those in power, media, the state and other powerful institutions are involved in an ongoing dialogue with one another, with the population reduced to the role of onlookers. The recent newspaper phone-hacking scandal in the UK, discussed in Chapter 7, provides, it might be argued, a particularly vivid illumination of such a situation.

Recent developments in digital and online media technology, however, may have profound implications for the engagement of private individuals in public culture and democracy and have prompted some to re-evaluate the relationship between media and the public sphere. While some regard digital and online environments as offering renewed hope for the development of engaged and participatory forms of culture and politics, others point to the endurance of commercial and corporate domination and the fragmentary and globalising possibilities of new media, regarding these as an impediment to the kind of shared societal identification some regard as crucial to an effective public sphere.

A DIGITAL PUBLIC SPHERE?

ONLINE PARTICIPATION AND DEMOCRACY

As we have seen, Habermas placed the blame for the decline of the public sphere on the expansion of instrumental reason, including the commercialisation of media. Yet the affordances of traditional mass media technologies such as radio and television also are deemed to have played their part. Such media have facilitated linear mass communication from the few to the many and while this may have been effective in the generation of national consciousness, it fits less well with facilitating the interactive exchange of culture and ideas by ordinary members of society. The hierarchical impact of concentrations of media power, then, may have been exacerbated by the one-directional bias of technologies (Mander 1978). Occasional examples of audience involvement such as phone-ins or participating studio audiences have significance and potential (Livingstone and Lunt 1994), but provide the exception that proves the rule.

In contrast, the digital transformation of media has led to a substantial growth of interactive communicative possibilities and offers, for some commentators, the potential to revive the public sphere. In particular, convergence between mass and interpersonal media, summarised in Spurgeon's (2008) notion of the internet as a medium of 'mass conversation', has led to optimistic predictions about the re-engagement of ordinary people and of the seizing back of power and influence from the establishment. For former US presidential candidate, Al Gore, the interactivity of the internet had the potential to herald a new era of public discussion and citizenship:

> In the world of television, the massive flows of information are largely in only one direction, which makes it virtually impossible for individuals to take part in what passes for a national conversation. Individuals receive, but they cannot send. They hear, but they do not speak. The 'well-informed citizenry' is in danger of becoming the 'well-amused audience….' Fortunately, the Internet has the potential to revitalize the role played by the people in our constitutional framework… It is the most interactive medium in history and the one with the greatest potential for connecting individuals to one another and to a universe of knowledge. It's a platform for pursuing the truth, and the decentralized creation and distribution of ideas… (Gore 2007)

More recently, theorist John Hartley (2009) has outlined a shift in the social role of television, from a broadcasting age where populations were spoken to and represented by a centralised media establishment, to an age of online democratised productivity, where everyone contributes to the creation of content and citizens increasingly can express themselves, both culturally and politically. Clay Shirky, too, has placed repeated emphasis on the potential for online interactivity, to 'spread' media production, enabling people to 'privately and publicly articulate and debate a welter of conflicting views' (2011).

Sure enough, the internet does enable an unprecedented combination of scale and interactivity, providing a limitless array of information, conjecture and culture for users to engage with and the possibility to produce, distribute and share content. According to Bakardjieva (2005: 127), such interactivity can enable citizens to experience political and media institutions as something within 'attainable reach' of their everyday lifeworld, something they can interact with and influence. Similarly, for Henry Jenkins, users and fans are finding that digital environments offer them more and more opportunities to 'take media into their own hands' (2008: 17) giving rise to new forms of influence and power with respect to media processes as well as the distribution of ideas and culture in a broader sense.

Such arguments are extended with a particular focus on blogging and social media by Zizi Papacharissi (2010). For Papacharissi, through combining an intimate embeddedness in the minutiae of individual everyday lives with the potential to participate in broader forms of public culture and debate, networked social media bring together private selves with broader society and politics. The informal and unstructured environments of Facebook, Twitter and parts of the blogosphere, she argues, enable private individuals to participate in matters of public and political importance in ways that challenge the more hierarchical spaces and agendas of traditional political engagement.

Papacharissi's emphasis on the private and individual-centred focus of social media spaces prompts her to envisage a shift away from more formal notions of a public sphere at the same time as drawing attention to how such channels are nevertheless contributing to greater vibrancy, inclusivity and democracy when it comes to political debate. The public content of major media content producers, meanwhile, is increasingly entangled with these private spheres of digital interaction. News, for example, increasingly is dependent for its circulation on the filtering and sharing practices of social media users and, in turn, such practices strongly influence what stories are covered and how. Thus, 'citizen gatekeepers' have the collective ability to 'endorse, reject or modify news agendas and potentially related policy and public agendas' enabling them 'direct access to an agenda they previously could only be passive observers of' (Papacharissi 2010: 153).

Perhaps, then, the internet is more suited than its predecessors to a situation in which society truly talks to itself, rather than being talked at by the powerful few? From resistant citizen journalists blogging inside war-torn or illiberal countries to global anti-capitalist movements and feminist protests against gender inequality, there are plenty of examples of interest groups or individuals effectively utilising the potential of the internet as a means of mobilising support for their perspective and thereby contributing to a broader political environment. Millions more interact with one another in relation to matters of everyday culture or politics via different forms of social media through sharing, appropriating, commenting and arguing in ways that sometimes can feed out of their private spheres and into more public ones.

ENDURING POWER DIFFERENTIALS

Yet we should be cautious before assuming contemporary digital environments are going to fundamentally transform power relations or prompt a full-scale resurgence of inclusive, effective democracy. From the companies that sell us our mobile devices, software and network connections, to those that provide popular content and services, the net has, in spite of its decentralised structure, become a highly effective means for large-scale corporations to maintain and develop their dominance. And sitting alongside new 'dot com' giants such as Google in this respect, are many of the companies who dominated the 'old' media environment, moving rapidly and effectively to establish online market share. Crucial though it may be as a socio-cultural development, it is worth remembering that much of the content created and published by ordinary internet users will only be engaged with by tiny audiences. In spite of notable exceptions such as the peer-produced Wikipedia and occasional examples of user-generated content that go sufficiently viral to generate significant interest, the most influential content still tends to originate with powerful organisations of one kind or another.

It is they, after all, who have the initial presence and means of promotion to consistently attract such attention. Even for optimists, such as Jenkins, it remains important to recognise that apparently democratising possibilities have been accompanied by 'alarming concentration of the ownership of mainstream commercial media, with a small handful of multinational media conglomerates dominating all sectors of the entertainment industry' (2008: 18). For Rheingold (2000), this replication of existing power relations on a new medium illustrates the danger in expecting fundamental social issues to be resolved by technology.

Not content merely to dispel what he sees as optimistic myths, Rheingold, alongside Lyon (1998) and others, also highlights how the enticing interactivity of the internet may increasingly subject those who publish, share or interact with content to surveillance and control by powerful interests. From the content of our email, to the sites we visit, links we share, items we purchase and music we stream, everything we do on the internet can be tracked and recorded. 'The spider spins the web in order to entangle and entrap the unsuspecting fly', suggests Lyon (1998: 33), who goes on to argue that 'without disputing whether inherently democratising possibilities lie latent in the internet, it is worth exploring the capacity of the 'Web' to capture and control, to target and to trap, to manage and to manipulate'.

As we saw in Chapter 9, the most obvious beneficiaries of this ability to track and monitor our every move online are advertisers, and the media and tech organisations who sell them access to consumers via their platforms or content. As more of our lives are lived out on these commercialised electronic networks, will our thoughts, conversation and creativity influence powerful commercial interests and hold them to account or, instead, be appropriated into helpful resources utilised by such institutions for their own ends? It may not be too much of a stretch of Habermas' thinking to suggest that, for all the potential benefits of digital environments, the commodification of everyday life, conversation and creativity in these thoroughly commercialised spaces of surveillance represents a particularly pervasive extension of the colonisation of the lifeworld by the system.

Of no less importance, meanwhile, is the increasing use of online surveillance by governments, police and security agencies. Following the 2015 Paris terrorist attacks, the UK government published draft legislation compelling internet service providers, mobile phone providers and others to retain records of a variety of core digital activities for all users and provide them to designated authorities on request subject to certain conditions. Nick-named the 'snooper's charter', the legislation effectively placed every citizen of the country under constant digital surveillance. Similar forms of legislation are being developed elsewhere. While such developments do not nullify the democratic or participatory possibilities of digital environments they offer a reminder of ongoing disparities of power and the ways technology can reinforce as well as challenge them (Dahlgren 2009).

FRAGMENTATION

For some theorists, however, the continued dominance of powerful media corporations and the location of interactions within commercialised spaces of surveillance do not represent the only reasons for pessimism about the potential of new media technologies to rehabilitate the public sphere. Such theorists also suggest that media digitalisation, alongside a broader climate of neo-liberal deregulation, is gradually diluting the national public culture they regard as so crucial for effective public engagement and debate. While Habermas himself became increasingly convinced that cultural togetherness was not essential for the regeneration of the public sphere, others ponder whether the erosion of societal belonging threatens to remove an important component of participation and citizen engagement. Either way, the apparent decline of national cohesion is a profoundly significant development.

The construction and facilitation of national identity by media in the twentieth century was reliant, as Scannell (1989) observed, on the common engagement of national populations with a limited range of content. Media bound society together, then, because a combination of spectrum scarcity and regulation meant that people had little choice but to watch or read the same things. The daily agendas and conversational topics of whole societies were strongly influenced by a small number of programme schedulers for universally targeted, mixed content channels. Such was the homogeneity of the broadcast experience that people could be confident of their ability to converse with peers, colleagues or even relatives across the country about the previous evening's viewing.

Digitalisation and deregulation, however, are reducing the number of media experiences that national populations share with one another. Rather than trying to offer something for everyone on broad mixed channels, a multitude of digital channels attract advertisers by delivering particular blends of programming oriented to specialist groups. For champions of national shared culture such as Scannell, even the first signs of such narrowcasting in the 1990s represented a threat to the notion of a unified national public:

> Generic programming fragments the general public that is still constituted in today's four national UK television channels into particular taste publics whom advertisers are increasingly keen to target. In so doing it destroys the principle of equality of access for all to entertainment, information and cultural resources in a common public domain. (1990: 26)

As well as offering an increasing range of specialist channels, of course, digitalisation increasingly is providing greater options to consume individual items of content on-demand. Personal video recording technologies (PVRs) enable pause and rewind of live television, easy recording of content for later viewing and libraries of on-demand programmes. Adherence to predefined programme schedules is further loosened by a range of online services, including YouTube, Netflix, Spotify and Amazon Prime, which enable viewers to stream content on demand. The individualisation of media consumption habits precipitated by this surely suggests a further dissipation of the common media experiences which predominated in the past (Dahlgren 2009).

If, at various points in their past, media have had a *centripetal* social impact by binding members of society together, then many commentators suggest the new media environment is more likely to have a *centrifugal* effect, facilitating social and cultural fragmentation (see Figure 10.1). Tracey connects the pluralisation of media with a 'retribalisation' of society and the demise of concern with shared culture or matters of common importance. 'Difference and diversity', he argues, 'may be socially formed, but they are helped along the way by new systems of communication, developed in the past two decades, which are profoundly individualistic and definitely not collective, public, shared or coherent' (1998: 263).

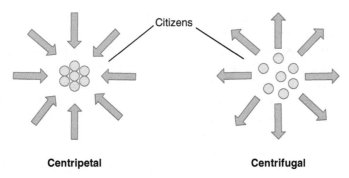

Figure 10.1   Illustration of centripetal/centrifugal media impact

When offered an increased range of choices over what to consume and when, it is argued that people gratefully accept the opportunity to opt out of any broader national public sphere in order to pursue specialist or individual interests and identities. For Christine Rosen (2005) all this amounts to a form of 'ego-casting' whereby media increasingly target each of us individually and we, in turn, become ever-more focused upon the minutiae of our individual tastes and preferences.

A similar picture of fragmentation may be taking place in relation to interactive forms of digital communication. Rather than encouraging people to share content with or engage with diverse groups of others as part of broad publics in inclusive spaces, the ability to select, filter and refine exactly what or who to engage with seems likely to favour the pursuit of particular interests or identities and association with narrower groupings, at least most of the time. This has two implications in relation to discussions of the public sphere. First, it is relatively easy for internet users to avoid contact with matters of public or societal importance such as current affairs and political controversies. Rather than encourage political interest, knowledge or participation among those for whom such subjects had little previous appeal, the internet, it might be argued, maximises the ease with which people can opt out of the broader public sphere in favour of their developing plethora of individualised tastes and interests.

Second, those who do continue to engage in political discussions may primarily do so through engaging with content and individuals sympathetic to their existing views. Rather than testing and developing their ideas and explanations in a rational, open-minded way against a range of others across society, then, conservatives, liberals, environmentalists and socialists may each end up conversing among themselves, preaching to the converted and strengthening both existing beliefs and collective hostilities towards those who differ (Sunstein 2002). While Hill and Hughes identified this sort of fragmentary trend as part of research on themed discussion groups in the early days of the internet (1998) others have identified similar tendencies in the more personalised worlds of blogging (Adamic and Glance 2005) and social media (Public Affairs Council 2013). Combined with the increasing specialisation of other media forms, this may result in a situation where, instead of having a shared public sphere, we find ourselves faced with a range of distinct and separate 'public sphericules' (Gitlin 1998). For Dahlgren (2009: 164–5) the danger here is that 'the lack of confrontation with information or arguments that may challenge existing world views' reduces 'the net's potential for promoting agonistic civic cultures characterised by robust civic talk'.

It is important to note some exceptions to this fragmentary picture, however. Recent evidence suggests that some social media networks can facilitate contact and debate between members of different clusters. A study by Conover and colleagues (2011), for example, established that, although networks of 'retweets' on Twitter clustered into clearly identifiable left- and right-wing networks, their examination of networks of Twitter 'mentions' revealed more contact between the two groups. While it seems likely such contact often consisted of members of each group criticising their opponents to a sympathetic audience of supporters, the study nevertheless illustrates contact between opposing views and individuals. There also remain circumstances in which large proportions of society are brought together through their engagement with particular content, news events or other activities. High profile sporting events like the Super Bowl still manage to cut across various interest groups as do global news events such as high profile terrorist incidents. Equally, through offering the ability to converse with numerous others at the same time as engaging with television or other forms of content, social media sometimes can facilitate particularly intense and interactive forms of shared media experience. The key question, perhaps, relates to how many such conversations cut across society rather than appealing exclusively to narrower interest groups.

GLOBALISATION

At the same time as generating potential for the internal fragmentation of national public culture, contemporary media form an important component of processes of globalisation, whereby national boundaries are bypassed by international flows of culture. Media are far from the only factor here, with the global expansion of capitalism as an equally significant driver. Meanwhile, the cheaper, faster movement of people has enabled substantial contact between cultures, contributing to internal diversity and intimate connections between migrant and minority groups and their countries of origin (see Chapter 12). In connection with such developments, however, the specific transfer from country to country of sounds, images and ideas has made a substantial contribution to transnational commonalities and connections.

Appadurai (1996) conceptualises the relationship between media, communication and other elements in the process of globalisation through five interrelated and overlapping global 'scapes'. *Financescapes* refers to the globalised worlds of commerce; and *ethnoscapes* to a world of people increasingly characterised by transnational movement, whether through tourism or migration. *Technoscapes* provides Appadurai's way of referring to the development and global distribution of technologies, including those which facilitate more efficient transnational communication. *Ideoscapes* constitutes the world of political ideas, images and ideologies which, to an extent, are also argued to have spread globally, in spite of a lingering focus upon the nation state here. The element which most directly concerns us here is his notion of *mediascapes*, which refers to the transnational media worlds with which we all engage. This is enabled by the global spread of the means to produce and receive media as well as the increasingly rapid transnational flows of content itself.

Consumers based around the world, then, can be expected increasingly to be consuming the same films, box sets and music tracks as one another, to say nothing of the global paraphernalia and celebrity culture associated with them. Global chains of influence also prompt the spread of successful narrative structures, programme formats and genres. And digital and online technologies are increasingly enabling collective global news experiences, whereby people across the world engage simultaneously with the same event. The Paris terrorist attacks in 2015 provide an excellent example whereby millions around the world engaged, in real time, with the same sets of sounds and images while, in many cases, conversing with one another about them. Perhaps more than any other medium, the internet offers its users potential access to seemingly infinite amounts of imagery, sounds, music, commerce and ideas from anywhere in the world.

We ought not assume, though, that an increase in transnational connections and similarities of experience necessarily equates to the development of a monolithic global mass culture, as envisaged in the cultural imperialism theories discussed in Chapter 6. There may be no shortage of global mass cultural products, from Hollywood blockbusters to high profile popular musicians. As well as being received differently by different national or regional populations, however, mass cultural goods account for only a proportion of the global mediascapes envisaged by Appadurai. Universal transnational super-products like Coca Cola and Justin Bieber are accompanied by a range of smaller-scale, specialist forms of expression that can have an equally transnational reach. Rather than global homogenisation, what is occurring may be more akin to a combination of fragmentation and globalisation, resulting in the expansion across national borders of distinct, specialist cultures as well as more standardised forms. As Hannerz once put it, 'What is personal, primary, and small-scale, is not necessarily narrowly confined in space, and what spans continents need not be large scale in any other way' (Hannerz 1996: 98).

Neither should it be assumed that national consciousness is automatically consigned to the past by such processes. While the increase in global flows is undoubted, a significant degree of national distinctiveness continues to pervade media channels and public discourse in most countries. This is particularly so in the case of news agendas, which continue to be dominated by a combination of domestic stories and distinctive national angles on international events. Meanwhile, even though the internet now forms their primary outlet, 'newspapers' continue to regularly remind readers of national affiliations through their news values, priorities and forms of address. And, where they continue to exist, public service broadcasters such as the BBC continue to explicitly construct particular forms of national shared experience as a key part of their remit.

It is also clear, however, that in their combination, fragmentation and globalisation imply a weakening of people's everyday participation in the broader national public cultures. We may be constantly reminded of our national identity to the extent that it is ingrained in our consciousness, but the intensive imagined sameness envisaged by Anderson may still be liable to recede at least a little as our everyday engagements with media and culture become more distinct from those of many of our fellow-nationals and more similar to those of like-minded media users elsewhere. And if, through such processes, our allegiance to national public cultures gradually erodes, it is not unreasonable to ask whether this has implications for our participation in national political cultures.

CONCLUSION: DECLINE OF THE NATIONAL PUBLIC

The discussions above suggest that, in spite of certain interactive possibilities, the notion of a national public may end up being further diluted by digital media environments that encourage cultural fragmentation, disengagement and transnational cultural flows. It is also unclear whether the increasingly commercialised nature of the media environment is compatible with democratic participation along the lines envisaged in Habermas' discussions. Yet if, for one reason or another, a unitary shared public sphere along such lines does look a distant prospect, should we lament this or celebrate it? For some critics, the notion of the public sphere has always been a problematic one.

The ideal of fully inclusive, equal and informed participation may sound laudable, such critics argue, but in practice, the rationalist version of public culture lauded by Habermas privileges an elite set of cultural ideas while excluding more marginalised forms of culture and expression. A particular target for criticism is the eighteenth and early nineteenth century bourgeois public sphere on which Habermas bases so much of his vision, which consisted exclusively of the perspectives, viewpoints and priorities of wealthy and powerful white males. 'Was it ever open to the scrutiny and participation, let alone under the control, of the majority?', asks Kevin Robins. 'If so, where were the workers, the women, the lesbians, the gay men, the African Americans' (Robins, cited in Morley 2000: 144).

Habermas may acknowledge these limitations of the bourgeois public sphere, but this does not prevent him, according to critics, from retaining significant elements of its elitist character in the vision he espouses. Some argue, for example, that the scientific reason which informs his ideal of rational critical discussion is itself derived from particular kinds of bourgeois, white and masculine ways of looking at the world which privilege some kinds of debate as legitimate, while excluding others (Morley 2000). Notably, there is no place in Habermas' rationalist vision for emotion, affectivity and subjectivity, all of which are dismissed as commercialised distortions oriented towards the realm of the personal rather than that of the public. Likewise champions of the public sphere who are critical of 'dumbing down' have tended to be particularly dismissive of content such as soap operas, reality television, game shows, popular news formats and celebrity culture, which tend to place emphasis upon emotion, identification and empathy and also to be disproportionately popular among women and the working class.

It is suggested, then, that while making proclamations of inclusivity and participation, some public sphere advocates end up excluding non-elite forms of expression. And this is argued to be particularly so for theorists who advocate the nurturing of cohesive national culture and identity as a base for political participation. This is because it is hard to envisage the defining of collective priorities, values or goals without the drawing of boundaries and the exclusion of those who fail to fit in, whether in relation to class, gender, sexuality or ethnicity. Likewise, attempts via public service media to provide unitary space for engagement with shared or national culture are unlikely to be able to avoid marginalising certain voices or identities. As Morley puts it:

> By the very way (and to the extent that) a programme signals to members of some groups that it is designed for them and functions as an effective invitation

to their participation in social life, it will necessarily signal to members of other groups that it is not for them and, indeed, that they are not among the invitees to its particular forum of sociability. (2000: 111)

Some advocates of the public sphere are more flexible than others in relation to these questions. Some, for example, recognise the value of a wide range of different forms of expression towards decentralised forms of public culture and debate (Dahlgren 1995; 2009). Others reject what they regard as the exclusionary project of national cultural cohesion, focusing instead on the possibility of a looser, more dynamic and diverse set of different spheres of culture and discussion (Downing and Husband 2005). Habermas, himself, meanwhile, has sought to move away from the notion of the public sphere as a national configuration and the assumption that it must rest upon any sort of deep cultural sameness. In light of trends towards fragmentation and globalisation, he calls for the development of post-national public spheres, discussing a pan-European sphere as a potential example (2001).

Habermas' vision of a pan-European public sphere is unconvincing, however, and it remains questionable whether his ideals of popular participation and engagement can truly be separated from the existence of at least some sort of cultural connection between the different segments of society. Will people across the cultural spectrum really be minded to participate regularly and substantively in politically-oriented discourse concerning the future of a broader society they feel little investment in and have limited contact or communication with? Even in diverse, decentralised media environments, then, might there still be value in the nurturing of at least some shared forms of public culture and communicative space that connect together the myriad groups and individuals which make up societies?

QUESTIONS/EXERCISES

1   What might be the role of media in the development of the public sphere? To date, how successful have they been in this respect?

2   a)   What does Anderson mean by 'imagined community'? In what ways have media contributed to the construction of national imagined community?

     b)   Analyse the content of the homepage of an online newspaper on a particular day. To what extent and in what ways does it address or construct a particular nation or national identity? Does it exhibit any of the banal references to nation identified by Billig in relation to daily newspapers?

     c)   Is the nurturing of common national identity and culture an essential prerequisite for the encouragement of political engagement in the public sphere?

(Continued)

(Continued)

3   a)   What does it mean to suggest media have shifted from being a largely centripetal force to a predominantly centrifugal one?

    b)   In what ways have recent developments in media contributed to processes of fragmentation? Are there any exceptions to this?

4   Has the increasing use of social media enhanced democracy and the public sphere or contributed towards their decline? Consider as many factors as you can.

5   a)   In what ways has the notion of the public sphere been argued to be an elitist idea that excludes and marginalises subordinate groups?

    b)   Can there ever be any such thing as a fully inclusive national public?

SUGGESTED FURTHER READING

Butsch, R. (ed.) (2007) *Media and Public Spheres*. London: Palgrave – Collection of chapters focused upon the relationship between media and a range of large- and small-scale publics.

Dahlgren, P. (2009) *Media and Political Engagement: Citizens, Communication and Democracy*. Cambridge: Cambridge University Press – Detailed examination of the role of media in facilitating and shaping civic engagement and political participation.

Morley, D. (2000) *Home Territories: Media, Mobility and Identity*. London: Routledge, Chapter 5 – Discussion of the links between media, the public sphere and exclusivist constructions of national identity.

Papacharissi, Z. (2010) *A Private Sphere: Democracy in a Digital Age*. Cambridge: Polity Press – Detailed argument that suggests social media, through connecting the intimate and the political, are forming a new participatory private sphere.

Scannell, P. (1989) 'Public Service Broadcasting and Modern Life', *Media, Culture and Society,* 11(2): 135–66 – A seminal defence of the role of public service broadcasting as a means of generating national togetherness.

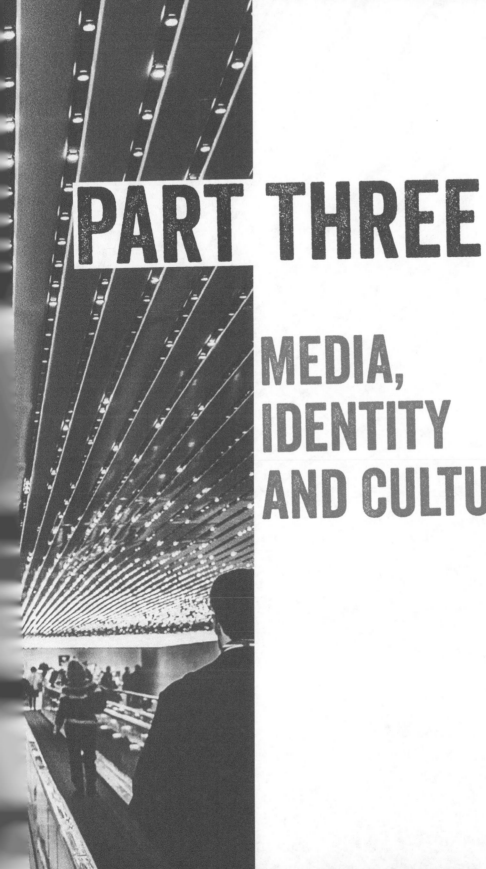

PART THREE

MEDIA, IDENTITY AND CULTURE

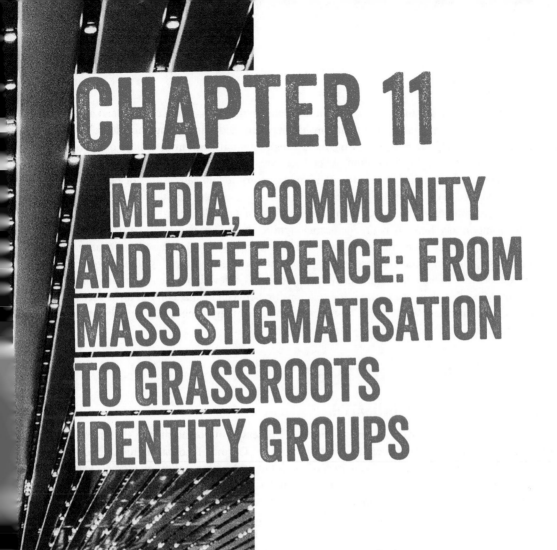

CHAPTER 11

MEDIA, COMMUNITY AND DIFFERENCE: FROM MASS STIGMATISATION TO GRASSROOTS IDENTITY GROUPS

FOCAL POINTS

- Understandings of media as homogenising or de-differentiating force
- Stereotypes, stigmatisation and the construction of difference
- Specialist media as facilitators of distinct community
- Interactive media and debates about 'virtual community'
- Case studies: class stigmatisation, youth subcultures, TV fan communities, LGBT groups

INTRODUCTION

Theories of media, culture and society sometimes focus on the ways media erode social and cultural difference. Some highlight the relationship between media and a singular 'public' or nation while others flag the potential of media to construct a universal mass culture or, conversely, a sort of mass individualisation, whereby distinct community attachments become eroded in favour of individual difference. Yet contemporary media can also – for better or worse – be involved in the construction of collective difference and the facilitation of minority or specialist communities. The representation of marginal or subordinate groups within mass media is of importance here, as is the increasing significance of specialist and participatory forms of media oriented to particular segments or communities, whether based on locality, consumer taste, fandom, political persuasion, or sexual orientation. Referring to a range of examples, including social class segments, youth subcultures, television fan communities and sexual minorities, this chapter examines the relationship between media, cultural differences and distinct communities. We'll begin, however, by looking at approaches that regard media as a homogenising or de-differentiating force.

MEDIA AS ERODER OF DIFFERENCE

HOMOGENISATION AND ATOMISATION

Media sometimes are regarded as part of broader processes of social change that erode collective differences. The nineteenth-century writings of German theorist Tönnies (1963) pointed to the gradual eclipsing of *gemeinschaft* (community) with *gesellschaft* (society) as the dominant mode of human association. Tönnies understood gemeinschaft as a grassroots form of collective unity premised upon the organic shared understanding, mutual dependence and self-sufficiency created by kinship, religion and the isolation of pre-industrial village life. Although media are not the main focus of Tönnies' account, gemeinschaft is deemed to have declined in prominence as a result of forces of modernity and industrialisation, including the movement of populations to large, anonymous cities, increased communication and trade between previously isolated localities, and the growth of capitalist modes of production. Such developments are deemed to have led to the prominence of gesellschaft, which is larger-scale, more disparate and centred on mechanical, rational relationships of convenience between self-interested individuals (Delanty 2003).

Tönnies' approach to gemeinschaft is adapted by Redfield (1955), who specifies that, as well as being organic rather than chosen, community implies a homogeneous group which is distinctive, bounded from the outside world and small enough to enable intense communication between members. It is not easy to find an example of so pure a community in modern societies, but the fictional depiction of local identity in UK soap operas such as *Coronation Street* or *East Enders* illustrates some of the features. On the basis of the accident of their shared locality, the characters know and depend on each other, socialise in the same handful of local cafes, bars and shops and proudly defend their distinct collective identity and values (Geraghty 1991). Such representations can strike a chord with audiences because, even if communities of this kind are increasingly rare, the ideal of folk community as distinctive, local, face-to-face and organic endures.

According to Bauman (2001), because it was dependent on isolation from the outside world, the traditional notion of community outlined by Tönnies and Redfield was undermined by the development of communications and media. Ever-more intensive contact with people in other places would blur insider/outsider boundaries while eroding distinctiveness and mutual dependence, rendering community a matter of choice rather than necessity. Others too have pointed to media as key to the demise of distinct communities. From the telegraph to the printing press, to television and the internet, emphasis is often placed on the ways media increase contact and shared experiences between people based in different settlements, villages, towns and even countries (see Anderson 1991; Bauman 2001; McLuhan 2001; Meyrowitz 1985). The implication is that the greater the penetration of media into people's lives, the more distinctive communities would dissolve into larger, more anonymous and de-differentiated societies.

MASS CULTURE

The argument is particularly stark in theories of mass culture. Such theories are best known for bemoaning the decline of elite high culture as a result of media propagation of superficial and highly standardised forms of culture to an increasingly homogeneous 'mass' of ordinary consumers. They are equally vocal, however, on the part played by such standardised mass media, alongside broader processes of industrialisation, in the erosion of distinctive grassroots folk communities. For MacDonald, folk culture, whose distinctiveness and substance had reflected the organic grassroots communication of ordinary people, was undermined by an artificial and undifferentiated mass culture imposed from above through media. This process is deemed to have led to 'a large quantity of people unable to express themselves as human beings because they are related to one another neither as individuals nor as members of communities' (MacDonald 1957: 59). Lamenting the decline of such folk communities and their distinctive traditions and values, he characterises 'the mass man' as 'a solitary atom, uniform with and undifferentiated from thousands and millions of other atoms…' From a slightly different perspective, the early Frankfurt School's neo-Marxist approach to mass culture also portrays media as a homogenising, atomising force that erodes cultural difference (see Chapter 6). Emphasising the underlying orientation of culture industries towards marketing standardised products to the largest possible audience, Adorno castigates the 'abstractness and self-sameness to which the world has shrunk' (1990: 57).

INDIVIDUALISATION AS DE-DIFFERENTIATION

While theories of mass culture emphasise the subsuming of collective difference into a top-down mass culture, notions of individualisation describe a different form of de-differentiation, centred on the fluidity of individual identities in a social and cultural world centred on seemingly infinite choices. From this point of view, through removing barriers of distance and offering connections across the social and cultural world, media have contributed alongside broader social change to the generation of an imperative to choose who or what to associate ourselves with. As media and popular culture have diversified, such choices have proliferated, rendering traditional forms of collective distinctiveness, such as those centred on locality, social class, religion or other aspects of social background, of less overall significance (Bauman 2001). As a consequence, individuals are left without stable roots or distinctive community belonging and are expected to forge their own identities through myriad choices. For Bauman (2000; 2001), an enduring desire for belonging prompts us to attach ourselves to myriad symbols and affiliations, many of which are related to media, advertising, consumption or popular culture. Instead of being defined by the locality, class or religion into which we were born, then, we may choose to identify as horror fans, golf supporters, gamers or celebrity watchers.

Crucially, because these media and consumer-related identities are elective, or chosen, they can be just as easily unchosen, so that attachments are always 'until further notice' (Beck and Beck-Gernsheim 2001). People buy into and then out of a multitude of partial and temporary attachments, it is argued, rather than committing themselves to genuinely distinct or lasting groupings. Instead of demonstrating genuine collective distinctiveness and commitment, then, the various 'groups' with which we temporarily associate ourselves are argued to be fleeting, superficial and subordinate to the shifting individual identities of those who float between them. From this point of view, the more extensive and expansive they become the more media contribute to what we might think of as a mass individualised society centred on ephemeral, multi-affiliated (and insecure) individuals rather than entrenched social differences or distinct communities (Bauman 2000).

An example can be drawn from recent perspectives on youth cultural identities. Many argue that diversifications in the operation of media and commerce have helped render youth identities increasingly complex and unstable. Instead of aligning themselves with distinct communities or subcultures derived from their background, young people, it is suggested, individually move between a variety of symbolic forms of cultural identity. A culture industry ever-more adept at promoting new styles, symbols and crazes offers little opportunity to form genuinely distinctive communities, leaving youth to pick and mix from the plethora of pre-mediated options (Polhemous 1997). Lacking community distinctiveness or substance, these media-constructed symbols are ideally suited to being quickly tried on and cast off, it is suggested; because there will always be a range of other styles to buy into, any groupings that do emerge are transitory and loosely bounded (Bennett 1999; Muggleton 1997). In this formulation, then, a culture saturated by media and consumption prevents the development of distinct forms of collective identity and thereby contributes to the dilution of collective social and cultural difference.

Although diverging in certain respects, then, the approaches and examples focused on here illustrate a tendency to characterise media as a significant factor in the erosion of collective differences. Yet, as we shall see, there are also a number of ways media can do the opposite. That is, they can play a key role in the construction or facilitation of difference and of particular forms of collective identity. This partly relates to the construction of small-scale forms of distinctive community by specialist forms of media but also to the construction of marginal communities through different forms of media stereotyping and stigmatisation.

STIGMATISING (AND AMPLIFYING) DIFFERENCE

The most obvious way media can amplify cultural difference is through their tendency to focus attention on particular segments of society and to represent them in a manner that underlines their otherness. From news websites to video games or Hollywood, media often use and repeat *stereotypical* depictions of identified social groups. This enables a degree of predictability and simplification that makes narratives more familiar for audiences, while also reflecting a tendency to amplify already circulating sets of assumptions. Stereotypes reduce the members of identified social groups to generalised and repeated sets of characteristics, holding the potential, according to Pickering, to 'render uniform everyone associated with a particular feature' (2001: 4). If the elderly are repeatedly depicted in a particular manner – as conservative and intolerant, or irrational, weak and helpless, for example – then audiences may come to associate such characteristics with all or most older people and to understand them as essentially distinct and different as a social group. Importantly, while media stereotypes of powerful groups undoubtedly exist, it is subordinate and minority groups who tend to be affected most acutely, both in terms of the pervasiveness of the stereotypes and the depth of their impact. 'Stereotyping reduces, essentializes, naturalizes and fixes "difference"', argues Stuart Hall and 'tends to occur when there are gross inequalities of power' (1997: 257–8). Furthermore, while some stereotypical representations may be regarded as relatively harmless, others can stigmatise in a manner that excludes and marginalises such groups from implicit notions of 'normal society' defined in its opposition to them.

POVERTY PORN? A STIGMATISED UNDERCLASS

A pervasive example of such stereotyping in recent years concerns the representation in news, television and other parts of popular culture of some aspects of lower working-class culture. Labelled by some as 'poverty porn', reality television shows focusing on the lives of the poorest members of society have been accused of stigmatising such groups and amplifying their difference from 'normal' society. In the UK, *Benefits Street* – a 2014 Channel 4 series focusing on the residents of a street in a deprived area of Birmingham – drew extensive criticism for reinforcing stereotypes of the urban poor as feckless, lazy and criminal. Though the show also included more nuanced depictions, the packaging of its characters as '*Benefits Street*' and emphasis on worklessness and welfare payments in its opening credits served to frame those represented primarily in terms of their receipt of tax-payers' money in a manner that cohered with a plethora of other television shows and with depictions of lazy welfare claimants in the popular press (Jensen 2014). For Tracy Jensen, the presence of more rounded or diverse depictions as part of the content did little to prevent the overriding stigmatisation of a lazy, semi-criminal underclass set apart from the 'normal society' being invited to look in on it:

> the national abjects of poverty porn serve to transform precarity into a moral failure, worklessness into laziness and social immobility and disconnection into an individual failure to strive and aspire. The recent swathe of poverty porn does not only play on existing shameless curiosity about poverty, it also positions the lives of the poor as a moral site for scrutiny, something to be peered at, dissected and assessed. (Jensen 2014: 2.7)

According to Jensen, the generalised setting apart of the poor as 'skivers' here represents just the most recent version of a set of established underclass stereotypes, including 'the single mother, the troubled family, the unemployed, absent or feckless father' (Jensen 2014: 2.6).

A particularly pervasive symbol of such stereotypes in the UK has been the figure of the 'chav'. Comparable in some ways to the Australian figure of the 'bogan', 'chav' emerged as a particular kind of reference to poor young people in the 2000s. For Hayward and Yar (2006: 17), representations of the chav as poor, stupid, dirty, lazy, vulgar and violent recalled notions of the 'great unwashed' of Victorian England, representing 'a soft semantic target for those keen to rebadge the underprivileged and socially excluded among us as a new form of feckless underclass'. Panicked about as an unruly threat, while simultaneously ridiculed for his/her impoverished cultural tastes, the chav formed a figure of scorn across reality television, comedy, news bulletins and opinion columns. For Imogen Tyler, the chav became a catch-all term for a variety of related stereotypes of working-class youth, as in the following extract she cites from a newspaper article about anti-chav websites:

> And we will know them by their dress… and trail of fag ends, sparkling white trainers, baggy tracksuit trousers, branded sports top, gold-hooped earrings, 'sovvy' rings and the ubiquitous Burberry baseball cap. Throw them together, along with a pack of Regal, and you have the uniform of what is being described as the UK's new underclass – the chav… They are the sullen youths in hooded tops and spanking-new trainers who loiter listlessly on street corners and shopping malls, displaying an apparent lack of education and an all too obvious taste for fighting; the slack-jawed girls with enough gold or gold-plated jewellery to put H Samuel out of business. They are the dole-scroungers, petty criminals, football hooligans and teenage pram-pushers. (The Scotsman 2004, cited in Tyler 2008)

Importantly, as well as creating generalised forms of stigmatisation and reinforcing difference, stereotyping such as this can contribute to social exclusion of a more material kind. As Jensen (2014) points out, the consistent framing of the lives of the poor by programmes such as *Benefits Street* – and the earlier stereotypes they reinforced – connected seamlessly with the rhetoric of mainstream politicians seeking to justify government cuts to welfare spending.

FOLK DEVILS, MORAL PANICS AND LABELLING

For Tyler (2008), Harwood and Yar (2006) and others, the figure of the chav represents a good example of a constructed media *folk devil*. Coined by Stanley Cohen (1972), this term draws attention to the tendency of media to construct caricatures of people or groups that come to symbolise perceived societal ills or problems – stigmatised outsiders who threaten ordinary society and offer its members 'visible reminders of what we should not be'. Cohen's own primary case study concerned a 1960s media *moral panic* surrounding violence between young mods and rockers. A stream of sensationalist headlines, reports and features about violence had the effect of exaggerating the magnitude of such events and stigmatising young people involved in the two subcultures as mindless, dangerous 'others', while prompting condemnation and calls for action from politicians and others. Importantly, as well as setting out the details of the exaggerated media coverage, Cohen comments upon the broader significance of media moral panics, both for the stigmatised groups and the rest of society.

The panic and stigmatisation relating to mods and rockers served to reinforce and police the perceived normality of mainstream values, through use of stereotyped outsider figures as something to define them against. But, crucially, the coverage is also deemed to have had an amplifying impact on the substance, distinctiveness and identity of mod and rocker sub-cultures themselves. The characteristics and meaning of each group, including their mutual animosity, became cemented in the minds of participants as a result of the media coverage, argues Cohen. Their distinctiveness as subcultures was strengthened, then, and the notoriety and excitement with which they were associated attracted new recruits while concentrat-ing the involvement of existing members. Resentment at media stigmatisation, meanwhile, prompted an amplification in the deviance of participants to the extent that aspects of their behaviour came to resemble the media representations. As Cohen puts it, 'the societal reaction not only increases the deviant's chance of acting at all, it also provides him with his lines and stage directions' (S. Cohen 1972: 137).

Cohen's seminal study forms part of a broader body of work centred on the transac-tional relationship between so-called deviant groupings and mainstream society. From Albert Cohen's (1955) examination of delinquent boys, through work on drug users by Howard Becker (1963) in the US and Jock Young in the UK (1971), such work centred on the way negative stigmatisation of marginal groups would tend to strengthen their resolve, commit-ment and distinctiveness. The experience of being collectively rejected and labelled, in other words, prompts those on the receiving end to become more tightly knit, different and hostile to the society doing the labelling – sometimes to the extent of developing ever-more deviant or counter-hegemonic approaches to life. If we take such understandings seriously, it becomes clear how negative media stereotypes of particular groups may not only represent but amplify cultural differences.

Since the classic works identified above, countless instances of moral panic and stig-matisation have taken place in different societies, with stereotyping and hysteria targeted at inner city youth, striking workers, new age travellers, binge drinkers, immigrants and various others. And studies sometimes have illustrated how such coverage can feed into and amplify difference. Sarah Thornton (1995), for example, demonstrates that media stigmatisation of 1990s' rave culture amplified the eventual size and distinctiveness of the movement. Panic-stricken headlines about drug-fuelled free parties, combined with the banning of records, police clamp-downs and repressive legislation are argued to have strengthened the commit-ment and unity of ravers, as well as attracting a wave of enthusiastic new participants.

The extent to which the same labelling argument could be applied to our earlier example of media stereotypes of welfare scroungers and chavs is not fully clear. We don't know, for example, how many people ever identified as chavs or what impact media representations had upon their identities. Most who have researched the subject regard the term primarily as a loaded caricature with little direct correspondence to positive forms of identification among disadvantaged young people themselves. What does seem clear, however, is that media stigmatisation of the feckless poor both reflects and amplifies existing prejudice among the majority with respect to aspects of lower working-class culture and that, in turn, this is liable to exacerbate the sense of exclusion, reliance upon one another and sense of collective identity of those on the receiving end. One way or another, then, it seems clear that negative media stigmatisation contributes to social difference.

Theories relating to stereotyping and labelling, then, may prove useful in illuminating the significance of media constructions of difference. It also should be acknowledged, however, that stigmatisation and moral panics can be as significant in their reinforcement and policing of the homogeneity of dominant or majority cultures as they are in the amplification of the difference of the stigmatised. They could be interpreted, then, as forces of homogenisation, at least in some respects. Amongst other things, this means that if we are to develop a more rounded understanding of how media construct and facilitate collective difference, we need also to examine the role of more positive forms of coverage in smaller-scale media oriented to distinct groupings.

TARGETING COMMUNITY

In the course of orienting themselves to particular sub-sections of society, specialist media often can contribute to the development or consolidation of distinct communities of one kind or another. While this is particularly important in today's fragmented digital environment, there are also examples that are neither new nor particularly high tech. Among the most obvious of these are local newspapers and radio.

LOCAL MEDIA

In spite of the prominence of national media in many countries, local newspapers, radio stations, television and websites can comprise an important part of the identity of regions, cities, towns and villages. With consumption confined to the particular areas they serve, such media typically construct a sense of collective exclusivity among their local audience through bringing residents into the same communicative space and enabling them to share an agenda of events, debates or forms of entertainment. Local media content often explicitly emphasises the significance of place, with outlets presenting themselves as champions of local opinion. The result can approximate a localised version of the national 'imagined community' discussed by Anderson (1991), with people continually reminded of their shared locality in a manner comparable to Billig's (1995) discussion of banal nationalism (see Chapter 10). Local media also facilitate direct contact between residents, meanwhile, enabling communities to speak to themselves. Whether they cover local politics, crime, school fetes or sports, articles and shows are full of the voices of residents themselves, while letters pages, phone-ins and online comment/discussion facilities offer forums for the exchange of views. Unlike their national cousins, local media also facilitate and publicise face-to-face events, whether through editorial coverage or through acting as community notice boards.

Writers such as Franklin and Murphy (1998) and Crisell (1998), however, express concern that the community value of local media has been eroded by market forces. Ownership by national or global corporations alongside the dominance of free media funded solely by advertising, argue Franklin and Murphy, have led to commercial-driven, populist agendas. Rather than providing in-depth examination of matters of local importance and constructing a sense of mutual support and responsibility, the suggestion is that local newspapers increasingly offer a bland, commercialised agenda dominated by crime and entertainment. And sometimes such pressures may lead to a decline in local distinctiveness, as in the case of the long-standing tendency to fill local commercial radio airtime with international pop music (Crisell 1998). Patchy levels of consumption among local populations as a whole, meanwhile, place limits on reach and impact. Nevertheless, the overall success of local media conglomerates such as Johnston Press and Local World amid steadily growing online audiences, as well as the considerable value placed on local media by its consumers, indicate an enduring market (Ofcom 2009). UK regulator Ofcom also notes that, while it has presented significant challenges to traditional local media, the internet has also enabled the development of new ultra-local media services, from online community television stations to street-oriented Facebook groups. Even if there are limits to its pervasiveness, then, the case of local media illustrates how media and communications can contribute to community distinctiveness.

NICHE MEDIA AND INTEREST GROUPINGS

While local media target the diversity of people who reside in a particular location, *niche* media court those united by particular characteristics, lifestyles or interests. Pre-dated by long-running high-brow newspapers aimed at particular social elites, the proliferation of *narrowcasting* coincided with the late twentieth century diversification of consumer culture. As outlined in Chapter 9, the mass market standardisation of *Fordist* approaches to commerce gradually gave way to a post-Fordist environment characterised by the development of a broader range of products and services, each carefully targeted at distinct consumer niches. An increasing emphasis on the symbolic value of goods for the identities of consumers, meanwhile, contributed to a broader shift towards the importance of leisure and consumption as the basis for both identity and community (Osgerby 2004). The shift was mirrored in many sectors of media. The final decades of the twentieth century saw a proliferation of magazines and ever-more specialist radio and television services oriented to a plethora of demographic and interest-based identity groups. Through their specialist orientation, such outlets were able to offer advertisers access to concentrated, specialist audience groups and cultivate a sense of collective distinctiveness and loyalty among participants that such advertisers were keen to associate themselves with. Subsequently, the digitalisation of television and radio, alongside the development of the internet, has taken the range of specialist media on offer to consumers to an entirely new level.

Sometimes the groups to which specialist media are oriented remain fairly broad. General categories of women's or men's magazines, for example, target markets that are clearly defined but non-cohesive, while consumer hifi or cooking magazines are specialist in content, but oriented towards interests that are relatively widespread. Other specialist media, though, covet more cohesive identity groups. Magazines, websites and other media oriented to minority activities such as rock climbing, snow-boarding, motorbike culture or model railways, for example, involve more tightly-knit and distinct audience groups with their own community values and sets of knowledges. Specialist media oriented towards intense fans of cult mass media products such as *Star Trek* or *Dr Who* provide an example. Here, niche

Figure 11.1   Consumer magazines © Torbjorn Lagerwall

media act as an intermediary between mass media products and particularly committed fan groups. Providing a range of inside information and gossip relating to scripting, special effects and casting decisions, they feed the enthusiasm of participants and encourage their self-differentiation from other members of the mass audience (Jenkins 1992). For Hills (2002) such fan-oriented publications, which include *Cult Times* and *Doctor Who Magazine*, commercially exploit the loyalty that characterises fan groups. Importantly, however, they also construct and amplify such loyalty. Sci-fi fans also have found themselves explicitly targeted by television narrowcasters such as *Syfy* as well as countless online magazines and a host of other internet resources, offering spaces of concentrated consumption and community.

Specialist music media can play a similar role, with sites and publications aligning themselves with particular genres and feeding collective identities. In some cases, these can play a substantial role in strengthening distinct scenes or communities. Sarah Thornton's (1995) seminal work on 1990s' rave culture suggests that, through operating in tandem with negative mass media coverage of the scene, positive coverage oriented towards insiders in youth lifestyle magazines such as *ID* and *Face* offered the subculture a key self-affirming space. The tone of such 'subcultural consumer magazines' (1995: 155) aligned itself with clubbers themselves, giving voice to their disdain for newspaper misunderstandings, while reinforcing subcultural rhetoric and values. Niche music media, Thornton argues, 'categorize social groups, arrange sounds, itemize attire and label everything... they baptize scenes and generate the self-consciousness required to maintain cultural distinctions (1995: 151). And since Thornton's work, the volume of specialist media available to music fans of different persuasions has multiplied across a range of platforms, with genre-specific music television channels, specialist online radio stations, streaming playlists and commercial websites all contributing to local, national and international music scenes.

LGBT-oriented media provide a further example of the role of specialist media in the construction and facilitation of community. An ever-expanding range of off and online lifestyle magazines, led by market leaders such as *OUT* and *Gay Times*, compete to offer spaces for expression, discussion and representation for groups often marginalised by mass media. There are also dedicated LGBT television channels, including *OutTV* in Canada, *Pink TV* in France and *Here TV* and *Logo* in the US, though the latter recently was criticised for diversifying its programming away from its LGBT focus. Such media court and construct particular versions of LGBT identity, complete with identifiable styles, tastes, perspectives and insider knowledges. In so doing, they can contribute to community commitment and cohesion and the establishment of norms and boundaries. For some years the most widely consumed LGBT media were dominated by a white, affluent, youthful form of gay male identity, while separate lesbian-oriented magazines such as *Diva* and *Curve* also had white, middle-class bias, something partly attributable to the value of affluent groups to advertisers. With the exception of more political and news-oriented publications such as *The Pink Paper*, working-class and ethnic minority LGBT people have sometimes been under-represented within commercial outlets, as have bisexual and trans-identities in some cases. At the same time as offering crucial forms of representation and inclusion, such media sometimes have, perhaps inevitably, contributed to the prominence of particular versions LGBT identity over others.

PARTICIPATORY MEDIA AND DIY COMMUNITY

In addition to the proliferation of commercial specialist media of various kinds, digitalisation and the rise of the internet have also precipitated a proliferation of smaller-scale 'DIY' or participatory media run by and for ordinary people, blurring the boundaries between producers and consumers. While such media take a variety of forms and are not necessarily 'subcultural' (Atton 2002), in many cases they are oriented to particular interest groups or communities and can play an integral part in the facilitation of such groups.

DIY PRINT MEDIA

The most talked-about form of DIY media prior to the days of digitalisation are fanzines or 'zines', defined by Leonard (1998: 103) as 'self-published, independent texts devoted to various topics including hobbies, music, film and politics [which are] usually non-profit making and produced on a small scale by an individual or small group of people...'. Preceded by early science fiction fan magazines and the larger-scale 'underground press' associated with 1960s' counter-culture, the growth of fanzines culminated in their extensive importance to punk subculture (Atton 2002). In the years that followed, fanzines remained a significant component of youth style subcultures, sports fan cultures, marginal political groups and a variety of sci-fi, horror and other media fan communities (Jenkins 1992). Typically distributed for free, sold at cost price, or exchanged for the publications of fellow producers, fanzines represent a decentralised form of communication close to the grassroots networks of communities (Leonard 1998).

Jenkins (1992) places emphasis upon the interactive and reciprocal nature of fanzine discourse in television fan communities, which included critical commentary and discussion, artwork and *fan fiction* based on the characters or context of television shows. Fanzine culture comprised an earlier version of what Jenkins later was to call 'participatory culture' (2006; 2008). Entry barriers to producing or contributing to 'zines were low and the boundary between production and consumption thoroughly blurred in an ongoing network of fanzine conversations whose participatory, DIY character contrasted with the operation of commercial niche media (Jenkins 1992). And it is clear that fanzines played a substantial role in constructing communities. In addition to Jenkins' early work on sci-fi culture, Thornton emphasises fanzines as a trusted means through which subcultural values were shared and reinforced within rave culture (1995). Similarly, my own work on the late 1990s' goth scene identified fanzines as a crucial communicative space for the subculture providing information and discourse about bands, events, fashion or controversies at a time when goth was largely ignored by the commercial music press (Hodkinson 2002).

ONLINE MICRO-COMMUNICATION

The internet has transformed and expanded the role of DIY media as a part of the contemporary communications environment. Many of those who may in the past have contributed to fanzines are today editing or submitting content to websites, blogs, forums and other online spaces. And as the production and distribution of online content has become more accessible, larger numbers of people are producing, distributing and sharing content, whether through the contribution of reviews, illustrations or stories to fan websites, participation in debates on discussion forums, posting of original music, photographs or videos in a variety of spaces or keeping a blog or journal. Far larger in scale than the previous DIY media landscape, this revolution in grassroots communication has prompted much debate about questions of power and influence (see Chapter 10) but also has implications for patterns of identity and community.

Offering the potential to connect interactively with anything or anyone we choose at the touch of a button, the internet may at first seem like a final nail in the coffin of the cohesive, distinctive and highly committed community. The unlimited possibilities make the world of online communication about as far removed as one could imagine from the geographically isolated communities of necessity discussed by the likes of Tönnies and Redfield. If we can watch, listen and talk about whatever we want when we want, then why would we confine ourselves to anything in particular? For this reason, some early internet commentators predicted that the internet would prompt individuals to develop multiple on-screen identities and play out several at the same time (Turkle 1995).

Rather than frantically searching for new things to do, however, most people use the internet as a means to extend their existing interests and relationships. Put simply, most of us respond to the amount of choice over what to access and who to engage with by focusing on what's already familiar. Studies of friendship and communication patterns on social media invariably indicate that most use such sites as an extension of offline friendships and interests (boyd 2014). To take a more specific community-oriented example, most goths interviewed during my research on the subculture said their use of the web was dominated by websites, forums and individuals connected to the scene (Hodkinson 2002; 2007). The efficiency of the web in enabling people to easily find what they choose maximises the ease with which those already interested in a topic or community can find one another and access content, while rendering it unlikely that many will accidentally stumble upon specialist content unfamiliar to them. This suggests, according to Lievrouw, that use of the internet is liable to 'reinforce people's identification with narrow interests' and 'their sense of difference from other groups' (2001: 22). Counter-intuitively, perhaps, on a medium that offers us instant access to anything, we may often be prompted to stick with what's familiar.

VIRTUAL COMMUNITIES?

Many early internet scholars focused on the possibility that the net could generate a resurgence of distinct communities. A body of research on so-called 'virtual communities' focused on specialist, all-to-all message forums oriented to political groupings (Hill and Hughes 1998), specialist rock fans (Watson 1997), soap opera enthusiasts (Baym 2000) and the like. Scholarship demonstrated how such forums had drawn together those with existing shared interests, providing a shared space for the grassroots establishment or reinforcement of community. In the case of fan cultures, they enabled the collective pooling of knowledge and reinforced the passion of individual fans by enabling everyday contact with like-minded others (Baym 2000; Jenkins 2002). Researchers also drew attention to the striking levels of belonging and commitment exhibited by group participants and the frequency and intensity of their communication with one another (Watson 1997). This sometimes led to strong familiarity between core participants, as in an email list for Kate Bush fans, dominated by 'long-term contributors who all knew one another well and often shared personal information and long-running jokes' (Vroomen 2004: 249).

Researchers also emphasise the clear and consistent values exhibited by such groups and their policing by group moderators and participants, with transgressions resulting in corrective measures. For Watson, the group responsibility indicated by such episodes 'strongly implies that sense of community in which individual actions are always executed within the known constraints of a forum...' (1997: 111). Such norm-maintenance also acted as a means through which groups 'vigorously and successfully defend their electronic boundaries' (Hill and Hughes 1998: 69). In contrast to notions of the internet as a boundless space, 'newbies' are often expected to earn the respect of other members over a period of time (Whelan 2006).

While most of the best-known studies of virtual communities were carried out over a decade ago, groups of like-minded people continue to cluster together on the internet in various ways, including on forums similar to those in earlier studies as well as social network site groups and other locations. Studies of virtual communities, however, have not been without their problems. In some cases, individual discussion groups were focused on in isolation from the broader identity groupings with which they were connected, and the overall lives of individual participants. Use of the term 'virtual community' implied a separation between these internet spaces and the 'real' communities or everyday lives of participants, rather than an examination of online communication as an integral part of everyday life (Miller and Slater 2000). We weren't told much about what Baym's soap fans or Watson's rock fans were doing 'off-list'. Did they converse with the same people about the same topics in their email, messenger, phone and face-to-face interactions, or were their communicative lives divided between different interests and networks?

Consideration of this final question has prompted some to question the strength of people's ties within online communities. According to Wellman and Gulia (1999), such groups typically play a partial role in participants' identities, competing for their attention with numerous other affiliations and networks. The interactions on discussion groups may be specific in topic-area, they argue, but rather than generating broadly based and committed *strong ties* between members, they encourage specialist, pragmatic exchanges confined to the subject in question. For Wellman and Gulia (1999) online communication was liable to extend the quantity of specialist *weak ties* that each of us generate across different spaces rather than generate more intense community-like attachments. Castells takes a similar approach, arguing that online communities are characterised by 'low entry barriers and low opportunity costs' and that each one typically forms just one component of complex individual 'portfolios of sociability' (Castells 2001: 132).

There remain some cases, however, where research has pointed to the facilitation of deep and strong attachments to tightly knit communities. In my study of goths, participants exhibited extensive levels of commitment to their subculture and individual relationships therein, which played themselves out across a range of physical and virtual spaces. Use of the internet enhanced the community by enabling participants to exchange information, take part in debate, generate enthusiasm, share or publicise music and strengthen subcultural friendships (Hodkinson 2003; 2007). Similarly, Jenkins (2002; 2006; 2008) shows how different forms of internet communication have been used to enhance committed forms of collective identity among a variety of different groups of intensive fans of television and film, including those producing and sharing their own forms of fiction and other content. Jenkins places particular emphasis upon the interplay and tensions between the infrastructure and values of such online fan communities – including *Harry Potter* and *Star Wars* fan fiction and film communities, for example – and the commercial producers of the mass media content on which their fandom is based (Jenkins 2008). Invariably, such tensions – often relating to intellectual property – served to further strengthen community bonds and values. Jenkins even compares the participatory fan communities he describes with long-standing notions of folk culture – his argument being that the internet is enabling new forms of grassroots creative community to come together and contribute through their discourse to the very construction of popular culture.

Examples of committed subcultural or creative communities such as these are not necessarily typical ones, of course. Many collective online spaces are not oriented to quite such committed communities, but to rather more widely dispersed subject matter: home repairs, sightings of celebrities, cheats for computer games or gardening advice, for example. Parenting-oriented sites such as Mumsnet and Netmums provide a further interesting example here. If one spends time conversing on the various discussion forums they house it is not difficult to identify the presence of particular values and boundaries in what people say and how they say it as well as, sometimes, demographic similarities between participants. Mumsnet, for example, is dominated by 30–40-year-old middle-class working mothers, and aspects of the content and discussion reflect this (Pederson and Smithson 2013). Yet it's equally clear that, aside from these broad similarities, there is a significant range of different people contributing – brought together by their parenthood and gender, but disparate in other respects. Likewise, it remains unclear how committed and emotionally attached most users of such sites are. Is participation limited to occasional pragmatic visits when a specific parenting need arises or are communication and relationships with the group stronger, more frequent and more intimate. Whether the likes of Mumsnet – ostensibly oriented to themes that cross-cut society – are sufficiently cohesive, committed and distinct to comprise discrete communities, then, may be a point of ongoing debate.

SOCIAL NETWORK SITES: COMMUNITY OR DE-DIFFERENTIATION?

Importantly, though examples such as Mumsnet illustrate how important they remain for some, the all-to-all discussion groups and related formats that feature in much virtual communities research have been over-shadowed in recent years by the rise of social network sites such as *Facebook*, *Twitter*, *Istagram* and *Tumblr*. Such sites sometimes include community facilities and the groups using these – which include anything from cancer sufferers to stay at home fathers to a plethora of interest and lifestyle groups – can exhibit similar features to those identified in the online community literature. Yet the core focal point of contemporary social media tends to be the personal identity of the individual user, who develops a constantly updated display of selected elements of their everyday self and identity oriented to personalised networks of followers (boyd 2008; Hodkinson 2015; Livingstone 2008). Rather than communicating in the shared, public space of a pre-defined community, then, this individual interacts primarily with an individually hand-picked set of friends and acquaintances that may connect to various aspects of their life.

This doesn't mean that social networking sites cannot facilitate community, however. If we were to examine the friends or follower lists of individuals heavily involved in a particular community, then it's likely that other members of this group would figure prominently – and that this close online association with one another could contribute to the overall strength and distinctiveness of their community (see Hodkinson 2007). Likewise, recent commentary on political communication on social network sites has indicated a distinct tendency for those of similar persuasion to cluster together, potentially concentrating in-group cohesion and social difference (Conover et al. 2011; Public Affairs Council 2013).

It is likely, though, that communication on social networking sites often involves a broader range of subject matter and friends from different spheres of life. When friends-lists or followers *collapse contexts* by mixing together friends, relatives, acquaintances and colleagues from different compartments of life, such networks may be more likely to cut across different communities than to reinforce their boundaries. Consistent with this, a study of youth cultural identifications among social media users by Robards and Bennett (2011) found that most placed themselves at an interface between different styles or subcultures rather than aligning themselves with any in particular. Context collapse also can present difficulties for individuals, as they seek to express their identities convincingly to diverse audiences with differing expectations (boyd 2014; Lincoln and Robards 2014). This may be particularly so if the majority of the people to whom we are connected tend to be loose acquaintances, or *weak ties*, rather than stronger, more committed relationships. Such acquaintances may be of considerable value to us, as sources of information, advice or support in specific situations (for example, Ellison et al. 2007), but there may be limits to the intimacy or boundedness of our interactions. Social media also present challenges to social privacy, argues boyd (2014), because of the ease with which what we say or share can be searched for, copied and recirculated beyond our intended audience. In this sense, the true audience on social media may sometimes be 'invisible' to us, she suggests. We'll discuss some of the implications of social media communication for individual identities further in Chapter 14.

CONCLUSION: COMMUNITIES OR LOOSE AFFINITIES?

Having started the chapter by outlining arguments that suggest media erode collective differences in society, this chapter subsequently identified a number of ways media can contribute to cultural distinctions and communities. The discussion has involved a recognition that, rather than being monolithic, different sorts of media work in different ways – and offer different possibilities for patterns of difference, identity and community. Negative mass media coverage can construct or amplify the stigmatisation and marginalisation of particular groups and may elicit a strengthening of their cohesion, distinctiveness or defiance. Conversely, the positive, exclusive tone of local and niche media can contribute to the provision of shared spaces for the ideas, interaction and collective identity of particular groups. Finally, participatory and DIY media – in their past and present guises – offer extensive possibilities for the bottom-up construction and facilitation of distinctive community, even if they can also contribute to rather less cohesive networks.

Substantial arguments remain about the levels of substance and meaning of the various 'media communities' we have discussed in the latter half of the chapter. Many would recognise the strength of identity and cohesiveness of certain sexual minority groups who tend to be excluded from or stigmatised by mainstream media and reliant upon niche and grassroots communication. Yet the situation may be rather less clear when it comes to the make-up of groups centred around particular leisure interests, lifestyles or roles, for example. Do extreme sports fanatics, sci-fi fans or online mums really constitute substantive distinct communities, or are such groupings too loose-knit, diverse and transitory to warrant such a description? The answer may well depend upon one's initial definition of community.

For some of those who take seriously traditional definitions such as those of Tönnies and Redfield, community implies a long-term togetherness and commitment which only exists in a situation of forced mutual dependence (Bauman 2001). The organic strength of genuine tight-knit communities is deemed to have reflected *ascribed* factors that people had no choice about, most notably geographical isolation, but also shared social class, ethnicity or religious traditions. From this point of view, the elective nature of many more media-facilitated forms of shared identity renders them superficial and temporary. The argument here – consistent with the individualisation theories described earlier in the chapter – is that true community can only exist in the absence of media because, through providing us with more and more choices, media contribute to a de-differentiated society centred upon floating multi-affiliated individuals (Bauman 2000).

The adoption of such a narrow view of community may not be necessary, however. If the term can only be applied to groups that are completely self-sufficient and exclusively committed as a result of forced mutual dependence, then as well as risking a romanticisation of the past, we may fail to recognise the presence of clear distinctive and communal features within contemporary groupings or to understand the role of media in their construction or facilitation. Rather than dismissing the significance of such groups on the grounds that they fail to live up to an idealised set of standards from the past, we should continue to explore the extent and nature of their communal features and the role played by different forms of media in providing the spaces, representations and interactions which contribute to their development. It is equally important, meanwhile, to continue to learn about the problematic ways that media stereotyping and stigmatisation can amplify social difference and division. In the following chapters, on ethnicity and gender respectively, we'll return to this particular theme.

QUESTIONS/EXERCISES

1   In what way do the following approaches tend to regard media as something which dilutes community?

   a) Theories of mass culture

   b) Theories of individualisation

2   Think of an example of recent media stigmatisation or stereotyping of a particular social group. In what ways might such coverage serve to amplify collective difference?

3   Conduct a close analysis of the content of a local newspaper or radio station. In what ways does the content construct or facilitate community?

4   a) What is it that makes the targeting of distinct identity groups by niche media a profitable exercise?

   b) Are the kinds of groups targeted by consumer magazines and specialist television stations close-knit enough to be regarded as communities? Does the availability of such media strengthen group attachments?

5   a) In what ways have theories of virtual community been criticised?

   b) In what ways might contemporary social media environments enhance community and difference? In what ways could they erode the boundaries between different groups?

SUGGESTED FURTHER READING

Bauman, Z. (2001) *Community: Seeking Safety in an Insecure World*. Cambridge: Polity – Theoretical analysis of the ongoing quest for lost community in an individualised society.

Baym, N. (2000) *Tune In, Log On: Soaps, Fandom and Online Community*. London: Sage – Classic study of online community focused on an internet discussion group oriented to avid soap opera fans.

Jenson, T. (2014) 'Welfare Common Sense, Poverty Porn and Doxography', *Sociological Research Online*, 19(3) – Analysis of the stigmatisation of welfare claimants by a number of recent UK reality television series and the popular press.

Robards, B. and Bennett, A. (2011) 'MyTribe: Post-Subcultural Manifestations of Belonging on Social Network Sites', *Sociology*, 45(2): 303–17 – Examination of the cultural affiliations of a sample of young users of social media which argues that such individuals tended to use such media to navigate between rather than align themselves to groups.

Thornton, S. (1995) *Club Cultures: Music, Media and Subcultural Capital*: Cambridge: Polity Press – Seminal study of rave culture which outlines the role of different forms of media in the construction of the subculture.

CHAPTER 12
MEDIA, RACE AND ETHNICITY

FOCAL POINTS

- Histories of media, race and exclusion
- Developing media representations of ethnic minorities and migrant groups
- Arguments about the promotion of 'positive' images of minorities
- Complexities of ethnic identity and the concepts of diaspora and transnationalism
- Use of specialist media by ethnic minority and transnational groups

INTRODUCTION

What is the role of media in the construction of minority ethnic identities and the development of race relations? Can they contribute to an atmosphere of mutual understanding and inclusion with respect to different ethnic groups, or are they more likely to exclude, foster misunderstanding and divide? Long-term and more recent patterns of migration have resulted in a situation where many countries have considerable ethnic diversity within their populations. Alongside the effects of war and natural disaster, the increasing globalisation of markets suggests such movements of people may be liable to increase. This chapter's exploration of the relationship between media and ethnic identities within contemporary societies begins with a focus on the connection between media constructions of nation and exclusionary or racist forms of discourse. We'll then focus more specifically on the question of representations of ethnic minority groups in media, engaging with debates about stereotyping and assessing different approaches to the improvement of the situation. Finally, we examine the use of media by different ethnic minority and migrant groups, focusing particularly on specialist and transnational media consumption. Here, we'll discuss the implications of such specialist media use for the facilitation of transnational ethnic communities and the relations between such groups and the broader populations among whom they reside.

RACISM AND EXCLUSION

The notion of racial difference is now widely accepted to be a cultural construct, based not on essential biological differences, but histories of human behaviour, thought and discourse. Historically-specific sets of interactions and representations established that, while some of the characteristics that differentiate humans are ignored, others, such as skin colour, form the foundation for collective racial types regarded as naturally distinct. Important in the development of such understandings were negative Western representations of the perceived character of non-white people during the days of slavery and colonialism. Whether through literature, music, drama, journalism or cartoon, racial exploitation was justified through the representation of those on the receiving end as irrational, animalistic, lazy, uncivilised, childlike and, depending on the context, either dependent slaves or savage natives (Pieterse 1992). Carlyle (1849), for example, wrote of 'a merry hearted, grinning, dancing, singing, affectionate kind of creature with a great deal of melody and amenability in his composition', while Kipling (1899) suggested that white men carried the noble burden of passifying 'fluttered folk and wild… sullen peoples, half devil and half child'. As well as establishing specific negative perceptions that were to permeate culture for years to come, such discourse contributed to an underlying and pervasive understanding of human beings as divided into internally homogeneous and externally distinct 'races' whose relative superiority or inferiority were rooted in their fundamental essence.

More recent forms of white racist discourse, developed in the context of the migration of populations from former colonies to Western countries, have drifted away from notions of natural or biological racial inferiority and towards the notion of essential differences of culture. Different ethnic communities, it is argued, have naturally distinct and incompatible collective values, allegiances and ways of living. This is deemed to make the co-presence of different groups within the same territory undesirable: a threat to each of their identities and a cause of natural hostility and conflict. Consistent with such emphasis on territory, Barker (1981) emphasised that this 'new racism', as he then called it, was intricately interwoven with constructions of national identity.

Political reactions to the migration of Caribbean, African and South Asian populations to the UK from the mid-twentieth century onwards provide a case in point. Anti-immigration rhetoric centred upon the encroachment of essentially different 'others' onto British territory and the resulting threat to (white) British cultural identity (Solomos 1993). Conflict was deemed an inevitable result. Calling for the repatriation of immigrants, Enoch Powell famously suggested in 1968 that whites were becoming strangers in their own country and that a bloody conflict was in danger of breaking out. A decade later, Margaret Thatcher lamented the potential 'swamping' of the 'British character' and more recently, the 'flooding' of British culture by a mixture of asylum seekers and economic migrants has been alluded to by various UK politicians and national newspapers. In 2015, large numbers of Syrian refugees seeking to enter the UK from France were described by the then Prime Minister, David Cameron, as a 'swarm' while the country's 2016 referendum on European Union membership also was dominated by an emphasis on national sovereignty and anti-migration rhetoric. Elsewhere, US presidential candidate Donald Trump placed language about the need to protect the US from Mexican and Muslim immigrants at the centre of a broader campaign about the decline of the US as a nation and the need to make the country 'great again'.

Such connections between constructions of nation and exclusionary, racist discourse have led some to criticise all forms of nationalism within media. The sense of shared experience and belonging necessary for meaningful nationalist expression is deemed to entail an inevitable boundary between insiders and outsiders. Identities, after all, are relational, which means every 'us' is reliant upon its differentiation from one or more 'thems' (Woodward 1997). In Enoch Powell's formulation, the 'us' consisted of a particular white British identity, given meaning by its essential difference from the culture of immigrants. And whilst contemporary representations of Britishness usually include some ethnic minorities, explicit and implicit discourses of racial exclusion persist while ethnic minorities continue to face marginalisation within national media channels.

As well as implying strong criticism of media themselves, arguments about the link between national identity and racism raise difficult questions for those who call for public service broadcasters to represent or foster a cohesive national public culture (see Chapter 10). Such objectives tend to be inclusive in their motivation, but is it possible to encourage a clear and meaningful sense of a national 'us' without also generating a marginalised 'them'? Depressingly for its advocates, evidence suggests that public broadcasters have often been rejected in favour of commercial alternatives by ethnic minority viewers, many of whom feel excluded from the national cultural agenda of the former (Morley 2000; Ofcom 2007b, 2013; Sreberny-Mohammadi and Ross 1995). A recent Ofcom survey showed, for example, that the BBC's main flagship channel, BBC1, is watched by 72% of white British respondents but only 46% of Asian Pakistanis, 40% of Asian Indians and 49% of Asian Bangladeshis. The figure for black Caribbean and African respondents was a little higher, at 63% and 68% respectively, but still lower than for white British audiences (Ofcom 2013).

REPRESENTATION

The apparent opting-out from mainstream national media of some ethnic minority audiences brings us onto some long-running discussions about representations of marginalised groups in the mass media outlets of the countries in which they reside. Such debates about representation concern the extent to which ethnic minorities are represented *at all* within such media and the particular ways they are depicted.

UNDER-REPRESENTATION

Media on both sides of the Atlantic have a history of under-representing ethnic minorities. Though their representation is greater than that for other minority ethnic groups, the proportion of African Americans on US television shows has historically been significantly lower than their proportion of the country's population. According to Stephanie Larson (2006), in 1952 only 0.4% of television performances were by blacks, a situation that improved only gradually in the decades that followed. For Larson (2006), the number of black characters only improved significantly with the development of newer cable and digital channels in the 1990s. Yet although African Americans achieved a high of 18% of speaking roles by 1999 (ibid.), other minorities, including Latinos and Asians, have continued to be severely under-represented. In 2015–16, for example, while 16% of characters on the major US networks were black, only 7% were Latino, less than half their proportion of the US population, which was 16% in the country's 2010 census (GLAAD 2015).

Minority groups appear to be particularly under-represented in video games. A study of 150 popular games by Dmitri Williams and colleagues (2009) found that black, mixed race and Hispanic characters were all significantly under-represented. As in the case of television, the figure for Latino characters was particularly striking, accounting for only 2.71% of characters. Those Latino representations that the study did pick up, meanwhile, were non-playable secondary characters. As Williams and colleagues point out, Latino children are actually more likely than their white counterparts to play video games, yet they and their older peers are left unable to play or interact with any people of their ethnicity inside these virtual worlds.

Ethnic minority media presence in UK media, meanwhile, was extremely low prior to the 1980s, when a period of racial unrest prompted a concerted attempt to adopt a more inclusive approach. In spite of substantial improvements in the decades which followed, Sreberny (1999) was minded to conclude in 1999 that 'If you flick through the national channels for ten minutes, everything is white, white, white' (1999: 27), a sentiment apparently confirmed in 2001 by BBC Director General Greg Dyke, who described his own corporation as 'hideously white'. Importantly, Dyke's criticism was directed as much at under-representation within the staff and higher management of the BBC as within the content of the corporation. If we examine representation from an institutional and industry point of view more generally, it is clear that the situation has improved but there remains significant under-representation in key decision-making roles. While Ofcom (2007a) reports in 2007 that they accounted for 9.3% of the employees of UK broadcasters as a whole, even by 2016 ethnic minorities occupied just one of 46 seats on the boards of the country's four major broadcasters (Phillips 2016).

STEREOTYPICAL REPRESENTATIONS

The question of under- or over-representation, however, comprises only part of the story. This is because, even when present, the roles in which ethnic minorities have been depicted in media have tended to be restricted and stereotypical (see Chapter 11), constructing a narrow and generalised version of the lives and identities of such populations.

Among the stereotypes that developed during the years of slavery and colonialism were the devoted and childlike 'Uncle Tom'; the lazy, ignorant 'Coon'; the larger than life 'Mammy'; the 'happy go lucky' entertainer; and the dangerous, animalistic native – all of whom presented those of African origin as irrational and inferior. Although the most overt expressions of white superiority gradually receded, for much of the twentieth century, depictions of black and other minority groups were restricted to a limited number of often-repeated character types. For some decades, African American film actors found they had little choice but to play stereotypical slaves, house-keepers or violent criminals in a white dominated media industry. The situation is parodied beautifully in the 1987 film *Hollywood Shuffle*, which includes a satirical advert for a 'Black Acting School' in which white instructors teach aspiring black actors how to play slaves, rapists and gang leaders, chastising their students for failing to authentically walk or talk 'black'.

One of the most prominent African American representations in early television was an adaptation of radio comedy show, *Amos and Andy*, whose presentation of the exploits of two uneducated black characters drew heavily on slavery-related stereotypes of ignorance and buffoonery (Corea 1995). While the television version at least involved black actors, the original radio production had featured white comedians, in keeping with the broader minstrel tradition in which white entertainers mimicked African Americans (Larson 2006). The civil rights movement of the 1960s and 70s, however, had a significant impact on media and the variety of roles in which African Americans were depicted slowly expanded. By the 1990s, it was common to see black actors as police, doctors, news readers, or even respectable situation comedy families. Meanwhile, in recent decades, black male Hollywood actors such as Denzel Washington, Will Smith, Samuel Jackson and Morgan Freeman have been cast in a range of starring Hollywood roles, including the latter as President of the United States in disaster block buster, *Deep Impact* in 1998, something that turned out to precede the election of a real black president in Barak Obama a decade later. More recently, *Star Wars: The Force Awakens*, one of the most keenly anticipated, talked about and watched blockbusters for years, featured black British actor, John Boyega, in one of the film's two lead roles.

That the casting of Boyega was so remarked upon, however, illustrated its unusualness, even in the contemporary media world. For, in spite of improvements, the overwhelming majority of lead and supporting roles in mainstream film and television drama remain white, even in relatively progressive examples such as *The Force Awakens*. Controversy erupted in 2016 about the continuing exclusion of minority characters from the Hollywood establishment when Oscar nominations, for the second year running, did not include a single non-white actor. Whether this reflected the ethnic make-up of Academy members, the lack of availability to ethnic minority actors of key roles in critically acclaimed films, or a combination of these, has been hotly debated. Most, though, were agreed that the episode vividly illustrated how much progress still needed to be made. The situation is particularly problematic for ethnic minority women, who with a few notable exceptions continue to be excluded from prominent roles in a clear illustration of how racial and gender disadvantages can intersect with one another.

Meanwhile, many of the most prominent representations of African Americans across media remain restricted and stereotypical. In the case of the music industry, for example, opportunities for black artists are largely restricted to R&B, hip hop and related genres. Meanwhile, in spite of significant signs of diversification in recent years, substantial portions of mainstream hip hop remain dominated by stereotypes of urban gang culture, depicting a blend of male criminality, violence and heterosexual aggression on the one hand and – sometimes – passive, sexualised and commodified female groupies on the other (Perry 2003). A far cry from the grassroots empowerment associated with some earlier and more specialist forms of hip hop, such images – illustrated strikingly in the 2006 documentary, *Beyond Beats and Rhymes* – continue to account for a significant proportion of the mediated representations of black culture seen in the United States and across the globe. And crucially, such representations are filtered, promoted and encouraged by a largely white-dominated music industry whose primary market is white consumers, prompting Tricia Rose to lament 'the destructive forces of commercialised manufacturing of ghetto street life' (Rose 2008: ix).

In the UK and Europe, images of ethnic minorities often relate closely to US representations, such are the ubiquity of Hollywood, hip hop and high profile US television drama. There are specific histories in different countries also, however. In the UK, depictions of Africans, Caribbeans and South Asians have centred consistently on criminality, violence and trouble, with images of angry young non-white men dominating news media moral panics about muggings in the 1970s (Hall et al. 1978), and urban riots, gang culture, shootings and stabbings in the decades that followed (Malik 2002; Alexander 2000). Most recently, the London riots of 2011 saw a notable return to newspaper front pages of young black men engaged in street violence. And the resonance of such images with broader stereotypes, such as those that dominate much commercial hip hop, has rendered them difficult to dislodge, in spite of substantial expansions in the overall range of representations of black and ethnic minorities in media over time. Black people are also often represented as athletes and sports people – as is the case in the US and elsewhere – though more rarely as coaches or sports presenters. Such sports representations may have potentially positive or counter-stereotypical implications in some respects, but simultaneously can reinforce stereotypes of black aggression and physical power, as against thought, intelligence and responsibility, for example.

It is also clear that opportunities for black, Asian and minority ethnic (sometimes shortened to BAME) actors remain restricted and that high profile lead roles in UK drama have been elusive. In a recent speech to a meeting at the UK Houses of Parliament, Idris Elba, one of the country's best known BAME actors, argued that he was forced to turn to the US television industry to move beyond bit-part roles such as 'best friends' and 'cop side-kick parts'. 'I knew I wasn't going to land a lead role', he said, 'I knew there wasn't enough imagination in the [UK] industry for me to be seen as a lead' (Elba 2016). Ultimately Elba did break through this glass ceiling, his prominent performance in US drama, *The Wire*, prompting a series of high profile roles in both the US and the UK, but it seems UK producers were unwilling to take a chance on him prior to this.

Representations of South Asians, who form a substantial part of Britain's ethnic minority population, have tended to defer to a few different stereotypes, meanwhile. In particular, recent

South Asian representations have also invoked themes such as religious conservatism, strict parenting, a refusal to 'integrate' with mainstream culture and arranged marriages, with South Asian women often depicted as quiet, passive and subordinated victims. Such stereotypical depictions remain pervasive, particularly in news media, in spite of their being accompanied by more nuanced examples. Nadiya Hussain's 2015 victory in the BBC's highly popular and nationally coded 'Great British Bake Off' competition, for example, broke through established stereotypes in the most mainstream of forums, achieving near universal popularity for the British Muslim housewife in the process, yet the amount of media discussion and comment (mostly positive) on her ethnicity betrayed the unusualness of such a scenario.

TERRORISM AND INTERNATIONAL EVENTS

One topic, however, has dominated discussions of the representation of South Asian populations in white-dominated parts of the world more than any other in recent years and that is the depiction of Muslims as religious extremists or terrorists. Extensive coverage of the 2001 New York World Trade Center attacks, subsequent terrorist incidents in Madrid, London, Paris and the broader activities of so-called ISIS have contributed to the repeated depiction of Muslims and Islam in association with fundamentalism and deadly political violence. Here, under-representation is not the problem, with studies indicating something of an explosion of largely negative coverage of Muslims and Islam over the last two decades. One content analysis classified 91% of 352 articles examined in 2006 as 'negative', with nearly half specifically referring to Muslims or Islam as a 'threat' and much of the rest referring to them in stories about threat or danger (Greater London Authority 2007). A subsequent study found that the most common nouns used in relation to British Muslims were 'terrorist', 'extremist', 'Islamist', 'suicide bomber' and 'militant' and that 'references to radical Muslims outnumbered references to moderate Muslims by seventeen to one' (Moore et al. 2008). Summarising his review of these studies, Chris Allen concludes that 'threat, otherness, fear and danger posed or caused by Muslims and Islam underpins a considerable majority of the media's coverage' (Allen 2012).

More generally, the operation of news values has a tendency to ensure media representations of non-white, non-Western parts of the world is sparse and dominated by high amplitude negative stories about conflict, famine or violence. Alongside romanticised depictions of exotic traditional cultures within tourist-oriented representations (Taylor 2007), such negative images tap into a broader form of orientalism: a fear and fascination with the exotic, irrational 'other' (Said 1978). As well as having implications for the populations of these countries, such representations also can reinforce domestic stereotypes of black, Arab or Asian minorities in white-dominated countries. Representations of East Asian or Arab populations in the US, Canada, Australia or Europe, then, may not be entirely unrelated to broader representations of East Asia or of the Arab world in international news, documentaries, films and the like.

THE REPRODUCTION OF SUBORDINATION

The impact of the under-representation and stereotyping of ethnic minorities is impossible to gauge in precise terms, but theorists are largely agreed that it has significant implications for race relations. First, such representations may adversely affect the way minority populations are viewed and treated by the dominant majority. Generalised and prejudiced expectations of black, Asian or South American people in Europe, North America or Australia may be reinforced and this may contribute to hostility or discrimination. As a result, minority populations may experience a consolidation of barriers to their achievement of employment or promotion, be more frequently stopped and searched by the police or refused tenancy. Stereotypical representations also can contribute to support for government rhetoric and policies that curb rights for minorities or restrict their cultural or religious expression.

Stereotypes may also impact the self-esteem and sense of belonging of members of the stereotyped group themselves. If all or most of the people who look and sound like you in the media display particular characteristics then this may increase the chances that you come to associate yourself in some way with these, whether you aspire to them or not. The absence of a range of representations and of successful role-models may compound existing socio-economic deprivation and everyday discrimination, further reducing hope. A further possibility is that the experience of media stereotyping and other forms of discrimination may prompt an active rejection among some of the values and goals of a society that has apparently rejected them. As with the stigmatised groups we examined in Chapter 11, the more such groups feel stigmatised and oppressed, the more they may be pushed into developing separate, oppositional values, identities or 'survival strategies' (Hall et al. 1978).

Because the interplay between representations and broader relations of power is a circular one, any concentration in majority prejudice or minority disaffection brought about by media stereotypes may feed back into future representations. There is a danger, then, of a self-perpetuating cycle, whereby the subordination of minority groups is reinforced by their representation in a white, bourgeois-controlled media where such stereotypical depictions are themselves reinforced by the concentrated subordination of minority groups (see Figure 12.1). In a broader sense, restricted or stereotypical media representations form one element of the process in which the cultural divisions between different ethnic groups are consolidated and hegemonic power relations reinforced (Hall 1997; Pickering 2001).

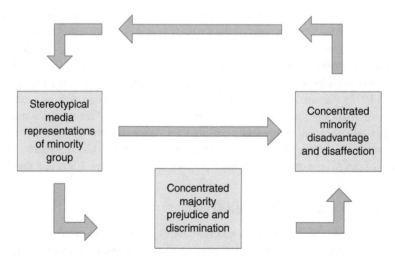

Figure 12.1   Simplified cycle of subordination

PROMOTING 'POSITIVE' IMAGES

Whilst most agree that stereotypes can be damaging, there has been much debate as to how to address the problem. Particularly from the 1970s and 80s onwards, various attempts have been made to actively promote 'positive' images of ethnic minorities, which, in one way or another, sought to reverse stereotypes (Hall 1997). Yet these attempts have differed with respect to which 'negative' images should be reversed and what exactly counted as positive.

REVERSING STEREOTYPES OF PASSIVITY

With respect to African Americans, some 1970s practitioners felt priority should be given to the reversal of the stereotypes of passivity, ignorance and deference which had derived from the days of slavery. A range of representations of black Americans emerged that sought to substitute subservience and ignorance with strength, assertiveness, rebelliousness and, sometimes, superiority over whites. A series of so-called 'blaxploitation' films, targeted primarily at black audiences, featured funk or soul sound-tracks, storylines centred on the ghetto and an emphasis on strong, black lead characters. Negative white characterisation was also sometimes a feature, whether in relation to corruption, criminality or merely being the object of humour.

Focusing on the most well-known film of the genre, *Shaft* (1971), which features the exploits of a strong, cocky, sexually successful police detective, Stuart Hall (1997) argues that such stereotype reversal can lead to its own problems. Consistent with the counter-stereotypical agenda, John Shaft occupies a position of authority and respect as well as being the film's hero. Meanwhile, his maverick, rule-breaking character – who has been compared with the likes of Dirty Harry – is anything but passive or subservient towards white colleagues and superiors, while retaining a clear attachment to his ghetto roots. The introductory theme music sums it up: 'He doesn't take orders from anybody, black or white, but he'd risk his neck for his brother man' (Hayes 1971). Yet as Hall explains, *Shaft*, like many of the other films in its 'blaxploitation' genre, ended up reinforcing a different set of black stereotypes, playing on the familiar theme of black male sexual prowess – 'He's a black private dick who's a sex machine with all the chicks' according to the introductory music – and depicting a ghetto full of stereotypical black pimps, drug dealers and gangsters. One set of stereotypes, then, was replaced with another:

> To reverse the stereotype is not necessarily to overturn of subvert it. Escaping the grip of one stereotypical extreme (blacks are poor, childish, subservient…) may simply mean being trapped in its stereotypical 'other' (blacks as motivated by money, love bossing white people around, perpetrate violence and crime… indulge in drugs, crime and promiscuous sex…). (Hall 1997: 272)

SUCCESSFUL, WELL-ADJUSTED, INTEGRATED

While blaxploitation films replaced subservience with black defiance and solidarity, a more common approach in recent years has been the promotion of images of ethnic minorities as successful and upstanding members of society. In the UK a concerted drive towards the inclusion of 'positive' ethnic minority representations in the media, which began in the 1980s, has borne some noticeable results, to the extent that it is now unremarkable to see black or Asian presenters of news broadcasts, documentaries, children's programmes and other respected forms of output. Similarly, ethnic minority actors often are cast as professionals such as doctors, teachers and police. Here, the promotion of 'positive' images implies replacing stereotypes of separatism and criminality with the depiction of ethnic minorities as integrated members of society who hold positions of influence and responsibility and have 'mainstream' aspirations.

A particularly important historical example of the approach is *The Cosby Show*, a US situation comedy featuring an all black cast which achieved extensive success among ethnically diverse audiences. Re-runs of the show have recently been pulled from some networks as a result of sexual assault allegations against the show's star, Bill Cosby, but it was first broadcast in the early 1980s. It features the Huxtables, a harmonious and amiable middle-class nuclear family who, with the exception of their ethnicity, are comparable to other mainstream sit-com families. Both husband and wife are successful professionals and caring parents, while their children are intelligent and well-adjusted. Through achieving such popularity for a programme depicting so successful a black family, the show had, according to Michael Dyson, 'permitted Americans to view black folk as human beings' (1993: 82). Yet, in spite of this, Dyson is not alone in criticising the series.

The issue is with whether, in its emphasis upon upper middle-class normality, *The Cosby Show* adequately represents what life is actually like for African Americans. They may be 'positive' from a certain viewpoint, but the levels of affluence depicted are far removed from the low socio-economic positions of the majority of blacks in the US. This prompts Miller (1988) to suggest that, rather than easing the country's racial problems, the show reinforces the myth of the American Dream, acting as a reassuring mask which hides the inequalities that prevent most blacks from achieving the social position enjoyed by the Huxtables (cited in Corea 1995; also see Larson 2006). While recognising the achievements of the show, Dyson (1993) questions its failure to address issues of inequality and racism, suggesting that, in elevating a particular middle-class version of black identity towards social acceptance, it may even have reinforced the marginalisation of the rest of black society.

Such criticism seems harsh when levelled at a single programme. After all, diversity may be valuable in itself and *The Cosby Show* certainly contrasted with many other representations of African Americans at the time. It also demonstrated that not every programme about black people had to be about poverty, crime or indeed race. The perspective of the critics is worthy of greater consideration, however, when it comes to broader attempts to promote integrated, successful and financially comfortable representations of ethnic minorities across media output. Unless pursued with great care, such a body of 'socially acceptable' representations may risk obscuring the poverty and disadvantage suffered by many ethnic minorities and implying that America or other Western societies are 'colour-blind' (Larson 2006). Furthermore, if pursued too stringently, the promotion of characteristics deemed 'positive' by mainstream society may privilege an assimilationist vision of race relations and implicitly label as 'negative' anything which looks or sounds more ethnically distinctive. As Dyson puts it, 'being concerned about issues that transcend race and therefore display our humanity is fine, but that does not mean we should buy into a vacuous, bland universality that stigmatizes diversity, punishes difference and destroys dissimilarities' (1993: 87).

There are two key points to take away from such debates. First, there are different versions of what constitutes a 'positive' or 'negative' image and it is far from easy to arbitrate between them (Malik 2002). To some, Shaft is positive because he is proudly and defiantly black, while for others he reinforces negative stereotypes of black promiscuity, separatism and violence. Likewise, some regard clean-cut middle-class conformist television personalities as positive while others regard the promotion of such images as part of a project whose emphasis on the merits of integration risks obscuring racial disadvantage and stigmatising distinctiveness. Second, whether or not it is a worthwhile enterprise, the promotion of 'positive images' may not always intersect with the promotion of a representative overall picture of the lives of particular ethnic minorities in a given country. The problem with stereotypes is that they select, exaggerate and disproportionately emphasise certain character types whilst systematically excluding others – and that is something that may also be true of some attempts to artificially promote 'positive' images (Pickering 2001).

THE BURDEN OF REPRESENTATION

A further problem with the 'positive' images approach is that it has encouraged the development of a *burden of representation* on ethnic minorities in the media and the arts who, as a result of being isolated within predominantly white media institutions, found themselves expected to stand for their entire ethnic group (Mercer 1990). Unlike whites, whose ethnicity tends to be rendered invisible in Western countries by their majority status, the attitudes and behaviour of ethnic minorities in the media are often in danger of being taken as representative of all those of their skin colour, origin or religion. Attempts to promote positive images can reinforce the pressure on writers, directors, artists and actors to ensure a socially acceptable impression is conveyed – and this can create limits on feasible character-types and storylines. Crucially, the operation of the burden of representation rests on broader assumptions that ethnic minority groups are sufficiently monolithic that they can be represented by a handful of media characters or personalities. Contemporary representations may (sometimes) be 'positive' in one sense or another, but audiences still tend to be encouraged to think of ethnic minority identities in *essentialist* terms: black people are regarded as essentially similar, and as collectively different to South Asian people, and so on. It is for this reason that Sarita Malik suggests that attempts to replace negative images with positive ones 'do little to displace the assumptions on which the original stereotypes are based' (2002: 29).

The problem is linked to that of *tokenism*, or the tendency to have a single token black or ethnic minority character, presenter or guest in order to give an inclusive impression. Isolated among a cast of whites, the ethnic difference of minority characters can stand out, which may further encourage audiences to associate their actions and storylines with their ethnicity, rather than more complex individual traits or contexts. Tokenism can also lead to a dearth of situations in which ethnic minority characters interact with one another as opposed to with white characters. UK entertainer Lenny Henry recently pointed this out in relation to BBC crime drama, *Luther*, in which, although Idris Elba plays the lead role (and therefore is more than merely a 'token'), his character is completely surrounded by white colleagues, friends and family. As Henry puts it 'An intellectual, troubled maverick cop who has no black friends or family. You never see Luther with black people. What's going on?' (BBC Online 2014).

Tokenism of a different kind can be found in some approaches to the reporting of racial issues in news and current affairs programming. In a well-intentioned attempt to refer to ethnic minority experiences and perspectives, journalists sometimes refer, in the singular, to 'the black community' or 'the Muslim community', reinforcing the impression of undifferentiated blocks of people who have a unified viewpoint. This is further reinforced through the use of 'spokespeople' or 'community representatives' for such groups who are regularly consulted for comment. Such references help ensure the inclusion of views that otherwise might be excluded, but risk further reinforcing the view of minority groups as essentially different, abnormal or *other*. Imagine the derision news in Western Europe or North America might face if it were to refer to 'representatives of white opinion'.

HYBRIDITY, DIASPORA AND TRANSNATIONALISM

SHIFTING ETHNICITIES

Partly in response to such problems, many theorists have shifted away from essentialist approaches in favour of an emphasis on the diversity and complexity of ethnic and racial identities. Associated with the work of Hall (1992) and others, the notion of *new ethnicities* sought to highlight the culturally constructed and malleable nature of race and ethnicity. If we regard ethnicity as a product of ongoing processes of human thought and representation rather than nature, then it follows that, rather than being a fixed state of *being*, ethnic identities are always developing, changing or *becoming*. They may retain stable features, but are constantly open to development and diversification according to changing circumstances – not least experiences of migration. The process of becoming involves ongoing encounters with new cultural influences as well as long-standing negotiations with intersecting aspects of identity such as class, gender, sexuality, locality, career and even strongly held leisure affiliations. The fluidity of ethnic identities, then, makes them subject to internal differentiation and external overlap.

Hall's approach focused attention on visible developments in the identities of second, third and fourth generation members of minority groups in countries such as the UK. The affiliation of these younger generations to their ethnic roots was increasingly becoming intertwined with the experience of growing up in urban, media-saturated Western environments. Rather than being simply 'Muslim', 'Chinese' or 'black' they were becoming distinctly 'black/Muslim/Chinese and British' in addition to their attachments to neighbourhood, age group, cultural interests and the like. These complex emerging identities have also been given expression in the form of hybrid forms of popular culture. The development and consumption by British Indian youth of Bhangra and post-Bhangra forms of music, for example, entailed a fusion of selected elements of traditional Indian music with Western urban dance rhythms and sequences (Huq 2006). The hybridity of Bhangra, along with a range of local variants of hip hop and other 'mixed' cultural forms, serves to illustrate the richly complex ethnic identities of those who created and consumed them and, specifically, the reconciling of heritage with everyday multi-racial local contexts (Back 1996; Gidley 2007).

In trying to think about new ethnicities, Hall and others were seeking to make sense of these youth cultural developments as part of a broader emphasis on the complexity of *all* ethnic identities. Amongst other things, this implies a move away from simplistic positive image campaigns or tokenistic approaches to media representation. If British Indian consists of countless different combinations of local, generational, age, gender, class and peer-group identities, then to speak of their representation by a single spokesperson, character or personality begins to look far-fetched. But this should not be taken to mean that people's ethnicity or origins are insignificant or do not engender crucial shared experiences and affiliations. In seeking to make sense of the interplay of individual and collective difference in a context of shifting patterns of migration and communication, some have turned to concepts such as diaspora and transnationalism.

DIASPORA

Diaspora refers to the dispersal around the globe of people who share a common point of origin, encompassing migrants themselves and their descendants who grow up within the destination or 'host' country. At the same time as allowing for the development of internal differences within diasporic populations – not least with respect to age, generation and contrasting destination country experiences – diaspora draws attention to enduring affinities with and attachments to the transnational diasporic community and, in particular, the place of origin, sometimes referred to as the 'mother country'.

For Paul Gilroy (1993), diaspora encompasses not just a mutual connection to shared *roots* in the mother country or continent, but the collective experience of migration itself – the sense of common *routes* across the globe. In the case of those of African origin we can envisage a triangle of historical migration routes across what Gilroy terms *The Black Atlantic*, consisting of forced movement between Africa, the Caribbean and US during the days of slavery and then voluntary post-war migration from both the Caribbean and Africa itself to countries in Europe. Meanwhile, migration routes from the Indian sub-continent have taken populations to Western Europe, North America and the Middle East, among other destinations. And the notion of diaspora has been used in relation to various other groupings, whose migration routes were formed in different ways at different times. As a concept, diaspora enables exploration of fluidities and differences within particular groups at the same time as recognising the sense of collective identification which can bind members together.

REPRESENTING DIASPORA

In contrast to positive image campaigns, some ethnic minority film-makers have sought to generate complex sets of representations of diaspora that are faithful to the shared realities of life for ethnic minorities at the same time as exploring complexities and differences. So-called 'diaspora films' often explore how characters negotiate their own path between cultural traditions associated with their ethnic heritage and elements of life within the society they live in. They tend to contest stereotypes and essentialism by presenting the trials, tribulations and conflicts of complex, rounded characters. Such films, whose depictions have sometimes involved the courting of controversy among sections of the ethnic minority groups depicted, include *My Beautiful Laundrette* (1985), *East is East* (1999), *Brick Lane* (2008) and two films directed by Gurinder Chadha on which we'll focus on briefly: *Bhaji on the Beach* (1993) and *Bend it Like Beckham* (2002).

Over 20 years old now, *Bhaji on the Beach*, offers a glimpse into the lives of a multi-generational group of South Asian women during a day out to the quintessentially English seaside town of Blackpool. The film's title, soundtrack and storylines point to negotiations between South Asian diasporic traditions and life in Britain, covering inter-generational and gender differences relating to teenage sexuality, domestic violence, marriage separation, multi-racial relationships, non-marital pregnancy, abortion and white racism. The themes of generational conflict and negotiating between cultures are taken up a decade later in Chadha's lighter, more mainstream *Bend it Like Beckham*. The plot centres on the love for football of teenage Sikh girl, Jess, and the tensions this creates with her parents. Both Jess and her older sister, Pinky, break their parents' rules, but while Pinky's hyper-feminine identity and pre-marital sex are channelled into a traditional marriage, Jess' ambitions are oriented to a professional football career and romance with her white Irish coach. A range of representations of young male Asian identity are encountered along the way, including Jess' gay best friend, Tony, and more peripheral laddish characters.

The varied representations presented in diaspora films have been built upon by other forms of media centred upon ethnic minority life, including comedy. The UK series *Goodness Gracious Me* presented a satirical interpretation of a range of distinctively British South Asian character types, referencing both diasporic heritage and negotiations with British life. Various facets of both young and old Asian identities are mocked from a knowing, insider point of view, as are aspects of established British culture, and its treatment of Asians. The show is of particular interest, according to Malik (2002: 103), because it goes 'inside the stereotype', tackling it head on and even at times colluding with it, but with a crucial knowing wink.

More recent examples of the representation of multi-generational diaspora groups include BBC show, *Citizen Khan*, which has attracted appreciable audiences since its debut in 2012 and been both lauded and criticised for its provocative fun-poking at British Muslims. The show's deliberate comic highlighting of stereotypical aspects of ethnic distinctiveness contrasts with *The Cosby Show*'s assimilationist approach but combines this with a diversity of characters with different orientations and a number of traits, themes and storylines familiar to more mainstream sit-coms. For commentator Saira Khan (2012), it was the show's invitation for British Muslims to laugh at themselves – and for the rest of the country's population to laugh at and with them – that made it so distinct from universally serious representations of Muslims elsewhere across media. In the US, meanwhile, 2011 series *All American Muslim* depicted the complex and varied lives of five different families in Michigan, explicitly drawing out both collective and individual distinctiveness as well as commonalities with non-Muslim Americans across eight episodes.

None of these forms of representation are beyond critique. Even in their desire to counter monolithic views of ethnicity, directors of diaspora films have sometimes ended up reinforcing familiar stereotypes (Hussain 2005). Images such as the repressive Asian husband and backward looking Asian parents and traditions tend to be reinforced in texts that can present crude dichotomies between established diasporic traditions and a younger generation keener to embrace Western culture. A further difficulty is that, with the exception of *Bend it Like*

Beckham, the emphasis on ethnic minority lives and identities tends to result in diaspora films being pigeon-holed as specialist ethnic minority texts. The distinct and deliberate 'Asianness' of *Goodness Gracious Me* and 'Muslimness' of *Citizen Khan* rendered these too, vulnerable to pigeon-holing. In spite of their range of characters and self-conscious humour, they may ultimately be viewed as amusing portraits of the curious ways of the 'other'. Nevertheless, such representations have played a role in a gradual trend towards a greater range of representations and, as part of this, more complex characterisations which refuse simple 'positive' or 'negative', 'integrated' or 'non-integrated' pigeon-holes.

TRANSNATIONALISM

While the concept of diaspora remains useful in making sense of the lives of long-standing, multi-generational minority groups, more recent patterns of migration have prompted some to turn to the concept of *transnationalism*. Though it partially overlaps with diaspora, transnationalism draws specific attention to groups of migrants who retain significant practical connections to their 'home' country, whose current location may be temporary and who, as a consequence, can occupy a somewhat liminal role as transnational subjects. Recent patterns of economic migration within the European Union offer a significant example here, with various individuals or groups moving between countries to work for a period of time while maintaining transnational networks – via media, travel, political engagement, financial transactions or other means – with friends, family and institutions in their home country. In some cases – as with the UK Polish population, for example – such migrants can form diaspora-like communities within their country of residence, while at the same time maintaining extensive ties with their home country. Through highlighting these ongoing transnational connections and networks, alongside the uncertainty of their conceptions of home, transnationalism theories offer a useful extension to thinking about minority populations in such circumstances (Faist 2010; Glick-Schiller et al. 1992; Mamattah 2006).

Representations of these more transitory groups of transnational migrants in media within their countries of residence tend to be considerably more limited than those for more established minority groups and largely confined to negative (and occasionally more positive) stereotypes about migration and migrants in news coverage. Alina Rzepnikovska's (2013) study of UK press coverage of Polish migrants found that initial stereotypes of efficient, hard-working labourers gave way to negative articles that presented them as an economic threat to UK workers and a social and/or criminal threat to the UK public. The latter representations, argues Rzepnikovska, involved the repeated construction of a racialised Eastern European 'other' associated with crime, drink and violence. Following up her textual analysis with interview research, Rzepnikovska argues the pervasiveness of such coverage had a profoundly negative impact on the lives of Poles living in the UK (ibid.).

MEDIA SEGREGATION?

Partly as a consequence of the ongoing marginalisation of minorities within mainstream channels, there has been a recent growth in the use by such communities of specialist media. The trend is connected to developments in media technologies and the broader pluralisation of media, and reflects the obvious appeal both to established ethnic minority communities and more transitory migrants of reinforcing connections with other members of their diaspora and/ or their home country. Myria Georgiou (2002: 3) explains that for dispersed populations, 'the construction of shared imagination, images and sounds have always been key elements of sustaining community'. As internet communication has evolved and become more widespread, her point has become even more apt.

NEWSPAPERS, FILM AND GLOBAL BOLLYWOOD

Of course, the use of specialist media by ethnic minority groups is not entirely a phenomenon of the digital age. Specialist newspapers have long formed an important part of minority communications networks, with local retailers within areas of high concentration for particular groupings often stocking such publications, some of which oriented specifically to such localised populations and others distributed globally. In the case of newspapers serving the Tamil diaspora, *Puthinam* is oriented particularly to Tamils based in London, while *Eelamurazu* is distributed across the diaspora throughout Europe and Canada (Antony 2009). Specialist local radio can also play an important role. Georgiou, for example, emphasises the significance of Greek London Radio as a source of community participation for members of the Greek diaspora located within the city (Georgiou 2001).

In her seminal 1990s study of the media use of Punjabi young people and their families in the London suburb of Southall, Marie Gillespie (1995) demonstrates the importance of film as a means of engaging with forms of media content associated with the diaspora. Such was the demand in Southall for Bollywood films, for example, that dedicated networks of specialist video hire stores had emerged. Gillespie explains how, as well as being used by parents to encourage their children to engage with their cultural roots, Bollywood and associated fashion and celebrity culture also had independent appeal for young people. Defying theories that suggest media globalisation is a one-way process, Bollywood has become a massively lucrative enterprise whose success partly rests on the large-scale export of films to communities associated with the Indian diaspora (often referred to as Non-Resident Indians or NRIs). Indeed, Bollywood, along with associated fashion, music and celebrity industries, has become increasingly oriented towards the potential of its export market, producing increasing numbers of films that explore NRI settings, characters and experiences. This orientation, alongside the gradual pushing of boundaries of taste and decency, has ensured that the NRI market includes younger as well as older generations, cementing its place in the shared cultural imagining of the diaspora. As Manas Ray (2003: 32) puts it, 'Bollywood representation establishes the "India" community as a national but global community'.

ETHNIC AND TRANSNATIONAL SPECIALISATION IN THE DIGITAL ERA

Recent transformations in media technology have substantially expanded the range of possibilities for specialist communication within particular ethnic or transnational groupings. Digital television services offer the potential to reject mainstream mixed channels in favour of more specialist alternatives defined partially or wholly by their ethnic orientation. Viacom's *Black Entertainment Television* network, for example, covers a blend of music, film, religious broadcasts and news targeted towards the US' African American population and in 2008 began to broadcast in the UK and Ireland. Meanwhile the *Zee TV* network broadcasts a mixture of drama, comedy, news, documentaries and films to South Asian audiences in the UK, Europe and the United States. Some mainstream broadcasters have also moved towards offering specialist minority-oriented services. *Radio 1 Extra*, for example, is oriented to a range of black music genres, and *BBC Asian Network*, covers music, culture and discussion oriented to British Asian youth. Given the corporation's historical emphasis on uniting the nation through universal programming, the development of such separate services represents a point for debate.

Of greatest significance, however, are the increasing possibilities of the internet with respect to the reinforcement and development of transnational or diasporic communications. Research by Ofcom (2013) indicates that internet use by ethnic minority groups tends to be higher than that of the UK's white British population. For example, 82% of the country's Indian Asian population had a broadband connection compared with 70% of its white British population. Qualitative research, meanwhile, suggests that the maintaining of transnational cultural connections constitutes a significant component of the internet use of some minorities and migrant groups. According to Georgiou (2002: 2), the internet allows communities disenfranchised within mainstream national media, to 'gain access and the right to speak in a transnational public'.

In her study of diaspora and transnational groups within Europe, Georgiou (2002) highlights extensive use of public internet resources, including information and news websites and interactive community forums where individuals could directly participate in the exchange of ideas. Typically hyperlinked together with networks of similarly oriented sites, the use of such resources can facilitate what we might conceive as specialist and ethnically distinct transnational imagined communities or public spheres (Dayan 1998). Similarly, the internet use of ethnic minority respondents in a Canadian study by Maria Bakardjieva (2005) was dominated by engagement with news websites, online radio stations and discussion forums oriented to their country of origin. According to Bakardjieva, such facilities enabled ethnic minorities in Canada to keep their country and culture of origin 'within attainable and restorable reach' (ibid. 125).

In addition to its role in the facilitation of minority public communication, the internet facilitates the development of disorganised sets of personal ties via more private forms of mediated interaction. In both Georgiou and Bakardjieva's studies, extended family and friendship networks were maintained across thousands of miles through email, instant messenger conversations and the exchange of images. Today, social media such as Facebook and Twitter provide even more effective and flexible means to reinforce transnational personal social networks, combining elements of private and public communication (boyd 2008; 2014). Such networks are of particular significance for more transitory migrant groups, enabling intensive forms of connection with fellow-nationals in their home country and elsewhere. Research by Komito and Bates (2009) demonstrates that use of social network sites by Polish migrants in Ireland has enabled vibrant and extensive Polish networks that included friends and acquaintances in Ireland,

Poland and around the world. Such is the significance of social media in this respect, they argue, that migrants' levels of contact with broader Irish society was reduced, underlining their status as mobile transnational subjects.

CONCLUSION: EMPOWERMENT OR GHETTOISATION?

In many respects, the increasing availability of specialist local and transnational forms of media to ethnic minority and transnational groups may be regarded as a positive note on which to end the chapter. Populations long under-represented, stereotyped and saddled with the burden of representation, alongside new groups of more temporary migrants, are increasingly able to engage with public culture, entertainment, discussion and ideas oriented specifically towards people of their ethnicity, nationality or status as well as to maintain regular personal contact with friends and relatives in a variety of locations. Their constant connection to these networks of representation, interaction and ideas suggests a reinforcement of shared belonging to distinct ethnic or transnational communities, with all the social and political benefits that may bring. For Downing and Husband (2005) the development of specialist ethnic minority media forms a key component in the positive affirmation of difference and self-determination by minorities, refusing establishment pressure to assimilate into mainstream culture. Governments should support the further development of such media, they argue, in the hope of expanding ethnic minority opportunities for expression and developing a new, disparate and multi-ethnic form of public sphere.

Although laudable in its rejection of assimilation, Downing and Husband's account might also have recognised some potential disadvantages of the media separatism they describe. If different ethnic groups increasingly participate in separate or parallel spheres of mediated communication, as is indicated in studies such as Komito and Bates' (2009) research above, could there be a danger that this bypasses rather than tackles the long-standing problems of prejudice and discrimination? As well as letting mainstream media off the hook with respect to the need to improve the services they offer minorities, increased segregation may mean that the long-standing issues created by physical ghettoisation of some minorities are exacerbated by a form of media ghettoisation.

The situation may not be quite as stark as this, however. Even in the case of those with the greatest commitment to specialist forms of content and communication, in most cases these form only part of overall media portfolios that encapsulate a range of tastes and interests. And although majority media consumption patterns do appear to differ from those of minorities, the most popular forms of content for the latter appear not to be particularly specialist. A recent UK television study, for example, found that, although their preferences differed from those of white audiences, the most watched television programmes for ethnic minority audiences were the BBC's New Year's Eve fireworks coverage, mainstream soap opera *East Enders*, and reality shows *The Great British Bake Off*, *X-Factor* and the *Apprentice* (Phillips 2016). Although lacking in detail, such figures bring a useful sense of perspective to arguments about ghettoisation, as well as indicating that, where mainstream shows do include significant minority characters or contestants in a manner that avoids stereotypes or tokenism, minority audiences tend to enthusiastically tune in. It also should be remembered that, if some ethnic minorities and migrants *are* rejecting broad mixed-content media in favour of specialist alternatives, then they are far from alone in doing so. As the digital revolution embeds itself more deeply, audiences are becoming more fragmented across the board.

It remains important that the obvious interest of many ethnic minority and migrant populations in specialist forms of communication does not result in their being excluded from more mainstream services. This makes it paramount to accelerate progress with respect to the need to include a diversity of representations and forms of culture across all types of media. Public service broadcasters such as the BBC, in particular, must ensure that they also continue to prioritise the needs of ethnic minority audiences across the range of services they offer and not just on segregated or specialist channels. Perhaps, in combination with the proliferation of specialist media, such a drive towards wider inclusivity might offer a balance between affirmations of distinctiveness and the erosion of essentialism and prejudice.

QUESTIONS/EXERCISES

1 In what ways are discourses of racism connected with those of nationalism? Should attempts to represent or construct national identity by public service broadcasters be abandoned on the basis that they are liable to promote exclusion?

2 a) To what extent do representations of ethnic minorities continue to be restricted in contemporary media?

   b) Choose an example of a media text (e.g. a video game, film, news article, television programme or music video) and analyse the ways in which different ethnic or racial groups are represented in its content. Does the text reinforce or challenge stereotypes?

3 a) As approaches to the development of more 'positive' representations, what is the difference between *Shaft* and *The Cosby Show*? Which approach is preferable do you think?

   b) What is meant by the 'burden of representation' and how does this connect to attempts to promote positive images?

4 a) What is meant by the following terms: *new ethnicities*; *diaspora*; *transnationalism*?

   b) Identify a media text you feel represents or illustrates one or more of these concepts and analyse it with respect to how ethnicity is constructed.

5 Is the increasing availability and use of specialist and/or transnational media by minority groups a positive or a negative thing? Why?

SUGGESTED FURTHER READING

Dyson, M. (1993) *Reflecting Black African-American Cultural Criticism*. Minneapolis: University of Minnesota Press – Detailed discussion of a range of black American expression, including critical analysis of *The Cosby Show*.

Georgiou, M. (2006) *Diaspora, Identity and the Media*. Hampton Press – Explores the role of a range of media in the facilitation of global diasporic networks and identities.

Hall, S. (1997) 'The Spectacle of the Other', in Hall, S. (ed.) *Representation: Cultural Representations and Signifying Practices*. London: Sage – Includes critical analysis of attempts to challenge stereotypical depictions through reversing them, as in films such as *Shaft*.

Larson, S. (2006) *Media and Minorities: The Politics of Race in News and Entertainment*. Lanham: Rowman and Littlefield – In-depth discussion of race and representation focused particularly on the US, covering a range of questions across different forms of media.

Williams, D., Martins, N., Consalvo, M. and Ivory, J. (2009) 'The Virtual Census: Representation of Gender, Race and Age in Video Games', *New Media and Society,* 11(5): 815–34 – Quantitative study that includes representations of different ethnic groups in video games, showing significant under-representation of ethnic minorities, particularly Hispanics.

CHAPTER 13
MEDIA, GENDER AND SEXUALITY

FOCAL POINTS

- Feminist criticism of media representations of gender
- Changing representations of femininity: from domestic goddess to glamorous action hero/career woman
- Studies of 'active' female media users and cultural producers
- Understandings of media representations of masculinity
- Arguments about the marginalisation of LGBT people in media

INTRODUCTION

Questions about the relationship between media, gender and sexuality have formed the basis for countless books, articles and dissertations. As in the case of race and ethnicity, discussions of the nature and possible impact of media representations have long been at the centre of such writings. We'll focus in some detail on such matters early in this chapter, outlining the contribution of a range of critical feminist studies of the depiction of women in popular media forms. We'll then look at contrasting approaches that question what they regard as an over-dismissive approach to forms of culture and representation enjoyed by millions of women. This leads us to a switch of focus towards audience studies oriented to the way women use, enjoy and make sense of commonly derided media forms such as romance genres, soaps, celebrity culture and fashion and beauty magazines. We'll then discuss a growing body of work on masculinity and media, before engaging with questions about the representation of LGBT identities in media.

Running through the chapter is the underlying notion that gender categories are culturally constructed. Our understandings and experiences of male, female, masculinity and femininity are, like our conceptions of black, white and Asian, products of a history of human discourse. Drawing on the work of Foucault (1990), Butler (1990) argues gender should be understood as a series of performances based on prevailing understandings of what it is to be male and female. Gender, then, can be thought of as something that we do rather than something that we are. Crucially, at the heart of these performances of male and female are an equally constructed set of understandings of sexuality, that centre on the predominance of heterosexual, opposite sex desire. Dominant constructions of masculinity and femininity, then, revolve around discourses of difference from and desire for the opposite sex and the marginalisation of same-sex desires and identities forms an integral part of this. Meanwhile, rather than being arbitrary or equal constructions, feminists argue that prevailing notions of masculinity and femininity form part of a patriarchal system which legitimates male power and female subordination.

CONSTRUCTIONS OF FEMININITY

MARGINALISATION OF WOMEN

Although women figure prominently within media content, their role often has been secondary to that of men. The number of blockbuster films or television series with a woman in the lead role, as opposed to one in which she functions as 'companion' and/or 'love interest' for a male star remains relatively low, a situation replicated across a range of other dramatic genres. Women are also significantly under-represented in particular types of media. Williams and colleagues' (2009) study of popular video games found that 85% of characters were male and just 15% female. Turning to the prestigious media sphere of news and current affairs, global content research by The Global Media Monitoring Project (2015) found that women accounted for just 24% of the people depicted within news overall and that just 10% of news stories had women as their central focus. Women formed the majority of those depicted in only four of 54 story categories that were analysed. Significantly, the study emphasises that there is little appreciable difference in these respects between more traditional outlets and newer online news services. Women also tend to be under-represented within key decision-making roles in media institutions. According to Trevor Phillips (2016) of the UK think-tank Policy Exchange, women accounted in 2016 for only 25% of board membership of the country's four major broadcasters. In spite of the importance of this continuing under-representation of women both in media content and institutions, much of what has been written about gender representation has focused upon an analysis of the particular roles in which women are depicted. Such analysis has frequently attacked media for reinforcing a patriarchal system in which women are subject to systematic male domination across society.

THE MALE GAZE

The best-known critique of the depiction of women in media is probably a short article by Laura Mulvey on 1970s' cinema. Drawing on developments of Freud's theory of psychoanalysis, Mulvey (1975: 6) argues that cinema reflects 'the unconscious of patriarchal society' and reinforces the subjugation of women to heterosexual male control and desire. Cinema, she argues, is centred upon *scopophilia*, a Freudian term for childhood voyeurism or the pleasure of 'taking other people as objects, subjecting them to a controlling and curious gaze' (1975: 8). In its stark separation of a darkened, anonymous auditorium from the world that unfolds on-screen, cinema functions as a voyeuristic medium, she argues, encouraging us to take pleasure from looking upon an objectified private milieu.

Crucially, this process is gendered, so that it is women who are set up as the object of scopophilia and men who bear the controlling – and sexually objectifying – gaze. This is ensured by the emphasis on visual sexual appeal in the construction and presentation of female characters:

> In their traditional exhibitionist role women are simultaneously looked at and displayed, with their appearance coded for strong visual and erotic impact so that they can be said to connote to-be-looked-at-ness... She holds the look, plays to and signifies male desire. (Mulvey 1975: 9)

The gender imbalance is exacerbated by another aspect to the operation of scopophilia in cinema, which relates to *narcissism*, or the gaining of pleasure through gazing at one's own image. In outlining the 'mirror stage' of child development, Lacan (2001) argues that the child enjoys in the mirror not a reproduction of himself, but something distinct, superior and closer to perfection – an external idealised image against which the self develops. For Mulvey, cinema replicates the role of this superior mirror image, constructing idealised on-screen images of human subjectivity for audiences to identify with and aspire to.

This narcissistic element is also deemed to be strongly oriented to the male audience. While female characters are optimised in their function as sexual objects for the male gaze, the cinematic depiction of males is as subjects of audience identification and aspiration: 'a male star's glamorous characteristics are thus not those of the erotic object of the gaze, but those of the more perfect, more complete, more powerful ideal ego conceived in the original moment of recognition in front of the mirror' (Mulvey 1975: 11). The male cinema-goer, then, projects his identity onto the active, powerful male star, colluding in his possession and objectification of women. In summary, Mulvey argues that cinema is systematically patriarchal: men are active, independent and in control of their destiny, while the role of women is to satisfy the male gaze and, ultimately, to be possessed.

PATRIARCHAL ROMANCE AND DOMESTICITY

Mulvey's notion of the male gaze and her broader emphasis on the media subjugation of women have proved enormously influential, forming part of a broader critique of gender representations. While critical feminist analyses of pornography, such as those focused upon in Chapter 7, applied the notion of female objectification to the most explicit media depictions of female sexuality (Dworkin 1981; MacKinnon 1988), other theorists examined more mainstream media depictions which presented women as subordinate to and dependent upon men, particularly within the domestic roles of wife and mother.

A study of advertising by Erving Goffman (1979) identified a series of themes pervading the representation of men and women in magazine advertisements. When heterosexual couples were presented together, men were either taller or higher up than women and the implied power difference was reinforced by an admiring gaze from the latter. Women also were frequently represented in submissive postures – lying down, bending their knees, canting their heads or smiling deferentially. Another common trait was 'licenced withdrawal', where women appeared to be distracted – avoiding eye contact, withdrawing their attention, daydreaming or fiddling with objects. Goffman notes that, while men's use of objects tended to be functional and definite, women frequently were shown caressing objects in a distracted, emotional or sexual way. Overall, Goffman concludes that men were presented as independent, rational and clear thinking, while women appeared subordinate, dependent, emotional and absent-minded.

The depiction of women within magazine representations has also been a focus for criticism. A study of teenage girl's magazine, *Jackie*, by Angela McRobbie in the 1970s illustrates a relentless emphasis upon heterosexual romance. Picture stories with titles such as 'As Long as I've Got You' depicted cliché-ridden tales of love between 'dewy eyed women' and 'granite jawed heros' (McRobbie 2000: 81). Getting and keeping a man was presented as the primary concern, a goal whose achievement involved reconciling this 'natural' female desire for romantic attachment with an equally innate promiscuous tendency in men. Other magazine features reinforced the theme, with pop music coverage focused upon the romantic potential of male stars and relentless emphasis on fashion and beauty predicated, argues McRobbie, 'upon the romantic possibilities it precipitates' (2000: 101). In a nod toward Mulvey, McRobbie emphasises that the Jackie girl 'is intended to be looked at' (2000: 76).

Emphasis on women's dependency forms one of a litany of complaints against media raised by Gaye Tuchman (1978), who argues that representations in news, television and adverts were responsible for the 'symbolic annihilation of women'. Reviewing a range of quantitative studies, she concludes that media misrepresented women by disproportionately confining them within the home, reinforcing their association with cooking and child-rearing and their financial dependence on men. Occasional appearances at work were restricted to subordinate roles such as nursing and clerical work and women within such roles, she claims, were often condemned or trivialised (1978: 8). Such conventions predominated, she argues, even within female-oriented media such as soap opera and women's magazines. While more prone to respond to progressive social change than television, the latter, for example, are ultimately deemed to have retained a clear emphasis on marriage, motherhood and domesticity (1978: 24).

POST-FEMINIST INDEPENDENCE?

THE GLAMOROUS CAREER WOMAN

Representations of women have changed considerably since the 1970s. In particular, the emphasis on domesticity and traditional romance identified by Tuchman has been at least partially replaced by more independent versions of femininity. Targeted at financially independent career women, magazines such as *Cosmopolitan* and *Glamour* have for some time constructed an image of women who, on the face of it, go out and get what they want, something expressed in their careers, disposable income and engagement in relationships and sex on their own terms. Sometimes referred to as 'post-feminist', this more confident, independent woman also appears frequently in advertising. Chanel's campaign for its *Allure* perfume range in the early 2000s, for example, featured images of assertive and successful women set against captions outlining their professional identity. And it sometimes extends to cinema and television. One of the most discussed examples in recent decades has been TV series, *Sex and the City*, which centres on the sexual exploits and dilemmas of a group of professional 30-something career women. The four women have different attitudes to sex and relationships but all have brief sexual encounters, periods of being single and longer-term relationships. And the show explicitly highlights their independence – they consume autonomously and are assertive in their relationships, while their female friendship group forms the most consistent and dependable aspect of their lives.

In comparison with earlier representations, the presence and popularity of images of single, financially and sexually autonomous women should not be under-estimated. It both illustrates and contributes to changing social attitudes about what it is to be a woman. Yet not everything has changed. She may be a professional success story rather than a domestic goddess and sexually assertive rather than romantically deferential, but two elements identified by earlier critics remain in many such depictions: the need to look good and the need for male attention. And the two are inextricably linked, of course, by Mulvey's notion of the male gaze. It is partly for this reason that Angela McRobbie (2008) argues that such images constitute a post-feminist masquerade: they emphasise particular versions of female independence, she suggests, while simultaneously reinforcing patriarchy.

If anything, the shift towards the confident city girl representation has further concentrated the emphasis on looking good through discerning consumption. According to an influential 1990s study by Ellen McCracken (1992), rather than being coincidental, this reflects a mutual dependency between media and the cosmetic and fashion industries. The editorial agenda of women's fashion/beauty magazines fits seamlessly with the need to sell advertising space to fashion and cosmetics companies. Such magazines link together the themes of looking attractive and consuming fashion and beauty products with a third one: (hetero)sexual attention and relationships. Even the pose of the model or celebrity on the cover of women's fashion and beauty magazines implies an out-of-shot male presence, argues McCracken, her confidence, status and beauty associated with being desired. The cover image of perfect femininity and sexual success acts as a 'window to the future self' of the reader if she takes heed of the magazine's advice and consumes the fashion and cosmetics of its advertisers (McCracken 1992).

Similar themes can be identified in *Sex and the City*. The identities and aspirations of the characters revolve around their extensive consumption – mostly of clothing and accessories – and their relationships with men. And, while relationship patterns undoubtedly contrast with previously dominant images, the non-attached lifestyles of the women are subject to greater uncertainty as the show progresses, with the more traditional theme of 'looking for Mr Right' lingering ever-larger (Gill 2007: 242). Amidst her short-term liaisons, the story of the show's central character, Carrie, is dominated by an on-off relationship with one man, 'Mr Big' and the show's climax involves him travelling to Paris to finally declare his love for her. As a consequence, Gill argues that *Sex and the City* 'works to re-establish and re-affirm precisely the boundaries it appears to threaten' (2007: 246).

The glamorous career woman trope also tend to be white, young, slim, glamorous, straight and wealthy, projecting a version of femininity that largely excludes larger, darker-skinned, non-straight and working-class femininities. As well as being marginalised in general, Cynthia Carter (2014) suggests that older and minority women are often confined to stereotypical roles that relate to the integration of their gender with age or ethnicity. The ways gender intersects with other characteristics in media representations provides an important reminder that women should not be understood or studied as a single, undifferentiated category.

THE SEXY ACTION HERO

Another form of female characterisation that has become relatively common-place in recent years is that of the sexy female action-hero. Typified by films such as *Lara Croft Tomb Raider*, *Underworld*, *Charlie's Angels*, *Wanted*, *The Avengers* and the depiction of Wonder Woman in *Batman versus Superman: Dawn of Justice*, this trope has been lauded for the plot centrality, toughness and independence of such characters, which contrast starkly with traditional love-interest characterisations in action movies. Yet they share with the glamorous career-woman trope an explicit emphasis on sex appeal. Such characters typically wear tight, revealing clothing and are immaculately made-up, while scenes and camera work are carefully choreographed

Figure 13.1   Wondermark comic, courtesy of wondermark.com, © 2009 David Malki!, http://www.wondermark.com/521

to emphasise sex appeal. As well as appearing in the world of film, sexy action women are prevalent within mainstream video-games, the appeal of playing or interacting with physically tough yet sexually objectified women – pioneered by the original video-game version of *Tomb Raider* – having been carefully cultivated to appeal to a male-dominated consumer base. Recent video analysis by Anita Sarkeesian (2016) demonstrates the extent to which depictions of playable female action protagonists across a range of games are depicted in a manner that draws obvious and repeated attention to their bottoms, for example.

DIVERSIFYING REPRESENTATIONS

Not all 'progressive' representations of women in recent decades fit into the glamorous career woman or sexy action hero stereotypes, however. Although their most frequent depiction of women continues to centre on some variant of the love interest and/or sex object role, some blockbuster movies have featured women as active, powerful characters in their own right. Ripley, in the classic *Alien* films, is infinitely tougher, cleverer and more determined than all her comrades of either gender and not primarily coded for sex appeal. Likewise, Sarah Connor develops into a tough female lead throughout the first two *Terminator* films and a spin-off series, without recourse to objectification. Interestingly, both the depictions in *Alien* and *Terminator* focus on another traditional feminine theme – that of motherhood – but the action-filled roles of Ripley and Connor are about as far as one could get from the passive domestic goddess.

More recently, lead female characters such as Katniss Everdeen in *The Hunger Games* movies and Rey in *Star Wars: The Force Awakens* have moved significantly beyond established or newer stereotypes, presenting as strong, independent heroes who are neither sexually objectified nor reliant on men. In the case of Katniss Everdeen, an emphasis on complex and sometimes confused romantic feelings and on nurturing qualities forms part of the characterisation, but integrated with this is an overall focus on her inner-strength, leadership and abilities. Rey, meanwhile, presents as determined, skilled and courageous throughout and is neither coded as a sex object nor a romantic interest. Rey's gender comes to the fore only in the context of her dismissive responses to attempts to look after and protect her by the film's male co-lead, Finn.

Characters such as Katniss and Rey remain exceptional in the world of blockbuster movies, something betrayed by the amount of discussion and analysis of them. And the omission of Rey from certain games and toys that featured characters from *The Force Awakens* offered a reminder of the embeddedness of the conventions being challenged by the character. Nevertheless, a greater range of female characters have been establishing themselves in the world of television drama for some years. In recent years, for example, *The Good Wife* has been praised by some for its balanced depiction of lawyer Alicia Florrick, in relation to her balancing of the demands of a demanding high profile career, those of parenting teenage children, and the expectations that come from having been married to a high profile politician. *The Walking Dead*, meanwhile, has included a rich variety of tough and non-sexualised female characters as part of its depiction of the struggle to survive in a post-apocalyptic world, even if the leader of the group depicted in the series is male.

Orange is the New Black, meanwhile, takes us several steps further, the setting of a women's prison offering the opportunity to explore a complex and diverse range of female characters of different ages and backgrounds, along with the relationships they develop with one another. Highly unusual in its overwhelmingly female cast and in devoting such time to intra-female relationships, the series breaks out of a tendency elsewhere for women primarily to be depicted interacting with men, or interacting with women about men. Famously observed in a 1980s comic written by Alison Bechdel, the dearth of meaningful or multifaceted female-to-female interactions in popular film or drama has given rise to what some now term the Bechdel test, as a means to assess depictions of women in popular culture. Quite simply, if two or more women interact with one another about something other than a man, then the series, film or advert passes the test.

ENDURING OBJECTIFICATION

Unfortunately, however, not only are there many media texts that fail the Bechdel test, but plenty of representations of women that are more unambiguously objectifying. The use of sexualised images of women as an easy form of 'click-bait' on some news websites, for example, has become commonplace in recent years, with *Mail Online*'s international commercial success owing partly to a right-hand side-bar dominated by images of the partially uncovered bodies of female celebrities and others. The broader emphasis on female celebrity bodies, meanwhile, often serves to reinforce some of the most entrenched gender stereotypes. Eric Meyers' (2014) analysis of celebrity gossip blogs and magazines suggests their emphasis on identifying flaws or secrets through intense focus on female bodies constantly polices femininity. As a case study, Meyers discusses gossip about possible celebrity baby bumps, based on the wearing of loose clothing or slight bulges in the stomach. For Meyers, such gossip simultaneously polices what the non-pregnant female body and clothing should be like (perfectly slim, tight clothing) and invokes stereotypes and judgements about fidelity and suitability for motherhood (Meyers 2014).

Elsewhere, in the world of video-games, heated debate has raged relating to representations of women. Alongside extensive emphasis on women's sexualised bodies through attire, posture and visual emphasis, video games have frequently featured women as objects of male violence, sources of motivation or reward for male protagonists or as 'Damsels in Distress' in need of male rescue (Sarkeesian 2013). While more complex, nuanced and positive female characterisations are increasingly visible (Carr 2006), gaming as a format continues to provide examples of the most regressive forms of gender objectification. Feminist criticisms of sexism within gaming culture from Anita Sarkeesian and others, meanwhile, have been greeted by some male gamers with online abuse, threats and intimidation.

ELITIST CRITICS?

In spite of the persistence of representations of women which might be deemed problematic, some feminists have urged a degree of caution with respect to exactly what is criticised and how, questioning what they regard as the over-dismissive approach of some of their peers, especially when it came to depictions of women in genres popular among female audiences. From the early 1980s, concerns have been expressed that the uncompromising criticism of writers such as Gaye Tuchman, for example, might have the inadvertent effect of denigrating lifestyles and media genres that were central to the everyday lives and identities of many ordinary women. There are three elements to this concern.

First, in labelling certain representations as 'negative' or inaccurate, some critics are argued to have ignored the elements of congruence between some such 'negative' images and the identities of millions of women (Pickering 2001). Calls for the replacement of 'negative' representations with 'positive' ones sometimes suffered, as did similar arguments in relation to ethnicity (see Chapter 12), from difficulties with respect to what exactly was 'positive', who was qualified to decide and what the relationship was between being 'positive' and faithfully representing the range of women's real lives, tastes and interests. At times, the approach of some early critics appeared to equate 'positive' exclusively with assertive, independent, powerful, and career-minded representations, something that meant, for example, that images of motherhood, domesticity, marriage and attachment to the family were in danger of being entirely dismissed as 'negative'.

Second, some feminist critics appeared to fall into an elitist dismissal of cultural texts enjoyed by millions of women, from fashion magazines, to romance genres and, more recently, celebrity gossip blogs. While their observations may not have been entirely invalid, the targeting of criticism at such genres carried the danger of establishing a gulf of perspective between such critics and many of the women they claimed to speak for. The implication sometimes was that such women were ignorant, duped or suffering from false-consciousness. For a recent example, we might consider protest and criticism relating to the 2015 film adaptation of *Fifty Shades of Grey*. Feminist commentators lined up to attack the film's damaging depiction, as they saw it, of wealthy entrepreneur Christian's aggressive sexual pursuit of college student Ana and his enticement of her into submissive forms of BDSM. Yet, whether or not their complaints were valid, the extent of the dismissal of the film among some feminists sat a little uncomfortably with the huge popularity of its depictions with female audiences, the book version of the title having achieved well over 100 million sales globally.

Some of the criticism of the gender depictions in *Fifty Shades of Grey* seemed also to connect with broader dismissals of the quality of the story and, by implication, those who chose to consume and enjoy it, providing a recent example of the concern that feminist critics sometimes have adopted a tone comparable to general attacks on vulgar mass culture, such as those of the Frankfurt School and contemporary critics of media 'dumbing down'. Often made by male academics or critics, these broader criticisms have tended to target types of media that are popular among women, including pop music, consumer magazines, daytime talk shows, soap opera, celebrity gossip and romance genres. Such criticism, some argue, yearns for a version of quality which satisfies a dispassionate, masculine, public agenda, while attacking the tastes and priorities of many women. By themselves attacking 'feminine' genres, some feminist media critics are deemed to have reinforced this denigration of female tastes and pleasures (Modleski 1982). Joke Hermes outlines her concern with the approach as follows:

> The feminist media critic is prophet and exorcist, even while being, as many claim, an 'ordinary woman' too. Feminists… speak on behalf of others who are, implicitly thought to be unable to see for themselves how bad such media

texts... are. They need to be enlightened; they need good feminist texts in order to be saved from their false consciousnesses and to live a life free of false depictions... of where a woman might find happiness. (Hermes 1995: 1)

This brings us to a third problem – that like many other deconstructions of ideology in media content, feminist critics sometimes assumed that the transmission of gendered meanings was predetermined, with the implication that audiences were being passively indoctrinated. In Mulvey's critique of cinema, for example, it is assumed the gaze of the audience is always positioned as male so that even female audience members are forced into this perspective. Greater consideration of audience dynamics surely would illustrate that there are various opportunities for women to gain visual or erotic pleasure, either via a heterosexual gaze focused on male characters, or a lesbian female-to-female gaze (Gauntlett 2008). The determination that a given representation or set of representations are definitively either patriarchal or counter-hegemonic, then, may take insufficient account of the way the texts in question are used by different consumers. A range of detailed studies of female audiences since the 1980s have sought to address this.

EMPOWERING POSSIBILITIES

READING THE ROMANCE

One of the first studies to focus in detail on female audiences was Janice Radway's analysis of the world of romantic fiction. Popular with some women, this literary genre had been subject to extensive feminist criticism – not entirely unlike the more recent and more explicitly erotic example of *Fifty Shades of Grey* perhaps. Such critics attacked the apparently standardised, patriarchal and heterosexist narratives of stories that invariably involved lost, unfulfilled women finding salvation and fulfilment in the arms of a tough, assertive male lover. Without fully rejecting such criticism, Radway (1987) asserts that in order to understand the significance of the genre we must examine how it is used and interpreted by readers. Using detailed qualitative interviews with members of a group of avid readers, Radway's study foregrounds the role novels played within everyday lives dominated by domestic responsibilities.

Radway learned that one of the most important motivations for reading was that the act of doing so enabled women to claim time and space within the home. It was 'a way of temporarily refusing the demands associated with their social role as wives and mothers' and even 'a declaration of independence' (Radway 1987: 9). Yet rather than being isolating, reading also connected them to broader communities of readers. Turning to their engagement with the content itself, Radway emphasises the sophisticated and informed choices made by women with respect to authors and plot types. Notably, their preferred endings tended to involve not only the submission of the heroine to the masculine sexuality of the male, but also his submission to her desire for more feminine forms of love. For Radway, such plots provided emotional replenishment for women who were constantly called upon to care for others, through offering a fantasy of being nurtured as well as sexually fulfilled. While this does not necessarily make the act of reading counter-patriarchal, Radway insists that the women enacted a small-scale appropriation of the texts, interpreting the plots in a way that resolved unsatisfactory elements of their everyday contexts.

SUBVERSIVE PLEASURES?

Radway's study is widely regarded as a pioneering contribution to the study of female audiences. Yet she is criticised by Ien Ang (1996) for having ended up too detached from the women in her study, interpreting the political significance of their accounts from an 'outside' feminist position rather than appreciating their enjoyment on its own terms. Ang's own work (1985) also examined audience responses to a popular and often derided product – the US soap opera *Dallas* – which, for many, was a symbol of the swamping of the globe with superficial US mass culture. Ang rejects such 'ivory tower' accusations while resisting presenting use of the text as a form of resistance for down-trodden audiences. Instead, she emphasises the fundamental importance of the everyday emotional pleasures associated with 'loving Dallas' – pleasures connected to the show's emotional realism which, rather than acting as an 'escape', became intricately interwoven with everyday life and identity.

Other theorists have focused more explicitly on soap opera as a significant female-oriented genre that offers progressive and empowering possibilities (Baym 2000; Brunsdon 1997; Fiske 1987; Geraghty 1991, 2006). Christine Geraghty argues that, through their emphasis on strong, influential female characters and perspectives, soaps explore women's lives, interactions and perspectives in a depth unusual elsewhere, allowing audiences to engage with discourses about 'the way in which relationships… between men and women could be differently organised on women's terms' (1991: 117). Notably, soaps replace linear 'climax' narratives ending with heterosexual love with ongoing multi-narrative structures, so that romantic arrangements are never complete and always subject to disruption and threat. They also are argued to be less overtly centred upon feminine spectacle than some other genres, with a greater focus on everyday life and, according to Fiske, on sexuality as 'a positive source of pleasure in a relationship, or a means of her empowerment in a patriarchal world' (Fiske 1987: 187). Studies of soap audiences, meanwhile, have illustrated the discerning, selective, engaged and critical nature of female viewers of the genre (Hobson 2006), as well as the ways the genre has given rise to online spaces for female-dominated audience reflection and interaction on the plots, narratives and issues they raise (Baym 2000). Geraghty sums up the conclusions of the body of work on soaps and women viewers as follows:

> If soaps, then, were women's fiction, these studies revealed that it was not just because of the stories they told or the heroines (and villainesses) they offered, but because of the way their viewers felt about these programmes… For many, soap viewing was accompanied by female-dominated talk… Even when men watched… it was claimed that women viewers defined the way in which the programmes were understood and their role in everyday life… (2006: 132)

Although they place emphasis on differential readings and uses, many audience studies have remained focused on the kinds of meanings audiences generate. In contrast, a study of women's magazine readers by Joke Hermes (1995) sought to focus primarily on the broader role of reading itself within everyday lives. A key finding was that readers themselves didn't always attach much importance to content, or take it particularly seriously. Most found some features useful either in practical or emotional terms and selectively integrated these into their lives, but Hermes' interviews were dominated by discussion of the compatibility of the act of magazine reading itself with everyday routines. They were deemed easy to pick up and put down and ideal for 'relaxation', through taking time out either from work, worries or other people.

Focusing more closely on readers' engagements with the specific content of magazines, Dawn Currie (2003) suggests teenage women's magazine readers tended to be sceptical about glossy ads and images and more focused on what they saw as the realism of textual articles such as advice columns, which they connected with their everyday lives. Currie also identified a 'pick 'n' mix' approach to reading whereby significant amounts of content are simply bypassed. This finding is replicated in a study by David Gauntlett (2008), which also identified a range of different attitudes to content. Some regarded fashion-related images and advice as providing goals and means for self-improvement, some enjoyed criticising the identities depicted, while others regarded the magazines as an escapist pleasure of little real-life relevance. Readers also displayed diverse views about the impact of magazines, with some sharply critical of the versions of femininity and masculinity they presented. Without fully rejecting feminist criticisms of magazine content, Gauntlett emphasises that such publications offer a more contradictory set of ideas than they are sometimes given credit for and that readers draw on these in a variety of ways.

FEMINIST PROSUMERS?

In recent years the focus for feminist media scholars increasingly has been on the activities of women who have challenged dominant gender relations not only as active audiences, but as critics, appropriators and producers. An early example that precedes the era of mass digital participation is the 1990s Riot Grrrl scene which countered male domination in the music industry through all-female bands who angrily repudiated traditional gender roles, flaunting an aggressive and uncompromising sexuality through music, imagery and on-stage performance. The scene was characterised by a punk-inspired DIY ethic in which, as well as being encouraged to pick up guitars or organise events, participants produced a substantial grassroots network of printed and eventually online zines featuring a range of content related to gender, sexuality and female empowerment (Leonard 1998: Schilt and Zobl 2008). Although the movement gradually shifted out of the public eye, Schilt and Zobl argue that the network of DIY communication it gave rise to continues to thrive underground in the form of websites, blogs and online forums (ibid.).

Studies of female popular media fan groups, meanwhile, have focused upon interactive fan activities that can subvert dominant gender representations. In a classic study, Constance Penley (1991) focused on the female-dominated phenomenon of 'fan fiction', whereby fans compose their own stories based on the setting or characters of existing television, film or novels. Penley's particular focus was on 'slash', a sub-genre focused on the development of romantic and sexual storylines. Typically, such stories subvert the patriarchal and hetero-sexual orientation of the original fiction by exploring same-sex encounters between male characters. As well as contesting dominant understandings of mainstream fictions such as *Star Trek* and *Harry Potter*, such interpretations allude to understandings of sexuality as flexible and unfixed. In their recent study of a Harry Potter fan fiction website, Karlsson and Ohlin-Scheller (2015) explore how traditional gender subject positions can be partially contested through the live, collaborative development of fan stories on the internet. While noting that, in the example they observed, heteronormative understandings ultimately prevailed, they note how interactions appropriated and played with standard gender tropes and how, in general, girls were considerably more active than boys in the fan story.

In spite of its significance, fan fiction remains something of a minority practice engaged in by unusually committed or engaged groups. Yet in recent years, social network sites, among other easily accessible interactive media, have become everyday forms of communication and gender expression for countless ordinary young women. Central to the use of such media are representations of oneself and one's friends via text, images and sometimes video. According to Amy Shields Dobson (2011; 2014), sharing self-representations and interacting with those of others via social media have become key components in how young people learn about and contribute to constructions of male and female. Focusing on the images young women foregrounded and shared on the MySpace profiles, Dobson identifies a complex mixture of representations that may be open to different interpretations with respect to their reinforcement and/or subversion of hegemonic gender categories.

With respect to the images foregrounded on their profile pages, Dobson identified in a number of examples of what she terms 'hetero-sexy' images that – at face value – presented objectified, sexualised images of heterosexual bodies (2011). These included sexualised images of idealised unidentified 'dream-girls' and female celebrities, depictions of heterosexual sex and images of themselves in poses that appeared to replicate the imagery of dominant fashion and beauty, advertising or soft-porn. While recognising how such images 'hold connotations of objectification and complicity with a masculinised gaze' and that profiles are often generated in an atmosphere of peer pressure, Dobson suggests the context of self-production here may complicate things somewhat, indicating at least a partially active embrace of 'gazing back', ironic or critical uses of such imagery and/or agentic communication of the pleasure of being seen (Dobson 2011).

In addition to such hetero-sexy images, however, Dobson (2014) also identifies a preponderance of what she calls 'performative shamelessness' in the form of laddish representations, particularly when it came to images users posted of their friends and friendships. Here, young women still are the focus of visual attention but, rather than seeking to approximate perfect constructions of feminine beauty, images tend to emphasise assertive, humorous poses and activities, including 'silly' or caricatured faces; wide open mouths and protruding tongues; displays of drunken and rowdy behaviour and exaggerated masculine postures: 'heads are back and bodies are sometimes doubled over in an antithesis of grace and modesty… poses with their limbs akimbo, spread out and space-occupying' (Dobson 2014: 150). Dobson explores the complex and contradictory implications of such imagery, noting the importance of sexual and even pornographic inferences at times as well as the apparently subversive, exaggerated caricatures of inappropriate and/or laddish forms of behaviour. She suggests such self-selected humorous and grotesque bodily representation on social network sites may represent a partial challenge to the fantasy feminine ideals emanating from the fashion and beauty industries, including those that could be identified elsewhere on their profiles (Dobson 2014).

IDENTIFYING AGENCY, REMAINING CRITICAL

Studies of the activities of female audiences and, more recently, prosumers, have been important in illustrating some of the limitations of feminist criticism of popular media texts and drawing attention to the agency of media users. Yet critical textual analysis ought not to be entirely abandoned in favour of a celebration of user pleasure and/or empowerment. Ang's endorsement of viewing pleasures, for example, may be lauded for celebrating ordinary pleasures but comes at the possible cost of letting media producers off the hook with respect to the ways they encode particular representations into texts. Similarly, although Hermes' emphasis on the validity of magazine reading as an active activity is illuminating, the strength of her dismissal of more critical and text-based approaches may underrate their enduring importance. Williamson's accusation that feminist audience studies were in danger of endorsing a 'pointless populism' (cited in Gill 2007: 16) is overly-harsh, but the warning therein that the study of media and gender must not lose its critical edge is pertinent.

The testimonies of female audience members illuminate a diverse range of engagements and, sometimes, critical negotiations with media texts, reminding us that the impact of content ought never be taken for granted. Meanwhile, the participatory activities of female media users, from fan fiction groups to individual social media users, illustrate that media industries do not have a monopoly on the construction of gender. Such details about users, though, do not preclude the possibility that consistent themes in widely circulated media representations might have a broader pervasive influence. If there are limits to the range of understandings of femininity readily accessible within the content of a given advert, magazine, film or television programme, and if these limits are consistent with dominant existing understandings, then it is not unreasonable to identify the text as having the potential to reinforce such understandings. The constructions of gender available within media content continues to warrant careful critical analysis.

MEDIA AND MASCULINITIES

Partly as a result of the substantial contribution of feminism to the study of gender and media, a good deal of what has been written on the subject has been centred upon women, something reflected in the structure of this chapter. Yet the way in which men and masculinity are constructed in media, alongside the role of men as media producers and audiences, is every bit as important to discussions about gender, sexuality and identity – and over the past two decades has been afforded a gradual increase in analytic attention.

MASCULINITY OR MASCULINITIES?

As Mulvey observes, the cinematic male lead is typically a dominant, powerful and sexually successful focus for male-centred audience identification. And in spite of elements of diversity, recent decades of popular film have been dominated by representations of active, powerful male characters who use their prowess – whether physical or otherwise – to overcome the forces stacked against them and, often, to win the love of the film's lead female. In the 1980s, Fiske (1987) argued that a key element of media representations of masculinity was a practical orientation towards the successful achievement of goals. The narrative structure of male-oriented television series, he says, tended to consist of a one-dimensional plot progression towards a climax of achievement induced by masculine performance. Most obviously, male power was emphasised, for Fiske, through the physical imagery of muscular bodies triumphing in fist fights and male control of trucks, fast cars and guns. While there has been significant diversification of narrative structures, representations and themes since the 1980s, it is not difficult to find an underlying emphasis on masculine purpose and/or toughness in many contemporary drama series (*24*, *Luther*, *Peaky Blinders*, *Game of Thrones*), blockbuster movies (*Spectre*, *The Amazing Spiderman*, *The Dark Knight Rises*) and, even more so, video games (where there are far too many examples to mention). Even when they are not portrayed in physically tough roles and where there is greater nuance to their characters, men regularly are represented as active, goal-oriented and competitive and as occupying positions of power, authority and responsibility.

Yet even the most overt versions of on-screen masculinity may entail ambiguities with respect to their social significance. The visual construction of extreme physical male prowess, for example, may lend itself in some cases to use as sexual objectification for a straight female or gay male gaze. Deliberate emphasis on the body of Daniel Craig walking out of the sea in swimming shorts in the marketing for *Casino Royale* represents just one example. Emphasis on the scarred, ripped physical body of Geralt at various points in the second and third instalments of hit video game series *The Witcher* is open to a similar reading, even if the series also places more predictable emphasis on female bodies too. The significance of representations of spectacular male physical power to heterosexual male audiences also entails ambiguities when we consider its relationship to everyday life. For Fiske, rather than reinforcing everyday male experience, such images are more likely to act as unrealistic fantasies when compared to the lack of independence, control or power which characterise most ordinary men's lives, particularly in the contemporary workplace (Fiske 1987; also see Harrison 2014; Price 2013). The ongoing decline of traditional male jobs in manufacturing industries has exacerbated the separation between most ordinary men and the physical exploits of their screen heroes, while the diversification of relationships and families, growth of female employment and changes in attitudes towards gender have also contributed to what some term a 'crisis' in the status of masculinity (Horrocks 1994).

Sometimes the changing reality of everyday masculinities is itself the subject of nuanced, complex representations. Stuart Price (2014) explores the significance of rhetoric and speech within 1999 hit *Fight Club* as a complex response to what the film's anti-hero, Tyler, perceives as a loss of authentic masculinity in a world of pointless white-collar jobs, feminised self-help groups and empty consumerism (also see Giroux 2002). While *Fight Club* represents – though does not entirely endorse – a violent and revolutionary reaction to the crisis of masculinity, media representations elsewhere embraced notions of the so-called 'new man', comfortable with gender equality, balancing work and domestic responsibilities, in touch with his emotional side and making considerable effort with his appearance (Harrison 2014). The latter is reflected in a rapidly expanding portfolio of advertisements for men's cosmetic and fashion products, and the significance of the cosmetics and clothing industries in promoting this more narcissistic, nurturing form of masculinity has prompted some to label it 'commercial masculinity' (Harrison 2014). Women's fashion and beauty magazines, meanwhile, sometimes placed emphasis upon the desirability for women of this more image-conscious, sensitive male. A further source for the 'softening' of male images was the phenomenon of the boy band, which re-emerged in the 1990s in the form of groups such as *Take That* and has continued to thrive since then in the form of *One Direction* and others. Oriented to young female and gay male audiences, the boy band combined some traditional elements of masculinity with style-conscious, sensitive and slightly built 'boy next door' features. Meanwhile, as Gauntlett points out, internationally popular sit-coms such as *Friends* frequently depicted men who combined selected established masculine qualities with 'characteristics of sensitivity and gentleness, and male-bonding' (2008: 65).

CONTRADICTORY REPRESENTATIONS: LADS AND BEYOND

Yet, far from moving seamlessly from a regime of aggressive, powerful stereotypes to one dominated by sensitive caring representations, the development of masculinities is full of conflicts and contradictions. While Connell (2000) argues there is, at any moment in time, a hegemonic version of masculinity that is more influential than others, Gill (2007) suggests identification of such a single dominant type is difficult given the range of competing and overlapping types of maleness. Developing representations of 'lad culture' in recent decades provide an illuminating illustration. Centred upon sex, drinking, cars, sport, gadgets and 'male' popular culture, so-called lad-mags became highly popular for a relatively short period during the late 1990s and early 2000s. Such publications presented themselves as a reassertion of authentic masculinity in the face of the 'new man', who was derided as feminine and/or homosexual. The narrative throughout the magazines emphasises the pragmatic use of women for sex while avoiding having masculinity compromised through permanent commitment to them (Jackson et al. 2001). Women, then, are presented as a source of pleasure but also as a threat to men's natural love for adventure, drinking, sport, cars and having a laugh with their mates.

Beneath the hysterical hyper-masculine exterior of babes, beer, fast cars, sport and laughs, however, were elements to the 'new lad' that sat less easily with traditional masculine confidence. The fashion and personal grooming of commercial masculinity were a constant feature, in connection with an array of cosmetic and clothing ads. Meanwhile, beneath their confident, cocky headlines, advice columns focused on health problems and relationship guidance suggested at least a degree of self-consciousness and insecurity. For Jackson et al., it is through adopting their hyper-masculine veneer that lad's magazines carried off the inclusion of such features. For Gauntlett, this makes representations of the new lad open to a range of possible meanings and uses, containing constant indications of male weakness, alongside what he takes as a playful and ironic hyper-masculine façade (Gauntlett 2008). Gauntlett's argument is compelling in its recognition of the complexity of representations within what initially appears as a one-dimensional text and the possibility of non-patriarchal readings, but ultimately comes across as a little complacent. As Jackson et al. (2001) point out, an ironic tone does not negate the possibility of reinforcing problematic gendered assumptions and may even act as a convenient device that deflects criticism (Jackson et al. 2001).

While some retain an online presence, major lad mags such as *FHM* and *Loaded* no longer exist in print-form, having fallen victim to the general decline in print media and a haemorrhaging of readers to other formats. Their laddish representations, however, are alive and well, pervading, for example, the BBC's internationally successful *Top Gear*, with its carefully blended combination of fast-car driving, competitiveness and exaggerated masculine antics and banter. The lad trope is equally prevalent in some forms of advertising and, most notably, betting commercials for companies such as Ladbrokes and Betfair that centre on familiar tropes of young men watching the game together and engaging in witty banter. Yet the less traditionally masculine aspects of male representation have also persisted and developed, albeit in conjunction with more reassuring forms of masculine imagery. While the lad magazine format appears to have been consigned to history, magazines such as *Men's Health* have continued to flourish, having successfully transitioned to online as well as print formats. With a mature orientation and tone, such titles typically combine traditional emphasis on sport, fitness and strength with a reflective focus on the male body and mind, from achieving a muscular torso to dressing effectively, eating healthily and dealing with stress and anxiety.

Consumer masculinity, meanwhile, continues to develop. For every lad-focused betting ad, there is a commercial focused upon men using cosmetics or clothing to work on their appearance. And the range of products previously only targeted to women and gay men is expanding. Claire Harrison's (2014) analysis of an example of a men's make-up website, provides a notable example. While using masculine colours and address, reassuring customers as to the difference between their products and women's make-up and placing particular emphasis on the health benefits of its products, the site constructed a version of masculinity centred on wearing make-up to look good. Harrison interprets this as a refocusing of the male gaze onto the male body itself, including through semi-naked images of attractive models encoded as ordinary men enhanced by the company's cosmetics. While examples such as this may be atypical, it is clear that media depictions of men are complex, contradictory and, in some respects at least, changing.

BEYOND HETEROSEXUALITY

Even though the range of representations of both masculinity and femininity are expanding, they both still tend to largely exclude non-heterosexual forms of identity. Opposite sex attraction and encounters between men and women lie at the core of the way media discourses construct masculinity and femininity and the marginalisation of LGBT orientations or identities forms an integral part of this heterosexual matrix, or hegemony (Butler 1990). Alluding to Tuchman's earlier attack on media representations of women, Gross (1995: 63) argues that same-sex desires and identities have been 'symbolically annihilated' or rendered invisible by mass media, adding that 'when they do appear, they do so in order to play a supportive role for the natural order' (Gross 1995: 63). In other words, media representations of minority sexualities have tended to reinforce the prevailing heterosexual hegemony. This is because sexual minorities have tended to be pigeon-holed within stereotyped roles and narratives.

Historically, many of the lesbian characters or personalities to make an appearance in mainstream media, for example, were aggressively dysfunctional or unhappy characters (Arthurs 2004). And Moritz (2004) identifies an ongoing tendency for fictional narratives involving lesbians to end up restoring heterosexual normality in a variety of ways. Typically, she argues, lesbian characters have tended to be positioned as troubled, dysfunctional or nasty characters who are ultimately either killed off, imprisoned or restored to happiness through a return to heterosexual femininity. In recent times, however, there has been a shift towards a different image of lesbianism – as young, glamorous and ultra-feminine. Lesbian-themed series such as *Sugar Rush* and the *L-Word* have been of importance here, alongside lesbian characters, romances and encounters in a range of other series, including *Buffy the Vampire Slayer*, *Guiding Light* and *Grey's Anatomy*. Such representations have the potential to blur some of the boundaries of dominant femininity and raise questions about the exclusive equation of feminine glamour with the male gaze.

Yet lesbianism within mainstream dramatic programming has often tended to consist of a moment of temporary exploration or a one-off relationship, followed by either a return to heterosexuality or an exit from the series, both of which function to restore the heterosexual equilibrium. The narrative conventions of soap opera, in particular, have sometimes marginalised long-term lesbian or gay characters due to an insufficient number of potential partners in the predominantly heterosexual local communities depicted. Meanwhile, although it challenges boundaries, the trend towards glamorous, feminine lesbian representations may reinforce dominant notions of female beauty and, particularly, depictions of femininity as sexualised display. In the world of the narrative, the male gaze may be secondary to female-to-female sexual attraction, but the spectacle of the young, glamorous lesbian encounter on-screen may also be read, in some cases, as sexualised display oriented towards the male viewer. Recently, *Orange is the New Black* has managed to avoid some of these shortcomings, however, its setting of a women's prison enabling exploration of a number of long- and short-term lesbian or bisexual relationships as well as incorporating a transgender character.

Gay men have probably been more frequently represented in mass media than lesbians and other sexual minorities, with a range of male game show hosts, pop stars and actors openly identifying as homosexual for many years, yet depictions of male gay intimacy remain rare. Stereotypes of feminine, camp eccentricity have dominated, often establishing the gay male as a mildly freakish, theatrical figure of fun, positioned at a safe distance from dominant masculinities. Male homosexuality also is frequently represented in its most white, middle-class, sanitised and unthreatening guise (Arthurs 2004). The dependable gay best friend and/or fashion expert has become a particularly familiar stereotype in female-oriented television series, including *Will and Grace* and *Sex and the City* as well as in romantic comedy and reality TV shows such as *Say Yes to the Dress*.

Such representations may be 'positive' in that they present gay men as likeable and friendly members of society, but as well as being guilty of pigeon-holing, their socially-acceptable orientation tends to exclude other elements of gay identities. Notably, the same-sex encounters or romances of the gay best friend tend to be somewhat marginalised and, in particular, explicit male-to-male intimate and sexual contact remains unusual across a range of genres and formats. A similar point could be made, perhaps, in relation to the numerous high profile gay male artists in the popular music industry, many of whom have tended to avoid explicit or clear expressions of their sexuality in lyrics, imagery, interviews or public appearances in order to ensure they remain sufficiently palatable to heterosexual consumers (Doty and Gove 1997).

The example of the gay best friend character also exemplifies a tendency for LGBT characters to be secondary to predominantly heterosexual, binary gender narratives. And according to Doty and Gove, even if homosexuality is positioned more centrally, it tends to be focused on from a heterosexual point of view. 'Heterocentric narrative construction', they argue, 'will, finally, structure the plot to revolve around how straight characters and culture respond to lesbians, gays and queers', so that 'we see these characters primarily through straight gazes and narratives' (Doty and Gove 1997: 88). And this connects to a further point – that the emphasis on attracting straight audiences invariably causes non-heterosexual characters to be isolated within overwhelmingly straight environments or communities. We rarely see much evidence of broader gay peer groups or communities, let alone involvement in collective activism (Arthurs 2004).

This tendency for gay narratives to be marginal and/or sanitised is not ubiquitous, of course. The 1990s UK series, *Queer as Folk* focused in detail on the lives, relationships and encounters of gay men, enabling exploration of a variety of different characters in the context of a gay scene. In contrast to sanitised depictions elsewhere, its narratives included controversial sides of the gay scene as well as overtly sexual storylines and a number of explicit depictions of sexual encounters. More recently, the cartoon series *Rick and Steve* presented a satirical focus on the gay scene, complete with comic storylines about threesomes, lesbian motherhood and even HIV. And non-stereotypical gay characters, complete with light forms of intimacy have been represented in a number of shows, including *The Wire*, *Empire* and *Game of Thrones*.

A particularly striking break from desexualised or secondary representations was provided by the Oscar winning blockbuster, *Brokeback Mountain*, which focused on a long-term love affair between two summer sheep-herders in Wyoming. The film's huge box office success enabled it to break out of the specialist gay content pigeon-holes within which some other productions have been restricted, reaching a large, diverse audience around the world. More recently *Blue is the Warmest Colour* achieved significant critical acclaim for its intense, erotic depiction of a lesbian love affair between a high-schooler and an art student. Encouraging though such examples may be, it remains the case that, outside of high-brow or specialist gay and lesbian media channels, non-heterosexual characters or personalities are often either invisible or stereotyped as a fixed and familiar 'other' (Foucault 1978).

While overt LGBT representations remain limited, there are many characters that are primarily coded as straight, but offer the possibility of queer audience readings (Doty and Gove 1997). What were taken as occasional hints at a lesbian relationship between the main characters of 1990s cult series *Xena Warrior Princess*, for example, prompted many fans to understand them as lesbian icons, even though they were not explicitly presented as such. This was then encouraged by the show's producers, who developed the lesbian sub-text through further hints as the series continued. Meanwhile, as we have already seen, groups of straight, lesbian and bisexual women engaged in online slash fan fiction communities have regularly created storylines centred upon queer interpretations of straight characters in a variety of mainstream series (Jenkins 2003). For Sonia Katyal (2006: 485), inherent to slash as a grassroots, participatory movement is a rejection of 'the notion that gender roles are fixed and predetermined' and an embrace of 'the idea that sexuality can be fluid and filled with various erotic possibilities'. Even back in the 1990s, the popularity among slash communities of 'queering' outwardly straight characters prompted Doty and Gove (1997: 89) to note that 'almost every figure on television might be "representing" queerness in some way, to some degree, for some viewer'. Once again, we are reminded of the need to recognise the range of audience responses to textual representations and the ways that, particularly in digital, participatory environments such interpretations can contribute to the subversion of dominant structures of meaning. It is not only, as Katherine Sender (2014: 209) puts it, that such environments may be offering to LGBT people the increasing possibility to find 'opportunities to speak, rather than be spoken for', but also that their creativity and participation may in some cases have influence on the producers of the shows they engage with (Jenkins 2003).

CONCLUSION: A BALANCED APPROACH

While studies of the depiction of women have dominated the development of studies of gender, sexuality and media, the growing body of research on masculinities has underlined the need to make sense of the media construction and living out of both female and male forms of identity. Meanwhile developing understandings of LGBT representations in media remind us, among other things, of the crucial link between the reinforcement of dominant understandings of sexuality and prevailing binary constructions of gender. And a rounded understanding is equally dependent upon a balance between emphasis on media representations and on the ways users construct gendered and sexualised identities through their uses of media. We should be cautious of both over-deterministic textual criticism and over-celebratory audience studies. Neither should the structure of media industries be omitted from our analysis, particularly with respect to the relationship between gender constructions and media profitability. After all, the media representations of masculinity and femininity that dominate our various screens normally are those that sell the most tickets, subscriptions and advertising space.

QUESTIONS/EXERCISES

1   a) Select an example of a recent blockbuster film and try to analyse the construction of its male and female characters using Laura Mulvey's framework. To what extent does your film illustrate or challenge her conclusions?

    b) How valid is Anita Sarkeesian's critique of the representations of women in video games?

2   What would a 'positive' representation of femininity look like and why? How about masculinity? Are the notions of negative and positive helpful or unhelpful as part of this discussion?

3 a) What contribution to debates about media and gender has been made by studies of female media audiences and users? If audiences are active and creative, do we need to worry about what is depicted in media content?

   b) What are Dobson's conclusions about young women's self-representation through images on social networking sites? Do you agree with her?

4 Identify four distinct masculine 'tropes' or 'stereotypes' in contemporary media, providing examples for each one. What are the differences and commonalities between the types you have identified?

5 Discuss the ways apparently straight characters or personalities have been read or reinterpreted by some audience groups as queer? What is the significance of such interpretations?

SUGGESTED FURTHER READING

Dobson, A. (2015) *Postfeminist Digital Cultures: Femininity, Social Media, and Self-Representation.* New York: Palgrave Macmillan – Detailed exploration of the digital media practice of teenage girls with particular focus on the ways young women represent themselves on social media and elsewhere.

Gill, R. (2007) *Gender and the Media.* Cambridge: Polity Press – Critical account of a broad range of debates and examples relating to media and gender.

Harrison, C. (2014) 'Studio5ive.com: Selling Cosmetics to Men and Reconstructing Masculine Identity', in Ross, K. (ed.) *Handbook of Gender, Sex and Media.* Oxford: Wiley-Blackwell, pp. 189–204 – Case study analysis of representations of masculinity on a male make-up website, identifying complex forms of address, including a refocusing on the male gaze.

Mulvey, L. (1975) 'Visual Pleasure and Narrative Cinema', *Screen*, 16(3): 6–18 – Highly influential article which first established the notion that media depictions of women are oriented to the male gaze.

Radway, J. (1987) *Reading the Romance: Women, Patriarchy and Popular Literature.* London: Verso – One of the first and most well-known feminist studies of the audiences of often-derided media forms popular with women.

CHAPTER 14
SATURATION, FLUIDITY AND LOSS OF MEANING

FOCAL POINTS

- The increasing saturation of contemporary life by media and consumer culture
- Arguments that saturation is blurring boundaries between representations and reality
- The notion that identities are becoming fluid, fragmented and media-centred
- The internet as a culture of image and simulation, or as an extension of everyday life
- Criticisms of postmodern interpretations of media saturation

INTRODUCTION

At various points during this book we have revisited questions about whether media should be regarded as a reflective mirror on the broader social and cultural world or as shapers of that world. The approach the book has advocated suggests that, rather than innocently mirroring society, media construct very particular representations of it and that the selectiveness of these mediated versions of reality have the capacity to influence future social relations, cultural values and so on. This circular way of thinking offers an improvement on the more partial and simplistic poles of reflection and shaping theory, providing a broad framework for making sense of the different topics we have covered. The selective representations approach, however, may itself be vulnerable to the criticism that, in spite of regarding the media–society relationship as a complex, two-directional one, it continues to place emphasis on a fundamental distinction between media representations and the 'real world' which they are taken to refer to and influence. This simplification may be valuable in helping us to make sense of how media work, but it is important to realise that, ultimately, media form an integral part of this real world rather than operating outside it (Alexander 2003).

Some theorists argue that media representations have become so central to everything we see, think, say and do that it is impossible to conceive of any reality that is separate from them. For some postmodernists, contemporary societies are so saturated by media that reality and representation are, essentially, one and the same – that reality consists of no more or less than a multiplicity of representations. Everything, from understandings of contemporary events to the construction of individual identities, is inseparable from media of one kind or another. This chapter examines such a possibility, through focusing on the proclamations and predictions of theorists who argue that the saturation of society by media has reached such an extent that truth, certainty and meaning are rapidly disappearing.

SATURATION AS LOSS OF MEANING

CONSUMERISM: EXPANSION AND SPEED-UP

Driven by a combination of profit making and new technologies, the amount of media communication and commercialism circulating within society has expanded rapidly in recent decades. Important here has been the transition outlined in Chapter 10 from a standardised *Fordist* economy to a *post-Fordist* one dominated by an ongoing and disorganised proliferation of different sorts of media and cultural products, each oriented to distinct consumer segments. The sharp growth of disposable income across developed societies, alongside intense competition within increasingly unregulated markets meant, according to postmodernist theorist Fredric Jameson, that the culture industries were increasingly focused on a constant drive to develop as many new and different things for us to consume as possible. As well as developing as many variations as possible within existing genres or product categories, this search for 'ever more novel-seeming goods' entailed an ongoing search for new markets and new forms of advertising with which to engage these (Jameson 1991: 4; Featherstone 2007).

As well as cultivating a proliferation of niche markets, media and commerce have penetrated into more areas of our everyday lives, routines and identities. Sure enough, it has become difficult to think of many cultural activities that are not now centred on media and profit-making interests. Popular sports fandom, for example, has become a thoroughly media-driven pursuit, whose every element is focused upon and shaped by money-making: auctioned television rights, replica shirts, club sponsorship deals, commercials at grounds, in-play online gambling, internet fan communities, branded calendars, computer games, mugs and so on. Participation in sports and outside activities is equally exploited with constant efforts to develop new and novel-seeming forms of equipment, clothing and a wide range of consumer and media items.

An accompanying theme is the ever-greater significance of symbolic value as part of this mediated consumer culture. If the primary role of our clothes, cars, mobile devices and household decor is to make a symbolic statement about who we are (see Chapter 10), then there are fewer limitations to the frequency with which we purchase such items. The triumph of symbolic value, then, drastically expands the intensity of consumerism. A rapid speed-up in the turn-over rates for new products and the cycles of fashion with which they were associated is argued to be a further key feature of contemporary media and commerce (Harvey 1989). The life span of any one set of products becomes shorter as companies compete to shift our attention and money elsewhere as soon as possible. What we have been seeing, it is suggested, is an increasingly frantic and chaotic proliferation of different symbolic products and services into all aspects of our lives.

INFORMATION OVERLOAD

Media, of course, have formed a key component in this ongoing expansion of post-Fordist consumerism and it is no coincidence that they also have proliferated and diversified in recent years. Aided by deregulation and the development of digital, internet and mobile technologies, media have shifted from a small number of products distributed to huge audiences towards a complex and ever-expanding array of content and services, many of which are interactive and/or on-demand. And this proliferation has been matched by an increase in the media saturation of contemporary life. We listen to radio as we get up, view billboards and digital displays around our towns and cities and engage with a range of content and friends via social media at various points throughout the day. We then spend our evenings watching television, playing video games and engaging with more social and online content. Alternatively, if we go out, we watch films in the cinema or engage with recorded music, television and/or the internet in cafes and bars. The increasing capacity of mobile media is crucial here, enabling many of us to take the internet, games, music and virtually any other forms of content everywhere we go. Wherever we are, then, multiple media messages from different sources are competing for our attention, to the extent that, according to Sherry Turkle, we now inhabit a world of simulation where 'what people mostly want from public space is to be alone with their personal networks' (2013: 14). Some of us even consume media to help us sleep.

For some, this everyday plethora of images and information is cause for celebration. Proponents of the deregulated free market regularly emphasise the choice on offer to us, while enthusiasts of digital democracy point to the emancipatory possibilities of such unprecedented access to information and interaction. However, for Jean Baudrillard (1988) – writing before the digitalisation of media but anticipating much that it was to bring – the proliferation of electronic media signalled the drowning out of substance by noise. According to this view, the more the channels of communication multiply, the more we suffer from information overload. For Nick Stevenson, the amount of simultaneous information with which we surround ourselves has reached the point where it 'exceeds the interpretive capacity of the subject' (2002: 162), leading to a replacement of understanding with a range of superficial surfaces. And such simultaneous media consumption has significantly intensified since Stevenson's comment. We semi-watch television while engaging with our mobile devices as we flick back and forth between numerous tabs, windows or apps, and we listen to music as we glance up and down between our personal online networks and an array of media messages in the spaces around us as we travel.

The content transmitted, meanwhile, becomes increasingly oriented, Baudrillard argues, to immediate stimulation and excitement, since it is only by doing so that it can hope to garner our attention amidst the din. Across genres, the emphasis is on fast-moving, ever-changing images which are almost immediately abandoned and replaced with something different. Rather than developing a complex, in-depth or coherent understanding of anything in particular, then, our attention constantly switches between myriad temporarily engaging images and representations. Context and history become increasingly unimportant, then, and our responses to the images placed before us are dominated by emotional reactions, snap judgements and, ultimately, a thirst for the next bite-sized snippet of content.

MEDIA = REALITY

For Baudrillard, the extent of the saturation of our lives by this barrage of media messages suggested there was no longer any distinction between such representations and society itself. Sure enough, the centrality of media to our everyday experiences means that their cumulative impact throughout our lifetimes is overwhelming – they define and dominate our broader cultural relations, values, experiences and understandings of the world. Even in those rare moments when we are not 'tuned in', our thoughts and activities are defined in relation to the myriad previous media experiences through which our lives are constructed. Similarly, each of our encounters with media in the present are defined by existing understandings that can be traced back to past media encounters. For theorists such as Baudrillard, this sort of multi-layered saturation makes it impossible to envisage any sort of real society, authentic cultural identity or truthful account of the world which lies beneath all the mediated images and representations. Active audience theories emphasise that engagement with media consists of a two-way engagement between media and the existing social and cultural contexts of consumers, but if these contexts are themselves inseparable from a history of previous media experiences then might the situation not be better described as an interaction of new sets of media representations with the outcome of previous ones?

Our understanding of public issues such as those concerning politics, wars, famines or the environment, then, should be regarded as entirely dependent upon layer upon layer of media representations, whether through news, documentaries, film, magazines, television series or the ways these are framed and interpreted via cascading social media commentary. As with many other events, we understood the Paris attacks in 2015 through a series of media representations in the form of television and online coverage that often were filtered or understood via a plethora of comments, shares, likes and arguments with people known and unknown to us via social media. In coming to judgements and interpretations of what had taken place there was no unmediated version against which to assess all this. Rather the only option open to us was to compare and contrast different mediated representations and interpretations with one another. And, of course, each of our interpretations was equally dependent upon the culmination of our past and ongoing media experiences: disaster films, TV drama, video games, previous news stories and all manner of narratives about victims, terrorists, goodies, baddies and war. When current sets of representations can only be understood through past representations, the notion of an unmediated truth or reality beneath it all, according to Baudrillard, is difficult to envisage. Famously, and controversially, he illustrated the point by declaring that the 1991 Gulf War did not happen – that there was no discernable external reality beneath the barrage of media images (Baudrillard 1995b).

Understandings of issues and experiences associated with the private sphere are no less media saturated. The ways we live out our relationships, family lives, interests, hobbies and everyday behaviour are developed in relation to past and present media representations of these aspects of life, not least in the form of novels, soap opera, films, magazines, news stories, chat shows and advertising, to say nothing of the ever-expanding range of reality TV programmes. Equally important, our own use of DIY media such as digital cameras and social networking sites increasingly form a core, integral and structuring part of our lives rather than merely representing them (Turkle 2013). One consequence of this is that the boundaries between private and public can become blurred, with more and more details of our intimate lives shared with diverse and, sometimes, unpredictable audiences (boyd 2014). Our private interactions with friends, meanwhile, take place increasingly within commercialised environments where what we say, like and share is recorded, archived and mined for information with which to more effectively target us with commercial messages (Cohen 2013). There is a strong case, then, for suggesting that, as well as dominating our perspectives on the broader world, media are equally integral to our everyday routines and dominate the values we live by and the ways we understand our place in the world. Our understandings of ourselves and our everyday lives, then, are as intertwined with media images as are our perspectives on the broader world.

FROM TRUTH, TO IDEOLOGY, TO SIMULACRA

Baudrillard (1995a: 6) locates media saturation as part of a four-phase transformation in the cultural role of images and representations – or more precisely, signs. In the first two phases, signs are counter-posed with 'a profound reality'. In the second two, the signs have proliferated to such an extent that they replace reality.

In phase one, images perform the traditional symbolic role of the sign, acting as a means to faithfully represent real facets of the world. To use the language of semiology, we could say that signifiers have a clear referent, an object which they refer to which is located in reality. In Baudrillard's second phase, instead of faithfully representing the real world, the predominant role for signs and images is to obscure or distort that reality. This phase equates with Marxist-derived notions of media as a form of ideology which blinds the population to the true nature of the circumstances in which they live (see Chapter 6). Crucially, although it is hidden by inaccurate representations, reality is still present beneath the images at this stage.

The transition to phase three is the crucial one in Baudrillard's schema. Here, the proliferation of images has proceeded to such an extent that there is no longer any unmediated reality underneath them all. Rather than either representing or misrepresenting reality, the image 'plays at being an appearance' (1995a: 6), misleading us into thinking that it is a representation of something real. Even in the act of obliterating reality through their very proliferation, then, images still present themselves to us as signifiers of the real. In so doing, they hide from us the fact that nothing is real anymore. For Baudrillard, television was particularly effective at masking the absence of reality. Its fast-moving blend of sound sequences and moving images invite us to experience it as a set of representations of an external world when, in fact, the world amounts to no more or less than a plethora of television images. Theme parks such as *Disney World* provide another example of this masking of unreality. *Disney World*, Baudrillard argues, presents itself to us as a miniature, fantasy representation of something real: America. Some might understand it, then, as a first phase symbol of reality, while others may suggest it is a second phase ideological distortion which blinds people to the failures and exploitations of US capitalism. For Baudrillard, however, the function of Disneyland is not to either represent or misrepresent the reality of America, but rather to conceal the absence of any such reality. Disneyland 'plays at being an appearance', then, when in fact there is no reality to represent because America consists of little more than the same images and signs from which the theme park is constructed. There are also more contemporary applications of Baudrillard's notion. Might we conceive, for example, of the way images and interactions on social media can appear to us as representations of our 'real' identity and social life when, it may be more accurate to regard our 'real' selves and friendships as increasingly defined through and by media?

This brings us onto a fourth and final phase which in Baudrillard's view was being quickly approached, in which images no longer even play at being representations and refer only to one another. They are not signs or symbols at all, only empty *simulacra* – images without referent, style without substance, surface without depth. In this world it is impossible to talk about the relationship between media and reality, about whether media are sufficiently real, truthful or accurate, or about whether they might be biased. Media do not reflect or shape society – they *are* society. This is Baudrillard's world of the *hyperreal*, in which there is no distinction between truth and falsehood, only a myriad of mediated stories, discourses, interactions, ideas and images. How can I discern whether an image, statement, interaction or story is 'true' if there is no longer any media-free reality to assess it against? There are all manner of examples we might use to illustrate the sort of depthless, self-referential images described by Baudrillard, covering a wide range of genres, both 'factual' and 'fictional'. One of the most obvious and illustrative case studies is provided by the phenomenon of celebrity culture.

CELEBRITY CULTURE AS HYPERREAL

In many respects celebrities are the ultimate media creation and as such embody the notion of simulacra. Since the early cultivation of familiar 'stars' as a mark of familiarity with which to market films and popular music many years ago, a huge industry has emerged whose primary role is the careful construction and publicising of the personality, brand and image of celebrities (Turner 2004). This industry intersects with a range of different media who utilise, reference and contribute to the manufacture of celebrities. Celebrities not only appear, 'in character' in film and television but also 'as themselves' in chat shows, magazines, adverts, news and on social media. More visibly than any other area, the celebrity industry revolves around media referring to other media, forming an interchangeable array of empty simulations which rarely refer to any reality outside themselves.

How else could we interpret the domination of news headlines or documentaries, for example, by the activities of Jennifer Lawrence, Kanye West, Benedict Cumberbatch or Kim Kardashian? All are, if we follow Baudrillard's way of thinking, media simulacra. The 'real' personalities emphasised so much in celebrity coverage are every bit as constructed as the 'fictional' roles some of them play in film or television, and yet the soap opera inhabited by such personalities increasingly dominates even those 'factual' genres of media that claim the closest relationship with reality. At times, celebrities even have been at the centre of enormous media events characterised by the outpouring of public emotion, most notably in the case of the deaths of Princess Diana, Michael Jackson or, more recently, David Bowie. For Baudrillard, the sight of such huge popular grieving in response to the death of someone who for everyone except their friends and relatives is little more than a set of media representations, surely would have represented a near-perfect example of hyperreality.

The role of celebrity in contemporary societies also can be used to illustrate Baudrillard's third phase, in which the image 'plays at being appearance', masking the absence of reality. The façade of a distinction between the 'real personalities' of film stars and the 'fictional' characters they play provides one example. We could also note that the branding of 'reality television' programmes such as *The Only Way is Essex* implies that the personalities depicted therein are somehow more authentic than other celebrities when arguably this association with 'reality' is merely part of the artificial branding of individuals whose lives are largely defined by a plethora of media discourse. Indeed the notion of 'reality television' itself is a media inversion, in the sense that it presents itself to us as media representation of the real when what it more plausibly demonstrates is the colonisation of real life by media. Yet there is still another more fundamental layer of phase three concealment in the case of the celebrity industry. In presenting itself to us as a separate world of media spectacle and fantasy, the celebrity industry may serve to obscure the extent to which the 'real' society which we inhabit every day is saturated by empty media symbols and images. The penetration of celebrity discourse itself within everyday lives, aspirations, understandings and identities represents just one example of such saturation.

IDENTITY: FRAGMENTATION AND FLUIDITY

Among the many implications of media saturation and hyperreality, for Baudrillard, is that the identities of individuals have become increasingly attached to the floating signifiers which circulate around us. That is, we define and differentiate ourselves from others on the basis not of the place we live, or the nature of the work we do, but through the symbolic value associated with things like clothes, cosmetics, music, household decor, cars and other consumables.

This focus on identities centred on media images and consumer goods has also been of importance for other theorists. Some are postmodernists while others avoid this particular label, but what unites them is a suggestion that, as a result of their symbolic relationship to the world of media and consumption, identities have become increasingly fragmented and unstable.

RECYCLING AND PASTICHE

Outlining what he describes as the 'postmodern condition', Jameson (1991) suggests that the increasingly fast proliferation and turnover of consumer goods makes it harder and harder to associate any of them with fixed meanings. From this point of view, use value had, even by the 1990s, been almost entirely replaced by symbolic value and symbolic value itself had become increasingly malleable and hard to pin down. One of the impacts of pressure to develop 'novel-seeming' consumables, for Jameson, is a constant reformulation and recirculation of styles and fashions from the past. It isn't hard to think of examples of this in the worlds of music and fashion, from individual items such as flares, tight jeans or leggings, to broader categories such as rock 'n' roll, glam, goth or new romantic. Crucially, the connection of such styles with their original contexts and symbolic meanings is argued to loosen more with each reuse.

Sometimes reuses might form a conscious revival, whereby selective caricatures of the style's original associations are embraced wholeheartedly or subjected to knowing kitsch or *parody*. Here there remains a clear reference to an original symbolic meaning, even if it is a loose or simplified one. For Jameson, however, parody had become less significant as a mode of reuse than another approach: *pastiche*. Here, instead of referring back to an original set of meanings, objects or styles are extracted from previous associations in the process of being fused together with one another to create new products in new contexts. Hebdige, for example, argues that music had by the 1980s become dominated by the 'raiding and pasting together of rhythms, images and sounds from multiple sources' (1988: 212). A particular focus for claims such as this, both in the past and more recently, has been the emphasis upon sampling, reusing and arranging sequences from a variety of sources, particularly in dance music genres and cultures (Connor 1997; Katz 2010). The broader implication according to some theorists, meanwhile, is that the more the ongoing process of recycling and pastiche continues, the more devoid of fixed or substantive meanings the newly manufactured hybrids can become. For Chambers, writing in the 1980s, such hybrids may no longer have had clear or fundamental meanings and instead were beginning to represent only 'their own transitory practice' (Chambers 1985: 199).

The implication, then, is that while previously the symbolic meanings of objects were deep and restricted, in recent decades we have been inhabiting something of a free-for-all where an endless stream of hybrid consumables can be selected and combined at will and associated with whatever meanings performers, consumers or others temporarily apply to them in the present. And, crucially, as our identities become more and more attached to floating, transitory, polysemic simulacra, it is argued that we ourselves may become increasingly hybrid and fluid, our understanding of self consisting of an ever-changing multiplicity of temporary styles and objects. We can adopt selected elements of punk style, it is argued, without attending a punk gig and listen to versions of hip hop with little knowledge of its origins. For Polhemous, in the postmodern 'supermarket of style' we might even come to regard authenticity and meaning as unimportant, revelling instead in the artificiality of it all: 'While fashion celebrated change and subcultural style celebrated group identity, the inhabitants of Styleworld celebrate the truth of falsehood, the authenticity of simulation, the meaningfulness of gibberish' (1997: 149–50).

Not everyone accepts that contemporary consumer goods and media images are quite this flexible with respect to their meaning or that consumers are no longer interested in meaning and authenticity. Nevertheless, the emphasis placed by postmodernists on the fragmentation and fluidity brought about by media and consumption coheres somewhat with more recent theories that emphasise the individualisation and liquidity that characterise modern life and identities. Without going as far as Baudrillard and Jameson with respect to the issue of meaninglessness, theorists such as Bauman (2000; 2007) and Beck and Beck-Gernsheim (2001) emphasise that identities are increasingly tied up, amongst other things, with fluid facets of life such as consumer and media habits and that, because of the vast choice of objects and symbolic meanings on offer to individuals, the extent of their attachment to any one coherent affiliation is liable to be both partial and temporary. Meaning here remains of greater importance than in some postmodern accounts, but identities nevertheless become more fluid, constantly in a state of reflexive construction.

THE INTERNET AS VIRTUAL PLAYGROUND

SIMULATED IDENTITY?

Not surprisingly, for some of its earliest theorists, the internet represented a particularly concentrated manifestation of the hyperreal culture of simulacra and meaninglessness described by Baudrillard among others. Describing the internet as 'a culture of simulation', Sherry Turkle suggested that in their on-screen lives, people consisted of no more than a set of arbitrary words and images – symbols, in other words, interacting with other symbols (1995: 10). And, for Turkle, the lack of physical presence rendered the extent of any connection between these virtual symbols and a substantive or 'real' person ambiguous. Given that limitations of physical presence and distance are removed, users were rendered free to develop their virtual identities in whatever way they desired. The internet allowed us to play at the construction of personalities, according to this view, adapting and adjusting our virtual gender, sexuality, ethnicity, nationality and all manner of other characteristics. Online freedom from physical constraints was argued to enable identities to become particularly malleable and fluid. Not only could the images and text that represent us on-screen change as often as we like, but we could also sustain multiple virtual identities at any one moment in time. Referring to the connection between Microsoft's operating system and the internet, Turkle claimed that 'the life practice of Windows is that of a decentred self that exists in many worlds and plays many roles at the same time' (1995: 14).

Rather than being a unified individual consisting of a stable inner core and physically located body, then, online selves are understood in this formulation as incoherent, multiply located and always shifting. And as greater and greater time, energy and emotions are exhausted on parallel virtual personas, it becomes increasingly unclear which identity is 'real' and which artificial. There may even be ambiguities as to whether the life of the person sitting at the screen is any more authentic than the actions and affiliations of their virtual on-screen personalities. Cyborg identities on the internet, then, were argued to be blurring the boundary between human and technology, authentic and artificial, real and representation. 'Are we living life on the screen or in the screen?' Turkle asks (1995: 21), going on to suggest that 'people are increasingly comfortable with substituting representations of reality for the real' (Ibid.: 23).

Although Turkle's early work was focused upon multi-user dungeons (MUDs) in the early days of the internet, her point can be illustrated in relation to more recent virtual environments such as *Second Life*. Here, users develop 'fictional' characters that explore, work, learn, play, buy, sell and develop relationships with other characters in an entire world of virtual spaces and places (Boellstorff 2008; Geser 2007a, 2007b; Johnson 2010). The question of interest to many sociologists is that, as they put more time and energy into these 'virtual' characters and their 'fictional' relationships, at what point, if any, do the latter become as 'real' as their identity off the screen? In 2008 a British couple – Amy Taylor and David Pollard – were reported to have got divorced in the 'real' world as a result of a virtual 'affair' between the husband's character on *Second Life* and the character of another user. Phylis Johnson (2010: xiii)), meanwhile, points out that establishing and using a particular place in *Second Life* as 'home' is of particular importance to many users: 'participants admit a sense of comfort by having a place to entertain company or return to before they sign off for the night'. The establishment of a virtual presence on the platform by an increasing number of 'real' businesses and other organisations adds further weight to suggestions the boundary between the real and the virtual has become ambiguous and complex.

Another theorist who focuses on the role of the early internet in a developing postmodern culture of simulation is Poster (1995; 2001). Poster regards the internet as part of a final stage in the decline of enlightenment notions of a coherent, autonomous individual subject who is able to observe, understand and act upon an external reality. In his first stage – the age of print media – an informed, critical, rational subject has been moulded by the contextual depth and individualistic orientation of books and newspapers, as well as their clear reference to an external world in relation to which the subject could act. In stage two – the age of broadcast media – the rational subject is still addressed and constituted as such by media producers but its ability to act in relation to an external world begins to be undermined by a proliferation of depthless television images that, consistent with Baudrillard's thinking, increasingly refer only to one another. In the final stage, the age of the internet, the notion of an observable external world implodes altogether, while the subject itself becomes fragmented. The internet precipitates a massive expansion in the range and volume of media content, while its interactivity diversifies the range of sources for such content. The division between consumers and producers is blurred and the greater the proliferation of content, the more self-referential such content becomes. Consistent with Turkle's account, distinctions between reality and representations are undermined online while depthless images or simulacra are ubiquitous. In other words, on the internet, everything is an image on a screen referring to another image on a screen and another and so on. The range of media simulacra on offer, meanwhile, fragment the collective audience so important to the broadcast age and prompt the breaking up of the individual subject, which at this point exists only as a set of different virtual roles being played out in a range of online spaces. There is no external 'real' world for the subject to observe or understand, only a limitless virtual world within which it is subsumed: 'the self is no longer a subject since it no longer subtends the world as if from outside but operates within a machine apparatus as a point on a circuit' (Poster 2001: 16).

INTERNET AS EXTENSION OF EVERYDAY LIFE

Though they make a number of salient observations, postmodernist approaches to the internet such as those described by Turkle and Poster tend to exaggerate the social impacts on which they focus. Such accounts present the technologies of the internet as primary instigators of social change, with insufficient weight afforded to the role of individuals, organisations and broader social contexts in their development and use. They also turn selective readings of the possibilities of the internet into confident and generalised predictions. It is assumed by Turkle, for example, that because internet technology creates the potential for people, under certain circumstances, to experiment with or expand their identities in wholly virtual environments, we can expect that identities across society will become fluid and fragmented and that online identities will be essentially separate from offline ones. But why should we assume that most people will be prompted to develop such parallel identities, especially when the internet offers equally strong possibilities to consolidate one's existing position in the world?

A further problem is that Turkle's emphasis on the distinctiveness of the virtual sphere as perfect embodiment of postmodern theory is confusing because it implicitly suggests that offline society fails to live up to such postmodern proclamations. One suspects that Baudrillard would have regarded Turkle's singling out of the internet as a move that serves to obscure the media saturation and hyperreality which he believed to characterise *all* social life. Interestingly, Turkle's more recent work on digital and media cultures (2013) comes closer to this sort of a view, in some respects at least. Here, her previous enthusiastic emphasis on the potential development of multiple and parallel virtual selves is replaced with a more pessimistic discussion of the total saturation of everyday life by virtual networks and digital devices, to the extent that substantive, meaningful face-to-face relationships are sacrificed (Turkle 2013).

Leaving aside the level of 'reality' or 'unreality' in the world as a whole, the presentation of the internet as parallel sphere tends now to be regarded as mistaken. Such an interpretation may have fitted with the experience of early 1990s MUDs (multi-user dungeons) and may retain usefulness in relation to contemporary environments such as *Second Life* and *World of Warcraft* in which participants develop identities, personalities and friendships that operate separately from those they live out elsewhere. For most contemporary users, however, the internet does not comprise an alternative world, but a set of communications tools that integrate increasingly seamlessly with their existing identities. For all the excitement about it, most of us use the internet to do mundane, everyday things connected with all sorts of aspects of our off-line lives: shopping, searching for jobs, researching essays, engaging with the news, checking railway timetables and, of course, sharing media content and conversing with people we know (boyd 2014; Wellman and Haythornthwaite 2002). Rather than offering a distinct 'virtual' world, then, we might better think of the internet as forming part of the broader saturation of everyday life by mediated communication.

That the internet is thoroughly embedded within everyday life, however, does not mean that we should dismiss the suggestions of Turkle, Poster and others out of hand. Poster's work, for example, usefully highlights the role of the internet as a catalyst for the increasingly disorganised proliferation of images and messages that are saturating culture and society, whether or not we accept his conclusions about the death of the subject and loss of the real. Neither should we abandon the suggestion that internet use might facilitate looser, more complex or changeable identities. Connecting the internet with the broader theoretical approaches of the likes of Bauman (2001; 2007), Wellman and Haythornthwaite explicitly suggest the internet encourages what they term 'networked individualisation', through enabling each of us to act as a social switchboard, at the centre of our own shifting set of personal networks (2002: 32). Apparently anticipating the subsequent explosion of social media, the argument here isn't that the subject is dead or that parallel selves coexist. It is that the increasing ubiquity of the internet and digital life may be contributing to a broader shift towards ephemeral individualised networks and identities.

CASE STUDY: SOCIAL MEDIA

The enormous popularity of social media such as *Facebook*, *Twitter*, *Instagram* and *Tumblr* provides a useful case study with which to explore the connections between internet use and people's everyday worlds and identities. Unlike older discussion forums and chat rooms, whose early prominence reflected their popularity among high-intensity early internet adopters, social media are now used by millions of ordinary people as a regular part of their everyday lives. According to the Pew Research Centre, in January 2014 some 73% of online US adults used *Facebook*, with 26% using *Instagram*, 28% using *Pinterest* and 23% *Twitter*. Meanwhile use of multiple social media platforms is on the rise, with 52% of online adults in the survey reporting they use two or more (Duggan et al. 2014). Use of social media, then, has become an ordinary part of many people's everyday lives.

Research on the subject confirms that such media tend to be seamlessly integrated within the broader lives and identities of individuals. Rather than meeting and interacting with large numbers of strangers, most of us primarily converse with people we already know (boyd 2014). And studies suggest that increasing numbers of users utilise privacy features such as 'friends-only' controls to establish boundaries around their online spaces, enabling only a hand-picked personal network dominated by people they know to engage with what they say or share (Hodkinson 2015). Friends also use other tactics to restrict their communication to those they know best, from user-names that are only shared with certain people, to informally coded ways of speaking (Lincoln and Robards 2014; Marwick and boyd 2014) (also see Chapter 11).

While content is varied, many people's communication on such platforms is dominated by statements or images related to mundane aspects of everyday life off the screen, whether in the form of reflections on the weekend, relationship dilemmas, comments about work or pictures of children. Sharing and conversing about media of various kinds forms a further key feature of social media use, of course, but even here, the kinds of material highlighted tend to cohere rather than contrast with our broader interests, opinions and concerns. Individuals may, of course, exaggerate certain features, events or achievements and play down others – and their overall presentation of self may differ somewhat between different online platforms they use as well as between on and offline spaces. Such variation of self-performance, according to context and audiences, however, is far from unusual and encapsulated by classic sociological theories relating to performance and everyday interactive behaviour in physical spaces (Goffman 1967).

While a certain amount of variation between spaces – and even trying on and experimenting with different facets of identity – is inevitable, the construction of identity on social media tends more often to centre on expressing, consolidating and making sense of one's existing place in the world. As with decorating the walls of the teenage bedroom, social media can enable young people to construct and perform a coherent and unified identity out of the range of contexts, interests and relationships that make up their lives (Hodkinson and Lincoln 2008; Lincoln and Robards 2014). Far from accelerating the postmodern decline of the self, then, their use is often a means of 'writing oneself into being' (boyd 2008) or making reflective sense of one's biography and identity (Robards 2014). And, consistent perhaps with the notion of networked individualism, social networking sites enable each user to act as a social switchboard, conversing from their own personal online space, or spaces with a variety of individuals and groups connected to different aspects of their past or present. Such sites can, it might be argued, comprise home territories that bring together the various aspects of people's lives and enable them to make sense of their identities (Hodkinson 2015).

In spite of their intimate connection with everyday life, the centring of social networking sites on the floating individual may still enable them to facilitate a degree of identity fluidity, as discussed in Chapter 11. In contrast to community forums, social media users are typically encouraged to illustrate their uniqueness as an individual through the display of an ever-developing collage of different interests, affiliations and everyday reflections. The unification of one's overall identity remains of central importance in this construction, but rather than being rooted in anything in particular, this identity may consist of multiple, shifting locations and focal points. Through making it easier for people to manage and develop such shifting identities, social networking sites could be said to contribute in some way towards identity fluidity, then, even if such sites also offer some possibilities for the furtherance of group attachments.

The widespread use of social networking sites also could be interpreted as a further example of the saturation of the social world with superficial images, messages and interactions. Whether they are focused on mundane activities, feelings and opinions or the sharing of countless images, clips and articles, the users of such sites consume and contribute to a never-ending barrage of mediated material. Often devoid of detail and context, the stream of updates on most users' news feed is so extensive that each message can only hope to retain our attention momentarily before being replaced by a torrent of new ones. Every now and again, sustained collective attention is devoted to something in particular but invariably even these instances quickly are replaced by something new. Everyday lives, then, are being populated with a multiplicity of ever-changing, superficial, momentary snippets of information, it might be argued. And if we connect this with the vast range of other images we encounter throughout our daily existence away from social media, then such platforms could be regarded as an extension of the information overload and hyperreality discussed by Baudrillard, Poster and others. Amongst all of the mediated chatter and clutter, how are we to identify, focus on and develop any understanding of messages of consequence?

As we have noted previously, in Sherry Turkle's recent work (2013), the problem relates particularly to the consequences of all this for the substance of the relationships we have with those closest to us. Through their combination, social media and mobile digital devices enable us to be in constant connection to personalised media networks to the extent that in physical spaces we increasingly find ourselves 'alone together' (ibid.). Whether at the dinner table, in cafes and bars or at work, we occupy the same space as those close to us while our attention is focused on the myriad ephemeral images and interactions in the mediated worlds we access through devices that accompany us everywhere. The essential superficiality of much that takes place in these digital worlds, Turkle suggests, cannot adequately replace the substantive, meaningful social relationships that are being sacrificed for them.

CONCLUSION: SATURATED BUT REAL?

The primary contribution of postmodern theories in relation to the concerns of this particular book may be the observation that, rather than being a separate, external mirror or shaper of social and cultural life, media lie right at the heart of society, saturating our understandings, values, lifestyles and identities. It is truly hard to envisage an activity, an event, a set of values or a group of people within the developed world that could be said to lie substantially outside of the world of image and communication. Meanwhile, emphasis on the sheer number of channels and messages surrounding us, and the increasingly superficial and momentary character of these has drawn crucial attention to the danger of assuming, when it comes to 'information', that more is always better. Similarly, postmodern theorists have provided insights into the speed-up and saturation of culture by a disorganised proliferation of commercial objects and images – and the drift towards layer upon layer of symbolic value, to the extent that we purchase images and messages which have little relation to anything outside of themselves. As a consequence, it also makes sense to conclude that a range of boundaries have become a little less clear than they used to be, not least distinctions between 'factual' and 'fictional' media, different cultural genres and styles, public and private, different sorts of identity and, finally, authenticity and artifice.

The problem is that postmodernists such as Baudrillard and Jameson tended to over-generalise the implications of what they observed into sweeping claims about wholesale loss of meaning, reality and subjectivity. For example, the valid observation of an intensification of the operation of symbolic value in society becomes exaggerated, as Strinati (2004) points out, into an implication that use value has all but disappeared. If we consider a range of examples of everyday consumables – from motor-cars to eye glasses to vacuum cleaners to electronic tablets – it becomes apparent that things are rather less clear-cut. To be sure, all of these items involve a substantial symbolic role as images about our identities. Yet to suggest that substantive forms of use and practical features are of no importance seems an unnecessary exaggeration.

Likewise, it is one thing to suggest that developed societies are increasingly saturated by media images – or even to recognise an increasing tendency for media representations to refer to one another – but another to claim that reality itself has entirely disappeared, that identities, lifestyles and understandings are meaningless and that self and subject are obliterated. The notion that reality and truth are entirely indistinguishable from artifice and the relativist implication therein that all representations and images should be regarded as equally valid is of particular importance here. Such a claim has great significance to the way we should understand and assess media, not least those which claim to be informational, such as news, documentaries, books, 'factual' websites and even academic papers and research reports.

Self-evidently, we *are* largely reliant upon layers of media representations and all such representations clearly *are* manufactured, making it difficult to gauge accuracy or reliability. But this does not mean that the representations on which we rely have no relationship whatsoever to real events, or that we have no possibility of judging between comparatively more or less faithful and honest accounts. Castigating Baudrillard for his infamous claim that the 1991 Gulf War consisted of nothing more than a media spectacle, Webster (2002: 256) argues that 'it is demonstrably the case that all news worthy of the term retains a representational character'. In other words, for Webster, the words and images in 'factual' media often do relate to very real events and situations and it is imperative that we do all we can to understand and assess the nature of this relationship.

Ultimately, as well as being an exaggeration, the argument that there is no reality or truth and only a myriad of equally valid symbols and representations is a contradictory and self-defeating one. The statement that there is no truth is, itself, a truth claim – about as big a truth claim as one could make in fact. If there is no possibility of discerning truth from fiction, then on what basis can Baudrillard ask us to accept his particular claims about that world over those of other theorists? Like many other postmodernist theorists, he denies the essential validity of all truth claims except for his own. Indeed, he is so confident in the latter that he is able to identify 'false' understandings of the world, such as those relating to Disneyworld, which mask the truth, as he asks us to see it (Larrain 1994).

The biggest problem with the more exaggerated postmodernist claims we have addressed in this chapter, however, is that even in those cases where they are critical of the media-saturated, meaningless situation we face, they risk undermining attempts to learn about and improve the situation. As a consequence, they all but exempt media from criticism or demands for improvement. After all, if one cannot judge between truth and fiction, honesty and dishonesty, quality and superficiality or valuable and harmful, then there seems little point in further analysis – we might as well all just make what we can of our fragmented, incoherent media-driven identities and enjoy (or not) participating in the show. The reader will not be surprised to hear, however, that this is not the conclusion of this chapter or this book. On the contrary, the increasing saturation of the social and cultural world by media renders it more important than ever to understand as definitively as possible how processes of communication work in all their forms and guises. It is equally important that such understandings be used to hold powerful media organisations to account and ensure that the operation of communications within society is such that its potential to enhance lives, identities and democracies is realised more than its potential to undermine them.

QUESTIONS/EXERCISES

1   Is it accurate to suggest contemporary culture and society are saturated by media and consumerism? Try to identify elements of private or public life which are not somehow defined or dominated by media.

2   a) Why does Baudrillard connect the media saturation of society with a loss of meaning and a gradual erosion of the relationship between media images and reality?

    b) What are the implications of Baudrillard's argument for the way we might assess the value of news media?

3   In what ways does the example of celebrity culture illustrate Baudrillard's concept of hyperreality? Try to identify some other examples.

4   a) To what extent does participation in virtual environments like *Second Life* suggest a postmodern fragmentation of the self and a blurring of boundaries between fiction and reality?

    b) How typical is the behaviour of users in such environments compared to that of internet users as a whole?

5   Does the use of social networking sites such as *Facebook*, *Instagram* and *Twitter* offer an illustration of postmodern theories of media or does it draw attention to the limitations of such theories?

SUGGESTED FURTHER READING

Baudrillard, J. (1995a) *Simulacra and Simulation*. University of Michigan Press. – Frequently cited discussion of the saturation of culture and society by simulacra and the loss of meaning.

boyd, d. (2014) *It's Complicated: The Social Lives of Networked Teens*. New Haven: Yale University Press – Influential research-driven account of the significance of social media for young people, covering a range of issues related to the playing out of identity in spaces where privacy can be compromised.

Featherstone, M. (2007) *Consumer Culture and Postmodernism – Second Edition*. London: Sage – Influential analysis of the expansion of consumerism through the lens of postmodern theory.

Johnson, P. (2010) *Second Life, Media and the Other Society*. New York: Peter Lang – Detailed analysis of the parameters, norms and significance of *Second Life*, connecting closely to questions about real/virtual and complexities of identity.

Turkle, S. (1995) *Life on the Screen: Identity in the Age of the Internet*. London: Phoenix – Early study of internet culture, drawing on postmodern theories in relation to the blurring of boundaries and multiple selves.

GLOSSARY

Agency
The ability of individuals to be self-determining. Often discussed in relation to the ways in which agency is constrained by social *structures*.

Agenda setting
The notion that, through their decisions about which issues and events on which to focus, news and other 'informational' media can shape the priorities of the public.

Alienation
Used by Marx to refer to the estrangement of workers from the objects which their labour produces within capitalist societies. For Marx, alienation from the object of one's labour effectively amounted to alienation from oneself.

Assimilation
The process whereby members of an ethnic minority or other marginal group are encouraged or required to adopt the way of life, cultural values and identity of the majority.

Asynchronous communication
Communication which does not take place in real time. Newspapers are asynchronous, as are books, letters and emails.

Audience ethnography
An approach to media research geared towards the development of a rich understanding of the role of media in the lives of users, usually through in-depth observation and/or interviews.

Bechdel test
A test first envisaged as part of an Alison Bechdel comic, designed to assess marginalisation of women within media content. The test asks whether, as part of a given piece of content (e.g. a film or a TV series), two or more women speak to one another about something other than a man.

Bias
Partiality or lack of objectivity in a person, an organisation, a statement, or a news report, etc.

Bourgeoisie
Used by Marx to refer to the capitalist ruling class, who own and control the means of production.

Branded content
Content produced by advertisers that is designed to be appealing and entertaining to audiences in its own right. Often the intention is to encourage audiences to voluntarily view, recommend and share the content on the basis of its inherent appeal.

Bricolage
Used in subcultural theory to refer to the forming of new styles by bringing together a disparate set of previously unconnected objects, each of which acquires subversive meanings in its new context.

Burden of representation
The constraining expectation on ethnic minority artists, directors, actors, presenters and other public figures that they or their work will be taken to represent their entire ethnic group. Also applicable to members of sexual or other minority groups.

Censorship
A form of regulation concerned with restricting or banning particular kinds of content, on the basis that they are offensive or socially harmful.

Centrifugal
Used in the study of media and society to refer to the process whereby a fragmented, plural media system contributes to the movement of different groups and individuals away from a common centre.

Centripetal
Used in the study of media and society to refer to the process whereby common media usage has the effect of drawing disparate individuals and groups together.

Citizen journalism
The active participation of ordinary members of the public in amateur journalistic practices, from taking and distributing newsworthy photographs, to conducting interviews, to posting reports or comment pieces on the internet.

Commodity fetishism
The separation of commercial objects from the social conditions in which they were produced. A social relationship becomes reified into a relationship between objects and money.

Community
A group of people who share a set of values, interests and experiences and feel a sense of affiliation and commitment to one another. Sometimes restricted to the most tightly-knit or isolated local communities, while other uses encapsulate a variety of different sorts of group.

Connotation
Used by Barthes to refer to the 'second order', associative or inferred meaning of a signifier or set of signifiers. Also see *denotation*.

Consumer culture
A culture saturated by the buying and selling of material goods, to the extent that consumerism dominates cultural life and consumption habits become markers of identity, status and happiness.

Content
The messages, discourse or cultural forms communicated via media technologies.

Content analysis
A systematic, quantitative approach to the study of content, focused upon the frequency with which designated types of content occur across statistically generalisable samples of texts.

Convergence
The process whereby the boundaries between previously distinct types of communication begin to blur.

Cool media
Used by McLuhan to refer to low intensity, high participation media forms such as, in his view, television.

Cultivation theory
George Gerbner's contention that, over a period of time, the versions of the world presented by television begin to dominate the symbolic realities of audiences, cultivating particular attitudes, opinions and understandings.

Cultural capital
Used by Pierre Bourdieu to refer to forms of cultural knowledge, taste and experience which confer status and socio-economic advantages on those who have them. Transmitted via one's milieu or habitus, cultural capital is deemed to contribute to the maintenance of class boundaries.

Cultural imperialism theory
A critical interpretation of processes of globalisation which emphasises the cultural domination of small countries by multinational companies distributing Western media and cultural products.

Cultural/Culturalist perspective
Connected with the broader discipline of cultural studies, cultural or culturalist is sometimes used to refer to an approach to the study of media which is deemed to focus particularly on questions of discourse and meaning, often through the detailed study of media texts or their interpretation by audiences. Often contrasted with *political economy*.

Culture
Complex term whose use here infers the ways of life associated with a particular society or group and/or the forms and practices of creative and artistic expression associated with a particular society or group.

Culture industry
Used by Adorno and Horkheimer to refer to the commercial mass production and distribution of standardised cultural products.

Denotation
Used by Barthes to refer to the 'first order' or most immediate and explicit meaning of a signifier or set of signifiers. Also see *connotation*.

Deregulation
The process whereby government-driven regulation of an industry is relaxed, enabling a greater role for market forces.

Diaspora
A group of people who share a common point of origin and identity and who have become dispersed around the globe as a result of patterns of migration.

Diaspora film
A film which depicts the life and experiences of *diaspora* populations.

Digitalisation
The process whereby analogue forms of media are replaced by digital communications.

Discourse Analysis
An approach to the study of content which focuses on the construction of meaning through verbal or written forms of language use. Critical discourse analysis concentrates on the role of discourse in the reinforcement of dominant ways of seeing the world.

DIY media
Amateur and usually small-scale forms of media. Also sometimes referred to as micro-media.

Economic determinism
The belief that economic or material relations drive the course of history and determine the non-material facets of society, including cultural norms, ideas, beliefs and forms of expression. Closely related to the notion of material determinism or materialism.

Effects research
An empirical approach to the study of audiences which focuses upon measuring the extent to which, and ways in which, media consumption influences attitudes or behaviour.

Ephemeral
Temporary, or subject to constant change.

False consciousness
The adoption by members of the proletariat (or other subordinate groups) of distorted sets of ideas and beliefs which reinforce the system which oppresses them.

False needs
Used by Marcuse to describe distorted sets of priorities whose internalisation by individuals – to the point that they are experienced and strived for as necessities – serves to reinforce oppression and subservience. Often used as a critique of consumerism.

Fan
An intensive, committed follower of a particular cultural form or set of cultural forms whose enthusiasm may form a significant part of their identity and/or involve participation in a fan community.

Fanzine
A small-scale amateur pamphlet or magazine associated with a particular topic or interest community.

Fluidity
Social or cultural instability, changeability or ephemerality.

Fraternity
Refers to a 'brotherhood' and sometimes is used by public sphere theorists to refer to the role of shared identity as part of the broader citizenship.

Fordism
An approach to the organisation of capitalist enterprise characterised, amongst other things, by the large-scale assembly-line production of standardised, universally targeted goods and the mass marketing of such goods to broad groups of consumers.

Fragmentation
Social fragmentation implies a breaking up of once cohesive societies into a plurality of comparatively disconnected individuals and groupings.

Functionalism
A perspective which seeks to explain different elements of the social world by reference to the role they play in contributing to the smooth functioning of society as a whole.

Gate-keeping

The process by which media organisations select which elements of the social world to include in their content. Often used to conceptualise news filtering processes.

Gemeinschaft

German term for community, used by Tönnies to refer specifically to the most intimate, affective and all-encompassing forms of collective unity and mutual dependence.

Genre analysis

An approach to the study of content which examines the relationship between individual texts and broader genres – or categories – which each have distinct sets of conventions and audience expectations.

Gesellschaft

German term for society, used by Tönnies to refer to a social entity which, in contrast to *gemeinschaft*, consists of a plurality of complex, pragmatic and self-interested relationships within a broad, disparate group of people.

Globalisation

The process, in which media form a key component, whereby different parts of the world become intensively interconnected, in terms of trade, finance, politics, social life and culture.

Global village

Term coined by McLuhan to refer to the effective shrinking of the globe as a result of increased international communication brought about by media technologies.

Hegemony

Hegemony, or sometimes cultural hegemony, is associated with the work of Antonio Gramsci and refers to domination over the realm of culture and ideas by the ruling class. Rather than being pre-determined by economic relations, cultural hegemony is constantly subject to ideological challenge and struggle.

Horizontal integration

The expansion of media corporations across different media sectors (e.g. television, newspapers, books, gaming, music, etc.) via take-overs and mergers. Also see *vertical integration*.

Hot media

Used by McLuhan to refer to high intensity, low participation media forms. Including most forms of print media, hot media were deemed isolating and undemocratic.

Hyperreality

Used by Baudrillard to refer to a situation in which society is so saturated by layer upon layer of simulacra that it becomes impossible to discern any sort of external reality or truth beneath all the empty images.

Icon
Semiological term: a signifier which bears a resemblance to its signified, for example through appearance or sound.

Ideological state apparatus
Used by Althusser to describe a set of institutions, including the family, the education system, religious organisations and media, which, although relatively autonomous, are determined by the economic base of society 'in the last instance' and function to reinforce dominant ideology.

Ideology
A set of ideas, beliefs and assumptions about the world. Often used (e.g. in Marxist theories) to refer specifically to dominant and/or misleading sets of ideas which reflect and reinforce prevailing power relations.

Imagined community
Used by Benedict Anderson to refer to the symbolic sense of shared identity experienced by those who share the same nationality, in spite of never meeting or knowing one another.

Index
Semiological term: a signifier which does not resemble but which is causally or sensorially connected with its signified and therefore not arbitrary.

Individualisation
The notion that individuals are increasingly detached from traditional sources of stability, security and direction and that, as a consequence, they float freely between a range of temporary and partial foci for identity.

Industry
Media industry refers to the body of organisations which dominate the development, operation and distribution of media.

Instrumental reason
Development and use of the human capacity for imagination, judgement, reasoning and rationality as a means to an end (for example, to increase productivity, efficiency or profit) rather than as an end in itself.

Interpersonal media
Media which enable interactive communication between small numbers of people.

Labelling theory
The argument that the negative labelling of 'outsider' groups or individuals by society (e.g. via media coverage) can amplify their sense of difference and cause them to identify more strongly with the values or individuals associated with the label.

Male gaze
The objectifying look of the heterosexual male voyeur to whom many representations of femininity are argued to be directed. Associated with Laura Mulvey's work on gender and cinema and widely adopted in other contexts.

Marxism
A perspective based on the ideas of Karl Marx, which focuses on the exploitative and alienative relations deemed to define capitalist societies and on the determination of non-economic spheres of society (e.g. culture, ideas) by economic relations. Marxist perspectives on media tend to focus on the way mass communications reflect and/or reinforce capitalist material relations.

Mass culture theory
Theories which lament the replacement of elite high culture and/or grassroots folk culture with a superficial and standardised mass culture attributable to mass media and consumer culture. Connected to notions of mass society, which emphasise the replacement of distinct participatory communities with an atomised mass.

Mass media
Usually used to refer to the one-directional distribution of media by powerful corporate institutions to large and demographically broad audiences.

Medium
The technological means through which content is communicated between an origin and a destination. e.g. telegraph, telephone, television, book, etc.

Medium theory
A theory which focuses on the ways in which communications technologies act as a force for social and cultural change.

Media
Plural of medium. Also sometimes used to refer to the collective make-up, activities or impact of large-scale media organisations.

Monopoly
A situation in which all or most of the products and services for a particular market are supplied by a single provider.

Moral conservativism
A political perspective focused upon protecting traditional moral values.

Moral panic
An intense societal reaction – usually fuelled by sensationalist media coverage – against a perceived threat to prevailing social values or ways of life. Those associated with the threat are invariably stigmatised, according to Stan Cohen, as 'folk devils'.

Myth
Used by Barthes to refer to broader sets of dominant or 'common-sense' understandings which are tapped into and reinforced by the connotations of individual texts.

Narcissism
The gaining of pleasure through gazing at and/or admiring one's own image. Associated with Lacan's 'mirror stage' of child development and adapted to discussions of the representation of gender in media.

Narrative analysis
An approach to the study of content which focuses on the role of structures and conventions of story-telling in media texts.

Narrowcasting
The distribution of media to clearly defined, specialist audiences.

Neo-liberalism
A political doctrine which revived some of the free market ideas of eighteenth and nineteenth century liberal economics, including the work of Adam Smith. Neo-liberal perspectives on media endorse the relaxation of state intervention, from controls on content to the funding of public service broadcasters.

Neo-Marxism
A perspective which adapts or amends the ideas of Karl Marx (see *Marxism*) in some way, as in the case of theorists such as Gramsci and Althusser, who diluted Marx's *economic determinism*.

Neo-tribe
Used by Michel Maffesoli to refer to loose-knit affinity groupings with porous boundaries and adopted by some youth cultural theorists as a replacement for the notion of subculture.

New ethnicities
Used by Stuart Hall to refer to the complex and fluid nature of ethnic identities. Particularly associated with research on multi-faceted ethnic identities of second and third generation ethnic minority youth.

News values
The set of priorities which form the basis of decisions made by news organisations about the selection, positioning and construction of stories.

Niche media
Forms of media which are targeted narrowly towards particular groups or types of consumers.

Oligopoly
A situation in which a particular market is overwhelmingly dominated by a small number of powerful companies.

Panopticon
A prison in which every cell is visible from a single watch tower. Often used as a metaphor to refer to the capacity of electronic media technologies such as the internet to subject individuals to surveillance throughout their everyday lives.

Paradigmatic analysis
An approach to semiological analysis concerned with comparing each element of a text with a paradigm of alternatives which might have been used in its place. Also see *syntagmatic analysis*.

Parody/pastiche
A distinction used by Frederick Jameson between ironic reuses of images which refer to the context of the original use (parody), and reuses which remove all reference to previous context by combining the image with a range of others (pastiche).

Patriarchy
Used here to refer to a social system centred upon male authority and female subordination.

Pluralism
A perspective or state of affairs whereby the coexistence of a range of voices and view-points is valued.

Political economy
A political economic perspective on media is one that focuses particularly on the workings of the media industry and the broader economic and political context in which it operates.

Polysemic
Semiological term referring to the capacity of a sign to have multiple meanings.

Population
The overall group of people or body of content which the *sample* in a research study is intended to represent.

Post-Fordism
A flexible approach to capitalist enterprise, characterised, amongst other things, by the precise targeting of niche markets and the capacity to rapidly develop and promote new and different kinds of product in response to market changes.

Preferred meaning
The meaning which the encoding of a media text is deemed to encourage.

Proletariat
Used by Marx to refer to the working class, by which he meant the non-wealth-owning majority, who sell their labour to make a living.

Pseudo-individualisation
Used by Adorno to refer to the guise of difference and originality with which standardised cultural products present themselves to us.

Public service broadcasting (PSB)
A form of broadcasting whose objective is to benefit society, an orientation usually achieved via government-driven funding and/or regulation.

Public sphere
A space for the collective exchange and development of ideas located between the realm of government and the domestic and commercial spheres of society. Often discussed in relation to the role of media in the facilitation of public debate and/or shared culture.

Reflection theory
An approach which suggests that media reflect or 'mirror' existing social values or relations.

Regulation
Controls imposed by government or government-appointed bodies on the activities of media organisations.

Reification
The transformation of what is human, subjective or social into an object or thing. For example, the dehumanisation of workers into cogs in the capitalist machine, or the theoretical decontextualisation of technologies from their human context by technological determinist theorists.

Relative autonomy
Used by Althusser to describe the partial independence of non-economic spheres of society – including the realm of culture and ideas – from the economic base.

Representation
Refers to the way media content symbolises or stands in for social or cultural phenomena. Often used to refer to the selective portrayal of events, people, groups, cultural trends, social relations, etc.

Retargeting
A term used in digital advertising to refer to the targeting of consumers with advertisements for products they recently have viewed online in order to turn their interest into a purchase.

Sample
A selection of people or content which is designed to represent the broader *population* in which a research study is interested.

Saturation

Media saturation refers to the domination of all or most facets of society, culture and everyday life by layer upon layer of mediated communication, information and imagery.

Scopophilia

The gaining of pleasure through subjecting others to a voyeuristic, objectifying gaze. Adapted from psychoanalytic understandings of childhood in Laura Mulvey's discussion of the significance of the *male gaze* in cinema.

Shaping theory

An approach which suggests that media have a direct influence on society.

Self-fulfilling prophecy

A prediction or representation whose own influence causes it to be fulfilled. For example, high profile media discussion about the likelihood of violence at a protest march may render violence more likely to occur by affecting the mood of participants.

Simulacra

Used by Baudrillard to refer to the meaningless images which, in his view, had saturated social and cultural life. Rather than referring to any sort of external reality or truth, simulacra refer only to one another.

Semiology

An approach to the study of media content which focuses on the generation of meaning through arrangements of signs.

Signified

Semiological term: the concept which is represented by a *signifier*.

Signifier

Semiological term: the means by which a concept, or *signified*, is represented.

Social democratic

A political perspective which embraces democracy and elements of market capitalism while endorsing substantial state intervention in the interests of equality, social justice and the public good.

Society

A network of institutions, relationships, interactions and culture within which individual lives take place.

Stereotype
A familiar and often-repeated characterisation of the members of a particular social group or category (e.g. ethnic, gender, age or sexual categories) whose prevalence has the effect of reducing, simplifying and generalising the features of the group as a whole.

Strong ties
Broad, substantive and sustained relationships which involve extensive individual familiarity and commitment and are sustained across numerous sites of interaction.

Structure/s
The set of established social institutions, groupings, hierarchies, norms and ways of living into which people are born. Often regarded as constrainers or shapers of individual lives and identities. Also see *agency*.

Subculture
Contested term associated with youth cultural theory which usually refers to a group of people characterised by a strong sense of identity and centred around a set of styles, values or tastes which differentiate them from the broader culture of which they are a part.

Symbol
Semiological term: a signifier which has no a priori relationship to its signified and is therefore arbitrary. Also used in a more general sense to refer to any sort of signifier.

Symbolic value
The value which derives from the symbolic meanings associated with a commodity. For example, an object may have significance as a marker of identity or status.

Synchronous communication
Communication which takes place in real time. A telephone call is synchronous, as is radio listening and TV watching.

Syntagmatic analysis
An approach to semiological analysis centred upon developing an understanding of the relationship between different elements of a text in the construction of meaning.

Technological determinism
The belief that technologies act as independent shapers of the social and cultural world and are the most important instigator of social change. Often used as a means to draw attention to the perceived short-comings of *medium theory*.

Technology

For media technology, see *medium*. In its broader sense technology refers to the practical application of scientific knowledge for a particular purpose and/or to the outcomes of such endeavour.

Tokenism

The inclusion of one or a small number of people from a minority or marginalised group in an organisation, an event or a cultural text in order to appear inclusive.

Two-step flow

A model of communication which suggests that media influence on people is channelled and filtered by influential members of their community.

Users

The range of ordinary people who utilise media, whether as audiences, as interpersonal interactants or as non-professional producers and distributors of content.

Uses and gratifications

A research approach focused upon the active selection and use of media by individuals in order to fulfil needs and achieve gratifications.

Use value

The value which derives from the practical function of a commodity.

Vertical integration

The expansion of media corporations – via mergers or take-overs – up and down the different stages of production and distribution. Also see *horizontal integration*.

Virtual community

Contested term, referring to a community which is primarily generated or sustained through internet communication.

Volunteer audience

An audience which is deemed wilfully to have chosen to consume a particular type of content (rather than to have accidentally stumbled upon it through channel hopping, for example).

Weak ties

Narrow and limited relationships which lack intensity or commitment and are often confined to a particular sphere of interest/commonality and/or a single site of interaction.

REFERENCES

Abercrombie, N. and Longhurst, B. (1998) *Audiences: A Sociological Theory of Performance and Imagination*. London: Sage.

Adamic, L. and Glance, N. (2005) 'The Political Blogosphere and the 2004 U.S. Election: Divided They Blog', in *Proc. 3rd Intl. Workshop on Link Discovery* (LinkKDD): 36–43. URL (accessed 2016): www.ramb.ethz.ch/CDstore/www2005-ws/workshop/wf10/AdamicGlanceBlogWWW.pdf

Adler, J. (2011) 'The Public's Burden in a Digital Age: Pressures on Intermediaries and the Privatisation of Internet Censorship', *Journal of Law and Policy*, 20(1).

Adorno, T. (1990), 'On Popular Music', in S. Frith and A. Goodwin (eds) *On Record: Rock, Pop and the Written Word*. London: Routledge (article first published 1941).

Adorno, T. (1991) 'The Schema of Mass Culture', in J. Bernstein (ed.) *The Culture Industry: Selected Essays on Mass Culture*. London: Routledge (article originally published 1944).

Adorno, T. and Horkheimer, M. (1997) *Dialectic of Enlightenment*. London: Verso (first published 1944).

Advertising Association (accessed 2015) 'Advertising Pays 3: The Value of Advertising to the UK's Culture, Media and Sport'. URL: www.adassoc.org.uk/publications/advertising-pays-3/

Alexander, C. (2000) *The Asian Gang: Ethnicity, Identity, Masculinity*. Oxford: Berg.

Alexander, V. (2003) *Sociology of the Arts: Exploring Fine and Popular Forms*. Oxford: Blackwell.

Allan, S. and Thorsen, E. (eds) (2009) *Citizen Journalism: Global Perspectives*. New York: Peter Lang.

Allen, A. and Zelizer, B. (2004) *Reporting War: Journalism in Wartime*. London: Routledge.

Allen, C. (2012) 'A Review of the Evidence Relating to the Representation of Muslims and Islam in the British Media', written evidence submitted to *All Party Parliamentary Group on Islamophobia*. URL (accessed 2016): www.birmingham.ac.uk/Documents/college-social-sciences/social-policy/IASS/news-events/MEDIA-ChrisAllen-APPGEvidence-Oct2012.pdf

Althusser, L. (1971) *Lenin and Philosophy and Other Essays*. London: New Left Books.

American Psychological Association Task Force on Violent Media (2015) *Video Games and Violence*. URL (accesssed 2016): www.apa.org/news/press/releases/2015/08/technical-violent-games.pdf

Anderson, B. (1991) *Imagined Communities*. London: Verso.

Anderson, C. W. (2011). 'Between creative and quantified audiences: Web metrics and changing patterns of newswork in local US newsrooms', *Journalism,* 12(5): 550–66.

Ang, I. (1985) *Watching Dallas: Soap Opera and the Melodramatic Imagination*. London: Methuen.

Ang, I. (1996) *Living Room Wars: Rethinking Media Audiences For a Postmodern Age*. London: Routledge.

Antony, R. (2009) *Second-Generation Tamil Youth in London*. Ongoing PhD Project, University of Surrey.

Appadurai, A. (1996) *Modernity at Large: Cultural Dimensions of Globalisation*. Minneapolis: University of Minneapolis Press.

Arthurs, J. (2004) *Television and Sexuality: Regulation and the Politics of Taste*. Maidenhead: Open University Press.

Arvidsson, A. (2005*) Brands: Meaning and Value in Media Culture*. Abingdon: Routledge.

Atton, C. (2002) *Alternative Media*. London: Sage.

Back, L. (1996) *New Ethnicities and Urban Culture: Racisms and Multiculture in Young Lives*. London: Routledge.

Bagdikian, B. (2004) *The New Media Monopoly*. Boston: Beacon Press.

Bakardjieva, M. (2005) *Internet Society: The Internet in Everyday Life*. London: Sage.

Baker, W. and Dessart, G. (1998) *Down the Tube: An Inside Account of the Failure of US Television*. New York: Basic Books.

Bakshy, E., Hofman, J. M., Mason, W. A. and Watts, D. J. (2011) 'Everyone's an Influencer: Identifying Influence on Twitter', WSDM, Hong Kong. URL (accessed 2016): http://snap.stanford.edu/class/cs224w-readings/bakshy11influencers.pdf

Baltruschat, D. (2011) 'Branded Entertainment', in Sussman, G. (ed.) *The Propaganda Society. Promotional Culture and Politics in Global Context*. New York: Peter Lang.

Bandura, A., Ross, D. and Ross, S. A. (1961) 'Transmission of Aggression Through Imitation of Aggressive Models', *Journal of Abnormal and Social Psychology*, 63: 575–82.

Bandura, A., Ross, D. and Ross, S. A. (1963) 'Imitation of Film-Mediated Aggressive Models', *Journal of Abnormal and Social Psychology*, 66: 31–41.

Banerjee, I. and Seneviratne, K. (eds) (2005) *Public Service Broadcasting: A Best Practices Sourcebook*. UNESCO.

Barker, M. (1981) *The New Racism: Conservatives and the Ideology of the Tribe*. London: Junction Books.

Barnett, S. (1998) 'Dumbing Down or Reaching Out: Is it Tabloidisation Wot Done It?', in Seaton, J. (ed.) *Politics and the Media: Harlots and Prerogatives at the Turn of the Millennium*. Oxford: Blackwell.

Barthel, M. (2015) 'Newspapers: Factsheet', *Pew Research Center*. URL (accessed 2015): www.journalism.org/2015/04/29/newspapers-fact-sheet/

Barthes, R. (1968). *Elements of Semiology*. London: Cape (first published 1964).

Barthes, R. (1972) *Mythologies*. New York: Hill and Wang (first published 1957).

Baudrillard, J. (1988) *The Ecstacy of Communication*. MIT Press.

Baudrillard, J. (1995a) *Simulacra and Simulation*. University of Michigan Press.

Baudrillard, J. (1995b) *The Gulf War Did Not Take Place*. Bloomington: Indiana University Press.

Bauman, Z. (2000) *The Individualized Society*. Cambridge: Polity.

Bauman, Z. (2001) *Community: Seeking Safety in an Insecure World*. Cambridge: Polity.

Bauman, Z. (2007) *Liquid Times: Living in an Age of Uncertainty*, Cambridge: Polity.

Baym, N. (2000) *Tune In, Log On: Soaps, Fandom and Online Community*. London: Sage.

BBC Online (2014) *Lenny Henry Calls for Ethnic TV Industry Boost*, URL (accessed 2016): www.bbc.co.uk/news/entertainment-arts-26626388

Beck, U. and Beck-Gernsheim, E. (2001) *Individualization*. London: Sage.

Becker, H. (1963) *Outsiders: Studies in the Sociology of Deviance*. New York: Free Press.

Bell A. (1991) *The Language of News Media*. Oxford: Blackwell.

Bennett, A. (1999), 'Subcultures or Neo-Tribes? Rethinking the Relationship Between Youth, Style and Musical Taste', *Sociology,* 33(3): 599–617.

Berelson, B. (1952) *Content Analysis in Communication Research*. New York: Free Press.

Berelson, B., Lazarsfeld, P. and McPhee, W. (1954) *Voting. A Study of Opinion Forming in a Presidential Campaign*. Chicago: University of Chicago Press.

Berkowitz, L. (1984) 'Some Effects of Thoughts on Anti- and Pro-Social Influence Of Media Events', *Psychological Bulletin,* 95(3): 410–27.

Billig, M. (1995) *Banal Nationalism*. London: Sage.

Boellstorff, T. (2008) *Coming of Age in Second Life: An Anthropologist Explores the Virtually Human*. Princeton University Press.

Bokzkovski, P. and Peer, L. (2011) 'The Choice Gap: The Divergent Online News Preferences of Journalists and Consumers', *Journal of Communication,* 61(5): 857–76.

Bordewijk, J. and van Kaam, B. (2002) 'Towards a New Classification of Tele-Information Services', in McQuail, D. (ed.) *McQuail's Reader in Mass Communication Theory*. London: Sage, pp. 113–24.

Bourdieu, P. (1984) *Distinction: A Social Critique of the Judgement of Taste*. London: Routledge.

boyd, d. (2008) *Taken Out of Context: American Teen Sociality in Networked Publics*. PhD Thesis, University of California. URL (accessed 2009): www.danah.org/papers/TakenOutOfContext.pdf

boyd, d. (2014) *It's Complicated: The Social Lives of Networked Teens*. New Haven: Yale University Press.

Boyd-Barrett, O. (1977) 'Media Imperialism: Towards an International Framework for the Analysis of Media Systems', in Curran, J., Gurevitch, M. and Woollacott, J. (eds) *Mass Communication and Society*. London: Arnold.

Brand, R. (2014) *Revolution*. London: Random House.

Briggs, A. (1961) *The History of Broadcasting in the United Kingdom: Birth of Broadcasting Volume 1*. Oxford: Oxford University Press.

Brighton, P. and Foy, D. (2007) *News Values*. London: Sage.

Bruns, A. (2008) 'The Future Is User-Led: The Path towards Widespread Produsage', *Fibreculture Journal*, 11.

Brunsden, C. and Morley, D. (1978) *Everyday Television: Nationwide*. London: BFI.

Brunsdon, C. (1997) 'Crossroads: Notes on Soap Opera', in *Screen Tastes: Soap Opera to Satellite Dishes*. London: Routledge, pp. 13–18.

Bull, M. (2005) 'No Dead Air! The iPod and the Culture of Mobile Listening', *Leisure Studies*, 24(4): 343–55.

Bull, M. (2007) *Sound Moves: iPod Culture and Urban Experience*. London: Routledge.

Butler, J. (1990) *Gender Trouble: Feminism and the Subversion of Identity*. New York: Routledge.

Butsch, R. (2007) (ed.) *Media and Public Spheres*. London: Palgrave.

Carlyle, T. (1849) 'The Nigger Question', *Fraser's Magazine*, December 1949.

Carr, D. (2006) 'Games and Gender', in Carr, E., Buckingham, D., Burn, A. and Schott, G. (eds) *Computer Games: Text, Narrative and Play*. Cambridge: Polity Press, pp. 162–78.

Carter, C. (2014) 'Sex/Gender and the Media: From Sex Roles to Social Construction and Beyond,' in Ross, K. (ed.) *The Handbook of Gender, Sex and Media*. Oxford: Wiley-Blackwell.

Cashmore, E. (2014) *Celebrity Culture – Second Edition*. New York: Routledge.

Castells, M. (2001) *The Internet Galaxy*. London: Oxford University Press.

Castells, M., Fernandez-Ardevol, M., Linchuan Qui, J. and Sey, A. (2006) *Mobile Communication and Society: A Global Perspective*. London: MIT Press.

de Certeau, M. (1984) *The Practice of Everyday Life*. Berkley: University of California Press.

Chambers, I. (1985) *Urban Rhythms: Pop Music and Popular Culture*. London: Macmillan.

Chandler, D. (1994a) 'The Transmission Model of Communication'. URL (accessed 2008): http://visual-memory.co.uk/daniel/Documents/short/trans.html

Chandler, D. (1994b) 'Semiotics for Beginners'. URL (accessed 2008): http://visual-memory.co.uk/daniel/Documents/S4B/

Chandler, D. (1995) 'Technological or Media Determinism'. URL (accessed 2008): http://visual-memory.co.uk/daniel/Documents/tecdet/

Cohen, Albert (1955) *Delinquent Boys: The Culture of the Gang*. London: Collier-Macmillan.

Cohen, N. (2013) 'Commodifying Free Labour Online: Social Media, Audiences and Advertising', in McCallister, M. and West, E. (eds) *The Routledge Companion to Advertising and Promotional Culture*. Abingdon: Routledge, pp. 177–91.

Cohen, S. (1972) *Folk Devils and Moral Panics: The Creation of the Mods and Rockers*. London: MacGibbon & Lee.

Collins, E. and Murroni, C. (eds) (1996) *New Media, New Policies: Media and Communications Strategies for the Future*. Cambridge: Polity.

Collins, R. (1990) *Culture, Communications and Political Economy*. Toronto: University of Toronto Press.

Connell, R. W. (2000) *The Men and the Boys*. Cambridge: Polity.

Connor, S. (1997) *Postmodernist Culture: An Introduction to Theories of the Contemporary – Second Edition*. Oxford: Blackwell.

Conover, M., Ratkiewicz, J., Francisco, M., Goncalves, B., Flammini, A. and Menczer, F. (2011) 'Political Polarization on Twitter', *Proc. Fifth International AAAI Conference on Weblogs and Social Media*. URL (accessed 2016): www.aaai.org/ocs/index.php/ICWSM/ICWSM11/paper/viewFile/2847/3275

Corea, A. (1995) 'Racism and the American Way of Media', in Downing, J., Mohammadi, A. and Sreberny-Mohammadi, A. (eds) *Questioning the Media: A Critical Introduction*. London: Sage.

Crisell, A. (1998) 'Local Radio: Attuned to the Times or Filling Time With Tunes?', in Franklin, B. and Murphy, D. (eds) *Making the Local News: Local Journalism in Context*. London: Routledge.

Cross, G. (2013) 'Origins of Modern Consumption: Advertising, New Goods and a New Generation 1890–1930', in McCallister, M. and West, E. (eds) *The Routledge Companion to Advertising and Promotional Culture*. New York: Routledge, pp. 11–23.

Croteau, D. and Hoynes, W. (2014) *Media Society: Industries, Images and Audiences – Fifth Edition*. Los Angeles: Sage.

Crystal, D. (2003) *English as a Global Language – Second Edition*. Cambridge: Cambridge University Press.

Curran, J. and Seaton, J. (2010) *Power Without Responsibility: The Press, Broadcasting and New Media in Britain – Seventh Edition*. New York: Routledge.

Currie, D. (2003) 'Girl Talk: Adolescent Magazines and Their Readers', in Brooker, W. and Jermyn, D. (eds) *The Audience Studies Reader*. London: Routledge.

Dahlgren, P. (1995) *Television and the Public Sphere: Citizenship, Democracy and the Media*. London: Sage.

Dahlgren, P. (2009) *Media and Political Engagement: Citizens, Communication and Democracy*. Cambridge: Cambridge University Press.

Danesi, M. (2006) *Brands*. London: Routledge.

Davies, N. (2008) *Flat Earth News*, London: Chatto & Windus.

Davis, A. (2013*) Promotional Cultures*. Cambridge: Polity.

Dayan, D. (1998) 'Particularistic Media and Diasporic Communications', in Curran, J. and Liebes, T. (eds) *Media, Ritual and Identity*. London: Routledge, pp. 103–13.

DCMS (2016) 'A BBC For the Future: A Broadcaster of Distinction', UK Government White Paper. URL (accessed 2016): https://www.gov.uk/government/uploads/system/uploads/attachment_data/file/524863/DCMS_A_BBC_for_the_future_linked_rev1.pdf

Delanty, G. (2003) *Community*. London: Routledge.

Department for Culture, Media and Sport (UK) (2015) *BBC Charter Review: Public Consultation*. URL (accessed 2015): www.gov.uk/government/uploads/system/uploads/attachment_data/file/445704/BBC_Charter_Review_Consultation_WEB.pdf

Devlin, P. (1963) *The Enforcement of Morals*. London: Oxford University Press.

Dinucci, D. (1999) 'Fragmented Future', Print 53 (4), URL (accessed 2016: http://darcyd.com/fragmented_future.pdf

Dobson, A. S. (2011) 'Hetero-Sexy Representation by Young Women on MySpace: The Politics of Performing an "Objectified" Self', *Outskirts: Feminisms Along the Edge*, 25.

Dobson, A. S. (2014) 'Laddishness Online: The Possible Significations and Significance of "Performative Shamelessness" for Young Women in the Post-Feminist Context', *Cultural Studies*, 28(1).

Dobson, A. S. (2015) *Postfeminist Digital Cultures: Femininity, Social Media, and Self-Representation*. New York: Palgrave Macmillan.

Dorfman, A. and Mattelart, A. (1971) *How to Read Donald Duck: Imperialist Ideology in the Disney Comic*. New York: International General.

Doty, A. and Gove, B. (1997) 'Queer Representation in the Mass Media', in Medhurst, A. and Munt, S. (eds) *The Lesbian and Gay Studies Reader*. London: Cassell.

Downing, J. and Husband, C. (2005) *Representing Race: Racisms, Ethnicity and the Media*. London: Sage.

Doyle, G. (2013) *Understanding Media Economics – Second Edition*. London: Sage.

Drabman, R. and Thomas, R. (1974) 'Does Media Violence Increase Children's Toleration of Real-Life Aggression?', *Developmental Psychology*, 10: 418–21.

Du Gay, P., Hall, S., Janes, L., Mackay, J. and Negus, K. (1997) *Doing Cultural Studies: The Story of the Sony Walkman*. London: Sage.

Duggan, M. and Smith, A. (2013) 'Cell Internet Use 2013', *Pew Research Centre*. URL (accessed 2016): www.pewinternet.org/2013/09/16/main-findings-2/

Duggan, M., Ellison, N., Lampe, C., Lenhart, A. and Madden, M. (2014) 'Social Media Update 2014', *Pew Research Center*. URL (accessed 2016): www.pewinternet.org/2015/01/09/social-media-update-2014/

Dworkin, A. (1981) *Pornography: Men Possessing Women*. London: Women's Press.

Dworkin, A. (1995) 'Pornography and Male Supremacy', in Dines, G. and Humez, J. (eds) *Gender, Race and Class in Media: A Reader*. London: Sage, pp. 237–43.

Dwyer, T. (2011) 'Net Worth: Popular Social Media as Colossal Marketing Machines', in Sussman, G. (ed.) *The Propaganda Society*. New York: Peter Lang.

Dyson, M. (1993) *Reflecting Black African-American Cultural Criticism*. Minneapolis: University of Minnesota Press.

Edwardson, R. (2008) *Canadian Content: Culture and the Quest for Nationhood*. Toronto: University of Toronto Press.

Elba, I. (2016) 'Diversity in Media', Keynote Address to UK Parliament. URL (accessed 2016): www.channel4.com/info/press/news/idris-elba-s-keynote-speech-to-parliament-on-diversity-in-the-media

Eldridge, J., Kitzinger, J. and Williams, K. (1997) *The Mass Media and Power in Modern Britain*. New York: Oxford University Press.

Ellison N., Steinfield C. and Lampe C. (2007) 'The Benefits of Facebook "Friends": Social Capital and College Students' Use of Online Social Network Sites', *Journal of Computer Mediated Communication*, 12: 1143–68.

Elstein, D. (1986) 'An End to Protection', in MacCabe, C. and Stewart, O. (eds) *The BBC and Public Service Broadcasting*. Manchester: Manchester University Press, pp. 81–91.

Fairclough, N. (1995) *Critical Discourse Analysis: The Critical Study of Language*. Harlow: Longman.

Faist, T. (2010) 'Diaspora and Transnationalism: What Kind of Dance Partners?', in Bauböck, R. and Faist, T. (eds) *Diaspora and Transnationalism: Concepts, Theories and Methods*. Amsterdam University Press.

Featherstone, M. (2007) *Consumer Culture and Postmodernism – Second Edition*. London: Sage.

Federal Communications Commission (FCC) (2016) 'Obscene, Indecent and Profane Broadcasts'. URL (accessed 2016): https://www.fcc.gov/consumers/guides/obscene-indecent-and-profane-broadcasts

Ferguson, C. (2015) 'Does Media Violence Predict Societal Violence? It Depends on What You Look At and When', *Journal of Communication*, 65(1): E1–22.

Feshbach, S. (1961) 'The Stimulating Versus Cathartic Effects of a Vicarious Aggressive Activity', *Journal of Abnormal and Social Psychology*, 63: 381–5.

Fiske, J. (1987) *Television Culture*. London: Methuen.

Fiske, J. (1990) *Introduction to Communication Studies – Second Edition*. London: Routledge.

Fiske, J. (1991a) *Understanding Popular Culture*. London: Routledge.

Fiske, J. (1991b) *Reading the Popular*. London: Routledge.

Fiske, J. and Hartley, J. (1988) *Reading Television*. London: Routledge (originally published 1978).

Foucault, M. (1990) *The History of Sexuality: Volume 1*. Harmondsworth: Penguin (first published 1976).

Franklin, B. (1997) *Newszak and News Media*. London: Arnold.

Franklin, B. and Murphy, D. (1998) 'Changing Times: Local Newspapers, Technology and Markets', in Franklin, B. and Murphy, D. (eds) *Making the Local News: Local Journalism in Context*. London: Routledge.

Fuchs, C. (2014) *Social Media: A Critical Introduction*. London: Sage.

Fulton, H., Huisman, R., Murphet, J. and Dunn, A. (2006) *Narrative and Media*. Cambridge University Press.

Gaber, I. (2012) 'Not Just the Murdoch Press', in Keeble, R. and Mair, J. (eds) *The Phone Hacking Scandal: Journalism on Trial*. Bury St Edmonds: Arabis.

Galtung, J. and Ruge, M. (1973) 'Structuring and Selecting News', in Cohen, S. and Young, J. (eds) *The Manufacture of News: Social Problems, Deviance and The Mass Media*. London: Constable.

Gans, H. (2004) *Deciding What's News*. Northwestern University Press.

Garnham, N. (1993) 'The Media and the Public Sphere', in Calhoun, C. (ed.) *Habermas and the Public Sphere*. London: MIT Press.

Garnham, N. (1995) 'Contribution to a Political Economy of Mass Communication', in Boyd-Barrett, O. and Newbold, C. (eds) *Approaches to Media: A Reader*. London: Arnold (article originally published 1979).

Gauntlett, D. (1998) 'Ten Things Wrong With the Effects Model', in Dickenson, R., Harindranath, R. and Linné, O. (eds) *Approaches to Audiences – A Reader*. London: Arnold.

Gauntlett, D. (2008) *Media, Gender and Identity: An Introduction – Second Edition*. London: Routledge.

Gellner, E. (1983) *Nations and Nationalism*. Oxford: Blackwell.

Georgiou, M. (2001) 'Crossing the Boundaries of the Ethnic Home: Media Consumption and Ethnic Identity Construction in the Public Space: The Case of the Cypriot Community Centre in North London', *International Communication Gazette*, 63(4): 311–29.

Georgiou, M. (2002) 'Diasporic Communities Online: A Bottom-Up Experience of Transnationalism', *Hommes & Migrations,* 1240: 10–18. URL for English version (accessed 2009): http://eprints.lse.ac.uk/26142/

Georgiou, M. (2006) *Diaspora, Identity and the Media*. Hampton Press.

Geraghty, C. (1991) *Women and Soap Opera: A Study of Prime-Time Soaps*. Cambridge: Polity Press.

Geraghty, C. (2006) 'Women's Fiction Still: The Study of Soap Opera in Television Studies', *Critical Studies in Television*, 1(1): 129–34.

Gerbner, G. (1956) 'Toward a General Model of Communication', *Audio Visual Communication Review IV*, (3): 171–99.

Gerbner, G. (1994) 'Reclaiming Our Cultural Mythology', *In Context*, 38.

Gerbner, G. (2002) 'Global Media Mayhem', *Global Media Journal*, 1(1). URL (accessed 2009): http://lass.calumet.purdue.edu/cca/gmj/fa02/gmj-fa02-gerbner.htm

Gerbner, G. and Gross, L. (1976) 'Living with Television: The Violence Profile', *Journal of Communication*, 26: 173–99.

Gerbner, G., Gross, L., Jackson-Beeck, M., Jeffries-Fox, S. and Signoreilli, N. (1977) 'TV Violence Profile No. 8: The Highlights', *Journal of Communication*, 27(2): 171–80.

Geser, H. (2007a) 'Me, My Self and My Avatar. Some Microsociological Reflections on "Second Life"', in *Sociology in Switzerland: Towards Cybersociety and Vireal Social Relations*. URL (accessed 2009): http://socio.ch/intcom/t_hgeser17.pdf

Geser, H. (2007b) 'A Very Real Virtual Society: Some Macrosociological Reflections on "Second Life"', in *Sociology in Switzerland: Towards Cybersociety and Vireal Social Relations*. URL (accessed 2009): http://socio.ch/intcom/t_hgeser18.pdf

Gidley, B. (2007) 'Youth Culture and Ethnicity: Emerging Youth Multiculture in South London', in Hodkinson, P. and Deicke, W. (eds) *Youth Cultures: Scenes, Subcultures and Tribes*. New York: Routledge.

Gilder, G. (1992) *Life after Television: The Coming Transformation of Media and American Life*. New York: Norton.

Gill, R. (2007) *Gender and the Media*. Cambridge: Polity Press.

Gillespie, M. (1995) *Television, Ethnicity and Cultural Change*. London: Routledge.

Gillespie, M. (2006) 'Narrative Analysis', in Gillespie, M. and Toynbee, J. (eds) *Analysing Media Texts*. Maidenhead: Open University Press.

Gillmor, D. (2006) *We the Media: Grassroots Journalism By the People For the People*. Sebastopol: O'Reilly Media.

Gilroy, P. (1993) *The Black Atlantic: Modernity and Double-Consciousness*. London: Verso.

Giroux, H. (2002) 'Private Satisfactions and Public Disorders: *Fight Club*, Patriarchy, and the Politics of Masculine Violence'. URL (accessed 2016): www.henryagiroux.com/online_articles/fight_club.htm

Gitlin, T. (1998) 'Public Sphere or Public Sphericules', in Liebes, T. and Curran, J. (eds) *Media, Ritual and Identity*. London: Routledge.

Gitlin, T. (2000) *Inside Prime-Time: Revised Edition*. London: Routledge.

GLAAD (2015) *Where We Are On TV 2015–16*. URL (accessed 2016): www.glaad.org/files/GLAAD-2015-WWAT.pdf

Glasgow University Media Group (1976a) *Bad News*. London: Routledge and Kegan Paul.

Glasgow University Media Group (1976b) *More Bad News*. London: Routledge and Kegan Paul.

Glasgow University Media Group (1982) *Really Bad News*. London: Writers' and Readers' Publishing Cooperative.

Glick-Schiller, N., Basch, L. and Blanc-Szanton, C. (1992) 'Transnationalism: A New Analytic Framework for Understanding Migration', *Annals of the New York Academy of Sciences*, 645: 1–24.

Global Media Monitoring Project (2015) *Highlights of Findings*. URL (accessed 2016): http://cdn.agilitycms.com/who-makes-the-news/Imported/reports_2015/highlights/highlights_en.pdf

Goffman E. (1967) *Interaction Ritual: Essays in Face-to-Face Behaviour*. Chicago: Aldine Publishing Company.

Goffman, E. (1979) *Gender Advertisements*. London: Macmillan.

Golding, P. and Murdock, G. (1991) 'Culture, Communications and Political Economy', in Curran, J. and Gurevitch, M. (eds) *Mass Media and Society – Third Edition*. London: Arnold, pp. 70–92.

Goldman, R. (1992) *Reading Advertisements Socially*. New York: Routledge.

Google (accessed 2015) 'Google Adwords', URL: www.google.co.uk/adwords/

Gore, A. (2007) *The Assault on Reason*. Bloomsbury Publishing.

Gramsci, A. (1971) *Selections From the Prison Notebooks*. London: Lawrence & Wishart.

Gray, A. (1992) *Video Playtime: The Gendering of a Leisure Technology*. London: Routledge.

Gray, J., Sandvoss, C. and Lee Harrington, C. (eds) (2007) *Fandom: Identities and Communities in a Mediated World*. New York University Press.

Greater London Authority (2007) 'The Search for Common Ground: Muslims, Non-Muslims and the UK Media', report for The Mayor of London. URL (accessed 2016): www.insted.co.uk/search-for-common-ground.pdf

Gross, L. (1995) 'Out of the Mainstream: Sexual Minorities and the Mass Media', in Dines, G. and Humez, J. (eds) *Gender, Race and Class in Media*. London: Sage, pp. 61–70.

Grzywinska, I. and Borden, J. (2012) 'The Impact of Social Media on Traditional Media Agenda Setting Theory – The Case Study of Occupy Wall Street Movement in USA', in Dobek-Ostrowska, B. and Wanta, W. (eds) *Agenda Setting: Old and New Problems in Old and New Media*. Wydawnictwo Uniwersytetu Wroclawskiego, pp. 133–55.

Gunter, B. (2000) *Media Research Methods*. London: Sage.

Habermas, J. (1987) *The Theory of Communicative Action, Volume 2: Lifeworld and System – A Critique of Functionalist Reason*. Cambridge: Polity Press (first published 1981).

Habermas, J. (1992) *The Structural Transformation of the Public Sphere*. Cambridge: Polity Press (originally published 1964).

Habermas, J. (1996) *Between Facts and Norms: Contributions to a Discourse Theory of Law and Democracy*. Cambridge: Polity Press.

Habermas, J. (2001) *The Postnational Constellation: Political Essays*. Cambridge: Polity.

Hall, S. (1973) 'The Determination of News Photographs', in Cohen, S. and Young, J. (eds) *The Manufacture of News*. London: Constable.

Hall, S. (1982) 'The Rediscovery of "Ideology": Return of the Repressed in Media Studies', in Gurevitch, M., Bennett, T., Curran, J. and Woollacott, J. (eds) *Culture, Society and The Media*. London: Routledge.

Hall, S. (1992) 'New Ethnicities', in Rattansi, A. and Donald, J. (eds) *Race, Culture and Difference*. London: Sage.

Hall, S. (1993) 'Encoding, Decoding', in During, S. (ed.) *The Cultural Studies Reader*. London: Routledge, pp. 90–103 (article originally published 1980).

Hall, S. (1997) 'The Spectacle of the Other', in Hall, S. (ed.) *Representation: Cultural Representations and Signifying Practices*. London: Sage.

Hall, S., Critcher, C., Jefferson, T., Clarke J. and Roberts, B. (1978) *Policing the Crisis: Mugging, The State and Law and Order*. London: Macmillan.

Halloran, J. (1970) *The Effects of Television*. London: Panther.

Hannerz, U. (1996) *Transnational Connections: Culture, People, Places*. London: Routledge.

Harcup, T. and O'Neill, D. (2001) 'What is News? Galtung and Ruge Revisited', *Journalism Studies*, 2(2): 261–80.

Harrison, M. (1985) *Television News: Whose Bias?* Berkshire: Hermitage.

Harrison, J. (2006) *News*. London: Routledge.

Harrison, C. (2014) 'Studio5ive.com: Selling Cosmetics to Men and Reproducing Masculine Identity', in Ross, K. (ed.) *The Handbook of Gender, Sex and Media*. Chichester: Wiley, pp. 189–204.

Hartley, J. (1982) *Understanding News*. London: Methuen.

Hartley, J. (2009) 'Less Popular But More Democratic? *Corrie*, Clarkson and the Dancing *Cru*', in Turner, G. and Tay, J. (eds) *Television Studies After TV: Understanding Television in the Post-Broadcast Era*. London: Routledge.

Harvey, D. (1989) *The Condition of Postmodernity: An Enquiry into the Logics of Social Change.* Oxford: Basil Blackwell.

Hayes, I. (1971) *Theme From Shaft.* Enterprise (music recording).

Hayward, K. and Yar, M. (2006) 'The 'Chav' Phenomenon: Consumption, Media and the Construction of a New Underclass', *Crime Media Culture*, 2(1): 9–28.

Hebdige, D. (1979) *Subculture: The Meaning of Style.* London: Methuen.

Hebdige, D. (1988) *Hiding in the Light: On Images and Things.* London: Routledge.

Herman, E. and Chomsky, N. (1998) *Manufacturing Consent: The Political Economy of the Mass Media.* London: Vintage (originally published 1988).

Hermes, J. (1995) *Reading Women's Magazines.* Cambridge: Polity Press.

Hesmondhalgh, D. (2006) 'Discourse Analysis and Content Analysis', in Gillespie, M. and Toynbee, J. (eds) *Analysing Media Texts.* Maidenhead: Open University Press.

Hesmondhalgh, D. (2007) *The Culture Industries – Second Edition.* London: Sage.

Hill, K. and Hughes, J. (1998) *Cyberpolitics: Citizen Activism in the Age of the Internet.* Oxford: Roman and Littlefield.

Hills, M. (2002) *Fan Cultures.* London: Routledge.

Hobson, D. (2006) 'From Crossroads to Wife Swap: Learning From Audiences', *Critical Studies in Television*, 1(1): 121–8.

Hodkinson, P. (2002) *Goth. Identity, Style and Subculture.* Oxford: Berg.

Hodkinson, P. (2003) 'Net.Goth: Internet Communication and (Sub)Cultural Boundaries', in Muggleton, D. and Weinzeirl, R. (eds) *The Post-Subcultures Reader.* Oxford: Berg, pp. 285–97.

Hodkinson, P. (2007) 'Interactive Online Journals and Individualisation', *New Media and Society*, 9(4): 625–50.

Hodkinson, P. (2015) 'Bedrooms and Beyond: Youth, Identity and Privacy on Social Network Sites', *New Media and Society*, online before print, DOI: 10.1177/1461444815605454

Hodkinson, P. and Lincoln, S. (2008) 'Online Journals as Virtual Bedrooms: Young People, Identity and Personal Space', *YOUNG*, 16(1).

Holmes, L. (2012) 'We've Seen Enough Breasts: Why I Started the No More Page 3 Campaign', *The Independent*. URL (accessed 2015): www.independent.co.uk/voices/comment/exclusive-weve-seen-enough-breasts-why-i-started-the-no-more-page-3-campaign-8159600.html

Homer, P. (2009) 'Product Placements', *Journal of Advertising*, 38(3): 21–31.

Horrocks, R. (1994) *Masculinity in Crisis: Myths, Fantasies and Realities.* London: Palgrave.

Huq, R. (2006) *Beyond Subculture: Pop, Youth and Identity in a Postcolonial World.* London: Routledge.

Hussain, Y. (2005) *Writing Diaspora: South Asian Women, Culture and Identity.* London: Ashgate.

Innes, H.A. (1951) *The Bias of Communication.* Toronto: University of Toronto Press.

Jackson, J. (2012) 'How Much Do Newspapers Think Their Audiences Are Worth?', *The Media Briefing*. URL (accessed 2016): www.themediabriefing.com/article/how-much-do-newspapers-think-their-audiences-are-worth

Jackson, P., Stevenson, N. and Brooks, K. (2001) *Making Sense of Men's Magazines*. Cambridge: Polity Press.

Jameson, F. (1991) *Postmodernism or the Cultural Logic of Late Capitalism*. London: Verso.

Jenkins, H. (1992) *Textual Poachers: Television Fans and Participatory Culture*. London: Routledge.

Jenkins, H. (2002) 'Interactive Audiences?', in Nightingale, V. and Ross, K. (eds) *Critical Readings: Media and Audiences*. Maidenhead: Open University Press.

Jenkins, H. (2003) '"Out of the Closet and Into the Universe": Queers and Star Trek', in Brooker, W. and Jermyn, D. (eds) *The Audience Studies Reader*. London: Routledge, pp. 171–80.

Jenkins, H. (2006) *Fans, Bloggers and Gamers: Exploring Participatory Culture*. New York: New York University Press.

Jenkins, H. (2008) *Convergence Culture: Where Old and New Media Collide*. New York: New York University Press.

Jensen, T. (2014) 'Welfare Commonsense, Poverty Porn and Doxosophy', *Sociological Research Online*, 19(3): 3.

Johnsen, P. (2010) *Second Life, Media and the Other Society*. New York: Peter Lang.

Karlsson, M. and Olin-Scheller, C. (2015) '"Let's Party!" Harry Potter Fan Fiction Sites as Social Settings for Narrative Gender Constructions', *Gender and Language*, 9(2).

Katyal, S. (2006) 'Performance, Property and the Slashing of Gender in Fan Fiction', *Journal of Gender, Social Policy and Law*, 14(3).

Katz, E. and Lazarsfeld, P. (1955) *Personal Influence*. New York: Free Press.

Katz, E. and Liebes, T. (1985) 'Mutual Aid in the Decoding of *Dallas*: Preliminary Notes from a Cross-Cultural Study', in Drummond, P. and Patterson, R. (eds) *Television in Transition*. London: British Film Institute, pp. 187–98.

Katz, E., Blumler, J. and Gurevich, M. (2003) 'Utilization of Mass Communication By the Individual', in Nightingale, K. and Ross, A. (eds) *Critical Readings: Media and Audiences*. Maidenhead: Open University Press (article originally published 1974).

Katz, E., Gurevitch, M. and Haas, H. (1973) 'On the Use of Mass Media for Important Things', *American Sociological Review*, 38: 164–81.

Katz, M. (2010) *Capturing Sound: How Technology Has Changed Music – Second Edition*. University of California Press.

Kellner, D. (1995) 'Advertising and Consumer Culture', in Downing, J., Mohammadi, A. and Sreberny-Mohammadi, A. (eds) *Questioning the Media: A Critical Introduction – Second Edition*. London: Sage, pp. 329–44.

Kerlinger, F. N. (1986) *Foundations of Behavioural Research*. New York: Holt, Rinehart and Winston.

Khan, F. and Mythen, G. (2015) 'Double Standards and Speech Deficits: What is Sayable for British Muslims After Paris', *Sociological Research Online*, 20(3).

Khan, S. (2012) 'Offensive? Racist? No, Just Funny and Oh So True', *Mail Online*. URL (accessed 2016): www.dailymail.co.uk/debate/article-2195459/Citizen-Khan-Offensive-Racist-No-just-funny—oh-true.html

Kipling, R. (1899) 'The White Man's Burden', *McLure's Magazine*, 12 February 1899.

Klein, N. (2000) *No Logo*. London: Flamingo.

Komito, L. and Bates, J. (2009) 'Virtually Local: Social Media and Community Among Polish Nationals in Dublin', *Aslib Proceedings*, 61(3): 232–44.

Kress, G. and Hodge, R. (1979) *Language as Ideology*. London: Routledge and Kegan Paul.

Lacan, J. (2001) *Écrits: A Selection*. London: Routledge (first published 1977).

Lane, D. (2005) *Berlusconi's Shadow: Crime, Justice and the Pursuit of Power*. Harmonsworth: Penguin.

Langer, J. (1998) *Tabloid Television: Popular Television and the 'Other News'*. London: Routledge.

Larrain, J. (1994) *Ideology and Cultural Identity*. Cambridge: Polity.

Larson, S. (2006) *Media and Minorities: The Politics of Race in News and Entertainment*. Lanham: Rowman & Littlefield.

Lasswell, H. (1948) 'The Structure and Function of Communication in Society', in Bryson, L. (ed.) *The Communication of Ideas*. New York: Institute for Religious and Social Studies.

Lazarsfeld, P., Berelson, B. and Gaudet, H. (1944) *The People's Choice*. New York: Columbia University Press.

Lee, A., Lewis, S. and Powers, M. (2014) 'Audience Clicks and News Placement: A Study of Time-Lagged Influence in Online Journalism', *Communication Research*, 41(4): 505–30.

Leiss, W., Kline, S. and Jhally, S. (1997) *Social Communication in Advertising: Persons, Products and Images of Well-Being – Second Edition*. New York: Routledge.

Leiss, W., Kline, S., Jhally, S. and Botterill, J. (2005) *Social Communication in Advertising: in the Mediated Marketplace –Third Edition*. New York: Routledge.

Leonard, M. (1998) 'Paper Planes: Travelling the New Grrrl Geographies', in Skelton, T. and Valentine, G. (eds) *Cool Places: Geographies of Youth Cultures*. London: Routledge.

Lewis, J., Williams, A. and Franklin, B. (2008) 'A Compromised Fourth Estate? UK News Journalism, Public Relations and News Sources', *Journalism Studies*, 9(1): 1–20.

Liebes, T. (1998) 'Television's Disaster Marathons: A Danger for Democratic Processes?', in Liebes, T. and Curran, J. (eds) *Media, Ritual and Identity*. London: Routledge.

Lievrouw, L. (2001) 'New Media and the "Pluralization of Live-Worlds": A Role for Information in Social Differentiation', *New Media and Society*, 3(1): 7–28.

Lincoln, S. and Robards, B. (2014) 'Being Strategic and Taking Control: Bedrooms, Social Network Sites and the Narratives of Growing Up', *New Media and Society*, online before print, DOI: 10.1177/1461444814554065.

Livingstone, S. (2008) 'Taking Risky Opportunities in Youthful Content Creation: Teenagers' Use of Social Networking Sites for Intimacy, Privacy and Self-Expression', *New Media and Society*, 10(3): 393–411.

Livingstone, S. and Lunt, P. (1994) *Talk on Television*. London: Routledge.

Longhurst, B. and Bogdanovic, D. (2014) *Popular Music and Society – Third Edition*. Cambridge: Polity.

Lule, J. (2001) *Daily News, Eternal Stories: The Mythological Role of Journalism*. Guilford Press.

Lury, C. (2011) *Consumer Culture – Second Edition*. Cambridge: Polity.

Lyon, D. (1998) 'The World Wide Web of Surveillance: The Internet and Off-World Power-Flows', *Information, Communication & Society*, 1(1): 91–105.

MacDonald, D. (1957) 'A Theory of Mass Culture', in Rosenburg, B. and White, D. (eds) *Mass Culture*. Glencoe: Free Press.

MacKinnon, C. (1988) *Feminism Unmodified: Discourses on Life and Law*. Harvard University Press.

MacRury, I. (2013) 'Back to the Future: Gifts, Friendships and the Re-Figuration of Advertising Space', in McCallister, M. and West, E. (eds) *The Routledge Companion to Advertising and Promotional Culture*. New York: Routledge.

Malik, S. (2002) *Representing Black Britain: Black and Asian Images on Television*. London: Sage.

Malm, K. and Wallis, R. (1993) *Media Policy and Music Activity*. London: Routledge.

Mamattah, S. (2006) 'Migration and Transnationalism: The Complete Picture? A Case Study of Russians Living in Scotland', *E-Sharp*, 6(2).

Mander, J. (1978) *Four Arguments for the Elimination of Television*. New York: William Morrow.

Marcuse, H. (1964) *One Dimensional Man: Studies in the Ideology of Advanced Industrial Society*. London: Routledge and Kegan Paul.

Marshall, P. D. (1997) *Celebrity and Power: Fame in Contemporary Culture*. University of Minnesota Press.

Marwick, A. and boyd, d. (2014) 'Networked Privacy: How Teenagers Negotiate Context in Social Media', *New Media and Society*, 16(7): 1051–67.

Marx, K. (1844) 'A Contribution to the Critique of Hegel's Philosophy of Right', *Deutsch-Französische Jahrbücher*, February.

Marx, K. (2000) 'Preface to a Contribution to a Critique of Political Economy', in McLellan, D. (ed.) *Karl Marx: Selected Writings*. Oxford: Oxford University Press.

McCallister, M. and West, E. (2013) (eds) *The Routledge Companion to Advertising and Promotional Culture*. New York: Routledge.

McChesney, R. (1999) *Rich Media, Poor Democracy: Communication Politics in Dubious Times*. New York: The New Press.

McChesney, R. and Nichols, J. (2010) *The Death and Life of American Journalism*. New York: Nation Books.

McChesney, R., Stole, I., Bellamy Foster, J. and Holleman, H. (2011) 'Advertising and the Genius of Commercial Propaganda', in Sussman, G. (ed.) *The Propaganda Society: Promotional Culture and Politics in Global Context*. New York: Peter Lang, pp. 27–44.

McCombs, M. and Shaw, D. (1972) 'The Agenda-Setting Function of the Press', *Public Opinion Quarterly*, 36(2): 176–87.

McCracken, E. (1992) *Decoding Women's Magazines: From 'Mademoiselle' to 'Ms'*. Basingstoke: Macmillan.

McDonnell, J. (1991) *Public Service Broadcasting: A Reader*. London: Routledge.

McGuigan, J. (2009) *Cool Capitalism*. London: Pluto Press.

McLuhan, M. (1962) *The Gutenberg Galaxy: The Making of Typographic Man*. Toronto: University of Toronto Press.

McLuhan, M. (2001) *Understanding Media*. London: Routledge (originally published 1964).

McQuail, D., Blumler, J. and Brown, J. (1972) 'The Television Audience: A Revised Perspective', in McQuail, D. (ed.) *Sociology of Mass Communications*. Harmondsworth: Penguin.

McRobbie, A. (2000) *Feminism and Youth Culture – Second Edition*. Basingstoke: Macmillan.

McRobbie, A. (2008) *The Aftermath of Feminism: Gender, Culture and Social Change*. London: Sage.

Mediawatch UK (2005) *Towards a Decent Society*. URL (accessed 2009): www.mediawatchuk.org.uk/index.php?option=com_content&task=view&id=155&Itemid=124

Mepham, J. (1990) 'The Ethics of *Quality* in Television', in Mulgan, G. (ed.) *The Question of Quality*. London: British Film Institute.

Mercer, K. (1990) 'Black Art and the Burden of Representation', *Third Text,* 10.

Meyers, E. (2014) 'Gossip Blogs and "Baby Bumps": The New Visual Spectacle of Female Celebrity in Gossip Media', in Ross, K. (ed.) *The Handbook of Gender, Sex and Media*. Chichester: Wiley, pp. 53–70.

Meyrowitz, J. (1985) *No Sense of Place: The Impact of Electronic Media on Social Behaviour*. New York: Oxford University Press.

Miles, S. (1998) *Consumerism as a Way of Life*. London: Sage.

Mill, J. S. (1975) 'On Liberty', in *Three Essays: 'On Liberty', 'Representative Government', 'The Subjection of Women'*. London: Oxford University Press (first published 1859).

Miller, D. (1995) (ed.) *Acknowledging Consumption*. London: Routledge.

Miller, D. and Slater, D. (2000) *The Internet: An Ethnographic Approach*. Oxford: Berg.

Miller, M. C. (1988) 'Cosby Knows Best', in Miller, M. C. (ed.) *Boxed-In: The Culture of TV*. Evanston: Northwestern University Press, pp. 69–78.

Modleski, T. (1982) *Loving With a Vengeance: Mass Produced Fantasies for Women*. New York: Routledge.

Moore, K., Mason, P. and Lewis, J. (2008) 'Images of Islam in the UK: The Representation of British Muslims in the National Print News Media 2000–2008', Cardiff School of Journalism, Media and

Cultural Studies. URL (accessed 2016): www.channel4.com/news/media/pdfs/Cardiff%20Final%20 Report.pdf

Moran, A. (1998) *Copycat TV: Globalisation, Programme Formats and Cultural Identity*. Luton: University of Luton Press.

Morgan, R. (1980) 'Theory and practice: Pornography and rape', in Lederer, L. (ed.) *Take Back the Night*. New York: William Morrow, pp. 134–40.

Moritz, M. (2004) 'Old Strategies for New Texts: How American Television is Creating and Treating Lesbian Characters', in Carter, C. and Steiner, L. (eds) *Critical Readings: Media and Gender*. Maidenhead: Open University Press.

Morley, D. (1980) *The Nationwide Audience: Structure and Decoding*. London: BFI.

Morley, D. (1988) *Family Television: Cultural Power and Domestic Leisure*. London: Routledge.

Morley, D. (1992) *Television, Audiences and Cultural Studies*. London: Routledge.

Morley, D. (2000) *Home Territories: Media, Mobility and Identity*. London: Routledge.

Muggleton, D. (1997) 'The Post-Subculturalist', in S. Redhead (ed.) *The Club Cultures Reader: Readings in Popular Cultural Studies*. Oxford: Blackwell.

Mulvey, L. (1975) 'Visual Pleasure and Narrative Cinema', *Screen*, 16(3): 6–18.

Murdoch, J. (2009) 'The Absence of Trust', MacTaggart Memorial Lecture, Edinburgh International Television Festival. URL (accessed 2015): http://www.thetvfestival.com/website/wp-content/uploads/ 2015/03/GEITF_MacTaggart_2009_James_Murdoch.pdf

Murdoch, R. (2001) 'Freedom in Broadcasting Versus the Public Service Tradition', in Franklin, B. (ed.) *British Television Policy: A Reader*. London: Routledge, pp. 38–40 (extract from 1989 lecture).

Murdock, G. (1992) 'Citizens, Consumers and Public Culture', in Skovmand, M. and Schroder, K. (eds) *Media Cultures: Reappraising Transnational Media*. London: Routledge.

Murdock, G. and Golding, P. (1995) 'For a Political Economy of Mass Communications', in Boyd-Barrett, O. and Newbold, C. (eds) *Approaches to Media: A Reader*. London: Arnold (article first published 1973).

Negroponte, N. (1995) *Being Digital*. New York: Vintage Books.

Nightingale, V. and Ross, K. (2003) 'Introduction', in Nightingale, V. and Ross, K. (eds) *Critical Readings: Media and Audiences*. Maidenhead: Open University Press.

Norman, E. (1988) *The Psychology of Everyday Things*. Basic Books.

Ofcom (2004) *Review of Public Service Television Broadcasting*. URL (accessed 2009): http://stake holders.ofcom.org.uk/broadcasting/reviews-investigations/public-service-broadcasting/psb-review-1/

Ofcom (2005) *Review of Public Service Television Broadcasting: Phase 3: Competition for Quality*. URL (accessed 2009): http://stakeholders.ofcom.org.uk/binaries/consultations/psb3/psb3.pdf

Ofcom (2007a) *The Promotion of Equal Opportunities in Broadcasting: 2007 Report*. URL (accessed 2008): http://stakeholders.ofcom.org.uk/broadcasting/guidance/equal-opps/equal-ops-report-07/

Ofcom (2007b) *Ethnic Minority Groups and Communication Services*. URL (accessed 2009): http://stakeholders.ofcom.org.uk/market-data-research/market-data/communications-market-reports/ethnic_minority/

Ofcom (2009) 'Local and Regional Newspapers in the UK: The View from Ofcom', *The Future of Local Media Conference*. URL (accessed 2016): http://stakeholders.ofcom.org.uk/binaries/research/tv-research/Salford_local_media.pdf

Ofcom (2013) *Ethnic Minority Groups and Communication Services*. URL (accessed 2016): http://stakeholders.ofcom.org.uk/binaries/research/cmr/ethnic-minority-groups/ethnic-minority-groups.pdf

Ofcom (2015) *Public Service Broadcasting in the Internet Age: Ofcom's Third Review of Public Service Broadcasting*. URL (accessed 2016): http://stakeholders.ofcom.org.uk/binaries/consultations/psb-review-3/statement/PSB_Review_3_Statement.pdf

Ofcom (2016) *The Ofcom Broadcasting Code*. URL (accessed 2009): http://stakeholders.ofcom.org.uk/broadcasting/broadcast-codes/broadcast-code/

Ong, W. J. (1977) *Interfaces of the Word*. Ithaca: Cornell University Press.

Osgerby, W. (2004) *Youth Media*. London: Routledge.

Papacharissi, Z. (2010) *A Private Sphere: Democracy in a Digital Age*. Cambridge: Polity.

Pederson, S. and Smithson, J. (2011) 'Mothers with attitude – How the Mumsnet Parenting Forum Offers Space for New Forms of Femininity to Emerge Online', *Women's Studies International Forum*, 38: 97–106.

Peet, R. (1989) 'The Destruction of Regional Cultures', in Johnston, R. and Taylor, P. (eds) *A World in Crisis? Geographical Perspectives*. Oxford: Basil Blackwell.

Peirce, C. (1931–48) *Collected Papers*. Cambridge, MA: Harvard University Press.

Penley, C. (1991) 'Brownian Motion: Women, Tactics and Technology', in Penley, C. and Ross, A. (eds) *Technoculture*. Minneapolis: University of Minnesota Press.

Perry, I. (2003) 'Who(se) Am I? The Identity and Image of Women in Hip Hop', in Dines, G. and Humez, J. M. (eds) *Gender, Race and Class in Media – Second Edition*. London: Sage, pp. 136–48.

Phillips, T. (2016) 'British Media: Not Quite Black and White', *Open Democracy UK*. URL (accessed 2016): www.opendemocracy.net/ourbeeb/trevor-phillips/british-tv-not-quite-black-and-white

Pickering, M. (2001) *Stereotypes: The Politics of Representation*. London: Palgrave.

Pieterse, J. P. (1992) *White on Black: Images of Africa and Blacks in Western Popular Culture*. Newhaven: Yale University Press.

Polhemous, T. (1997) 'In the Supermarket of Style', in S. Redhead (ed.) *The Club Cultures Reader*. Oxford: Blackwell.

Poster, M. (1995) *The Second Media Age*. Cambridge: Polity.

Poster, M. (2001) *What's the Matter With the Internet?* Minneapolis: University of Minnesota Press.

Postman, N. (1987) *Amusing Ourselves to Death: Public Discourse in the Age of Show Business*. London: Methuen.

Postman, N. and Powers, S. (1992) *How to Watch TV News*. Penguin Books.

Price, S. (2014) 'Rhetorical Masculinity: Authoritative Utterance and the Male Protagonist', in Ross, K. (ed.) *The Handbook of Gender, Sex and Media*. Chichester: Wiley, pp. 118–34.

Propp, V. (1968) *Morphology of the Folktale*. Austin: University of Texas Press.

Public Affairs Council (2013) 'Does Social Media Drive Polarisation?', *IMPACT*. URL (accessed 2016): http://pac.org/wp-content/uploads/Impact_2013_02.pdf

Radway, J. (1987) *Reading the Romance: Women, Patriarchy and Popular Literature*. London: Verso.

Ray, M. (2003) 'Nation, Nostalgia and Bollywood: In the Tracks of a Twice Displaced Community', in Karim, K. (ed.) *Media of Diaspora*. New York: Routledge.

Redden, G. (2007) 'Makeover Morality and Consumer Culture', in Hellar, D. (ed.) *Makeover Television*. I.B. Tauris & Co.

Redfield, R. (1955) *The Little Community*. Chicago: University of Chicago Press.

Reisman, D. (1953) *The Lonely Crowd: A Study of the Changing American Character*. Garden City: Doubleday.

Rettie, R. (2009) 'SMS: Exploiting the Interactional Characteristics of Near-Synchrony', *Information, Communication and Society*, 12(8).

Rheingold, H. (2000) *The Virtual Community: Homesteading on the Electronic Frontier – Revised Edition*. London: MIT Press.

Richards, B., MacRury, I. and Botterill, J. (2000) *The Dynamics of Advertising*. Harwood Academic Publishers.

Robards, B. (2014) 'Digital Traces of the Persona Through Ten Years of Facebook', *M/C Journal*, 17(3).

Robards, B. and Bennett, A. (2011) 'MyTribe: Post-Subcultural Manifestations of Belonging on Social Network Sites', *Sociology*, 45(2): 303–17.

Rock, P. (1973) 'News as Eternal Recurrence', in Cohen, S. and Young, J. (eds) *The Manufacture of News: Deviance, Social Problems and the Mass Media*. London: Constable, pp. 73–80.

Rojek, C. (2005) 'P2P Leisure Exchange: Net Banditry and the Policing of Intellectual Property', *Leisure Studies*, 24(4): 357–69.

Rose, T. (2008) *The Hip Hop Wars*. Basic Civitas Books.

Rosen, C. (2005) 'The Age of Egocasting', *The New Atlantis*, Fall 2004/Winter 2005: 51–72.

Rosengren, K. E. and Windahl, S. (1972) 'Mass Media Consumption as a Functional Alternative', in McQuail, D. (ed.) *Sociology of Mass Communications*. Harmondsworth: Penguin.

Ruggiero, T. (2000) 'Uses and Gratifications Theory in the 21st Century', *Mass Communication & Society*, 3(1): 3–37.

Rzepnikovska, A. (2013) 'Media Representations of Polish Migrants in Spain and in Britain: A Comparative Approach', Conference Paper, *Ethnicity, Race and Nationalism in European Media and Film*. URL (accessed 2016): www.academia.edu/6918894/Media_representations_of_Polish_migrants_in_Spain_and_in_Britain_A_comparative_approach

Safer Media (2013) 'Block Porn Campaign'. URL (accessed 2015): http://www.safermedia.org.uk/blockporn.htm

Sandvoss, C. (2005) *Fans: The Mirror of Consumption*. Cambridge: Polity.

Said, E. (1978) *Orientalism*. London: Routledge and Kegan Paul.

Sarkeesian, A. (2013) 'Damsels in Distress Part 1', *Tropes Versus Women in Video Games*. URL (accessed 2016): www.youtube.com/watch?v=X6p5AZp7r_Q (also see Parts 2 and 3).

Sarkeesian, A. (2016) 'Strategic Butt Coverings', *Tropes Versus Women in Video Games*. URL (accessed 2016): www.youtube.com/watch?v=ujTufg1GvR4

de Saussure, F. (1974) *Course in General Linguistics*. London: Fontana (originally published 1915).

Scannell, P. (1989) 'Public Service Broadcasting and Modern Life', *Media, Culture and Society*, 11(2): 135–66.

Scannell, P. (1990) 'Public Service Broadcasting: The History of a Concept', in Goodwin, A. and Whannel, G. (eds) *Understanding Television*. London: Routledge.

Schiller, H. (1976) *Communication and Cultural Domination*. International Arts and Sciences Press.

Schiller, H. (1992) *Mass Communication and American Empire*. Westview Press.

Schilt, K. and Zobl, E. (2008) 'Connecting the Dots: Riot Grrrls, Ladyfests and the International Grrrl Zine Network', in Harris, A. (ed.) *Next Wave Cultures: Feminism, Subcultures, Activism*. London: Routledge.

The Scotsman (2004) 'Sites to Check Out if you Chav What it Takes'. URL (accessed 2016): www.scotsman.com/news/uk/sites-to-check-out-if-you-chav-what-it-takes-1-922184

Segal, L. (1992) 'Introduction', in Segal, L. And McIntosh, M. (eds) *Sex Exposed: Sexuality and the Pornography Debate*. London: Virago Press.

Sender, K. (2014) 'No Hard Feelings: Reflexivity and Queer Affect in the New Media Landscape', in Ross, K. (ed.) *The Handbook of Gender, Sex and Media*. Chichester: Wiley, pp. 207–25.

Shannon, C. and Weaver, W. (1949) *The Mathematical Theory of Communication*. Illinois: University of Illinois Press.

Shirky, C. (2008) *Here Comes Everybody: The Power of Organising Without Organisations*. London: Penguin.

Shirky, C. (2011) 'The Political Power of Social Media: Technology, The Public Sphere and Political Change', *Foreign Affairs*, January/February 2011. URL (accessed 2016): www.foreignaffairs.com/articles/2010-12-20/political-power-social-media

Smith, A. (1904) *An Inquiry into the Nature and Causes of the Wealth of Nations – Fifth Edition*. London: Methuen and Co. (originally published 1776).

Smythe, D. (1981) 'On the Audience Commodity and its Work', in *Dependency Road: Communications, Capitalism, Consciousness, and Canada*. Norwood, NJ: Ablex, pp. 22–51.

Solomon, S. (1976) *Beyond Formula: American Film Genres*. New York: Harcourt Brace Jovanovich.

Solomos, J. (1993) *Race and Racism in Britain*. Basingstoke: Macmillan.

Spurgeon, C. (2008) *Advertising and New Media*. Abingdon: Routledge.

Sreberny, A. (1999) *Include Me In: Rethinking Ethnicity on Television*. London: Broadcasting Standards Council.

Sreberny-Mohammadi, A. and Ross, K. (1995) *Black Minority Viewers and Television: Neglected Audiences Speak Up and Out*. Leicester: Centre for Mass Communications Research.

Stevenson, N. (2002) *Understanding Media Cultures – Second Edition*. London: Sage.

Strinati, D. (2004) *An Introduction to Theories of Popular Culture – Second Edition*. London: Routledge.

Sunstein, C. (2002) 'The Law of Group Polarization', *Journal of Political Philosophy*,10(2): 175–95.

Talbot, M. (2007) *Media Discourse: Representation and Interaction*. Edinburgh: Edinburgh University Press.

Taylor, T. (1997) *Global Pop: World Music, World Markets*. London: Routledge.

Taylor, T. (2007) *Beyond Exoticism: Western Music and the World*. Duke University Press.

Temple, M. (2006) 'Dumbing Down is Good For You', *British Politics*, 1(2): 257–73.

Thompson, J. (1990) *Ideology and Modern Culture: Critical Social Theory in the Era of Mass Communication*. Cambridge: Polity Press.

Thornton, S. (1995) *Club Cultures: Music, Media and Subcultural Capital*. Cambridge: Polity Press.

Todorov, T. (1978) *The Poetics of Prose*. Ithaca: Cornell University Press.

Tomlinson, J. (1991) *Cultural Imperialism: A Critical Introduction*. London: Pinter.

Tönnies, F. (1963) *Community and Society*. New York: Harper and Row.

Tracey, M. (1998) *The Decline and Fall of Public Service Broadcasting*. Oxford: Oxford University Press.

Tuchman, G. (1978) 'Introduction: The Symbolic Annihilation of Women by the Mass Media', in Tuchman, G., Kaplan Daniels, A. and Benet, J. (eds) *Hearth and Home: Images of Women in the Mass Media*. New York: Oxford University Press.

Turkle, S. (1995) *Life on the Screen: Identity in the Age of the Internet*. London: Phoenix.

Turkle, S. (2012) 'Connected but Alone?', TED Lecture (Technology, Entertainment and Design). URL (accessed 2016): www.ted.com/talks/sherry_turkle_alone_together/transcript?language=en

Turkle, S. (2013) *Alone Together: Why We Expect More From Technology and Less From Each Other*. New York: Basic Books.

Turner, G. (2004) *Understanding Celebrity*. London: Sage.

Tyler, I. (2008) '"Chav Mum, Chav Scum": Class Disgust in Contemporary Britain', *Feminist Media Studies*, 8(1): 17–34.

Vroomen, L. (2004) 'Kate Bush: Teen Pop and Older Female Fans', in Bennett, A. and Peterson, R. (eds) *Music Scenes: Local, Translocal and Virtual*. Nashville: Vanderbilt University Press.

Watson, N. (1997) 'Why We Argue About Virtual Community: A Case Study of the Phish.Net Fan Community', in S. Jones (ed.) *Virtual Culture: Internet and Communication in Cybersociety*. London: Sage.

Webster, F. (2002) *Theories of the Information Society – Second Edition*. London: Routledge.

Wellman, B. and Gulia, M. (1999) 'Virtual Communities as Communities: Net Surfers Don't Ride Alone', in Smith, M. and Kollock, P. (eds) *Communities in Cyberspace*. London: Routledge, pp. 163–90.

Wellman, B. and Haythornthwaite, C. (2002) 'The Internet in Everyday Life: An Introduction', in Wellman, B. and Haythornthwaite, C. (eds) *The Internet in Everyday Life*. Malden: Blackwell, pp. 3–44.

Westley, B. and MacLean, M. (1957) 'A Conceptual Model for Communication Research', *Journalism Quarterly*, 34: 31–8.

Whelan, A. (2006) 'Do U Produce?: Subcultural Capital and Amateur Musicianship in Peer-to-Peer Networks', in Ayers, M. (ed.) *Cybersounds: Essays on Virtual Music Culture*. Peter Lang Press.

Williams, D., Martins, N., Consalvo, M. and Ivory, J. (2009) 'The Virtual Census: Representations of Gender, Race and Age in Video Games', *New Media and Society*, 11(5): 815–34.

Williams, R. (1974) *Television: Technology and Cultural Form*. London: Collins.

Williams, R. (1980) 'Advertising: The Magic System', in *Problems in Materialism and Culture*. London: Verso.

Williams, R. (1988) *Keywords: A Vocabulary of Culture and Society*. London: Fontana Press.

Williams, R. (1989) *Resources of Hope: Culture, Democracy, Socialism*. London: Verso.

Williamson, J. (1978) *Decoding Advertisements: Ideology and Meaning in Advertising*. London: Marion Boyars.

Willis, P. (1990) *Common Culture: Symbolic Work at Play in the Everyday Cultures of the Young*. Milton Keynes: Open University Press.

Wimmer, R. and Dominick, J. (2006) *Mass Media Research: An Introduction – Eighth Edition*. Belmont: Thomson Wadsworth.

Woodward, K. (1997) *Identity and Difference*. London: Sage.

Young, J. (1971) *The Drug Takers: The Social Meaning of Drug Use*. London: Paladin.

INDEX

Figures are indicated by page numbers in bold print.